COME, LET US SING
A CALL TO MUSICAL REFORMATION

ROBERT S. SMITH

The Latimer Trust

Come, Let Us Sing: A Call to Musical Reformation © Robert S. Smith 2020. All rights reserved.

ISBN 978-1-906327-60-6

Cover photo: 'Hymnal.' By BillionPhotos.com on Adobe Stock

Published by the Latimer Trust April 2020.

The Latimer Trust (formerly Latimer House, Oxford) is a conservative Evangelical research organisation within the Church of England, whose main aim is to promote the history and theology of Anglicanism as understood by those in the Reformed tradition. Interested readers are welcome to consult its website for further details of its many activities.

The Latimer Trust

London N14 4PS UK

Registered Charity: 1084337

Company Number: 4104465

Web: www.latimertrust.org

E-mail: administrator@latimertrust.org

CONTENTS PAGE

PREFACE

My hope for this book is identical with George Whitefield's aim in publishing *A Collection of Hymns for Social Worship* in 1753: 'That we all may be inspired and warmed with a like divine Fire whilst singing below, and be translated after Death to join with them in singing the Song of Moses and the Lamb above'.[1] So although the following pages contain plenty of biblical exegesis and theological argumentation, the ultimate purpose of this book is practical: *the ongoing reformation of the musical and liturgical dimension of church life.* This will be clear at numerous points along the way, where I suggest applications and tease out implications, but especially when we get to chapter eleven, the conclusion and the appendices.

The embryonic form of this book was an article written in 2012 on 'The Role of Singing in the Life of the Church'.[2] That article was subsequently developed into a series of conference talks. These in turn have been expanded to form Part Two of this book (chapters five to ten). As I began work on these chapters, however, it became apparent that behind much of the confusion over *why we sing* was a more basic confusion over *why we gather.* Addressing this question, therefore, is the burden of Part One of this book (chapters two to four). For those with eyes to see, the two questions are also closely related to the title – *Come* (why we gather), *let us sing* (why we sing)!

Partly because much of this book was written in 2017 – the year of the 500th anniversary of the Protestant Reformation in Europe – and partly because of the theological, liturgical and musical riches of the Reformed heritage, I have deliberately engaged with the Reformed tradition throughout and made a particular point of invoking Martin Luther's wisdom on music and song. The subtitle of the book – *A Call to Musical Reformation* – also serves as a reminder that, this side of the

---

[1] George Whitefield, 'Preface' to *A Collection of Hymns for Social Worship: More particularly design'd for the Use of the Tabernacle Congregation, in London* (London, 1753).
[2] Robert S Smith, 'The Role of Singing in the Life of the Church', *The Briefing* 401 (September-October, 2012), 15-21.

consummation, the task of reform is ongoing: *ecclesia reformata, ecclesia semper reformanda* ('the reformed church is the church that is always reforming'). As we will see, there are also reasons why the musical side of church life needs renewed attention at the present time.

Although a reformed evangelical first and foremost, I am also a committed Anglican, an ordained Anglican Minister and am writing this book for The Latimer Trust! For these reasons, I have attempted to give the book a distinctively Anglican flavour (at least at various points), mostly by interacting with the musical side of the English Reformation and by occasionally illustrating from the *Book(s) of Common Prayer*. Rather than alienating non-Anglicans, my hope is that this will prove both illuminating and instructive, especially given that historic Anglicanism is a vital part of our Reformed heritage and a part from which we can learn a great deal – both for good and ill.

I am grateful to Prof Gerald Bray, Dr Mark Burkill and The Latimer Trust Council for inviting me to explore a subject so important for God's people and so close to my own heart. I am also thankful to Margaret Hobbs and Grace Raven for their gentle enquiries regarding progress and their patient encouragements to persevere. I also wish to register my debt to Dr Claire Smith, Dr David Peterson, Dr Alan Mugridge, Dr Alan Thompson, Dr Geoff Harper, Dr James Hely Hutchinson, Andrew Court, Trevor Hodge, Megan Ng and Amanda Mears for reading various chapters and/or appendices, and for offering numerous valuable comments and not a few necessary corrections.

As music ministry has been a large part of the work the Lord has given me to do (at least thus far), this book represents something of a life's work. In it I have sought to distil the fruits of several decades of reading, learning, singing, song-writing, teaching, training and experience. At the same time, and despite impressions to the contrary, I have also tried to avoid taking what some call 'the kitchen sink approach'. There is much more that could have been said at most points and other avenues that could have been explored. But I trust that what I have written will prove sufficient for the task at hand: that of calling God's people to ongoing musical reformation.

Robert S. Smith
March, 2020

1. The Path to the Present

In order to set the stage for the biblical, theological, pastoral and practical discussions that will occupy the bulk of this book, it is important to place these discussions in context – their historical context. This will not only help us understand where we have come from, but also where we are and why we have many of the confusions and conflicts we do. To this end, we begin with a brief history of the musical and liturgical reformation in the Church of England and the way this has impacted church life and ministry in the English-speaking world. I'm aware that history is not everyone's 'thing' and am, of course, totally unable to prevent readers from jumping straight to Chapter Two. But history is important – as well as being both interesting and instructive. So I urge the wary to proceed (or, at the very least, to return at a later point). We start our journey in the sixteenth century.

*   *   *

For several months after Elizabeth I's accession to the English throne in November 1558, it was unclear which way things would go. Would she continue the Catholicism blazed by her sister, 'Bloody Mary', or would she return to the path of Protestantism forged under Edward VI? In 1559, the passing of a new Act of Supremacy (in which Elizabeth was declared to be the 'Supreme Governor' of the Church of England), a new Act of Uniformity (which re-introduced a slightly modified version of the 1552 *Book of Common Prayer*), and a set of royal *Injunctions* answered that question. Based on a similar series published under Edward VI in 1547, the *Injunctions* did much to define and establish the Protestant nature of the English church from this point on. In the course of their dealing with the practice of ministry and the conduct of church services, Item XLIX makes the following pronouncement:

> And that there be modest and distinct song, so used in parts of the Common prayers of the Church, that the same may be as plainly understood, as if it were read without singing. And yet, nevertheless, for the comforting of such as delight in music, it may be permitted, that in the beginning, or in the end of Common Prayers, either at morning or evening, there may be sung, an hymn,

3

or suchlike song, to the praise of Almighty God, in the best sort of melody and music that may be conveniently devised, having respect that the sentences of the hymn may be understood and perceived.[1]

The road to this point had been a rather circuitous and conflicted one, with a number of early English reformers expressing a deep distrust of church music. William Tyndale, for example, feared 'that antichrist could manipulate music's affective capabilities to ease the consumption not of true doctrine, but of a perverted and corrupt parody of the same'.[2] Hugh Latimer likewise believed that the gospel was obscured when it was turned into 'piping, playing, and curious singing'.[3]

Myles Coverdale, on the other hand, was convinced that 'songs of praise and thanksgiving were a natural and irresistible act for the godly'.[4] His desire, therefore, was to reform church music, not to abolish it. Consequently, in 1535, Coverdale produced a collection of 41 English hymns, canticles and versified psalms (largely Lutheran in origin) which he believed to be 'the very word of God' in song-form. Its title is instructive: *Goostly psalms and spirituall songes drawen out of the holy Scripture, for the comforte and consolacyon of soch as loue to reioyse in God and his worde.*[5] In the preface to the collection, he also contested the idea that the singing of Old Testament saints provides little or no precedent for new covenant believers:

> Why should not we then make our songs and mirth of God, as well as they? Hath he not done as much for us as for them? Hath he not

---

[1] W H Frere and W M Kennedy (eds.), *Visitation Articles and Injunctions of the Period of the Reformation* (London, 1910), 3.

[2] Jonathan P Willis, *Church Music and Protestantism in Post-Reformation England: Discourses, Sites and Identities* (Farnham: Ashgate, 2010), 51.

[3] Hugh Latimer, 'Letter to Sir Edward Baynton, c. 1531', in G E Corrie (ed.), *Remains of Bishop Latimer* (For the Parker Society; Cambridge: Cambridge University Press, 1865), 348.

[4] Willis, *Church Music and Protestantism in Post-Reformation England*, 51.

[5] Or in contemporary English, *Ghostly* [i.e., inspired] *psalms and spiritual songs drawn out of the holy Scripture, for the comfort and consolation of such as love to rejoice in God and his word.*

delivered us from as great troubles as them? Yes, doubtless. Why should he not then be our pastime, as well as theirs?[6]

How much Coverdale hoped his collection might be used in congregational life is not clear.[7] What is clear is that he believed the singing of such 'godly psalms and songs of God's word' had a four-fold purpose: 'namely, to comfort a man's heart in God, to make him thankful, and to exercise him in his word, to encourage him in the way of godliness, and to provoke other men unto the same'.[8] Regrettably, neither church nor crown was quite ready for such developments and, by 1546, Coverdale's collection of *Goostly Psalmes* had been condemned to the flames.

Sometime after his appointment as Archbishop in 1532, Thomas Cranmer also began to experiment with hymns in the vernacular. This is not surprising, as he had not only been exposed to Lutheran influences during his time at Cambridge in the 1520s but had become personally acquainted with Lutheran hymn-singing during his time in Germany in the 1530s.[9] One of Cranmer's early efforts was an English version of the Litany, designed to be either said or sung. Upon its completion, he wrote a letter to the king containing the following advice:

> [A]fter your highness hath corrected it, if your grace command some devout and solemn note to be made thereunto, ... I trust it will much excite and stir the hearts of all men[10] unto devotion and

---

[6] Myles Coverdale, 'Goostly psalms and spirituall songes drawen out of the holy Scripture, for the comforte and consolacyon of soch as loue to reioyse in God and his worde', in George Pearson (ed.), *Remains of Myles Coverdale, Bishop of Exeter* (For the Parker Society; Cambridge: Cambridge University Press, 1846), 539.

[7] From a variety of statements made in Coverdale's 'Preface', Andrew Shead deduces that he 'probably expected them to be sung during daily devotions in the home, before and after the Bible was read'. See Andrew G Shead, 'Is There a Musical Note in the Body? Cranmer on the Reformation of Music', *RTR* 69.1 (April, 2010), 7.

[8] Coverdale, 'Goostly psalms and spirituall songes', 539.

[9] Cranmer had been sent to Germany as something of an 'ecclesiastical diplomat' in order to look into the King's 'Great Matter' (i.e., Henry's desire to annul his marriage to Catherine of Aragon).

[10] When quoting from historic sources I have retained the use of generic masculine terms.

godliness: but in mine opinion, the song that shall be made thereunto would not be full of notes, but, as near as may be, for every syllable a note; so that it may be sung distinctly and devoutly.[11]

While Cranmer was probably doing no more here than suggesting a potential mode of chant, it is clear that in order to make things 'most easy and playne for the understandynge' (as he would later put it in the 'Preface' to the 1552 *Book of Common Prayer*), he was keen 'to do away with the meandering melismas of the later medieval period'.[12] Edification required understanding, understanding required clarity, and clarity required a good 'fit' between text and tune.

Most of Cranmer's labours, however, were focussed on translations and revisions of Latin hymns. These had originally been intended for inclusion in a 'Reformed Breviary' (i.e., a book of daily services for the clergy), but instead ended up in the King's Primer of 1545 (i.e., a book of daily services to be used by the laity).[13] The purpose of Cranmer's English translations, as well as his intention for them to be sung, is clear from his (unpublished) Preface to the Primer:

> Now prayer is used or made with right and perfect understanding, if we sing with our spirit, and sing with our mind and understanding; so that the deep contemplation or ravishing of the mind follow the pithiness of the words, and the guiding of reason go before: lest when the spirit doth pray, the mind take no fruit at all, and the party that understandeth not the pith or effectualness of the talk, that he frankly maketh with God, may be as an harp or pipe, having a sound, but not understanding the noise that itself hath made.[14]

---

[11] Thomas Cranmer, 'Letter to King Henry VIII, 7 October, 1544', in J E Cox (ed.), *Miscellaneous Writings and Letters of Thomas Cranmer, Archbishop of Canterbury* (For the Parker Society; Cambridge: Cambridge University Press, 1846), 412.
[12] Willis, *Church Music and Protestantism in Post-Reformation England*, 52.
[13] Diarmaid MacCulloch, *Thomas Cranmer: A Life* (New Haven: Yale University Press, 1996), 332-333.
[14] Thomas Cranmer, 'A Preface made by the King's most excellent Majesty unto his Primer Book' (1545), in J E Cox (ed.), *Miscellaneous Writings and Letters of Thomas Cranmer, Archbishop of Canterbury* (For the Parker Society;

Despite the banning and burning of Coverdale's hymnbook, the late 1540s saw a number of fresh attempts to translate the psalms into English rhyming verse. The most important of these renderings was Thomas Sternhold's collection of 19 metrical psalms, published in 1547. By 1549, a second edition had appeared containing 37 of Sternhold's translations plus another seven by John Hopkins, mostly written in what was (at the time) a rather novel metre – 8.6.8.6. or 'fourteener'. Due to the broad acceptance of Sternhold and Hopkins' Psalter, this metre not only became extremely popular but was so often imitated that it soon become known as 'Common Metre'.[15]

At the same time that these seeds of congregational hymnody were being sown, other aspects of church music were being condemned.[16] With the accession of Edward VI in 1547, further indictments were issued not simply against the popish misuse of music, but against music itself! In *The Jewel of Joy*, for instance, Thomas Becon argued that 'music was little more than a drain on virtue, manliness and time which was better spent in honest study and edification'.[17] He even went so far as to claim that it was neither a divine gift, nor 'so excellent a thing, that a Christian man ought earnestly to rejoice in it'.[18] What, then, of the biblical calls to psalm singing and music making? These were 'to be interpreted ghostly'

Cambridge: Cambridge University Press, 1846), 497. In the final form of the Primer, Cranmer's Preface was replaced by the royal injunction.

[15] In the same year (1549), Robert Crowley produced an entire metrical Psalter in Common Metre. The accompanying music was similar to the Gregorian tones of the Latin Sarum Rite Psalter. A single note was given for each syllable in each verse, in keeping with Cranmer's instruction for the reformed Edwardian liturgy. The aim of such simplicity, and likewise the omission of complex vocal ornamentation, was to encourage attentiveness to the words that were being sung.

[16] For example, writing of the destruction of 'the great prostitute' in his 1544 commentary on the book of Revelation, John Bale denounced 'the sweet organs, ... great bells, ... fresh descant, ... counterpoint, ... lascivious harmony and delectable music' as 'provoking the weak hearts of men to meddle with thy abominable whoredom by the wantonness of idolatry of that kind'. See John Bale, 'The Image of Both Churches', in H Christmas (ed.), *Select Works of John Bale* (For the Parker Society; Cambridge: Cambridge University Press, 1849), 534-546.

[17] Willis, *Church Music and Protestantism in Post-Reformation England*, 53.

[18] Thomas Becon, 'The Jewel of Joy', in John Ayre (ed.), *The Catechism of Thomas Becon with other pieces written by him on the reign of King Edward VI* (For the Parker Society; Cambridge: Cambridge University Press, 1844), 429.

(i.e., spiritually).[19] As Becon himself put it, 'A Christian man's melody consisteth in heart'[20] and was (supposedly) meant to stay there!

It is sentiments like these (and the curious theology lying behind them) that perhaps best explain why, despite Cranmer's dabbling in hymnody and the popularity of Sternhold and Hopkins' Psalter (which had gone through nine reprints by 1553), 'the Edwardian church made no official move towards the incorporation of vernacular metrical psalmody into its liturgy'.[21] While this state of affairs has sometimes been blamed (wrongly) on the teaching of John Calvin,[22] it was more likely a result of Heinrich Bullinger's influence upon the English church.[23] In fact, it was the influence of Calvin and Bucer on the Protestants who fled to Geneva during Mary's reign that 'in the long run helped save English church music from Bullingerian austerity'.[24]

Whatever the case, the Elizabethan Settlement not only resolved the theological direction of the English church but set the course for congregational singing for the foreseeable future. Capitalising on the labours of the exiles (although dropping roughly half of their additions), a complete metrical Psalter was published by John Daye of London in 1562. It contained 86 new translations, mostly written by Hopkins, although four were posthumously discovered works written by Sternhold. Once again, the full title of the volume is instructive: *The whole booke of*

---

[19] John Bale, 'The Examination of William Thorpe', in H Christmas (ed.), *The Select Works of John Bale* (For the Parker Society; Cambridge: Cambridge University Press, 1849), 102.

[20] Becon, 'The Jewel of Joy', 429.

[21] Willis, *Church Music and Protestantism in Post-Reformation England*, 54. In fact, Shead ('Is There a Musical Note in the Body?', 11-14) makes a compelling case for seeing Cranmer as a cautious but committed advocate of church music in general and psalm singing in particular.

[22] So, for instance, Peter Le Huray, *Music and the Reformation in England, 1549-1660* (Cambridge: Cambridge University Press, 1967), 28.

[23] Bullinger had a well-known antipathy for music and song. See Diarmaid MacCulloch, *The Later Reformation in England, 1547-1603* (Basingstoke: St Martin's Press, 1990), 60.

[24] Willis, *Church Music and Protestantism in Post-Reformation England*, 55. Evidence of this can found in the fact that Sternhold and Hopkins' Psalter steadily grew in the hands of the Marian exiles, going through several Genevan editions – 1556 (51 Psalms), 1558 (62 Psalms), 1560 (65 Psalms) and 1561 (90 Psalms).

psalmes collected into English meter by T. Sternhold, I. Hopkins, and others; conferred with the Ebrue [Hebrew], with apt notes to sing them withal; set forth and allowed to be song [sung] in all churches, of all the people together before and after Morning and Evening prayer, as also before and after sermons and moreover in private houses.

Although Elizabeth is said to have dismissively referred to the metrical psalms (or, at least, their tunes) as 'Geneva jigs',[25] she did not oppose their use. *The whole booke of psalmes* was indeed 'allowed to be song in all churches' and, consequently, unaccompanied psalm singing quickly became both an accepted feature of congregational life and a welcome supplement to the formality of the Prayer Book services. In fact, such was the popularity of the practice that metrical psalms fast became 'the religious folk ballads of ordinary people as well as the precursors of freely composed hymns in English'.[26]

But the day of the English hymn was still some way off. In fact, for nearly two centuries after the Reformation there was no book of hymns for use in the English churches. While psalm singing continued, it also degenerated over time.[27] Less and less attention was given to the words and the number of tunes employed reduced down to a mere handful. Worse, 'through a process of oral tradition the tunes became progressively slower and rhythmically lifeless, until they were sung as a kind of dirge'.[28] Worse still, in numerous country parishes, where many were illiterate, the Psalms were sung by 'lining out'.[29] This involved a clerk reading each line aloud, so that the congregants could commit it to

---

[25] Horton Davies, *Worship and Theology in England: From Cranmer to Baxter and Fox, 1534-1690* (Grand Rapids: Eerdmans, 1996), 387.
[26] John Swarbrick, 'Jesus the Soul of Musick Is: Music and the Methodists'. A lecture read at the Methodist Sacramental Fellowship Public Meeting during the Methodist Conference of 2003 at Llandudno, 5: http://www.sacramental.org.uk/uploads/5/0/0/9/50096105/jesus_the_soul_of _musick_is_-_john_swarbrick.pdf.
[27] Parts of the following paragraphs have been adapted from sections of Robert S Smith, 'The Hymnody of John Wesley and George Whitefield', in Ian J Maddock (ed.), *Wesley and Whitefield? Wesley versus Whitefield?* (Eugene: Wipf & Stock, 2018), 219-242.
[28] Swarbrick, 'Jesus the Soul of Musick Is', 5.
[29] Frederick John Gillman, *The Evolution of the English Hymn* (London: George Allen, 1927), 198.

memory before attempting to sing it together. Not surprisingly, *The whole booke of psalmes* had its detractors. One, John Wilmot (1647-1680), the Earl of Rochester, cast his criticisms in verse:

> Sternhold and Hopkins had great qualms
> When they translated David's psalms,
> To make the heart right glad;
> But had it been King David's fate
> To hear thee sing and them translate
> By God! 'twould set him mad![30]

Musically speaking, the seventeenth century was a time of extremes. On the one hand, the music of the Chapel Royal was flourishing, with numerous English anthems and canticles being set to highly complex music. [31] On the other hand, in the large majority of parishes, congregational singing was in a sorry state and in bad need of reform. Early attempts to produce a hymnal had little success, mostly because 'the public singing of texts not directly from the Bible was still regarded by many as an "error of popery"'.[32] However, as the century progressed, a number of hymns began to gain traction, particularly those developed out of the writings of people like Richard Baxter and John Bunyan.[33] By the end of the century hymns were being freely written and (at least in some of the nonconformist churches) freely used – the Baptists being the pioneers.[34]

---

[30] Cited in William J Reynolds and Milburn Price, *A Survey of Christian Hymnody* (Carol Stream, Illinois, 1987), 37.

[31] See Andrew Wilson-Dickson, *The Story of Christian Music: From Gregorian Chant to Black Gospel, An Authoritative Illustrated Guide to All the Major Traditions of Music for Worship* (Oxford: Lion, 1992), 105-109.

[32] Wilson-Dickson, *The Story of Christian Music*, 110.

[33] Bunyan's 'To Be a Pilgrim' (now known as 'He who would valiant be'), which first appeared in Part 2 of *The Pilgrim's Progress* (1684), is a clear case in point. Baxter is also known to have written over 20 hymns.

[34] Benjamin Keach (1640-1704) was the most notable innovator. Keach not only wrote some 400 hymns but was also the first English minister to introduce regular hymn singing into the life of an English congregation. He also wrote a thorough defence of the practice of hymn singing with the instructive title: *The Breach Repaired in God's Worship: or, Singing of Psalms, Hymns and Spiritual Songs, proved to be an Holy Ordinance of Jesus Christ. With an Answer to all Objections* (1691).

However, the shift away from 'exclusive psalmody' and toward the inclusion of 'hymns of human composure' (i.e., songs not taken directly from Scripture) was given its greatest impetus by the Independent minister, Isaac Watts (1674-1748). Although not quite deserving to be called the 'father' of the English hymn, there is no question that he stood against the deplorable state of church music like no other before him.[35] To this end, Watts wrote over 600 hymns and published two principal collections: *Hymns and Spiritual Songs* (1707) and *The Psalms of David Imitated in the Language of the New Testament* (1719). The opening sentence of the 'Preface' to the former not only reveals the purpose of the volume but the larger problem that Watts was seeking to address:

> While we sing the Praises of our God in his Church, we are employ'd in that part of Worship which of all others is the nearest a-kin to Heaven; and 'tis pity that this of all others should be perform'd the worst upon Earth.[36]

As an Independent, Watts' most immediate influence was upon other nonconformist churches and dissenting hymn-writers (e.g., Philip Doddridge). Nevertheless, his concerns were shared and his hymns cherished by many in the Church of England.

And yet, over-shadowing all other eighteenth century contributions to the development of English hymnody is that of the two Anglican clergymen, John and Charles Wesley. In fact, their 'Charlestown Hymnbook', *A Collection of Psalms and Hymns* (1737), was the first hymnbook to be compiled for use in the Church of England. Moreover, by the time of John's death in 1791, the Wesleys had published some 60 separate hymnals, 36 of which contained his and Charles' hymns alone.[37] Erik

---

[35] In Louis Benson's words: 'He does not stand alone, but his personality commands the situation, his mind plans the remedy purely from personal resources, and his strong will overcomes the force of tradition, of conviction, of sacred associations, of habit, of prejudice, and, not least, of indifference'. See Louis F Benson, *The English Hymn: Its Development and Use* (London: Hodder & Stoughton, 1915), 217.

[36] Isaac Watts, 'Preface' to *Hymns and Spiritual Songs* (London: J. Humphreys, for John Lawrence, 1707), iii.

[37] Tim Dowley, *Christian Music: A Global History* (Oxford: Lion, 2011), 118. For example, *A Collection of Hymns for the Use of the People Called Methodists* (1780), contained 525 hymns in total, all but ten of which were written by

Routley's assessment, therefore, is not overstated: 'Watts taught his congregations to sing about Christ; the Wesleys taught the whole country to do so'.[38]

Hymn singing also made an enormous contribution to the Evangelical Revival – the songs having at least as great an effect as the sermons. Thus, in many ways, Methodism, like Lutheranism, was a movement born in song and bred by song. Much of this was due to the extraordinary ability of Charles Wesley (1707-88), who was not only adept at paraphrasing Scripture, but at versifying the whole range of Christian doctrine and evangelical experience. He was also remarkably prodigious in his poetic output, authoring somewhere 'between six thousand and nine thousand hymns and sacred poems (depending upon what one is willing to call a hymn or poem)'.[39]

Like his older brother, John, Charles was a man so soaked in Scripture that his hymnody, quite literally, oozed biblical language, biblical imagery and, above all, biblical truth. Indeed, it has been claimed that 'A skillful man, if the Bible were lost, might extract much of it from Wesley's Hymns'.[40] Of course, Charles was not only concerned that his hymns reflected scriptural *doctrine*, but that they expressed scriptural *devotion* as well. Many were, therefore, written as personal prayers or praises to God, and consequently voiced in the first-person. In other words, his hymns 'are not only theological statements about God, they are experientially-based affirmations made to God'; they are both theology and doxology.[41] And yet, 'Wesley's purpose was not the expressive *venting* of feeling but rather the evangelical *directing* of feeling'.[42] Consequently, as Methodist theologian, Thomas Langford, writes:

---

members of the Wesley family. It also contained 19 of John's translations of Moravian or Pietist hymns.

[38] Erik Routley, *A Short History of English Music* (Oxford: Mowbrays, 1977), 44.

[39] John R Tyson, *Assist Me to Proclaim: The Life and Hymns of Charles Wesley* (Grand Rapids: Eerdmans, 2007), vii-viii.

[40] J Ernest Rattenbury, *The Evangelical Doctrines of Charles Wesley's Hymns* (London: Epworth, 1941), 48.

[41] John R Tyson, 'The Theology of Charles Wesley's Hymns', *Wesleyan Theological Journal* 44.2 (Fall 2009), 70.

[42] Routley, *A Short History of English Music*, 79.

Charles Wesley's theology is 'a theology one can sing.' In this sense it is a theology with which one can praise; it is a theology with which one can pray, a theology with which one can teach; it is a theology which one can use to initiate, to guide, and to envision the final hope of Christian existence.[43]

It is for good reason, then, that John Wesley described *A Collection of Hymns for the Use of the People Called Methodists* (1780) – a volume dominated by Charles' hymns – as 'a little body of experimental and practical divinity'.[44]

Following in the wake of the Wesleys, the eighteenth century saw an explosion of hymns and hymnals, with more than 250 separate publications pouring forth from the presses. The educative effects were profound. 'The evangelical hymn writers greatly increased the vocabulary of their congregations and their ability to cope with complex theological language and thought'. [45] However, despite the fact that Church of England ministers had been steadily introducing such hymns ever since the 1730s, the practice was still not authorised by parliament and, at least until the end of the eighteenth century, was generally regarded as illegal. Even as late as 1820, one Sheffield parish attempted to initiate court proceedings against its vicar, Thomas Cotterill, for his use of hymns in church services. Wisely, the court refused to interfere.[46] This outcome led to hymn singing becoming even more widely accepted in the established church, with the result that during the remainder of the nineteenth century, an additional 200 different hymn-books appeared in the Church of England alone.

---

43 Thomas A Langford, 'Charles Wesley as Theologian', in S T Kimbrough Jr. (ed.), *Charles Wesley Poet and Theologian* (Nashville: Abingdon, 1992), 97.

44 John Wesley, 'Preface' to *A Collection of Hymns for the Use of the People Called Methodists* (1780), paragraph 4. As John Tyson explains: 'The word "experimental" focuses our attention on the lived and experiential dimension of hymns as theology. The term "practical" simply serves to intensify the emphasis; it draws our attention to Christian practice as a matrix for doing theology'. See Tyson, 'The Theology of Charles Wesley's Hymns', 61.

45 Mark Evans, *Open Up the Doors: Music in the Modern Church* (London/Oakville: Equinox, 2006), 35.

46 Nicholas Temperley, *The Music of the English Parish Church: Volume I* (Cambridge: Cambridge University Press, 1979), 3.

Two further nineteenth century developments are worthy of brief comment. The first concerns the rise of the Oxford (or Tractarian) Movement, with its desire to revive the ritualistic and symbolic aspects of pre-Reformation church life. Due to the Movement's influence on church music, in many parishes organs were purchased, gallery musicians dismissed, the metrical psalms abandoned, and a new type of Gregorian chant (known as Anglican chant) proposed as a vehicle for congregational song. While not all of these changes were inherently problematic, the net effect was deleterious for congregational singing. In addition to this, the rise of 'sacred music' in cathedral settings put further pressure on parishes. Not only were trained choirs needed to emulate cathedral music, but congregational participation threatened to spoil its performance.[47] At the same time, the Oxford Movement was also responsible for the publication of *Hymns Ancient and Modern* (1861). This rather eclectic collection of hymns, which was in general conformity to the *Book of Common Prayer*, proved so popular that by the end of the century it had sold 60 million copies.[48]

The second development was the burgeoning of North American evangelical hymnody and the development of a new type of congregational song; the 'gospel song'. Gospel songs were 'free in form, emotional in character, devout in attitude, evangelistic in purpose and spirit ... and develop a single thought, rather than a line of thought. That thought usually finds its supreme expression in the chorus or refrain which binds the stanzas together in a very close unity'.[49] Such songs played a large role in the transatlantic missions of Dwight L Moody (preacher) and Ira D Sankey (song-leader and soloist). In fact, following a mission to England in 1872, Moody and Sankey published a small booklet of songs used in the mission with the title, *Sacred Songs and Solos*. As their ministry continued, so the booklet grew. By 1903 it contained some 1,200 songs.[50] Still in use today, *Sacred Songs and Solos* has possibly had the largest circulation of any evangelical song book ever published.

---

[47] Wilson-Dickson, *The Story of Christian Music*, 133-136.
[48] Wilson-Dickson, *The Story of Christian Music*, 136.
[49] Edmund S Lorenz, *Church Music: What a Minister Should Know About It* (New York: Fleming H Revell, 1923), 342.
[50] Wilson-Dickson, *The Story of Christian Music*, 138. Fanny Crosby (1820-1915) is probably the best known, and was certainly the most prolific, of the 'gospel song' writers of the period. Blind from birth, she composed over 8,000 hymns

Despite the near eclipse of psalm singing in the late nineteenth century, the early twentieth century saw a number of attempts to revive the practice, particularly in Presbyterian circles and particularly in the United States.[51] The major development taking place in England, however, was the construction of *The English Hymnal*. Sponsored by a committee that was somewhat dissatisfied with *Hymns Ancient and Modern*, the new hymnal was lyrically edited by Percy Dearmer, vicar of St Mary's Primrose Hill, who, in turn, enlisted the help of composer, Ralph Vaughan Williams (1872-1958), as musical editor. This began an association between the two men that lasted over 30 years and resulted not only in *The English Hymnal* (1906; rev. 1933), but also in *Songs of Praise* (1925; rev. 1931) and *The Oxford Book of Carols* (1928).[52] Of particular interest are the following words penned by Vaughan Williams in the musical 'Preface' to the 1906 edition of *The English Hymnal*.

> The music is intended to be essentially congregational in character, and this end has been kept in view both in the choice of tunes and in the manner of setting them out. Fine melody rather than the exploitation of a trained choir has been the criterion of selection: the pitch of each tune has been kept as low as is consistent with the character of the melody.[53]

---

and is deservedly known as 'the mother of modern congregational singing in America'.

[51] For example, in 1909 a Joint Committee from nine churches of the Presbyterian family in Canada and the United States in North America began work on a new metrical psalter. The result was the 1912 publication of *The Psalter: With Responsive Readings*. Unlike the *Genevan Psalter*, it employed texts set largely to regular meter and, in so doing, resembled those psalters originating in the British Isles. Such was its influence that many of the psalms found in it appeared in later Reformed hymnals, including the *Psalter Hymnal* (1934), the *Hymnbook* (1955), and the *Trinity Hymnal* (1961). See Bert Polman, 'The History of Worship in the Christian Reformed Church', in Emily R Brink and Bert F Polman (eds.), *Psalter Hymnal Handbook* (Grand Rapids: CRC Publications, 1998), 116-117.

[52] Julian Onderdonk, 'Hymn Tunes from Folk-songs: Vaughan Williams and English Hymnody', in Byron Adams and Robin Wells (eds.), *Vaughan Williams Essays* (Abingdon: Routledge, 2016), 103.

[53] Ralph Vaughan Williams, 'Preface: The Music', to *The English Hymnal* (London: OUP, 1906), x: https://www.ccel.org/ccel/ccel/eee/files/enghml.htm.

As the hymnal's popularity testifies, Vaughan Williams evidently understood what makes for a good hymn tune. His incorporation of music by Gustav Holst (1874-1934), a number of his own compositions, and especially 43 (mostly English) folk melodies, all helped to set a new standard for congregational hymnody. [54] The folk melodies were especially significant. For, although himself an agnostic, Vaughan Williams was convinced that folksong was 'the spiritual life-blood of a people'.[55] His employment of it was part of a larger desire to build a grass roots national musical culture.[56] In other words, his attempt to marry the sacred and the secular was musically, rather than religiously, motivated.[57]

Later in the century, a parallel synthesis was attempted but, this time, for more explicitly Christian reasons. In the early 1960s, The Jubilate Group (as it was later called) was founded by Michael Baughen (soon to be Rector of All Soul's, Langham Place, London, and later Anglican Bishop of Chester) and a number of colleagues closely involved in work among young people. According to Canon Michael Perry, 'the group pooled their talents to meet the challenge of a new generation in the UK who wished to extend their singing beyond the foursquare ways of metrical hymnody and the unpredictability of Anglican chant'.[58] Their efforts resulted in the production of *Youth Praise* (1966) and *Youth Praise 2* (1969). In 1973, they also published *Psalm Praise*, a contemporary effort to revitalize the psalm-singing in the English churches. This volume not only broke new ground in terms of creativity and singability but was immensely popular throughout the 70s and 80s.[59]

These initiatives, however, were simply a small (and relatively conservative) response to much larger cultural and musical developments

---

[54] Wilson-Dickson, *The Story of Christian Music*, 234.

[55] Ralph Vaughan Williams, *National Music and Other Essays* (Oxford: OUP, 1987), 23.

[56] Matthew Riley and Anthony D Smith, *Nation and Classical Music: From Handel to Copland* (Woodbridge: The Boydell Press, 2016), 40.

[57] Onderdonk, 'Hymn Tunes from Folk-songs', 104.

[58] Cited in Andrew Butler, 'History of Hymns: "Blessed Be the God of Israel"', *Discipleship Ministries: The United Methodist Church* (n.d.): https://www.umcdiscipleship.org/resources/history-of-hymns-blessed-be-the-god-of-israel.

[59] In 1990, The Jubilate Group produced two other collections that followed the same approach: *Psalms for Today* and *Songs from the Psalms*.

in which the delineation between the secular and the sacred was becoming increasingly blurred.[60] While this process was fuelled by a range of social changes, one precipitating factor was the rise of a distinctive 'youth culture' in the post-war period. Unlike that of their parents, the culture of the 'baby-boom generation' (as it came to be known) was hedonistic, consumerist and anti-establishment. Furthermore, the 'alternative discursive world' that nurtured it 'was being manufactured by a bohemian and "delinquent" minority, based around Elvis Presley and rock-and-roll from 1956, and skiffle music in 1958-60, and centred on underground cafes, town hall dances and art colleges'.[61] Not surprisingly, music was at the very centre of the baby-boomers' self-understanding.[62]

In order to minister effectively to church-going youth who were inevitably being immersed in such a culture, a new approach to youth ministry was urgently needed. Because music was such a significant shaper and identity marker, a new approach to Christian music was needed as well. The rationale was clear: 'a generation that sought its youthful identity in music searches for its religious identity in music as well'.[63] In an attempt to compete, if not 'spoil the Egyptians', evangelicals 'began to construct parallel worlds of Christian record companies, festivals and organisations'.[64] This led not simply to Christian adaptations of 'beat music' but, in time, to the emergence of 'Jesus Rock' or 'Contemporary

---

[60] Evans, *Open Up the Doors*, 38.

[61] Callum G Brown, *The Death of Christian Britain: Understanding Secularisation 1800-2000* (London/New York: Routledge, 2009), 174.

[62] Michael S Hamilton, 'The Triumph of the Praise Songs: How Guitars Beat Out the Organs in the Worship Wars', *Christianity Today* (July 12, 1999), 30.

[63] Hamilton, 'The Triumph of the Praise Songs', 30. Such an understanding is reflected, for example, in Baughen's introduction to the first volume of *Youth Praise*: 'This book has been compiled to try to meet the evident need for a composite youth music book in Christian youth groups of many kinds. Its purpose is not to provide "musical entertainment with a religious flavour", but the provision of words and tunes, in adequate number and variety, to allow contemporary expression of youth praise and prayer and worship' (Michael Baughen [ed.], *Youth Praise* [London: Falcon Press, 1966], v).

[64] Pete Ward, *Selling Worship: How what we sing has changed the Church* (Milton Keynes: Paternoster, 2005), 13.

Christian Music' (CCM) – music that was secular in style but lyrically 'geared towards evangelism, apologetics, and entertainment'.[65]

It also led to the rise of 'Contemporary Worship Music' (CWM), which, like CCM, also traced its roots back to the Jesus People movement of the 1960s.[66] Historian, Michael Hamilton, divides the pioneers of CWM into 'reformers' and 'revolutionaries'. 'The reformers began with church music forms and sought to incorporate baby-boom values; the revolutionaries began with baby-boom music forms and baby-boom values, and sought to adapt these to the Christian faith'.[67]

---

[65] Larry Eskridge, 'The "Praise and Worship" Revolution', *Christianity Today* (October,2008): http://www.christianitytoday.com/history/2008/october/praise-and-worship-revolution.html. None of this was inherently problematic. Christians are called to engage the world around them and, in virtually every age, have sought to use culturally appropriate 'means' to do so (see David W Bebbington, *Evangelicalism in Modern Britain: A History from the 1730s to the 1980s* [London: Unwin Hyman, 1989], 41). The risk, of course, is that the medium will compromise the message. Critics of Christian pop claim that this is precisely what has happened. For example, Calvin Johansson contends that rather than proving to be a useful vehicle for gospel proclamation, 'Jesus rock' has instead produced music that is 'concerned with quantity (mass production), material profit, novelty, immediate gratification, ease of consumption, entertainment, the lowest common denominator, success first of all, romanticism, mediocrity, sensationalism and transience' – in short, qualities that are antithetical to the gospel (Calvin M Johansson, *Music & Ministry: A Biblical Counterpoint* [Peabody: Hendrikson, 1984], 55). This may well be true of the worse examples, but it is certainly not true of the best. Indeed, what is often missed by critics is the fact that, in the original context of the 1960s, much of the new Christian music was profoundly *counter-* cultural. It attempted to capture 'a style of music that had been used to express nihilistic philosophy and self-indulgence and turned it into praise of the God of Scripture' (John M Frame, *Contemporary Worship Music: A Biblical Defense* [Philipsburg: P&R Publishing, 1997], 57-58). This does not mean that every attempt has done this successfully. But when critics dismiss all without distinction, it's usually an indication of a personal preference for 'high art' over 'pop art'.

[66] Unlike CCM, however, CWM (at least in its initial phase) had more of 'the spirit of the folk hootenanny, and the ambience of a prayer meeting' (Eskridge, 'The "Praise and Worship" Revolution').

[67] Hamilton, 'The Triumph of the Praise Songs', 32.

One early reformer was Erik Routley, a Scottish Congregationalist minister and one of Britain's premier organists. Routley gathered a group of likeminded musicians around him who 'experimented with new poetic structures for the hymn lyrics and new instrumentation to accompany hymns. But most of all they tried to connect church singing to the contemporary social issues that preoccupied the baby boomers'.[68] This led naturally to the revising and modernising of older hymnals,[69] and to 'a phenomenal outpouring of new English-language hymnody that dovetailed perfectly with baby-boom concerns'.[70] Another influential reformer was Ralph Carmichael, 'an evangelical musician whose compositions "He's Everything to Me" (1964) and "Pass It On" (1969) – amongst others – suddenly permitted worshippers to choose between the historical hymns and more culturally relevant pieces'.[71] If there was one thing that united the various types of reformers, however, it was their tendency to remain 'comfortably inside the taste culture of formal church music'.[72]

The same could not be said of the revolutionaries. 'Ground zero' for this stream of CWM was Calvary Chapel, a modest Pentecostal church in Costa Mesa, California. Under the leadership of Chuck Smith, Calvary Chapel was not only one of the first churches to welcome the counterculture, but one of the first to embrace its music. As a consequence, a host of new songs began to emerge which were not constrained by the traditional conventions of hymnody. In fact, some congregation members even started to put Christian words to things like

---

[68] Hamilton, 'The Triumph of the Praise Songs', 31.

[69] Routley himself was responsible for editing a number of hymnals: *Congregational Praise* (1951), *Dunblane Praise* (1962), *Cantate Domino* (1968), *New Church Praise* (1972), *Ecumenical Praise* (1977), and *Rejoice in the Lord* (1985). *Hymns for Today's Church* (London: Hodder & Stoughton, 1982), which was the work of The Jubilate Group, is another important example. Edited by Michael Saward, it was one of the first hymn books to be published in completely modernised English.

[70] Hamilton, 'The Triumph of the Praise Songs', 31. Routley's move, in 1975, to become Professor of Church Music at Westminster Choir College in Princeton, New Jersey, not only helped disseminate the fruits of the British hymn explosion, but profoundly impacted American hymnody in the latter part of the twentieth century.

[71] Evans, *Open Up the Doors*, 38.

[72] Evans, *Open Up the Doors*, 32.

Coca Cola commercials![73] Others, like Karen Lafferty, trod an even more productive path. In fact, her 1971 composition, 'Seek Ye First', soon became 'a major hit at Calvary Chapel and quickly spread by song-of-mouth to Jesus People homes, coffeehouses, and "fellowships" all over Southern California – and then across the country. By the mid-1970s, it had also begun to pop up in a number of mainstream evangelical congregations as well'.[74] Following the success of a 'best of' Calvary Chapel album, *The Everlastin' Living Jesus Music Concert* (1971), Maranatha! Music Inc. was formed to help spread the new music to churches around the world.

Since then, CWM (which came to be known as 'Praise and Worship' music) has barely looked back. As Mark Evans writes: 'What began as a revolution has become big business; in fact praise and worship music is now a massive industry worldwide'.[75] Today, the major producers and distributors of the revolutionary stream of CWM include Hillsong, Vineyard, Bethel Music and Soul Survivor.

In historic mainstream churches, the Charismatic Renewal Movement (which likewise erupted in the late 1960s) also gave rise to a massive surge of new Christian music – both personal and congregational. One major strand of this music has sought to express a kind of 'romantic intimacy' between believer and Saviour, often characterised by emotional intensity, non-rationality and even elements of eroticism.[76] The other major strand has worked hard to re-express biblical truths in fresh, memorable and musically innovative ways. During the 1970s and 1980s, this strand was greatly aided by the various *Scripture in Song* volumes.[77]

---

[73] Eskridge, 'The "Praise and Worship" Revolution'.
[74] Eskridge, 'The "Praise and Worship" Revolution'.
[75] Evans, *Open Up the Doors*, 39.
[76] James H S Steven, *Worship in the Spirit: Charismatic Worship in the Church of England* (Carlisle: Paternoster, 2002), 123. See also Martyn Percy, 'Sweet Rapture: Subliminal Eroticism in Contemporary Charismatic Worship', *Theology & Sexuality* 6 (1997), 71-106.
[77] These were produced by a New Zealand couple, Dave and Dale Garratt. *Scripture in Song* was originally the name of a recording company registered by the Garratts in 1973. Their aim was to write, gather and record songs that effectively incorporated Scripture into contemporary musical forms. Through the various *Scripture in Song* albums and songbooks, the Garratts became key figures in the musical side of the Charismatic Movement. They have since gone

Since that time, not only have both of these strands continued, developed and sometimes intertwined, but choruses have given way to more fully formed songs with a variety of different structures and components. Key to this transition was Graham Kendrick, author of such songs as 'The Servant King' (1983), 'Meekness and Majesty' (1986), 'Shine Jesus, Shine' (1987) and 'Amazing Love' (1989) and, arguably, Britain's most successful contemporary 'Praise Maker'.[78]

Another important development of the 1980s was a move away from hymnbooks and songsbooks to the use of overhead projectors. By the 1990s, these began to be replaced by computers and big-screen video projectors. These developments not only enabled congregations to express themselves with greater physical freedom (given that they no longer needed to hold hymnbooks) but allowed a broader range of material to be sung by individual churches and new songs to be easily introduced and incorporated into a congregation's repertoire.[79]

Since the dawn of the third millennium, there has been a new burst of freshly written hymns. Stuart Townend and Keith Getty have distinguished themselves as leaders in this revival of traditional hymnody. 'In Christ Alone' (2001) – their best-known and best-loved collaboration – even has its own Wikipedia page![80] While Townend and Getty use a variety of song-forms (and don't always write together), their consistent aim is to provide twenty-first century churches with theologically rich lyrics and emotionally stirring church music. Not surprisingly, Getty and

---

on to become leaders in the global school of ethnodoxology, a discipline that helps indigenous cultures understand and express biblical truth in their own languages and musical forms.

[78] See, for example, Cole Moreton, 'Interview: Graham Kendrick – The Praise Maker', *Independent* (26 December, 1999): http://www.independent.co.uk/arts-entertainment/interview-graham-kendrick-the-praise-maker-1134491.html.

[79] In 1998, in order to deal with this phenomenon, the Christian Copyright Licensing International (CCLI) group was established. Its purpose was to allow churches to track which songs they were using and, via CCLI licencing programmes and distribution formulas, to pay an appropriate amount to writers and publishers for their usage.

[80] 'In Christ Alone': https://en.wikipedia.org/wiki/In_Christ_Alone.

his wife, Kristyn, admit to finding much of their inspiration in their collection of old hymn books.[81]

Psalm singing is also, once again, experiencing something of a renaissance. In 2008, for example, Sovereign Grace ministries held a conference entitled, 'Rediscovering the Psalms'. According to the 'Press Release', the aim of the conference was to explore 'how the Psalms model worship that is God-glorifying, Christ-centered, emotionally engaging, full of faith, relevant, and lived out every day'.[82] An album of 12 psalm-based-songs was also released at the conference. In addition to this, various websites are now providing resources for those who would like to learn more about psalm singing, and numerous blogs discuss and promote the relevance of the Psalter to the life and gatherings of the church.[83] Some churches are even making strategic plans to train their members in psalm singing.[84]

Aided by technological developments (especially new audio and video software, and various internet distribution networks), the last couple of decades has also witnessed an explosion of CWM from a range of quarters – e.g., Hillsong Worship (Australia), Bethel Music (US) and Soul Survivor (UK). While many songs 'come and go as quickly as any other ephemeral cultural thing', and some are theologically problematic, others have already become 'standards', and may well endure for some years to come.[85] This is particularly the case with those that have both a strong anthemic character and greater theological depth – e.g., 'How Great is

---

[81] Bob Smietana, 'Modern hymn writers revive lost art of Christian music', *USA Today* (April 16, 2013): https://www.usatoday.com/story/life/music/2013/04/16/christian-hymn-writers/2089271.

[82] Cited in Joshua Otte, 'WorshipGod 08 Conference', *Eucatastrophe* (27 February, 2008): https://eucatastrophe101.wordpress.com/page/16. At the conference, speakers addressed such topics as 'Praising God with Psalmist' (Bob Kauflin), 'Expressing Emotion with the Psalmist' (Thabiti Anyabwile), and 'Enduring Hardship with the Psalmist' (David Powlison).

[83] For a particularly useful list of such resources, see David Taylor, 'Resources for Exploring the Psalms', *Fuller Studio* (2017): https://fullerstudio.fuller.edu/resources-exploring-psalms.

[84] See Appendix 2 for more details.

[85] Brett McCracken, 'The Best New Worship Songs of the 2010s,' *TGC: US Edition* (September 21, 2019): https://www.thegospelcoalition.org/article/best-new-worship-songs-2010s.

Our God', Chris Tomlin (2004), '10,000 reasons (Bless the Lord)', Matt Redman (2011), 'Man of Sorrows', Hillsong (2013), 'O Praise The Name (Anastasis)', Hillsong (2015) and 'Living Hope', Phil Wickham (2018).

Finally, throughout the 2000s, there has also been a conscious effort on the part of many writers and producers to ensure a high degree of biblical faithfulness in lyrical content, matched with a commitment to contemporary tunes and arrangements, as well as quality production. The way here was led by Sovereign Grace, Emu Music, Townend and the Gettys, and has been continued by Matt Boswell, Dustin Kensrue, City Alight and many others. At the same time, numerous criticisms of CWM remain – e.g., its uncritical use of rock idioms, its emphasis on subjectivity, and the fact that both the style and (often) the volume suggest performance rather than participation.[86]

✽   ✽   ✽

Much more could be said about the contemporary scene, as it could about each of the steps and stages that have led to it. But I trust we now have a sufficient sense of both *where we have come from* and *where we presently are* to set the backdrop for the remainder of this book. For one of the lessons that emerges from any survey of the history of church music is that each generation has to deal with a number of *recurring temptations* and also with its own set of *unique challenges.*

The major *recurring temptations* are four:

(i) to side-line the practice of congregational singing (either by ignoring or misunderstanding the Bible's teaching);

(ii) to lose the clarity of the Word of God in our songs (either by singing untruthfully or unintelligibly);

(iii) to deprive the congregation of its central role in singing (either by turning it into an audience with excessive 'performance music' or by attempting songs that are unsuitable or unsingable); and

---

[86] Gary A. Parrett, '9.5 Theses on Worship: A Disputation on the Role of Music', *Christianity Today* 49.2 (February, 2005), pp 38-42.

(iv) to fight and divide over secondary matters (usually the style of music and/or the use and types of instruments).

The *unique challenges* are particular cultural manifestations of these recurring temptations. For example, due to the role that music has come to play in both personal and group identity formation over the last half century or more, many churchgoers no longer sort themselves by theological conviction or denominational affiliation, but by musical preference. [87] Many churches are, therefore, divided along various demographic lines – given that musical affinity tends to tie-in to age, ethnicity, culture and sub-culture.

What this effectively means is that our *aesthetics* are exercising an undue influence on our *ethics* and, in turn, our *theology*. This is a reversal of the classical Christian understanding of the ontological order between the three great 'transcendentals' – the *true* (theology), the *good* (ethics) and the *beautiful* (aesthetics). [88]

It also means that while the 'worship wars' have often been characterised as conflicts between the doctrinal merits of differing worship theologies (the *true*) and the edificatory advantages of differing approaches to congregational singing (the *good*), there is a third layer of conflict that needs to be appreciated – the aesthetic appeal of different musical genres (the *beautiful*). Indeed, truth be told, many of our 'worship wars' are, in fact, contests between competing aesthetics. [89] When we map on to this the fact that our musical tastes never develop in an ahistorical or purely individual fashion, but arise from the profoundly relational experience of singing and making music together, we begin see how practice entrenches bias and traditions become self-reinforcing. [90]

---

[87] Hamilton, 'The Triumph of the Praise Songs', 29.

[88] For in classical Christian understanding the *true* (theology) defines the *good* (ethics) and *good* defines the *beautiful* (aesthetics). See, for example, Peter Kreeft, 'Lewis's Philosophy of Truth, Goodness and Beauty', in David Baggett, Gary R Habermas and Jerry L Walls (eds.), *C. S. Lewis as Philosopher: Truth, Goodness and Beauty* (Downers Grove: IVP, 2008), 25.

[89] Jonathan Dueck, *Congregational Music, Conflict and Community* (Abingdon/New York: Routledge, 2017), 2. See also Mark Porter, *Contemporary Worship Music and Everyday Musical Lives* (Abingdon: Routledge, 2017).

[90] Dueck, *Congregational Music, Conflict and Community*, 4.

All of this suggests that we can easily be blinded by our preferences and prejudices, and easily miss the log in our own eye when trying to take the speck out of another's! It also alerts us to the possibility that some of our 'theological convictions' about church music may not be as theological as we think they are.

What then is the way forward?

Although her answers may leave something to be desired,[91] Marva Dawn's questions surely point us in the right direction:

> Can we find some way to prevent discussions about worship styles from becoming fierce and bitter battles waged between two entrenched camps? Can we instead find common criteria by which to assess what we are doing in worship, so that we can bring together opposing sides of various arguments, so that we can truly be the Church as we talk together about our worship practices?[92]

Of course, the only way to find *Christian* 'common criteria' is by bringing everything to Scripture, testing everything by Scripture and being led and guided by living Word of the living God in Scripture. It was for good reason that *ad fontes* ('to the sources'), the motto of the Renaissance humanists, became the motto of the Protestant Reformers. They understood that the key to the ongoing reform of the church is to keep going back to the Bible – the one divinely inspired written source of truth (*sola Scriptura*). Only the Bible can show us where we are right and where we are wrong, where we are wise and where we are foolish, where we are free and where we are bound. If we, as heirs of the Reformers, intend to follow in their footsteps, we must understand the same and do the same. *Ecclesia reformata, ecclesia semper reformanda.* This is certainly how I will be seeking to address the two issues we will be exploring in the two parts of this book – *Why we gather* and *why we sing*.

To that end, and with the task of ongoing musical reformation before us, my prayer is Cranmer's prayer – that Almighty God would continually inspire His people 'with the spirit of truth, unity, and concord: And grant,

---

[91] See John M Frame, '*Review of Marva Dawn*, Reaching Out Without Dumbing Down', in Frame, *Contemporary Worship Music*, 155-174.
[92] Marva J Dawn, *Reaching Out Without Dumbing Down: A Theology of Worship for This Urgent Time* (Grand Rapids: Eerdmans, 1995), 3.

that all they who do confess thy holy Name may agree in the truth of thy holy Word, and live in unity, and godly love'.[93]

---

[93] 'Prayer for the Church Militant', in 'The Order of the Administration of the Lord's Supper, or Holy Communion', *Book of Common Prayer* (1662).

PART ONE:

WHY GOD'S PEOPLE GATHER?

Oh come, let us sing to the LORD;
let us make a joyful noise to the rock of our salvation!
Let us come into his presence with thanksgiving;
let us make a joyful noise to him with songs of praise.
Psalm 95:1-2

From Exodus 15 onward, Scripture reveals that the singing of joyful and thankful songs of praise has always been a natural and fitting response to who God is and what He has done. Not surprisingly, the people of God – those who know His name and are the recipients of His grace – have always been a singing people. Moreover, if the pictures of heavenly worship that we are shown in Revelation 4 and 5 give us any indication of what will take place before the throne of God and the Lamb in the world to come, then we have every reason to expect that singing will also be a part of our eternal service of the triune God in the New Jerusalem (Revelation 22:3).

Nevertheless, in many churches today, confusion abounds regarding the place and importance of congregational singing and the purposes it is designed to accomplish in our gatherings. Is it an act of worship directed to God or an act of encouragement given to others? Should we only sing songs taken 'straight from Scripture'? Or are we free to sing songs of 'mere human composure' (to quote the *Scottish Metrical Psalter* of 1673)? How much singing should we do? Is it ever appropriate not to sing? These are only some of the more obvious questions and points of contention.

Needless to say, we are not the first Christians to wrestle with these issues, nor the only ones to get ourselves in a tangle over them. Virtually every generation of believers has had to grapple with such matters and endeavour to answer the questions raised by its own particular historical circumstances and unique cultural and ecclesial contexts. There is much, therefore, that we can and should learn from the past. But, even more importantly, we need to listen afresh to Scripture and apply it faithfully to the present. This book is a modest attempt to do just that.

Since a large part of the confusion over why and how we should engage in congregational singing is bound up with a broader level of confusion over why and how we should gather as God's people, it is both theologically prudent and practically necessary to address this broader question first before turning to an examination of the role and importance of singing in such gatherings. Consequently, coming to grips with why we meet together as Christians is the purpose of the first part of this book.

2. THE NEW WORSHIP

1. Answers Old and New

Why do Christians gather together? What do we meet to do? In the late
1970s, when I was a teenager in Youth Fellowship, an answer to that
question was provided in a song we used to sing with some regularity. In
fact, the very opening lines of the song, which were repeated three times,
left us all in no doubt: 'We have come into his house and gathered in his
name to worship him'.[1] But is this right? Leaving aside the question of
whether the church building (or, in our case, the church hall) is really
God's house, is this why we have come? Is 'worship' the most helpful and
biblical way to describe what we have met together to do?

1.1. The traditional answer

To the surprise of many, the traditional Protestant answer to these
questions is a resounding 'Yes'. The 1662 *Book of Common Prayer*
(*BCP*), for example, repeatedly speaks of the purpose of our coming
together as being for 'Divine worship' or 'Divine service'. The 'Preface' of
the *BCP* makes plain that all of its 'rites and ceremonies' have the same
aim: 'the procuring of reverence, and exciting of piety and devotion in the
publick worship of God'. The 'Orders' for both Morning and Evening
Prayer further elaborate on the nature of such public worship, declaring
that God's people 'assemble and meet together to render thanks for the
great benefits that we have received at his hands, to set forth his most
worthy praise, to hear his most holy Word, and to ask those things which
are requisite and necessary, as well for the body as the soul'.[2] It is clear

---

[1] Bruce Ballinger, 'We have come into his house' (©1976, Sound III and All
Nations Music).

[2] It has sometimes been suggested that a significant theological difference exists
between the 1552 *BCP* and that of 1662. For example, Mark Ashton comments
that, while not being a 'nomenclature purist', in the 1552 edition Cranmer 'does
not use the word worship to refer to church services', and suggests that 'such a
detail had important theological implications' (Mark Ashton with C J Davis,
'Following in Cranmer's Footsteps', in D A Carson [ed.], *Worship by the Book*
[Grand Rapids: Zondervan, 2002], 72). He may well have a point, for the term
'worship' is nowhere to be found in Cranmer's 'Preface' to the 1552 *BCP*, whereas
it does appear in the 'Preface' of the 1662 *BCP*. But the point is only a small one.

from such an exposition that the language of 'worship' is being used with a broader meaning than that which is normally intended by the primary Hebrew and Greek 'worship' words – *hishtachavah* (Heb) and *proskynein* (Gk). These terms, which account for over 80% of the occurrences of the word 'worship' in most English Bibles, usually mean, quite specifically, 'to bow down' or 'to pay homage'. However, there are several other Hebrew and Greek terms (which can also be translated by our English word 'worship') that cover a broader range of responses and so help us form a more general concept of 'worship'.[3] For various historical reasons, it is this more general concept that has given rise to the use of 'worship' as a systematic theological category covering any and every human response or approach to God – both individually and corporately. So the Westminster Confession of Faith affirms that 'God is to be worshipped everywhere, in spirit and truth; as, in private families daily, and in secret, each one by himself; so, more solemnly in the public assemblies' (XXI: VI). Along these lines, I Howard Marshall defines worship as 'the action of humans expressing homage to God because he is worthy of it. It is a human response to a gracious God'.[4]

For not only does Cranmer's 'Preface' use the parallel language of 'Divine Service', but (as per 1662) the 'orders' for Morning and Evening Prayer specify the same reasons for gathering as noted above. Moreover, the language of worship is used liberally throughout the rest of the 1552 *BCP*. For example, in 'The Order for the Administration of The Lord's Supper, or Holy Communion', we find the prayer: 'We prayse thee, we blesse thee, we worshippe thee, we glorifye thee, we geve thanks to thee for thy greate glorye, O Lorde God heavenly kyng, God the father almightie'. Clearly, then, in Cranmer's reckoning, worship is one of the activities that God's people are engaged in, and one of the ways of describing the purpose (or, at the very least, one of the purposes) for which they have gathered.

[3] Chief among these words are: (i) *yare'* (Heb)/*phobeō* or *sebō* (Gk) = to fear; (ii) *'abad* (Heb)/*latreuō* (Gk) = to serve; (iii) *sharat* (Heb)/*leitourgeō* (Gk) = to minister. Furthermore, while each of these word groups has its own semantic range, they can all function either more narrowly or more broadly, depending on context. This is true even of *hishtachavah* (Heb)/*proskynein* (Gk), which can occasionally refer metonymously to actions that would often accompany bowing down – such as offering sacrifice (e.g., Genesis 22:5; Jeremiah 1:16) or singing praise (e.g., Psalms 29:2; 66:4). It can also be used more broadly to mean devotion, service and submission (e.g., Nehemiah 9:6; John 4:20-24).

[4] I Howard Marshall, 'Worship', in I H Marshall, A R Millard, J I Packer and D J Wiseman (eds.), *New Bible Dictionary* (Leicester: IVP, 1996), 1250.

The traditional Reformed Protestant answer, then, sees and speaks of church gatherings as part of the broader response that, according to the apostle Paul, all Christians are called to make 'in view of God's mercies' (Romans 12:1). It follows, then, that the primary purpose of such gatherings (using Paul's language) is 'spiritual worship' or 'rational service' of a corporate or congregational kind.[5]

1.2. The revisionist challenge

In recent decades, however, the helpfulness of such a practice and the understanding that lies behind it have been roundly challenged. Marshall himself was one of the early voices to question the appropriateness of referring to church gatherings as occasions of 'worship', claiming that it is at odds with both the language and theology of the New Testament. He elaborated as follows:

> It is true that Christian meetings can be described from the outside as occasions for worshipping God and also that elements of service to God took place in them, but the remarkable fact is that Christian meetings are not said to take place specifically to worship God and the language of worship is not used as a means of referring to them or describing them. To sum up what goes on in a Christian meeting as being specifically for the purpose of 'worship' is without New Testament precedent. 'Worship' is not an umbrella-term for what goes on when Christians gather together.[6]

For Marshall, this was not an inconsequential observation of interest only to terminological pedants. Rather, he believed that to 'speak of a Christian meeting as being "a service of worship" with the implication that everything which takes place must somehow be related directly to this

---

[5] Paul's expression in Romans 12:1, *logikē latreia*, is variously translated (e.g., 'spiritual act of worship' [NIV], 'reasonable service' [AV and RV], 'spiritual worship' [NRSV and ESV], 'spiritual service of worship' [NASB]). Such variation is due to the fact that both of Paul's terms have a certain breadth or flexibility to them. For this reason, writes Leon Morris, 'we cannot feel confident that either "spiritual" or "rational" is absent from the adjective or that "worship" or "service" is lacking in the noun' (Leon L Morris, *The Epistle to the Romans* [Grand Rapids: Eerdmans, 1988], 434).

[6] I Howard Marshall, 'How Far Did the Early Christians Worship God?', *Churchman* 99.3 (1985), 220.

primary purpose is *to depart seriously from the NT pattern*'.[7] Such a verdict amounts to a very strong criticism of the 'we go to church to worship' tradition. Nor is Marshall alone in making such a denouncement.[8]

Building on his insights, others have brought a broader range of biblical theological considerations to bear on the discussion and argued that the terminological issues identified by Marshall are, in fact, reflective of significant differences between old and new covenant understandings of worship. In light of these differences, it is suggested that referring to church gatherings as occasions for worship perpetuates an error made by the early church; an error that involved

> the reintroduction of an Old Testament temple conception of worship: that 'church' is a formal public religious event to which the individual worshipper came in order to draw near to God (in a way that he couldn't or didn't otherwise) to approach him through various activities conducted by human mediators, in order to make some offering to him, in the expectation of being blessed by him.[9]

1.3.   A new 'worship' reformation?

So what are we to make of all this? Is such a critique justified? Certainly, as Tony Payne argues, where 'worship' is 'contracted to refer to our devotion to God alone in church alone, we develop an interest in such false paths as 'the holiness of beauty', the numinous, the symbolic, ritual observances and our offering to God'.[10] Likewise, where 'worship' is contracted further to singing alone (as in much contemporary usage and popular Christian literature), then evangelicals are in genuine danger of embracing a kind of 'temple model' of church, where 'worshippers' are

---

[7] Marshall, 'How Far Did the Early Christians Worship God?', 266-267 (emphasis mine).
[8] See, for example, John P Richardson, 'Is "Worship" Biblical?', *Churchman* 109.3 (1995), 197-218; Tony Payne, 'Why do we worship as we do?', *The Briefing* 299 (2003), 15-20; idem, 'Church and worship: Some questions and answers', *The Briefing* 301 (2003), 15-18; idem, 'The gathering: thinking afresh about church', *The Briefing* 302 (2003), 13-18.
[9] Payne, 'Why do we worship as we do?', 19-20.
[10] Peter F Jensen, 'The Lord and His Church', in *Church, Worship and the Local Congregation*, ed. B. G. Webb (Homebush West: Lancer, 1987), 118.

guided through the 'outer courts' by songs of praise into the 'holy of holies' to sing songs of worship.[11] Payne is right that this is nothing short of a modern day example of the 'reintroduction of Old Testament style human mediation into the way of relating to God'.[12]

Are we, then, in need of a new 'worship reformation' – if not at the level of our theology, at least at the level of our language? Certainly, some changes are necessary. For example, as D A Carson has argued, the popular 'notion of a "worship leader" who leads the "worship" part of the service before the sermon (which, then, is no part of worship!) is so bizarre, from a New Testament perspective, as to be embarrassing'.[13] Our gatherings cannot be neatly compartmentalised like that, any more than they can be siloed off from the rest of life.

But is it really the case that to 'speak of a Christian meeting as being "a service of worship" with the implication that everything which takes place must somehow be related directly to this primary purpose is to depart seriously from the NT pattern'?[14] Does this way of talking about our gatherings inevitably lead 'to their structure being determined in terms of what we offer to God in and through Christ', rather than the other way round?[15] Or is this to misconceive the issues? Might it even be the case that something of significance is lost if we abandon altogether the traditional answer to the question?

2.   Jesus and the Worship Revolution

To answer these questions, we need to appreciate the distinctive nature of new covenant worship and, in particular, the 'worship revolution' that the coming of Jesus has introduced. One particularly fruitful way to gain this appreciation is through an exploration of Jesus' teaching on worship in the Gospel of John.

---

[11] See, for example, T L Pedigo, *Worship Music in Three Dimensions: How to Sing Down the Presence and Power of God* (Colorado Springs: Winning Edge Publications, 2004).
[12] Payne, 'Why do we worship as we do?', 20.
[13] D A Carson, 'Worship Under the Word', in D A Carson (ed.), *Worship by the Book* (Grand Rapids: Zondervan, 2002), 47.
[14] Marshall, 'How Far Did the Early Christians Worship God?', 226-227.
[15] Marshall, 'How Far Did the Early Christians Worship God?', 227.

2.1. Worship in Spirit and truth

Under the old covenant, while the Israelites' broader 'call to worship' clearly encompassed every aspect of their life as God's people, the primary focus of their worship of God had to do with what went on in the temple in Jerusalem. In other words, worship was fundamentally tied up with the performance of certain sacred activities (e.g., the appointed sacrifices), made possible by certain sacred people (e.g., the appointed priests), at certain sacred times (e.g., the appointed festivals) and at a certain sacred location (e.g., the temple). This understanding is confirmed by none other than Jesus Himself in His conversation, recorded in John 4, with the Samaritan woman. Under the old covenant, as Jesus affirmed, Jerusalem was indeed 'the place where people ought to worship' (v 20).

However, as the conversation continues, Jesus reveals that with His own arrival a 'worship revolution' has taken place. He spells out the nature and implications of this revolution as follows:

> [21] ... Woman, believe me, the hour is coming when neither on this mountain nor in Jerusalem will you worship the Father. [22] You worship what you do not know; we worship what we know, for salvation is from the Jews. [23] But the hour is coming, and is now here, when the true worshipers will worship the Father in spirit and truth, for the Father is seeking such people to worship him. [24] God is spirit, and those who worship him must worship in spirit and truth. (John 4:21-24)

Neither on this mountain (Mount Gerazim in Samaria), nor in Jerusalem (Mount Zion, where the temple was located), but from now on 'in spirit and truth'. This is the character of the new worship.

But what exactly does Jesus mean by 'in spirit and truth'? The Gospel of John does not leave us guessing as to the answer. First, Jesus (as the Prologue tells us) is not only 'full of grace and truth' (1:14) but reveals the truth of the unseen Father (1:18). Indeed, He has come not only to bear witness to the truth (18:37), but He is the truth itself (14:6). 'Truth', then, refers to Jesus. Second, Jesus (as both He and John the Baptist tell us) is the one who will baptise in/with the Holy Spirit (1:33), giving the Spirit freely to all who believe in Him (7:37-38; cf. 3:5-8, 14-16). Later in John's Gospel, the intimate relationship between the Spirit and Jesus is further emphasised by the fact that Jesus calls Him 'the Spirit of truth' (16:13), because He will bring glory to Jesus by revealing the truth about Jesus to others (15:26). 'Spirit', then, refers to the Holy Spirit. Summing up: to worship the Father 'in spirit and truth' means to worship Him in and by the Holy Spirit, whom Jesus gives to all who believe in Him, and in and through Jesus Christ, whom the Father has sent into the world to 'teach us all things' (4:25) and to be 'the Saviour of the world' (4:42).[16]

2.2.   The arrival of the new temple

But there's even more to it than this. In fact, John has been laying the groundwork for us from the very beginning of his Gospel. He tells us that by entering into our humanity, the eternal Word has 'tabernacled' (Gk. *eskēnōsen*) among us (1:14). This language is far from accidental. It is chosen to communicate that with the coming of Jesus Christ, God has now fulfilled His promise to build a new temple, so that He might dwell with His people and they might worship Him forever. This is underscored by the fact that the same verse tells us that the disciples saw 'his glory' – indicating that the divine glory which once filled the tabernacle (and later the temple), signifying God's presence with His people, has now come to reside in a visible, physical, personal and permanent form in Jesus Christ. Indeed, His is a surpassing glory – 'glory as of the only Son from the Father', so that He might make the Father known to us (v 18). The implication of this for the 'old worship' is straightforward: in pitching the ultimate 'tent of meeting' on earth, Jesus has made the old tabernacle/temple redundant.[17]

The idea that Jesus is both the fulfilment and replacement of the temple re-emerges in John 1:51. In His conversation with the guileless Nathanael, Jesus refers back to the account of the Patriarch Jacob in Genesis 28:12ff. Here Jacob dreamt that he saw the angels of God ascending and descending upon a stairway or ladder that formed a bridge between heaven and earth. At the top of the ladder stood the Lord who there spoke to him reaffirming the promises He had made to Abraham. When Jacob awoke from his dream he said: 'Surely the LORD is in this place, and I was not aware of it'. Afraid he said, 'How awesome is this place! This is none other than the house of God; this is the gate of heaven' (28:16-18).

---

[16] From here on, then, when referring to Jesus' words in John 4:23-24, 'spirit' will be capitalized (so NIV) to make clear that Jesus' language refers to the Holy Spirit.

[17] D A Carson, *The Gospel According to John* (Leicester: IVP, 1991), 182.

When Jesus then says to His disciples: 'I tell you the truth, you shall see heaven open, and the angels of God ascending and descending on the Son of Man' (John 1:51), He is clearly claiming to be the fulfilment of what Jacob saw: the *true* house of God (i.e., the ultimate place of worship) and the *true* gate of heaven (i.e., the final meeting point between heaven and earth).[18]

These themes continue into John 2. In verses 1-11, Jesus performs His first sign (turning water into wine), which reveals that He is the one in whom the religion of the Jews finds its fulfilment. It is not surprising, then, that John tells us that by this act Jesus 'manifested his glory' (v 11). In John 2:13-22, Jesus cleanses the temple, which was rightly understood as a Messianic act, aimed at purifying the worship of God's people. This leads to the Jews' demand for a sign for Him to prove His authority to do such a thing. Jesus' answer in v 19 is deliberately obscure ('Destroy this temple and I will raise it again in three days'), because the temple that He would raise up was 'the temple of his body' (v 21). Jesus, then, clearly intended His disciples to understand (even if such understanding came only after He was raised) that He, as the Messiah, was not only going to *build* the new temple, but *be* the new temple! The Jerusalem temple, therefore, was now obsolete. The true temple had arrived.

2.3.   The gift of living water

One final passage from John's Gospel demands brief consideration: John 7:37-39. Here Jesus is teaching in the temple itself. The time is noted by John; it is the last and greatest day of the feast of tabernacles (v 37). The reason this is significant is because one of the key features of this particular feast was a water pouring ceremony that culminated on the last day, and that was understood to be a symbolic anticipation of the 'spiritual water' (i.e., the gift of the Spirit) which God would pour out in the Messianic age.[19] In this context, then, there can be little doubt as to the general thrust of Jesus' statement: 'If anyone thirsts, let him come to me and drink. Whoever believes in me, as the Scripture has said, "Out of his heart will flow rivers of living water"' (vv 37-38). Whether 'his heart' refers to Jesus' heart or the believer's heart, it is clear that Jesus is the source

---

[18] 'True' in the sense of His being the eschatological reality and final fulfilment of the OT types.
[19] Carson, *The Gospel According to John*, 321ff.

from which the believer may drink.[20] Moreover, verse 39 reveals that the 'living water' is none other than the Spirit.

Putting all this together, Jesus is the true temple from which the living water – the Spirit – flows to the believer (cf. Ezekiel 47; John 4:10). For, as we have already seen, He, as the Spirit-anointed Messiah, is the one who is equipped to baptise others in the Spirit and so bring them to the Father as true worshippers. This is why Jesus described the 'living water' He offered to the Samaritan woman as water that would become 'a spring of water welling up to eternal life' (John 4:14). It is also why He told Nicodemus, 'unless one is born of water and the Spirit, he cannot enter the kingdom of God' (3:5). To worship the Father 'in Spirit and truth', then, is to worship in and through Jesus, the new temple, and in and by the Holy Spirit, the gift of life that flows out from Him.

In 7:39, John adds one final piece of important information. When Jesus spoke the words recorded in verses 37-38, the giving of the gift of living water still lay in the future. The reason was because 'Jesus was not yet glorified'. In other words, He first needed to be glorified before He could function as the new temple and pour out the gift of the Spirit. As the Gospel goes on to make plain, this glorification takes place on the cross, for it is there that Jesus discloses the ultimate revelation of God and performs the ultimate function of the temple; i.e., to take away the sin of the world (John 1:29). In short, the cross is the place where the revelation of God's glory is fully and finally displayed, and the reconciliation of sinners fully and finally accomplished. Thus, it is only as Jesus is 'lifted up from the earth' that all people will be drawn to Him (John 12:32), the true temple, and are thus enabled to become true worshippers of the Father. In this action lies the fulfilment of Isaiah's vision of all people being drawn to the new temple to worship the Lord in truth (Isaiah 2:1-4).

Conclusion

Although there is much more that could be explored, we have seen enough to appreciate the larger dimensions of Jesus' words in John 4:23-24. To worship the Father 'in Spirit and truth' is to worship in and

---

[20] My own view is that v 38 refers to the believer's heart. See Carson, *The Gospel According to John* (322-326) for the arguments in support of this position.

through Jesus, the new temple and final place of sacrifice, and in and by the Holy Spirit, the gift of living water that flows from the new temple.

Behind this 'worship revolution' is the fact that Jesus has provided three things: (i) a *full revelation* of the unseen Father in all His grace and truth (John 1:17); (ii) a *final reconciliation* between God and sinners by taking away the sins of the world (John 1:29); and (iii) *spiritual regeneration* for all who believe in Him by the gift of the Holy Spirit. In so doing, Jesus has opened up a whole new era of worship; what He calls 'worship in Spirit and truth'. This is Jesus' function as the new, true temple.[21] The theological and practical implications of the ensuing 'worship revolution' are immense. David Peterson sums them up in the following way:

> In effect, the exalted Christ is now the 'place' where God is to be acknowledged and honoured. He, rather than a renewed temple in Jerusalem or on some other holy mountain, is the 'place' of eschatological pilgrimage for all the nations. The Father cannot now be honoured unless Jesus is given all the honour due to him as the Son (cf. 5:22-23; 8:49).[22]

As we will see in subsequent chapters, this 'worship revolution' also has numerous implications for both the content and direction of our praising, praying and proclaiming as God's new covenant people.

But at this point there are still some questions to be answered. How, for instance, do we come to this new place of worship? What does worship 'in Spirit and truth' look like in practice? (We'll explore these questions in chapter three – 'The New Wine'.) And what are the ecclesiological implications? That is, in what ways should new covenant church gatherings be different from the gatherings that once took place in Israel's temple? Does the 'worship revolution' that Jesus introduced mean that it is 'a mistake to regard the main or indeed the only purpose of Christian

---

[21] W S Salier, 'The Temple of God in the Gospel of John', in T Desmond Alexander & Simon Gathercole (eds.), *Heaven on Earth: The Temple in Biblical Theology* (Carlisle: Paternoster, 2004), 126-127.
[22] David G Peterson, *Engaging with God: A Biblical Theology of Worship* (Leicester: IVP, 1992), 100.

meetings as being the worship of God?'[23] (We'll explore these questions in chapter four – 'The New Wineskins'.)

---

[23] Marshall, 'How Far Did the Early Christians Worship God?', 227.

3. THE NEW WINE

1. The Difference Jesus Makes

'Six days of work and one day of worship – that's the biblical pattern'. Or so I was told as a young Christian. But is that right? Is it that simple? Is there nothing more to be said?

While it's not my aim here to explore the purpose of the Sabbath command, nor to open up the debate about its application to Christians, I'm not convinced the above statement adequately summarises even the Old Testament's teaching on the matter, let alone that of the New.[1] As the meaning of the word suggests (*Sabbath* = 'to cease from exertion'), the primary purpose of the Sabbath day was rest from work ('On it you shall not do any work', Exodus 20:10). This is why it naturally became a day of assembly (or 'holy convocation', Leviticus 23:3) and a day on which additional sacrifices were offered – twice as many as on other days (Numbers 28:8-10).

Of course, the obedience of God's old covenant people was not restricted to the Sabbath day, nor was their service of Him confined to what took place in the tabernacle or (later) temple.[2] What was tied to the tabernacle/temple, however, was the central part of their worship – the offering of sacrifices. These, as we learn from the book of Exodus, were the key to God's continuing presence with Israel (Exodus 29:38-46). Why so? Because they were 'the means by which God made it possible for a sinful people to draw near to him, to receive his grace and blessing, without desecrating his holiness and so incurring his wrath against them.'[3] Place was critical too (Deuteronomy 12:5-14). This explains the

---

[1] For a thoughtful, helpful and, to my mind, convincing treatment of this subject, see Thomas R Schreiner, *40 Questions About Christians and Biblical Law* (Grand Rapids: Kregal, 2010), 209-218. For a more substantial collection of essays on the question, see D A Carson (ed.), *From Sabbath to Lord's Day: A Biblical, Historical and Theological Investigation* (Grand Rapids: Zondervan, 1982).
[2] Carson, 'Worship Under the Word', 36.
[3] Peterson, *Engaging With God*, 49.

words spoken by the people of Reuben, Gad and Manasseh to the rest of the Israelites in the days of Joshua

> Far be it from us that we should rebel against the LORD and turn away this day from following the LORD by building an altar for burnt offering, grain offering, or sacrifice, other than the altar of the LORD our God that stands before his tabernacle! (Joshua 22:29)

The sacrifices that took place at the tabernacle/temple, then, were essential to old covenant worship. In fact, so integral were they that the prophets frequently spoke of Israel's future salvation and the purified worship of the new covenant not apart from but precisely in terms of the offering of renewed sacrifices in a restored temple.[4]

So what difference, then, does the coming of Jesus make?

1.1. The new covenant temple

One of the chief consequences of the 'worship revolution' that Jesus introduced is that 'the thought of sacrifice has been transposed across a double line – from cultic ritual to everyday life, [and] from a previous epoch characterised by daily offering of animals to one characterised by a whole-person commitment lived out in daily existence'.[5] In other words, with the coming of Christ and the sending of the Spirit, true worship of God has now been opened up to embrace the *whole* person in *all* of life. It is no longer tied to sacred times and sacred places. Consequently, 'under the terms of the new covenant, worship is no longer primarily focused in a cultus shaped by a liturgical calendar, but it is something in which we are continuously engaged'.[6] Not surprisingly, the apostle Paul offers the following exhortation to the Christians in Rome:

> [1] I appeal to you therefore, brothers, by the mercies of God, to present your bodies as a living sacrifice, holy and acceptable to God, which is your spiritual worship. [2] Do not be conformed to this world, but be transformed by the renewal of your mind, that by testing you

---

[4] Isaiah 2:2-3; 56:6-7, 60:7; Jeremiah 33:10-18; Ezekiel 20:40-41, 40:1-47:12; Malachi 3:1-4.

[5] James D G Dunn, *Romans 9-16* (Dallas: Word, 1988), 710.

[6] Carson, 'Worship Under the Word', 38.

may discern what is the will of God, what is good and acceptable and perfect. (Romans 12:1-2)

Two things are clear from Paul's words. The *first* is that under the new covenant the appropriate sacrificial response to the revelation of God's mercy in Jesus Christ is not the offering of animals but the offering of our *whole selves* ('body' = the total person in all aspects of life, cf. Romans 12-15). The *second* is that such a response requires both a *renewed mind* so that God's will might be discerned and a *regenerated spirit* so that God's will might be done (Romans 8:13). Therefore, while it is vitally important not to minimise the fact that old covenant worship also touched 'all of life', nor to downplay the 'significant continuities between the faith of ancient Israel and the early church',[7] it needs to be acknowledged that new covenant worship is radically different from old covenant worship in a number of important respects. Herman Ridderbos spells out the key points of contrasts:

> The New Testament knows no holy persons who substitutionally perform the service of God for the whole people of God, nor holy places and seasons or holy acts, which create a distance between the cultus and the life of every day and every place. All members of the church have access to God (Romans 5:2) and a share in the Holy Spirit; all of life is service to God; there is no 'profane' area.[8]

As we've seen, the theological reason for this dramatic revolution is that *the new covenant temple (and so the new place of worship) is no longer a building, but a person; the Son of God Himself.* Moreover, this person is no longer physically located on earth, but has ascended bodily into heaven.

What this means in practice is that if a person 'comes to Jesus' (by calling upon His name), if they are 'in Christ' (by believing in Him), then they have come to God's true temple, are permanently a part of the 'structure', and are (or, at least, ought to be) worshipping all the time. For this reason, the New Testament can speak of all Christians as a corporate priesthood,

---

7 Daniel I Block, *For the Glory of God: Recovering a Biblical Theology of Worship* (Grand Rapids: Baker, 2014), 5.
8 Herman Ridderbos, *Paul: An Outline of His Theology* (Grand Rapids: Eerdmans, 1975), 481.

called to spiritual sacrifices in a new, spiritual temple. The apostle Peter puts it this way:

> ⁴ As you come to him, a living stone rejected by men but in the sight of God chosen and precious, ⁵ you yourselves like living stones are being built up as a spiritual house, to be a holy priesthood, to offer spiritual sacrifices acceptable to God through Jesus Christ.
> (1 Peter 2:4-5)

Peter here takes us even further in our understanding of the new covenant temple. *It* (or rather *He*) is not only *something* (or better *someone*) we come to, but something/someone we actually *become part of.* Paul speaks similarly of 'Christ Jesus himself being the cornerstone, in whom the whole structure, being joined together, grows into a holy temple in the Lord' (Ephesians 2:20b-21). He then adds: 'In him you also are being built together into a dwelling place for God by the Spirit' (v 22). Little wonder he asks the Corinthians: 'Do you not know that you are God's temple and that God's Spirit dwells in you?' (1 Corinthians 3:16). This reality is true of every church and, indeed, of every individual believer (1 Corinthians 6:19)!

1.2. Spiritual sacrifices

In light of this, the New Testament's picture of new covenant worship has been summed up as follows:

> Sacred times and places are superseded by the eschatological public activity of those who at all times and in all places stand 'before the face of Christ' and from this position before God make the everyday round of so-called secular life into the arena of the unlimited and unceasing glorification of the divine will. At this point the doctrines of worship and Christian 'ethics' converge.[9]

This convergence can be seen by taking a closer look at Peter's own exposition of the 'spiritual sacrifices' mentioned in 1 Peter 2:5. For Peter, 'worship' and 'ethics' are indeed two sides of the one coin. J Ramsay Michaels puts it this way:

---

[9] Ernst Käsemann, 'Worship and Everyday Life. A note on Romans 12', in *New Testament Questions of Today* (London: SCM, 1969), 191.

In 1 Peter, as in Hebrews, the 'spiritual sacrifices' are first of all something offered up to God as worship [...] and, second, a pattern of social conduct. The two aspects cannot be separated, and the priority is always the same. The pattern of social conduct implicit in the 'spiritual sacrifices' dominates the central section of 1 Peter in its entirety, but the primary Godward reference of the phrase is reinforced at several crucial points as well: first in the phrase, 'acceptable to God through Jesus Christ' in the immediate context, and the expression, 'to sound the praises of him who called you,' in v 9; then in such expressions as 'glorify God' in 2:12 and 4:16, 'revere Christ as Lord' in 3:15, 'reverence toward God' in 2:17, 'conscious commitment to God' in 2:19, 'grace before God' in 2:20, and a spirit 'precious in the sight of God' in 3:4.[10]

That there should be a Godward or vertical dimension to the spiritual sacrifices of the new covenant ought not to surprise us. What is a little more surprising (at least for some) is the clear social or horizontal dimension that 'dominates the central section of 1 Peter in its entirety' (i.e., 2:11–4:19). This section begins with the following exhortation in 2:11-12:

> [11] Beloved, I urge you as sojourners and exiles to abstain from the passions of the flesh, which wage war against your soul. [12] Keep your conduct among the Gentiles honorable, so that when they speak against you as evildoers, they may see your good deeds and glorify God on the day of visitation.

Clearly, then, the vertical and horizontal dimensions of our spiritual sacrifices are profoundly related. The purpose of believers living good lives among their pagan contemporaries is not simply to silence their accusations (by showing them to be baseless), but ultimately to bring their accusers to repentance, so that they might join the chorus of praise to God on the last day (2:12).[11] In this sense, Christian living ought to lead others to worship of the living God.

---

[10] J Ramsay Michaels, *1 Peter* (Waco: Word, 1988), 101-102.
[11] Peter's expression, 'on the day he visits us' (or, more literally, 'in the day of visitation') is almost certainly a reference to the last day; i.e., the day of Jesus' return. See Ramsay Michaels, *1 Peter*, 118-120. *Pace* Wayne A Grudem, *1 Peter*

At an even deeper level, the social conduct of believers is itself 'worship' of God, for it expresses trust and hope in God. Consequently, the reason why believers ought not to retaliate is because we are to imitate Christ who 'entrusted himself to him who judges justly' (2:23). Likewise, the reason wives are to be submissive to their husbands is in imitation of 'the holy women of the past who put their hope in God' (3:5). In other words, Peter's ethics, far from being pragmatic or utilitarian, are both *deontological* (i.e., to do with what is right) and *teleological* (i.e., with a view to God's judgement). They also have a clear *virtue* dimension (i.e., to do with the development of character). For all of these reasons, says Peter, 'even if you should suffer for what is right, you are blessed' (3:14).

In terms of their social outworking, the 'spiritual sacrifices' that Christians are called to offer include: (i) submitting to the governing authorities (2:13-17); (ii) slaves submitting to their masters – even to those who are unjust! (2:18-25); (iii) wives submitting to their husbands – even to those who are unbelievers! (3:1-6); (iv) husbands caring for their wives (3:7); (v) living harmoniously with one another (3:8); (vi) doing good – even in the face of persecution (3:9-14, 17); (vii) our efforts at evangelism and apologetics (3:15-16); (viii) fighting against sin (4:1-5); (ix) our prayer, hospitality, and ministry to one another (4:7-11); and, finally, (x) our rejoicing in suffering (4:12-19).

Understandably, some have seen the coming of Christ and the sending of the Spirit as having brought about a radical desacralisation of the old covenant notions of temple and sacrifice. Certainly, the Christian believer (who has become a living stone in God's temple) has been permanently united to Christ (the cornerstone) and is therefore engaged in divine service 24/7. However, 'desacralisation' is a potentially misleading word, for all time and space have now been sacralised under the new covenant (cf. John 4:21-24).[12] Every sphere of life is not just a sphere of secular obedience, but a sphere of temple worship. Peterson is therefore right to conclude: 'Worship in the New Testament is a comprehensive category describing the Christian's total existence. It is coextensive with the faith-response wherever and whenever that response is elicited'.[13]

(Leicester: IVP, 1988), 116-117. But clearly this implies the conversion of those on view sometime before the last day.

[12] Carson, 'Worship Under the Word', 40.

[13] Peterson, *Engaging with God*, 18-19.

2. Worship and Coming Together

2.1. The 'worship' moratorium

It follows from all of this that when we come together as Christians, we clearly don't come in order to *start* worshipping – our worship started the moment we came to (and became part of) the true temple, Jesus Christ! If anything, we come together to *continue* worshipping. But (as we will see shortly) the distinctive thing is that we come to do this *with one another* and *with a particular goal*.

Because worship is a much bigger idea than 'what we do when we come together' some have expressed considerable nervousness about using worship language in connection with church. Surely to apply the word 'worship' to our gatherings is to turn the clock back, to resacralise a particular time and place and to reinforce the idea that worship is all about cultic activity and not ethical behaviour?[14] To make matters worse, in contemporary usage (as we've already noted) the meaning of 'worship' has been further narrowed to refer to congregational singing or (in some cases) certain types of singing. In light of this, John Richardson goes so far as to claim that our current notion of 'worship' is not only 'not biblical', but 'has taken on a meaning and a momentum of its own which threaten to distort our entire understanding and practice of the Christian life'.[15] Thus, the only way to counter such reductionistic distortions is to stop using worship language to describe anything we do in church.

In support of such drastic action, it is often pointed out that 'in the New Testament the vocabulary of worship is used remarkably infrequently in the descriptions of Christian meetings'.[16] This is certainly true and may even be one outworking of the revolutionary reapplication of Old Testament cultic language to new covenant all-of-life service that we've outlined in the previous pages. But infrequency is not the same as total absence. Moreover, these occasional instances reveal that there is no inherent conflict between the use of worship language for what takes place both outside and inside the Christian assembly.

---

[14] See, for example, Richardson, 'Is "Worship" Biblical?', 216-217.
[15] John P Richardson, 'Neither "Worship" nor "Biblical": A Response to Alastair Campbell', *Churchman* III.I (1997), 16.
[16] Marshall, 'How Far Did the Early Christians Worship God?', 217.

2.2.   Two important passages

So what are these 'occasional instances' and what do we learn from them?

(i) 1 Corinthians 14:24-25 contains an interesting use of *proskynein* language as Paul contemplates the scenario of an 'outsider' (*idiotēs*) entering a Christian gathering. Through the revelatory activity of prophecy – whereby God's Word is intelligibly spoken to all present – Paul envisages the unbeliever being convicted of both his sin and the reality of God's presence, and so falling on his face in 'worship' (*proskynēsei*). The use of such language clearly implies the conversion of the unbeliever, his falling down being an expression of humble repentance and submissive faith.

While Paul's teaching, in context, has a quite particular purpose (i.e., to discourage the use of uninterpreted tongues and to encourage the gift of prophecy), a number of important implications can be seen to flow from it. *First*, God is powerfully present among His people when they gather together. *Second*, His presence is recognised as His Word is heard and understood. *Third*, such a hearing takes place through the ministry of the members of the church as they speak the Word of God to one another. *Fourth*, the desired and, indeed, appropriate response of an unbeliever to such a ministry is to recognise and worship the God who is really among His people. *Fifth*, if this is so for the unbeliever, then the response of the believer to the ministry of God's Word ought to be exactly the same.

Marshall resists this last implication, first by claiming that 'worship is 'the 'outsider's' word rather than Paul's own description of what took place' and, second, by noting that 'worship' 'does not describe the action of the Christians but rather the reaction of the outsider'.[17] The first of these points is simply mistaken, for even in Paul's scenario the word 'worship' (*proskynēsei*) is not found on the lips of the 'unbeliever', but is Paul's own descriptor. As to the second point, it is hard to see why a believer would be exempt from responding similarly to the reality of God's presence through the hearing of His Word. The worship of God is incumbent upon all people.

As we'll see further shortly, while believers ought to use their gifts to edify others to the greatest effect, this is not as a substitute for divine worship,

---

[17] Marshall, 'How Far Did the Early Christians Worship God?', 219.

but as an expression of divine worship. Moreover, what 1 Corinthians 14:24-25 reveals is that the very act of edification has a purpose beyond itself: to enable divine worship. In other words, the effective edification of others in the assembly ought to *result* in true worship of God – either for the first time (in the case of the unbeliever) or in an ongoing way (in the case of the believer).

(ii) In Acts 13:2 the prophets and teachers (and perhaps other members) of the church in Antioch are described as 'worshipping (*leitourgountōn*) the Lord'. Although the verb *leitourgein* could be used to refer to non-cultic public service, the LXX usually applies it to service in the temple, as does Luke himself (cf. the noun form in Luke 1:23).[18] In Acts 13:2, it clearly 'refers to the kind of service in which these prophets and teachers were generally engaged in the church at Antioch'.[19] But what *kind* of service is on view? Craig Keener suggests that because the term inevitably retained its cultic associations from the LXX, 'it is helpful to think of spiritual sacrifices of worship'.[20] This is confirmed by the object of the verb: for irrespective of whether *leitourgein* is translated as 'worshipping' (ESV and NIV) or 'ministering' (NASB and HCSB) or 'serving' (as Marshall prefers), it has a clear Godward reference in this context: it is directed 'to the Lord' (*tō kuriō*).[21]

Given that the term is also here paired with fasting (v 2), which is then linked with prayer (v 3), some commentators have suggested that corporate prayer is now being regarded as the cultic activity of the new covenant, and thus a replacement for the sacrificial approach to God characteristic of the old.[22] While there is some merit to this suggestion (as we'll argue in a moment), it has against it the fact that prayer was just as much an old covenant activity both inside and outside of temple worship. Others have, therefore, suggested that *leitourgein* here refers to

---

[18] See Ben Witherington III, *The Acts of the Apostles: A Socio-Rhetorical Commentary* (Grand Rapids: Eerdmans, 1998), 393; Craig S Keener, *Acts: An Exegetical Commentary: Volume 2: 3:1-14:28* (Grand Rapids: Baker, 2013), 1991.
[19] Guy Prentiss Waters, *Acts: EP Study Commentary* (Holywell: EP Books, 2015), 304.
[20] Keener, *Acts,* Vol. 2, 1991.
[21] Peterson, *Engaging with God*, 68.
[22] I Howard Marshall, *Acts* (Leicester: IVP, 1980), 215. See also K. Hess, 'Serve, Deacon, Worship', in Colin Brown (ed.), *Dictionary of New Testament Theology,* Vol 3 (Exeter: Paternoster, 1978), 552.

the activities of teaching and, in particular, prophesying (vv 1-2).[23] In other words, it is the exercise of these ministries among God's people that is being regarded as a particular way of worshipping God under the new covenant. This is surely nearer the truth but may be needlessly reductionistic. In view of the natural connection between prayer and prophecy (1 Corinthians 11:4-5), it is most likely that Luke is using the term to refer *both* to the prophetic ministry that took place (and whatever prayer was a part of it) *and* to the prayer that naturally flowed out of it (v 3).[24]

Either way, the significance of this text, for our purposes, is clear. Not only can the activities of teaching, prophesying and (most likely) praying be described *as* worship, but given that the believers on view clearly gathered to engage in such activities, the purpose of their gathering may legitimately be described as being *for* 'worship' or 'service'. Peterson agrees: 'Acts 13:2 indicates the appropriateness of describing as worship a meeting for prayer and/or the exercise of gifts'.[25] Thus, Marshall's assertion that 'nothing suggests that "service" could be used to refer specifically to the character of a Christian meeting as a whole', goes against the evidence. Surely, that is precisely what Luke is doing, at least in this instance!

Therefore, Marshall's concluding claim – that 'to sum up what goes on in a Christian meeting as being specifically for the purpose of "worship" is without New Testament precedent' – cannot be upheld. Acts 13:2 provides such a precedent, and Paul likewise (as we've seen) regards divine worship not simply as one of the *fruits* of edification but as its *ultimate purpose*. In light of these observations, *'worship' is one biblically sanctioned way of speaking of the proper response to the living Word of the present Christ in the Christian assembly.* It is, therefore, a thoroughly

---

[23] David G Peterson, 'The Worship of the New Community', in I Howard Marshall and David G Peterson (eds.), *Witness to the Gospel: The Theology of Acts* (Grand Rapids: Eerdmans, 1998), 388. This is supported by the mention of prophets and teachers in v 1, and the fact that the divine directive must have come through one (or more) of them.

[24] Although using a different term (*latreuō*), Luke has also previously characterised prayer and fasting as an act of divine worship (see Luke 2:37).

[25] David G Peterson, 'Further Reflections on Worship in the New Testament', *RTR* 44.2 (1985), 36.

legitimate way (even if not the only way) of describing the purpose of the Christian gathering.[26]

3.   The Importance of Edification

3.1.   Congregational worship with a particular goal

If we wish to imitate this stream of biblical thought and language, there is a good case for speaking of our gatherings as '*congregational* worship' (as opposed to *personal* or *familial* worship). The addition of the adjective 'congregational' not only minimises potential confusion but has the advantage of stressing the fellowship dimension of our gatherings without obscuring their fundamental Godward orientation. Certainly, some such expression seems necessary. For, as Carson argues, 'if one uses the term worship only in its broadest and theologically richest sense, then sooner or later one finds oneself looking for a term that embraces the particular activities of the gathered people of God described in the New Testament'. Carson therefore opts for 'corporate worship', while recognising 'the ambiguities inherent in it'.[27]

Using such language creates no necessary conflict with the reality that all of life is worship or service of God. Jesus' words in John 4 certainly do not imply that God's people will no longer meet to worship, simply that their worship will no longer be centred on a single, sacred, earthly location (i.e., Jerusalem).[28] John Frame helpfully suggests that 'the difference between worship in the broader sense and worship in the narrower sense is a difference of degree'.[29] Otherwise put, our gatherings as God's people are (or, at least, ought to be) a corporate and focussed expression of our daily worship. Herman Ridderbos agrees:

---

[26] John Frame's judgement is balanced on this point. He writes: 'we may describe the New Testament meeting as 'worship', as long as we use other terms to differentiate between the different kinds of worship. Or, we can withhold the term worship from the Christian meeting – but then we must find other terminology to express the divine presence in the meeting and the special homage given there to God' (John M Frame, *Worship in Spirit and Truth: A Refreshing Study of the Principles and Practice of Biblical Worship* [Phillisburg: P&R Publishing, 1996], 32).
[27] Carson, 'Worship Under the Word', 49.
[28] Block, *For the Glory of God*, 16.
[29] Frame, *Worship in Spirit and Truth*, 34.

However much the 'liturgy' must be seen as a spiritual worship of God embracing the whole of life (Rom. 12:1, 2), this does not alter the fact that the indwelling in and communion of Christ with the church have their point of concentration and special realization in its unity as assembled congregation.[30]

Richardson may well be right in saying that God is not 'more "present" in church than anywhere else'.[31] Doubtless, Jesus' promise in Matthew 28:20 is not restricted to our church gatherings, as He has promised to be with us 'always' (*pasas tas hēmeras*). But that does not change the fact that our gatherings function as 'the focus-point of that whole wider worship which is the continually repeated self-surrender of the Christian in obedience of life'.[32] Our gatherings, likewise, are marked by a concentration or intensification of the Lord's presence, due to the fact that we meet to engage with Him *together* and encounter Him in and through *one another.*[33]

3.2. Applying the edification test

All of this begs an important question. Why, in 1 Corinthians 14, does Paul speak more of edification or mutual upbuilding (*oikodomē*) than of worship? The reason is straightforward. Paul is not so much contrasting edification and worship (for the first should lead to the second, as we've seen), but self-edification and church-edification (v 4). This is where the Corinthian Christians (like many contemporary Christians) were going badly wrong. Their self-centred focus on gifts that edify only the user meant that they were not edifying one another and, therefore, not helping others to worship God. Paul therefore urges them to 'strive to excel in building up (*oikodomēn*) the church' (v 12), to ensure that when they gather together, they will minister the Word of Christ to one another in an ordered and intelligible way. For apart from such speech, Christ's voice is not heard and understood, His presence is not acknowledged, and His person is not worshipped. Edification, then, is the ideal way to describe the *immediate goal* of the exercise of the 'grace gifts' (*charismata*), given

---

[30] Ridderbos, *Paul*, 486.

[31] Richardson, 'Is "Worship" Biblical?', 217.

[32] Charles E B Cranfield, *A Critical and Exegetical Commentary on the Epistle to the Romans: Introduction and Commentary on Romans IX-XVI and Essays*, Vol 2 (Edinburgh: T & T Clark, 1979), 602.

[33] Peterson, *Engaging with God*, 220.

'for the common good' (1 Corinthians 12:7), within the Christian gathering. Alistair Campbell, therefore, is right to say:

> Worship is offered to God, but it can be evaluated only by reference to men and women. Practices that do not help those assembled cannot be justified by reference to their supposed reverence nor excused by saying that they were offered to God and not to man. The one who does not bless the brother or sister whom he can see, will not bless God whom he cannot see![34]

This is precisely why I've spoken of edification as the 'goal' of our gatherings. A goal is something *measurable* (e.g., Have others been edified by the use of my gifts or not?). Goals are also *necessary to achieve a greater aim* (e.g., Have they been encouraged to trust God more deeply?). However we conceive of the interrelationship between edification and worship, the fact remains that our horizontal responsibilities to one another do not eclipse our vertical response to God – as if the second commandment ('love your neighbour as yourself') displaces the first and greatest commandment ('love the Lord your God'). Rather, the two work together; for not only does our service of others lead to the worship of God, but God is glorified as we serve one another (1 Corinthians 10:31-33). In that sense, we do not have to choose between edification and worship.[35] Rather *edification is the mode our worship takes with respect to one another, as we engage with God together*. For as we lovingly exercise the gifts God has given us, faithfully and intelligibly ministering His Word to each other, Jesus Himself is building His church (Matthew 16:18). In other words, the way Jesus is calling and shaping true worshippers, those who worship the Father in Spirit and truth (John 4:23), is as His body builds itself up in love (Ephesians 4:16).

---

[34] Alistair Campbell, 'Once More: Is Worship "Biblical"?', *Churchman* 110.2 (1996), 139.

[35] This is why Paul says: 'if you give thanks with your spirit [by speaking in an uninterpreted tongue], how can anyone in the position of an outsider say "Amen" to your thanksgiving when he does not know what you are saying? For you may be giving thanks well enough, but the other person is not being built up' (vv 16-17). Conversely, if a person's thanksgiving is understood by others then not only is God glorified, but others are edified as well.

Conclusion

I must not conclude this chapter without registering the obvious but important point that *the edification of others ought to be our goal in all of life.* Like the worship of God, it can hardly be confined to the Christian assembly, but encompasses every sphere of the believer's existence (1 Corinthians 8:1; 10:23; Ephesians 4:12).

Nevertheless, as we've seen, the pursuit of edification when we gather together will have clear implications for the way we approach 'congregational worship'. For example, Paul's teaching in 1 Corinthians 12-14 challenges the assumption that church services should be designed primarily to facilitate the believer's private communion with God. Such an assumption still occasionally reveals itself, as I discovered one Sunday morning when the 'service leader' asked us all to take a moment to greet those sitting around us. One man, clearly unhappy with this instruction, said in audible protest, 'I come to church to worship God, not to meet people!'

Paul would beg to differ – at least in what is being denied by such a protest. He envisages believers coming together precisely in order to meet each other and speak the Word of Christ to one another. This explains his two over-riding injunctions – 'Let all things be done for building up' (1 Corinthians 14:26) and 'Let all things be done decently and in order' (1 Corinthians 14:33) – both of which have the same desired outcome: 'so that all may learn and be encouraged' (1 Corinthians 14:31).[36] C S Lewis saw this clearly: 'Whenever we edify, we glorify, but when we glorify, we

---

[36] As we'll discuss further in chapter six, this does not mean that believers should never close their eyes when they sing. Most of us do this in corporate prayer and if that is thought to be unproblematic (which it ought to be), then there is no reason why it should be frowned upon in corporate praise. However, there is a certain tension between the call to engage with God and the call to engage with others that needs to be wrestled with here. Closing one's eyes may help with the first, but perhaps not greatly with the second. Having said that, it can sometimes be encouraging for others to see someone evidently engaging with the Lord with eyes closed. Therefore, wisdom would suggest that there is a need for both freedom of expression (not forced conformity) and also a flexibility of practice, determined by what is most edifying to others.

do not always edify'.[37] This is why edification must be our goal.

Nevertheless, as I've sought to argue in this chapter, none of this means that we are forced to choose edification instead of worship. To the contrary, our ministry to one another in our gatherings is, as Peterson notes, 'an important aspect of our service or self-giving to God'.[38] More than that, '[o]ne part of our meeting cannot be 'the worship time' (prayer and praise) and another part 'the edification time' (preaching and exhortation), since Paul's teaching encourages us *to view the same activities from both points of view*'.[39]

Let us gather, then, both for the purpose of divine glorification and for that of the church's edification, understanding the necessity of latter to achieve the former. For the only kind of public worship that truly glorifies God, is that which simultaneously edifies others.

[37] C S Lewis, 'On Church Music', in Walter Hooper (ed.), *Christian Reflections* (London: Geoffrey Bles, 1967), 94.
[38] David G Peterson, *Encountering God Together: Biblical Patterns for Ministry and Worship* (Leicester: IVP, 2013), 41.
[39] Peterson, *Encountering God Together* (emphasis his).

4. THE NEW WINESKINS

1.   What's at Stake in the 'Worship' Debate?

As often happens in passionate discussions about important matters, the debate over whether 'worship' is an appropriate way to describe the purpose of the Christian gathering has sometimes generated more heat than light. This is regrettable. 'Terminological questions are never matters of life and death', writes Frame. 'Modern English is different from Old Testament Hebrew and New Testament Greek, and it is rarely possible to achieve a perfect correspondence between an English expression and the expression found in the Bible's original languages'.[1] Furthermore, the New Testament has no singular way of describing either the individual activities that Christians engaged in when they met together, or their gatherings as a whole. Consequently, we should allow, if not encourage, some diversity in the language and descriptions we use.

1.1.   The primacy of God's action

That said, the discussion and the search for 'an alternative name that will better express what we are doing' (as Marshall puts it) has also been beneficial.[2] It has helped to clarify a number of important theological concerns lying behind recent debates; concerns that have often been responsible for their intensity. For example, one of the significant issues for Marshall is that worship language not only backgrounds the horizontal dimension of church but obscures the fact that the primary 'movement' in our gatherings is 'the God-man movement, downward rather than upward, in which God comes to his people and uses his human servants to convey his salvation to them, to strengthen and upbuild them'.[3] This is a laudable concern. To prioritise human action over divine action is to obscure the grace of God and turn the gospel on its head!

---

[1] Frame, *Worship in Spirit and Truth*, 32.
[2] Marshall, 'How Far Did the Early Christians Worship God?', 228.
[3] Marshall, 'How Far Did the Early Christians Worship God?', 227.

But does referring to Christian gatherings as occasions of 'worship' or 'service' actually do this? If it did, then Luke's choice of words in Acts 13:2 would have to be regarded as a major theological blunder. (Surely, an unthinkable thought!)

But Luke's description, like all such biblical descriptions or purpose statements, is a description of the human activities ('as *they* were worshipping the Lord ...'), not of God's action ('the *Holy Spirit* said ...'). Clearly then, it is not wrong to describe our gatherings in terms of what God calls us to do together in response to His mercies. But more importantly, as Acts 13 reveals, God's speaking and our ministry are not independent or even sequential activities. The Holy Spirit did not speak *after* the believers had finished 'worshipping the Lord', but *while* they were doing so (v 2). Indeed, He spoke *through* the ministry (i.e., the prophesying) of the members of the body!

An appreciation of this marvellous and gracious reality – of *divine action through human action* – is actually reflected in Marshall's own conclusion that 'teaching and upbuilding are primary', precisely because 'ministry is the means by which God presents his grace and worth to us and we celebrate the revelation by our response of praise and thanksgiving'.[4] In other words, while God's ministry toward His gathered people is logically and theologically prior to our response, it is chronologically simultaneous and practically inseparable. The same is also true of our response to God and our ministry to one another. For, as we saw at the end of our last chapter, it will simply not do to label prayer and praise as 'worship' and preaching and exhortation as 'ministry', since Scripture 'encourages us *to view the same activities from both points of view*'.[5]

1.2. The three-way movement

As Marshall's thinking unfolds, however, it emerges that his ultimate desire is not so much to find a term that better expresses 'what *we* are doing', but one that effectively communicates *all three movements* – i.e., God to us, us to God, and us to each other. In light of our observations above about the interconnectedness of the three movements, this is neither easily done, nor ultimately necessary. Nonetheless, here is where he considers the merits of the word 'service'. In my view, his case for

---

4 Marshall, 'How Far Did the Early Christians Worship God?', 228
5 Peterson, *Encountering God Together*, 41 (emphasis his).

adopting it is a strong one, as it is a word that works in all directions; i.e., when we gather God serves us, we serve Him, and we serve each other.[6] And yet Marshall retreats from the term on the grounds that 'the traditional associations of the word [i.e., that it is primarily about us serving God] are probably ineradicable'.[7] Instead he opts for 'church meeting', claiming that this brings out the fact that 'God's people are meeting with him'.[8]

But does it? Not obviously, to my mind. And even if it did convey this to some, such language says nothing about the *purpose* of the meeting. Meeting to *what end?* Meeting to *do what?* This highlights two related issues. The first is the need for God's people to be taught from Scripture (and taught regularly and thoroughly) about why we come together and what we ought to do when we are together. We simply cannot expect congregations to intuit this, no matter how clearly we describe our gatherings or label the various 'elements' within then. The second issue is that there is no perfect term or phrase that is going to solve all our problems and remove all potential confusion about why we've come together and what we've met to do. Whatever language we use will have its upsides and downsides, and will require clarification and elaboration.

For example, one of my preferred descriptions of the purpose of our gatherings is that *we come together to encounter God in the presence of one another and to encourage one another in the presence of God.*[9] But even this description needs to be unpacked if it is not simply to beg questions. How, for instance, do we encounter God together? Here is where the teaching of the *Book of Common Prayer* is particularly strong:

---

[6] Marshall, 'How Far Did the Early Christians Worship God?', 228. For the same reason, we could also consider words like 'blessing', 'fellowship' or 'love'. For each of these terms also works in all directions. And yet they are all sufficiently broad as to beg for further clarification. What manner of blessing? Fellowship in what? Love of what kind?

[7] Marshall, 'How Far Did the Early Christians Worship God?', 228.

[8] Marshall, 'How Far Did the Early Christians Worship God?', 228.

[9] Interestingly, the thesis of David Peterson's most recent book on this subject, *Encountering God Together*, is along similar lines. Richardson's issues with the language of encounter have more to do with how God is thought to be encountered in certain charismatic circles, than with the fact that He is genuinely encountered as His Word is heard and His people respond in faith and thanksgiving (Richardson, 'Is "Worship" Biblical?', 213-214).

it is as we 'render thanks for the great benefits that we have received at his hands, [...] set forth his most worthy praise, [...] hear his most holy Word, and [...] ask those things which are requisite and necessary, as well for the body as the soul'. What about encouraging one another? What does that mean in practice? Here, by way of contrast, the Anglican liturgical tradition is not so strong. In fact, it has been suggested that '[a]ll ministrations in the congregation referred to in the Prayer Book are performed by either bishops, priests or deacons, and there appears to be no concept of any ministry by individual lay persons within the congregation'.[10] This is certainly true in a formal or official sense.[11] But, as we noted in our introduction, by comparison with the medieval liturgies, 'Cranmer's services had a huge amount of congregational praying and involvement'.[12] Indeed, his liturgy 'has a much more corporate emphasis than some informal services today (where many individuals may make their own contribution, but people do less together)'.[13] Be that as it may, mutual encouragement has many facets (e.g., urging, exhorting, comforting) and can take many forms (given that it is linked to many of the 50+ 'one another' commands in the New Testament). Indeed, it is itself an expression of the overarching command to love one another.

As well as elaboration, my description also requires some supplementation. We don't simply encounter God in the presence of one another, but *in fellowship with one another as we minister to one another*. Likewise, we don't simply encourage one another in the presence of God, but *by the power of God as we exercise the gifts given to us by God*. This highlights the inevitability of having to provide further teaching. Still, the main point ought to be clear: we meet together *both* to encounter God together – drawing near with a true heart in full assurance of faith (Hebrews 10:22) – *and* to encourage one another – stirring up one

---

[10] Donald W B Robinson, 'What Theology of Order and Ministry do the Anglican Formularies Teach?', in *Donald Robinson: Selected Works: Volume 2, Preaching God's Word* (Sydney: Australian Church Record, 2008), 406.

[11] Article XXIII ('Of Ministering in the Congregation') of the *Thirty-Nine Articles of Religion* is clear on this point: 'It is not lawful for any man to take upon him the office of public preaching or ministering the sacraments in the congregation, before he be lawfully called and sent to execute the same'.

[12] Mark Ashton with C J Davis, 'Following in Cranmer's Footsteps', 73.

[13] Ashton with Davis, 'Following in Cranmer's Footsteps', 73-74.

another to love and good deeds (Hebrews 10:24).[14] In both of these movements (i.e., us to God and us to each other), the work of God's Word and Spirit (i.e., God's movement toward us) is vital. For we can only respond to God truly in the light of His self-revelation and by the illumination of His Spirit, and we can only minister to each other faithfully as we are instructed by His Word and enabled by His Spirit.

1.3. The place of 'offering to God'

The last issue raised by those who wish to question the appropriateness of using worship language for Christian gatherings, has to do with the place of 'offering to God' in such gatherings. Richardson, for example, has expressed considerable angst that 'worship' is 'increasingly regarded as the thing we offer to God, the means by which we receive *from* God and the context for an encounter *with* God'. Such ideas, he claims, not only reflect 'the craving to return to the familiar "bondage" of a recognizable cultus (Gal 4:8-10)' but are 'leading us away from biblical Christianity into mysticism and, potentially, idolatry'.[15] He goes even further:

> One reason for the present emphasis on worship is surely as old as religion itself, namely the natural, but false, assumption that there must be something we can or should do for God on a *quid pro quo* basis. Human nature is such that this tendency will always threaten to replace our reliance on God's grace. It is seen in Paul's constant need to set faith in its right relationship to works. However, it is

---

[14] Perhaps with Hebrews 10:19ff in mind, Peter Jensen makes the interesting suggestion that instead of using the words 'fellowship' and 'worship' in connection with church, we should speak rather of 'love' and 'faith' – faith 'because it focuses immediate and proper attention of [*sic*] Jesus Christ as head of the church, and his Word as that which shapes human response to his presence and lordship', and love 'because it focuses attention on our brethren and demands that we serve them as Christ our Head directs'. He concludes with his own suggested 'purpose statement' for our gatherings: 'We gather to meet Christ in the presence and for the good of one another' (Jensen, 'The Lord and His Church', 119).

[15] Richardson, 'Is "Worship" Biblical?', 211. Tony Payne expresses similar concerns (see Payne, 'Why do we worship as we do?', 19-20).

also seen in the frequent assertion that worship means 'giving worth to God'.[16]

We would be foolish to underestimate the reality of the dangers Richardson identifies. We must constantly guard against the 'perennial New Testament problem: of not holding firm to the utter sufficiency and fullness of who Christ [is] and what he has done, but wishing to reinject human religion and mediation in some form as an additional element'.[17] Christian history likewise reveals just how vulnerable we are to such a temptation. That said, is there anything inherently problematic with viewing 'worship' (whether by lip or by life) as something we offer to God? Hardly. The New Testament itself speaks this way (e.g., Hebrews 12:28), and even reappropriates sacrificial language to underscore the point (e.g., Hebrews 13:15). Of course, we don't literally 'give worth' or 'glory' to God (in the sense of 'adding something to Him'), any more than we literally 'magnify' or 'exalt' Him (i.e., make Him greater or lift Him higher). But we do *proclaim* His worth, *recognise* His glory, *declare* His greatness and *acknowledge* His exaltedness. Such ideas are embedded in the very heart of the biblical notion of 'worship' (expressed in the physical action of bowing down in homage).

What about the thought that 'worship' is 'the means by which we receive *from* God'? Is this a dangerous idea? Well, it all depends what is meant. Richardson is rightly alarmed at the prospect of worship being seen as 'a "softening up" process directed at God'.[18] Where such ideas do exist, they are pagan, not Christian. But does this danger become reality just because 'prayers of supplication are deliberately preceded by "a time of worship"'?[19] Surely not. Everything has to do with the understanding that undergirds these activities, not with their order per se. This highlights, once again, the need for patient teaching of the truth and gentle correction of false ideas about how and on what basis we can approach God. Furthermore, because God is generous, 'corporate worship' is very often a 'means of grace' whereby we receive from God – whether by being rebuked for our sins or reminded of His mercies or encouraged to trust Him. In this sense, our gatherings are, most assuredly, 'the context for

---

[16] Richardson, 'Is "Worship" Biblical?', 211.
[17] Payne, 'Why do we worship as we do?', 19-20.
[18] Richardson, 'Is "Worship" Biblical?', 212.
[19] Richardson, 'Is "Worship" Biblical?', 212.

an encounter *with* God' (to use Richardson's phrase), and a truly transforming one at that!

Marshall's concerns on this front are considerably milder than those of Richardson. He has no issue with the notion of offering to God, readily acknowledging that the 'spiritual sacrifices' offered by the Christian priesthood in the new covenant temple (1 Peter 2:4-5), while not confined to church meetings, are 'no doubt focussed in them'.[20] He likewise concedes that worship is 'obviously *an element* in Christian meetings'.[21] What then is his concern? It is one of order and emphasis. According to his reading of the New Testament, 'it is simply not the case that the purpose of Christian meetings was understood as being *primarily and directly* worship, homage and adoration addressed to God'.[22] Added to that, his view is that church meetings 'are for the benefit of the congregation and so indirectly for the glory of God. Worship in the sense of giving praise to God is thus logically secondary to ministry in the sense of God's ministry to us'.[23] This is why he regards teaching and upbuilding as primary and suggests 'the broad structure of proclamation of the Word leading to response to the Word is the right one'.[24] He admits, however, that 'this does not necessarily mean that these two elements must always be present in rigid chronological order'.[25]

In response to this, let me simply say that it is vital that we view our worship of God as being secondary to God's ministry to us. Marshall is absolutely right about this. In fact, given the constant temptation to see our own actions as initiatory (if not propitiatory) and meritorious (if not efficacious), this cannot be stressed enough. Consequently, songs that speak of us welcoming God into our gatherings or the quasi-pagan idea that we can 'sing down the presence of God' are profoundly unhelpful, if not heretical. Our self-offering is only ever a response to Christ's own self-offering (Romans 12:1-2; Ephesians 5:1-2), our spiritual sacrifices only ever acceptable to God through the saving sacrifice of Jesus Christ (Hebrews 13:20-21; 1 Peter 2:5), our worship only ever a grateful

---

[20] Marshall, 'How Far Did the Early Christians Worship God?', 225.
[21] Marshall, 'How Far Did the Early Christians Worship God?', 228 (emphasis mine).
[22] Marshall, 'How Far Did the Early Christians Worship God?', 226.
[23] Marshall, 'How Far Did the Early Christians Worship God?', 227.
[24] Marshall, 'How Far Did the Early Christians Worship God?', 229.
[25] Marshall, 'How Far Did the Early Christians Worship God?', 229.

acknowledgement of His gracious presence (1 Corinthians 14:25; Hebrews 12:28-29). Nevertheless, as we've seen, God's ministry to us through our ministry to one another can, quite legitimately, be captured under the rubric of 'worship' or 'service' (Acts 13:2), as well as having the aim of provoking and enabling true worship (1 Corinthians 14:25; 1 Peter 4:10-11). Indeed, both the work of Christ for us and our service of one another in His name have the same ultimate aim of glorifying God for His mercy (Romans 15:5-9; 1 Peter 2:9-10).

Marshall's concern to ensure that our praise of God is (and is understood to be) in response to God's ministry to us is, therefore, a valid and important one. But, as he himself realises, the best way to address it is not by insisting upon a rigid sequence of events within our gatherings (e.g., sermon always first, singing always second). Rather the solution lies in right understanding, and therefore in the biblical content of what is taught, both in sermons and in songs. Only gospel-filled preaching and praising will create grace-filled hearers and singers.

2.   Singing, Worship and Edification

2.1.   Three-dimensional church

Whatever we decide is the best way to describe the reasons for our coming together, the reality is that there will be 'a three-way movement' within our gatherings: 'from God to man, from man to God, and from man to man'.[26] This makes it necessary for us to think of our gatherings as three-dimensional events and to speak of what happens in them in tri-directional terms. It also highlights the need to appreciate what is distinctive about each dimension or movement, as well as what unites them and how they interrelate in practice.

In broad outline, the three movements we have noted are these: *First*, God, by His Word and Spirit, ministers to us. He does this as His saving and sanctifying Word is read, taught, spoken, prayed or sung to and by His people and as His Spirit opens our hearts to receive it. *Second*, we respond (both personally and corporately) to God's Word with repentance and faith, in prayer and in praise. *Third*, and as part of our response to

---

[26] Marshall, 'How Far Did the Early Christians Worship God?', 227.

God, we minister to each other – serving and encouraging one another in faith, hope and love.

Whether we realise it or not, everything we do when we gather together will fit somewhere into this threefold process, and most things will participate in at least two of these movements at the same time. For example, when the Word of God is taught truthfully and clearly, God is ministering to His children (movement 1) and the teacher is serving his brothers and sisters (movement 3). It could also be added that the teacher's faithful exposition is an expression of his own worship of God (movement 2). Likewise, when a member of the body prays intelligibly and helpfully, they are simultaneously speaking to God (movement 2) and edifying the other members of the body (movement 3). Again it could be added that if they are praying biblically (e.g., by praying about biblical concerns or by incorporating biblical content into their prayers) then God is also teaching us through their prayer (movement 1).

2.2.   Tri-directional singing

What about singing? How do 'psalms, hymns and spiritual songs' fit in to the picture we've just outlined? Given that the second half of this book is all about the place and role of congregational song, this is a key question. The short answer to it is that they fit in (or, at least, can fit it) everywhere; that is, congregational singing is an inherently tri-directional activity. Therefore, the longer answer is necessarily threefold. *First*, when we sing, provided the words of our songs convey the truth of God's Word, our songs participate in the ministry of God's Word to us (movement 1). *Second*, our songs are part of our responding to God in faithful prayer and thankful praise (movement 2). *Third*, again assuming our songs faithfully and clearly convey God's Word, singing is also a way of ministering to one another – e.g., by instructing and exhorting, confessing and reminding, encouraging and strengthening each other in the truth of the gospel (movement 3).

Paul's exhortation in Colossians 3:16 (a verse to which we will have cause to return more than once in the second half this book) beautifully illustrates the inherent tri-directionality of congregational singing:

> Let the word of Christ dwell in you richly [movement 1], teaching and admonishing one another in all wisdom, singing psalms and

hymns and spiritual songs [movement 3], with thankfulness in your
hearts to God [movement 2].

Here we see that movement 1 (the rich indwelling of the Word of Christ
in His church) is accomplished by movement 3 (the teaching and
admonishing that take place as the Word of Christ is sung). At the same
time, and by the same actions, movement 2 (giving thanks to God) also
takes place. So the three movements are profoundly interrelated and
wonderfully united, the one activity (in this case singing the Word of
Christ) accomplishing three goals simultaneously.[27] This is why, as we've
already stressed, we must strive for clarity in our communication of God's
truth (whether spoken or sung); for without it God's Word will not be
heard, His people will not be edified and God Himself will not be truly
worshipped.

2.3. The corporateness of congregational song

Finally, we come to the important fact that congregational music and song
open up possibilities for many (if not all) of the members of the body to
make a vital contribution. For example, those with skills on various
instruments can employ their gifts for the blessing of both God and
others, and all who are able to sing can use their voices to the same ends.[28]

---

[27] We ought not be puzzled by the fact that it is believers who are responsible for
the movement of God to us – by our 'letting' or 'ensuring' that the Word of Christ
dwells in us. This is not because our actions cause God to act, but because God
has graciously chosen to act in and through our obedient actions (cf. Philippians
2:12-13) and to speak through our faithful speech (1 Peter 4:10-11). This is one
reason why it is entirely appropriate to describe the purpose(s) of our gathering
in terms of what *we* have come together to do.

[28] There are those who have sought to argue that Christian congregational
singing should be done 'a cappella' (i.e., without instrumental accompaniment).
Their case is usually based on an argument from silence (i.e., that the New
Testament provides no clear evidence of musical instruments being used in
church life) and the assumption that every aspect of Israelite temple worship has
been abolished by the work of Christ. This latter assumption is transparently
groundless, given that singing, Scripture reading, and teaching are common to
both Old Testament temple worship and New Testament church gatherings. As
to the former argument, John Frame's verdict is difficult to gainsay: 'I know of
no passage of Scripture in which singing occurs that is demonstrably
unaccompanied' (Frame, *Worship in Spirit and Truth*, 128). Furthermore, even
it could be shown that every New Testament church sang 'a cappella', this would

Congregational singing, therefore, is a form of corporate worship that is simultaneously *of* the body, *by* the body and *for* the body, and yet all for the glory and praise of God.

None of this means that there is no place for believers to be sung to. As we see in Scripture, some songs were designed to be sung antiphonally (e.g., Deuteronomy 27:12-13) and certain psalms in call-and-response fashion (e.g., Psalm 136). In fact, over a third of the Psalms are addressed 'To the choirmaster', which may indicate that they were sung by the choir only – if not in whole, at least in part.[29] Further, there are a number of references to individuals singing in the midst of the congregation (e.g. Psalms 22:22, 25; 35:18; 111:1; Hebrews 2:12). The apostle Paul also countenances the possibility that a member of the church may come with a hymn to sing to the rest of the church (1 Corinthians 14:26). So there is clearly a place for solo or group 'items' in church, provided it is the Word of Christ that is being sung. Frame's conclusion is therefore apt: 'It is good to sing; it is also good to meditate while others are singing'.[30]

Having said that, and as we'll argue in more detail later, it is a great shame when congregations are sung to more than they sing. Such an imbalance strains against the emphasis of the exhortations of the New Testament, which urge *all* of God's people to sing Christ's Word and to praise Him *together with one voice*. An imbalance here not only encourages passivity – turning participants into listeners – but robs the body of a unique opportunity to minister to itself *en masse* and so be strengthened in its unity. Getting the balance right, therefore, is crucial. We should *prioritise corporateness*.

Conclusion

I titled this chapter 'The New Wineskins' because 'The New Wine' (i.e., the spiritual sacrifices of the new covenant) that flows from 'The New Worship' (i.e., the new way of serving God made possible by Jesus) has not only given new content to the gatherings of God's people, but has

---

not make it normative for subsequent generations. Description does not necessarily imply prescription, and, in this case, the evidence falls well short of description.

[29] J A Smith, 'Which Psalms Were Sung in the Temple?', *Music & Letters* 71.2 (1990), 167.

[30] Frame, *Worship in Spirit and Truth*, 129.

necessarily generated new forms of corporate response.[31] This would seem to be an inevitable implication of both the parable in which Jesus uses this imagery (Matthew 9:16-17; Mark 2:21-22; Luke 5:36-37) and the transposition of Old Testament temple theology that takes place in the New Testament.[32]

But this does not mean that the new has no connection with what has gone before. Not only is the new covenant the fulfilment of the old (Matthew 5:17), but there is considerable overlap between old and new covenant worship. This is why Jesus' disciples are to bring out of their storeroom 'new treasures as well as old' (Matthew 15:52).[33] It is important, then, that we do not draw too sharp an antithesis between the old covenant and the new,[34] otherwise we may needlessly forfeit many treasures.

We will return to this point at the beginning of the next chapter, as we consider the ongoing relevance of the Psalter to Christian congregational singing. For a further implication of rightly understanding the relationship between the old covenant and the new is that not all of the activities that took place in Israel's temple are irrelevant to Christian congregational gatherings. The general point, however, is that we simply need to appreciate *both* the difference that Jesus makes *and* the fact that

---

[31] See, for example, Jim Peterson, *Church Without Walls: Moving Beyond Traditional Boundaries* (Colorado Springs: NavPress, 1992), 141-162; Payne, 'The gathering: thinking afresh about church', 13-18.

[32] For an older but insightful exploration of this theme see Howard A Snyder, *The Problem of Wineskins: Church Structure in a Technological Age* (Downers Grove: IVP, 1975).

[33] Cranmer understood this, as is clear from the *BCP* 'Preface'. On the one hand, he was in no doubt that 'Christ's Gospel is not a Ceremonial Law, (as much of Moses' Law was,) but it is a Religion to serve God, not in bondage of the figure or shadow, but in the freedom of the Spirit'. But, on the other, he remained committed to 'those Ceremonies which do serve to a decent order and godly discipline, and such as be apt to stir up the dull mind of man to the remembrance of his duty to God, by some notable and special signification, whereby he might be edified' ('Of Ceremonies, why some are abolished and some retained').

[34] See the discussion in D A Carson, 'Matthew', in F E Gaebelein (ed.), *The Expositor's Bible Commentary: Volume 8: Mathew, Mark, Luke* (Grand Rapids: Zondervan, 1984), 227-228, 331-333.

'whatever was written in former days was written for our instruction' (Romans 15:4).

As for the 'worship word wars', I am not so naïve as to think that my analysis in this and the preceding chapters will, once and for all, bring these to an end. Not only is the temptation to quarrel over terminology a strong one (1 Timothy 6:4; 2 Timothy 2:14), but a certain amount of ongoing discussion and debate is needed to keep the key issues before us and to help us see them in proper biblical perspective. Nevertheless, I am hopeful that I've brought some additional clarity to a number of sticking points that have impeded previous discussions. Of course, my main contention is far from original. Over twenty years ago, Peterson expressed it succinctly and eloquently:

> [T]he God-directed ministry of prayer or praise and the notion of edification are intimately linked. Even 'psalms and hymns and spiritual songs,' which are *expressions of faith and thankfulness to God*, are to be considered simultaneously as the means of *teaching and admonishing one another*. This does not mean that our prayer or praise is a means to an end, namely edification. We worship God because of who he is and because of his grace towards us. However, participating in the edification of the church is an important expression of our devotion and service to God. God is glorified by the growth of the church towards the goals he has set for it.[35]

With these things understood, we are now ready to dive into the second part of this book and to explore what I consider to be the three principal purposes of congregational singing – i.e., praising, praying and preaching. But the biblical-theological foundations we have laid in this first half of the book are vital to appreciate, as they undergird everything that follows. For this reason, we will occasionally have cause to revisit or make reference to them, for they will help us grapple with some of the richness and complexity of (for example) praise, and the way it can function simultaneously as both divine adoration and evangelistic proclamation. But more on that shortly.

---

[35] David G Peterson, 'Worship in the New Testament', in D A Carson (ed.), *Worship: Adoration and Action* (Grand Rapids: Baker, 1993), 80 (emphasis his). For a more recent summary by the same author see Peterson, *Encountering God Together*, 41.

PART TWO:

WHY GOD'S PEOPLE SING

> [1] I will give thanks to the Lord with my whole heart;
> I will recount all of your wonderful deeds.
> [2] I will be glad and exult in you;
> I will sing praise to your name, O Most High.
> *Psalm 9:1-2*

One of the chief things that Christians are renowned for, universally and historically, is the singing of psalms and hymns and spiritual songs. This reputation goes back to the earliest times. For example, when Pliny the Younger, governor of Pontus and Bithynia (111-113CE), wrote to the emperor Trajan describing the activities of the early Christians, he mentions the fact that 'they were accustomed to meet on a fixed day before dawn and sing responsively a hymn to Christ as to a god' (*Letters* 10.96-97).

Christians may still sometimes fight over matters of *substance* (i.e., *what* to sing) and issues of *style* (i.e., *how* to sing), but we have rarely fought about *whether* to sing. As were God's old covenant people, we are a people of the song, as the whole rich history of Christian 'sacred music' – from monophonic plainsong to megaphonic Hillsong – bears witness. Moreover, it is a history that stands in marked contrast to (say) Islam, where music is regarded with considerable suspicion, if not as *haram* (forbidden), and where singing is not normally a feature of Mosque practices.[1]

---

[1] Although the Quran nowhere directly prohibits music or song, a number of the hadiths (i.e., records of the sayings of Muhammad and his companions) suggest that they are dangerous, most likely because of a supposed link to sexual immorality (e.g., Sahih Al-Bukhari, Vol. 7, *Book of Drinks*, Hadith 5590).

While the proportion of Christian congregational singing has varied from time to time and from place to place, most contemporary western churches devote about a third of their gatherings (and sometimes more) to the practice of singing and making melody to the Lord. They likewise invest a considerable amount of thought, effort and money into making sure that the musical side of church life is done skilfully and effectively.

Why is this? What can account for the importance accorded to 'church music'? There are numerous reasons why Christians (like Israel of old) are 'people of the song'. Indeed, Scripture reveals that congregational singing has several distinct purposes. It also has a number of concomitants or associated benefits – for example, it strengthens the bonds of Christian unity and helps God's people to engage emotionally with the truths they confess.

My aim in this second part of the book is not to say everything that could be said about church music. Rather it is to focus on (what I described at the end of chapter four as) 'the three principal purposes of congregational singing' – i.e., as a way of *praising*, a way of *praying* and a way of *preaching* – and to reflect on some of the associated benefits along the way.

5. SINGING AS PRAISE I:
NATURE AND OBSTACLES

Our focus in this and the following chapter is on what is, arguably, the central purpose of singing in Scripture: that of giving praise to almighty God. That praise should be central to our singing (in fact, to the very purpose of our existence!) should come as no surprise to attentive readers of the Bible. For praise, as Walter Brueggemann rightly affirms, 'is the duty and delight, the ultimate vocation of the human community; indeed of all creation'.[1] But what exactly does it mean to praise God? What are the aspects and entailments of the biblical depictions of praise? What is the precise relationship between praise and singing? And what, more pointedly, should our corporate praises look like, sound like and feel like today, in light of the Bible's teaching? These are the kinds of questions we will be seeking to answer.

1. The Relevance of the Psalter

Before delving into these questions directly, however, there is a prior matter that first needs to be addressed. As I will be drawing heavily on the Psalter in this part of the book, it will help us to clarify the applicability of both the theology and exhortations of the canonical psalms to new covenant congregational worship.

Church history reveals that Christians can tend to jump too far in one direction or another on this issue. For example, some so stress the continuity between the covenants that they underplay the significance of the salvation historical developments noted in part one of this book. Others so stress the discontinuities between old and new covenant worship that they end up with a quasi-Marcionite regard for the Old Testament in general and the Psalms in particular. Consequently, any suggestion of commonality between what once took place in Israel's temple and what should now take place in Christian churches is viewed as a retrograde step, if not a serious theological blunder.

---

[1] Walter Brueggemann, *Israel's Praise: Doxology Against Idolatry and Ideology* (Philadelphia: Fortress, 1988), 1.

As we have already seen, errors of this kind have not always been avoided – even by Reformed, Evangelical Protestants. A church building, for example, should not be described as 'the house of God', nor called a 'temple' – contrary to the 'Second Book' of Homilies.[2] The new covenant temple is none other than Jesus Christ and, by extension and inclusion, His people. Likewise, Christian clergy are not a mediatorial priestly class, and song-leaders even less so. Jesus Christ, our one and only great high priest, is the director of our worship and the leader of our praise (Heb 2:12; 4:14; 8:2). Accurately reflecting New Testament thought, Bishop J B Lightfoot put it this way:

> The kingdom of Christ ... interposes no sacrificial tribe or class between God and man, by whose intervention alone God is reconciled and man forgiven. Each individual member holds personal communion with the Divine Head. To Him immediately he is responsible, and from Him directly he obtains pardon and draws strength.[3]

It is vitally important, then, that such salvation-historical realities not be obscured, nor the newness of the new covenant in any way compromised.

But it is simply not the case that the arrival of the new covenant renders everything that took place in Israel's temple irrelevant to Christian gatherings. To the contrary, it is clear from the New Testament that all kinds of activities carried over from temple to synagogue to church assemblies – notably, public prayer, the reading of Scripture, preaching and teaching and congregational singing. Moreover, Paul twice urges the singing of 'psalms, hymns and spiritual songs' (Ephesians 5:20; Colossians 3:16), language which, as we shall argue in a later chapter, at the very least, includes the canonical psalms.[4]

I make no apology, then, for plundering the Psalter and, following the lead of the New Testament writers themselves, applying its teaching to

---

[2] See, for example, Homily III: 'For repairing and keeping clean the Church'.

[3] J B Lightfoot, 'The Christian Ministry', in *Saint Paul's Epistle to the Philippians* (London: MacMillan and Co, 1927), 181.

[4] So J B Lightfoot, *The Epistles of St Paul: Colossians and Philemon* (London: Macmillan, 1875), 223; Gordon D Fee, *God's Empowering Presence: The Holy Spirit in the Letters of Paul* (Peabody: Hendrickson, 1994), 654.

the life and gatherings of the churches of Jesus Christ.[5] For while I am not persuaded by either the philological or theological arguments for 'exclusive psalmody',[6] there can be little doubt about the authority and relevance of the Psalter for our subject. Indeed, it is, quite uniquely, 'God's canon of praise, each Psalm inspired by God and the entire Book of Psalms collected under the Spirit's direction for use by the Church',[7] as its title bears witness (*sefer tehillim* = 'The Book of Praises'). Patrick Miller expresses the point helpfully:

> In the hymns of Israel the most elemental structure of the Old Testament faith is set forth. So in the praises of this people the foundation stones of both theology and piety in the Judeo-Christian tradition are laid down. In what was said we learn of the one we call Lord. In the way it was said – both in shape and tone – we are given a model for our own response to God.[8]

This is precisely why the singing of the Psalms, historically speaking, has proved to be such a blessing to the Christian church, and why the widespread neglect of this heritage, at least in many contemporary evangelical congregations, is something of a bewildering departure from the historic practice of the saints.[9] For example, the great fourth century Archbishop of Constantinople, John Chrysostom, was so convinced of the

---

[5] According to the UBS *Greek New Testament* 'Index of Quotations', a total of 58 verses from 40 different Psalms are quoted in the NT, some several times.

[6] For a sympathetically argued case against 'exclusive psalmody' see Frame, *Worship in Spirit and Truth*, 123-127.

[7] 'The Psalms in the Worship of the Church', a paper submitted to the Synod of the Reformed Presbyterian Church of North America, June 2004 by Synod's Study Committee on Worship, 9:
http://www.reformedprescambridge.com/articles/Psalms_in_worship_final_version.pdf.

[8] Patrick D Miller, *Interpreting the Psalms* (Philadelphia: Fortress Press, 1986), 64.

[9] The word 'heritage' is important here. For as John Kortering rightly argues: 'Heritage must not be confused with tradition. Traditionalists hold onto the past just because they refuse all change. If we see psalm singing as a heritage, we hold onto psalm singing as a divine mandate, but recognize that it too must be adapted to the singing of each generation. In this way we hold a healthy appreciation for the work of the Spirit'. See John Kortering, 'Psalm Singing: A Reformed Heritage' (16 July, 2000): http://www.prca.org/pamphlets/pamphlet_37.html.

value of psalmody that he advocated their use morning and evening and in every sphere and season of life:

> The grace of the Holy Ghost hath so ordered it, that the Psalms of David should be recited and sung night and day. In the Church's vigils – in the morning – at funeral solemnities – the first, the midst, and the last is David. In private houses, where virgins spin – in the monasteries – in the deserts, where men converse with God – the first, the midst, and the last is David. In the night, when men sleep, he wakes them up to sing; and collecting the servants of God into angelic troops, turns earth into heaven, and of men makes angels, chanting David's Psalms.[10]

In terms of the Anglican heritage, Cranmer was of the same view, appointing several Psalms to be said each day, at both Morning Prayer and Evening Prayer. The goal was for Christian people to read through the entire Psalter every month![11]

We will have much more to say about the unique value of the Psalter in the pages and chapters that follow, but with the question of its relevance behind us, we now turn to an exploration of the nature of biblical praise.

2. The Nature of Biblical Praise

2.1 The parameters of praise

The Old Testament presents us with a wide range of Hebrew words that can either be translated as 'praise' or are related to the concept and practice of praise. Here, listed alphabetically, is something of a 'Top 20':

1. *'Alatz* = to exult, rejoice, triumph
2. *Barak* = to bless God as an act of adoration
3. *Basar* = to announce, preach, publish, tell forth good news

---

[10] John Chrysostom, Homily 6, 'On Penitence'. Cited in Terry Johnson, 'The History of Psalm Singing in the Christian Church', in Joel R Beeke and Anthony T Selvaggio (eds.), *Sing a New Song: Recovering Psalm Singing for the Twenty-First Century* (Grand Rapids: Reformation Heritage Books, 2010), 45.

[11] See 'The table and kalendar expressynge the ordre of the psalmes and lessons, to be sayed at the mornyng and evening prayer throughout the yere, excepte certayn proper feastes, as the rules followynge more plainlye declare', in the 1552 *BCP*.

4. *Gadal* = to advance, boast in, increase, lift up, magnify, promote
5. *Giyl* = to rejoice, shout in exultation, leap for joy
6. *Hālal* = to boast, praise, celebrate
7. *Kabad* = to glorify, honour, promote, make great or weighty
8. *Macha* = to clap or strike hands together in exultation
9. *Nagad* = to tell, announce, praise, profess, rehearse, report, show forth, utter
10. *Nasa* = to lift up (e.g., hands), exalt
11. *Ranan* = to emit a loud sound, to shout or sing for joy or gladness
12. *Rua'* = to shout aloud, make a joyful noise
13. *Safar* = to recount, declare, tell forth
14. *Salal* = to extol, exalt, lift up, raise up
15. *Samach* = to rejoice, be cheerful, make merry
16. *Shabach* = to commend, rejoice, sing praises, extol
17. *Tehillah* = praise, a song of praise
18. *Todah* = thanksgiving, thank-offering
19. *Yadah* = to praise, confess
20. *Zamar* = to sing praise, play an instrument

The Greek New Testament, similarly, has a broad vocabulary of praise related terms. So here again is something of an alphabetical 'Top 20':

1. *Adō* = to sing, to praise or proclaim in song
2. *Agalliaō* = to jump for joy, to leap or exult
3. *Aineō* = to praise, acclaim or commend
4. *Allelouia* = an adoring exclamation (lit. praise to Yahweh)
5. *Chairō* = to rejoice, congratulate, be glad, cheerful, happy or blessed
6. *Doxazō* = to glorify, esteem, honour, magnify
7. *Epaineō* = to praise, laud, acclaim or express admiration
8. *Euaggelizō* = to announce, preach, publish, tell forth good news
9. *Eucharisteō* = to be grateful, to express gratitude, to give thanks
10. *Eulogeō* = to speak well of, bless, thank, praise
11. *Hallomai* = to jump, to gush, leap, spring up
12. *Homologeō* = to confess, acknowledge, give thanks, promise
13. *Hosanna* = a shout of praise (lit. help or save)
14. *Humneō* = to sing a hymn, celebrate God in song, praise
15. *Kauchaomai* = to boast, glory, brag about, take pride in
16. *Megalunō* = to declare great, extol, magnify, praise

17. *Psallō* = to play a stringed instrument, make melody, sing psalms
18. *Skirtaō* = to jump, sympathetically move, leap for joy
19. *Thriambeuō* = to make an acclamatory procession, celebrate, triumph
20. *Timaō* = to honour, value, revere, show high regard for

Neither of these lists is anything close to exhaustive. It is also important to realise that the Bible writers can sometimes talk about or engage in praise without employing any of the usual vocabulary for praise.[12] But inasmuch as the two normally go together, what the lists above reveal is that the biblical concept of praise is rich, deep and broad, embracing the attitudinal, devotional, verbal, emotional, physical, gestural, behavioural and musical aspects of divine glorification.

When viewed as a whole, the central idea expressed by the biblical words for praise (whether it is being offered to God, idols or humans) is this: *praise is the expression of respect, admiration or gratitude by the declaration of the greatness, goodness or worthiness of the one praised.* Thus, in regard to divine praise, Miller writes: 'The act of praise, which in a most basic way is the goal of existence, means both to acknowledge and to confess who God is and, in so doing, to render honor and glory to the one who is the object of praise'.[13]

2.2   The two faces of praise

In biblical usage, the language of divine praise has two faces or aspects to it: that is, we can *praise God to God* (the *adoration* aspect) and we can *praise God to others* (the *advertising* aspect).[14] This bi-dimensionality or dual-directionality is not unique to human-to-divine praise, but equally

---

[12] Psalm 8:1 ('O LORD, our Lord, how majestic is your name in all the earth') is a notable example. See the discussion in James Hely Hutchinson, 'The Psalms and Praise', in David G Firth and Philip S Johnston (eds.), *Interpreting the Psalms: Issues and Approaches* (Downers Grove: IVP, 2005), 86-87.

[13] Patrick D Miller Jr, '"Enthroned on the Praises of Israel": The Praise of God in Old Testament Theology', *Interpretation* 39 (January, 1985), 11.

[14] I've borrowed the language of 'advertising' from Tony Payne, 'Confessions of the Teenage Praise Junkie', *The Briefing* (20 February, 1996): http://gotherefor.com/offer-search.php?pagetype=search&changestore=true&page=163&store=AU.

applies to human-to-human praise. For instance, I can praise my wife either by telling *her* how kind and thoughtful she is or by telling *others* how kind and thoughtful she is. Both are acts of praise. Of course, there is no either/or in God's case; He is both omniscient (all-knowing) and omnipresent (everywhere) and therefore never 'out of the room' or 'out of earshot'. So even when He is praised to others, He is always present to receive His praise. Furthermore, while it is clearly possible to praise God privately – as did David when lying on his bed or during the watches of the night (Psalm 63:5-6), Scripture indicates that the heavenly hosts are both aware of our praise and constantly engaged in praise of their own (Psalms 103:20; 138:1; 148:1-2; 1 Corinthians 4:9; 11:10; 1 Timothy 5:21; Revelation 4-5).[15] Therefore, whether we realise it or not, *it is actually impossible not to praise God to a wider audience, even when our praise appears to be private*. The two faces of praise, then, necessarily entail one another.

One of the implications of this is that our public praise of God (particularly, but not only, when it is sung) inevitably has an evangelistic dimension to it, for it bears witness to who God is and what He has done. Conversely, our evangelism (i.e., the many and varied ways we communicate the grace of God and His gospel to others) is also an act of praise, for it inevitably glorifies God – irrespective of the response of the hearers. So while we should be careful not to erase the distinction between the two faces of praise – i.e., *divine adoration* and *public proclamation* – or to diminish the priority of the former, the two cannot ultimately be separated. For, as the following psalms illustrate, just as divine adoration will inevitably spill over into public proclamation, so public proclamation is designed to increase divine adoration.

> Sing praises (Heb. *zamar*) to the LORD,
>   who sits enthroned in Zion!
> Tell (Heb. *nagad*) among the peoples his deeds!
>
> *Psalm 9:11*

---

[15] For a clear and helpful discussion of the role of angels in divine glorification and the need for believers to be aware of them in our daily lives, see Wayne A Grudem, *Systematic Theology: An Introduction to Biblical Doctrine* (Grand Rapids: Zondervan, 1994), 404-405.

> For this I will praise (Heb. *yadah*) you, O LORD,
>> among the nations,
>> and sing (Heb. *zamar*) to your name.
>
> *Psalm 18:49*

> Sing (Heb. *shir*) to him, sing praises (*zamar*) to him;
>> tell (Heb. *siach*) of all his wondrous works!
>
> *Psalm 105:2*

> I will give thanks (Heb. *yadah*) to you, O LORD,
>> among the peoples;
>> I will sing praises (Heb. *zamar*) to you among the nations.
>
> *Psalm 108:3*

What all this means is that our singing as God's people is not a retreat from the world but a key part of our witness to the world. This is so even when it takes place in what is, arguably, '*the most appropriate locus of praise*'; the congregational setting.[16]

This was brought home to me recently as I stood outside St Andrew's Cathedral in Sydney, waiting for a friend to arrive, and noticed how many passers-by were arrested by the sound of the praises of God emanating from the congregation within. David Barker is, therefore, right: 'Doxology is to evoke, as well as climax in, mission'.[17] Of course, the converse is also true: mission is to evoke, as well as climax in, doxology (e.g., Psalm 67).[18]

2.3   The need for holistic praise

The texts cited above, and many others like them, all link praise specifically with singing. But before we unpack the significance of this link, we need to note that *praise is not reducible to singing*. The heart of praise is an inward desire for God to be acknowledged, honoured and thanked, whatever form that might take. Of course, it is both natural and healthy for our inner thoughts and feelings to express themselves in

---

[16] Hely Hutchinson, 'The Psalms and Praise', 88 (emphasis his).

[17] David G Barker, 'Praise and Praxis: Doxology as the Context for Kingdom Ministry', *Baptist Review of Theology* 3:1 (Spring 1993), 5.

[18] As John Piper has memorably expressed it: 'Mission exists because worship doesn't' (*Let the Nations Be Glad! The Supremacy of God in Missions* [Grand Rapids: Baker, 2003], 17).

audible utterances and outward gestures. That is why praise, right throughout the Bible, invariably involves *verbal expressions* – like speaking, shouting and singing – and accompanying *bodily actions* – clapping, hand-raising and dancing (Psalms 47:1; 63:3-4; 149:3). But the inward desire is (or, at least, should be) the source of these outworkings.

The integration of the inner and the outer, then, is critical: for words without deeds can be hollow (James 2:14-16) and both words and actions without heart are necessarily hypocritical (Isaiah 29:13; Matthew 15:8). Furthermore, the alignment of public acts of worship with everyday acts of obedience is equally indispensable, for Scripture reveals that the latter are, in some sense, superior to the former and the former are worthless without the latter (Matthew 5:23-24; 23:23). That is why all attempts to substitute ritual acts for moral deeds are roundly condemned by the Bible writers in the strongest possible terms. As the prophet Samuel said to King Saul:

> Does the LORD delight in burnt offering and sacrifices as much as in obeying the voice of the LORD? To obey is better than sacrifice, and to heed is better than the fat of rams. For rebellion is like the sin of divination, and arrogance like the evil of idolatry. (1 Samuel 15:22-23)[19]

Similarly, the caustic words of the prophet Amos tell us in no uncertain terms what God thinks of the sung praises of His people when they are not matched with holiness of life and compassion for the needy:

> Take away from me the noise of your songs;
>   to the melody of your harps I will not listen.
> But let justice roll down like waters,
>   and righteousness like an ever-flowing stream.
>
> *Amos 5:23-24*

We should, then, be under no illusion: beautiful, skilful, even fervent singing is no guarantee of genuine praise. For praise to be authentic it must be *holistic* – involving heart, soul, mind and strength, love of neighbour as well as love of God. Indeed, all we think, say and do should be to the glory and praise of God (1 Corinthians 10:31). Such a view is

---

[19] Cf. Amos 5:21-27, Hosea 6:6, Isaiah 1:10-17; 66:1-4 and Micah 6:6-8.

helpfully captured in the *BCP*'s 'General Thanksgiving', which urges us to declare God's 'praise not only with our lips, but in our lives; by giving up ourselves to [His] service, and by walking before [Him] in holiness and righteousness all our days'.

None of this takes away from the fact that *the mode of praise in Scripture is consistently verbal.* J C Lambert is right: 'utterance is natural to strong emotion, and the mouth instinctively strives to express the praises of the heart'.[20] So when human beings praise, their praise is almost always articulated or announced, spoken or sung.[21] This reality is reflected in the well-known words of David (picked up in the *BCP* orders for Morning and Evening Prayer): 'O Lord, open my lips, and my mouth will declare your praise' (Psalm 51:15).

To praise, then, is to make a statement, to declare an opinion. It is in this sense that Brueggemann is right to speak of praise as both polemical and political, for divine praise 'insists not only that this is the true world, but that other worlds are false. The church sings praises not only toward God but against the gods'.[22] To engage in praise, then, is effectively to take sides, to declare one's allegiance, to nail one's colours to the mast! Karl Barth expressed it like this:

> It is in his spoken word that man, like God, comes out into the open, making himself clear, intelligible and in some way responsible, venturing forth and binding and committing himself. In his word man hazards himself. And it is demanded of him that in his word he shall continually hazard himself to God's glory, coming out into the open as a partisan of God.[23]

---

[20] J C Lambert, 'Praise', *International Standard Bible Encyclopedia Online.* http://www.internationalstandardbible.com/P/praise.html.

[21] Hely Hutchinson notes that because '*the activity of praising in the Psalter is essentially vocal* ... it would not be the norm for Yahweh to be praised silently, in a corner!' ('The Psalms and Praise', 86-87 [emphasis his]).

[22] Brueggemann, *Israel's Praise*, 27. Both quotes.

[23] Karl Barth, *Church Dogmatics: Volume III, Part 4* (trans. A T Mackay et al; eds. Geoffrey W Bromiley & Thomas F Torrance; Edinburgh: T & T Clark, 1961), 75.

2.4   The importance of singing praise

One obvious way a human being can 'hazard himself to God's glory' is by singing. Indeed, from the Bible's point of view, there is no escaping the fact that singing is a vital, if not the most common, form of praise. As Lambert suggests, 'the spirit of praise is a spirit of song. It may find expression in other ways – in sacrifice (Le 7:13), or testimony (Ps 66:16), or prayer (Col 1:3); but it finds its most natural and its fullest utterance in lyrical and musical forms. When God fills the heart with praise He puts a new song into the mouth (Ps 40:3)'.[24]

The reason for this is straightforward: *singing is a natural way of expressing joy*. As James writes: 'Is anyone joyful? Then let him sing songs of praise (Gk. *psalletō*)' (James 5:13). As we've already noted, Scripture repeatedly presents the following pattern: when God saves His people, His people are filled with joy, and when His people are filled with joy, they cannot help but sing songs of praise.[25] But there is even more to it than this. According to Brueggemann,

> Praise articulates and embodies our capacity to yield, submit, and abandon ourselves in trust and gratitude to the One whose we are. Praise is not only a human requirement and a human need, it is also a human delight. We have a resilient hunger to move beyond self, to return our energy and worth to the One from whom it has been granted. In our return to that One, we find our deepest joy. That is what it means to 'glorify God and enjoy God forever'.[26]

Singing, however, is not simply a *spontaneous* form of praise; it is also a *commanded* one. The Hebrew word *zamar* (which is one of the most common Hebrew words for praise) not only means 'to sing praise' but also frequently appears in the imperative mood.[27] Consequently, *if praise never takes the form of singing then* (from the Bible's point of view) *something strange, if not deficient, if not disobedient, is going on!* This may come as a challenge to those who, for one reason or another, find

---

[24] Lambert, 'Praise'.

[25] This connection is seen repeatedly throughout the Psalms (e.g., Psalms 5:11; 27:6; 33:1; 43:4; 63:7; 65:13; 67:4; 71:23; 81:1; 84:2; 92:4; 96:12; 98:8; 105:43; 149:5).

[26] Brueggemann, *Israel's Praise*, 1.

[27] See, for example, Psalms 9:11; 30:4; 47:6-7; 68:4, 32; 98:4-5; 105:2; Isaiah 12:5.

singing difficult.[28] But the fact remains that God repeatedly calls upon His people to sing His praise.

This is why many Scriptures (particularly many psalms) not only directly link praise with singing,[29] but also link the two faces of praise together, piling up the imperatives one upon another. The opening verses of Psalm 96 illustrate the links:

> [1] Oh sing (Heb. *shir*) to the Lord a new song;
>   sing (Heb. *shir*) to the LORD, all the earth!
> [2] Sing (Heb. *shir*) to the LORD, bless (Heb. *barak*) his name;
>   tell (Heb. *basar*) of his salvation from day to day.
> [3] Declare (Heb. *safar*) his glory among the nations,
>   his marvelous works among all the peoples!
> [4] For great is the LORD, and greatly to be praised (Heb. *halal*);
>   he is to be feared (Heb. *yare'*) above all gods.
>
> *Psalm 96:1-4*

The point could not be clearer. Scripture calls upon us to sing *to* the Lord, blessing His name, and to sing *of* the Lord, declaring His salvation to others. The first face of praise leads to the second, which in turn leads back to the first. More than that, the first includes the second just as the second also includes the first. For when we sing *to* the Lord, others hear our praise and when we sing *of* the Lord, He is present to receive His praise! Such is the marvellous symbiosis of the two faces of biblical praise.

3.   The Battle for Biblical Praise

3.1   The paradox of praise

The fact that Scripture is replete with commands for God's people to praise Him begs the question as to why such commands are necessary. Do not the redeemed have endless reasons to give God glory? Do we not long for a thousand tongues to sing our great redeemer's praise? If so, do

---

[28] It is important to appreciate that some of God's people do find singing difficult, either for physical reasons or, more commonly, for emotional reasons. Either way, professional and pastoral help should be sought, for in many cases real progress can be made – especially through singing therapy.

[29] For example, 2 Samuel 22:50; 2 Chronicles 20:21-22; Psalms 7:17; 9:2; 18:49; 21:13; 30:12; 66:2; 71:22; 104:33; 135:3; 138:1; 146:2; 147:1; 149:1; Isaiah 42:10; Jeremiah 20:13; 31:7; Romans 15:9; 1 Corinthians 14:15; Hebrews 2:12; James 5:13.

we really need to be told repeatedly to do so? In fact, can praise really be genuine if it has to be solicited?

Although understandable, such questions fail to appreciate both our need for commandments of all kinds – after all, loving God is described as 'the great and first *commandment*' (Matthew 22:38) – and also the work of God's Spirit, who both transforms us from within and exhorts us from without! Both works are necessary, as the writer of Psalm 119 understood: 'I will run in the way of your commandments when you enlarge my heart!' (v 32).

At the same time, it is also important to realise that not all biblical commands are of the same kind. Some are simply encouragements for God's people to do either what they are already doing or are only too eager to do (e.g., Galatians 2:10; Philippians 2:12; 1 Thessalonians 4:1-8). Many of the Bible's 'calls to praise' are, no doubt, of this kind (e.g., Psalms 9:11; 30:12; 34:3; 47:6-7; 66:2; 95:1-2). But not all. Indeed, the *illocutionary force* of a command may be deliberately left open precisely because the intended *perlocutionary effect* may depend on how it encounters us; that is, on our degree of receptivity to it. Of course, by their nature, God's commands are always life-giving and, if rightly received, never burdensome (Psalms 19:7-11; 1 John 5:3). But the reality is that praise does not always come easily to God's people and sometimes, without a command, may not be forthcoming at all.

We need, then, to grapple with the paradox of praise – i.e., its *naturalness* (on the one hand) and its *difficulty* (on the other). For despite the reality of our redemption, the workings of God's Spirit and the occasional spontaneity of our praise, there are often many obstacles that inhibit genuine praise. The scriptural injunctions to praise, then, are far from superfluous. If nothing else (although there is plenty else) they effectively serve to highlight the fact that, in this present age – as we battle against sin, the flesh and the devil – praise will not always be straightforward for God's people. It will usually need to be encouraged and will sometimes require hard work.

This should not surprise us. For if it is God's will that His people should praise Him with both lip and life, in speech and in song, then, like all other aspects of Christian obedience, this is bound to be an arena in which we will be tempted to be neglectful and will have to fight to be faithful.

Consequently, we should expect periodic, if not perpetual, battles with praise.

So how do these battles manifest themselves? What are some of the obstacles that can prevent praise, or at least make it difficult?

3.2   A time to mourn

The first obstacle is an entirely legitimate one. For various reasons, God's children can find themselves in places where, like the writer of Psalms 42-43, they simply cannot praise. Of course, the primary reason why this is so for the psalmist is because he, quite literally, is a long way from the place of praise: the temple in Jerusalem (42:6).[30] However, there is more to it as well. As we read on we discover that the psalmist's deepest distress lies in the fact that God appears to have 'forgotten' him (42:9) or may even have 'rejected' him (43:2). This is why he finds his enemies' question – 'Where is your God?' (42:3, 10) – so vexing. He feels forsaken. It is this sense of abandonment, even judgement, that gives rise to his plaintive and heartfelt cry: 'all your waves and breakers have swept over me' (42:7). Little wonder that as much as he yearns to do so, he cannot sing the Lord's praise in such a place or in such a state.

And yet even at this low ebb his ability to remember great days of praise is the very thing that awakens his hope; hope that God will not leave him in such a predicament, but will send forth His 'light' and 'truth' that they might lead him back to His 'holy mountain' (43:3). In fact, confidence that God will, in due course, reverse his circumstances is the basis for his thrice-repeated self-exhortation: 'Put your hope in God, for I will yet praise him' (42:5, 11; 43:5).

While members of the new covenant cannot be separated from the new covenant temple – Jesus Christ, we are strangers and exiles in this world, presently separated from our heavenly homeland. Furthermore, Jesus' followers can certainly know times when, because of their failures, they (as the Westminster Confession reminds us) 'fall under God's fatherly

---

[30] Possibly the captive of 'an unfaithful nation' (43:1), he speaks of being oppressed by enemies (42:9), taunted by adversaries (42:10) and surrounded by men who are 'deceitful and wicked' (43:1). This, then, is why he is unable to 'go to the house of God under the protection of the Mighty One with shouts of joy and praise among the festive throng' (42:4).

displeasure and not have the light of His countenance restored to them, until they humble themselves, confess their sins, beg pardon, and renew their faith and repentance'.[31]

Furthermore, even when we are not responsible for our trials, there are times when, like the apostle Paul, we can feel as though we have 'received the sentence of death' (2 Corinthians 1:9). So, for a whole variety of reasons, there are times when it is entirely appropriate for God's children to mourn, rather than rejoice, and in such times our song (if we have one at all) will be one of lament rather than one of praise.

Lament and praise, however, are not quite the polar opposites they might first appear to be. 'In the lament, a recurring element is the vow to praise (the promise that if God will answer the prayer, the psalmist will praise God for that deliverance)'.[32] More than that, lament should be seen not only as the first step on the path to praise, but as a kind of 'praising in the dark'.[33] In addition to this, as well as learning to sing our griefs before the throne of grace, there is a need for God's children to learn to rejoice in our sufferings, with an appropriate appreciation of what suffering accomplishes for us under our heavenly Father's good, wise and loving hand (Romans 5:3-5).

Therefore, although it can be difficult to praise in the midst of pain, it is important that we learn to do so, even if our songs are mingled with tears and praise takes the form of lament. Indeed, as we'll see further in chapter seven, the laments psalms are a great gift to us in this regard. Not only do they enable us to sing out our pain with the aid of divinely inspired words, but in so doing they help us progress toward praise as they strengthen our faith and awaken our hope. As Craig Broyles notes: 'A lament psalm ... is a set poetic prayer aimed to present a need to God so that he may resolve it and further his praise ... Praise should have the last word'.[34]

---

[31] Westminster Confession of Faith, XI, V.

[32] Rolf Jacobson, 'The Costly Loss of Praise', *Theology Today* 57:3 (October, 2000), 376.

[33] See Appendix 1 where these issues are discussed more fully.

[34] Craig C Broyles, 'Psalms of Lament', in Tremper Longman III and Peter Enns (eds.), *Dictionary of the Old Testament: Wisdom, Poetry and Writings* (Downers Grove: IVP Academic, 2008), 384.

3.3 Diabolical distraction

The next obstacle I've labelled 'diabolical distraction'. The reason for this description is that there is an array of spiritual powers, headed up by Satan himself, utterly committed to robbing God of His glory and, therefore, to distracting God's people from giving Him the praise that is rightfully His. This is one of the foundational themes of the Bible's meta-narrative from Genesis 3 onward. Succumbing to this temptation and refusing to 'glorify God and give thanks to him' is of the very essence of human rebellion (Romans 1:21). We should be under no illusions then: the battle for true worship of God is at the heart of all our spiritual warfare.

This reality comes clearly into view in Matthew's account of Jesus' temptation. After showing Jesus 'all the kingdoms of the world and their glory' (Matthew 4:8), Satan says to Him: 'All these I will give you, if you will *fall down and worship me*' (v 9). Jesus refuses on the firm ground of Scripture, replying: 'it is written, 'You shall worship the Lord your God and him only shall you serve' (v 10; citing Deuteronomy 6:13). This, of course, is simply another way of stating the first commandment: 'you shall have no other gods before me' (Exodus 20:3). Because the Lord alone is God He will neither tolerate rivals nor allow His relationship with His people 'to be violated by the entry of any third party'.[35] As Psalm 148 reminds us, this principle applies equally to praise: 'Let them [i.e., all created things] praise the name of the LORD, for his name *alone* is exalted' (v 13).

The point, then, is this: *Satan wants the worship that only God deserves, and just as he is determined to deprive God of His praise, so he is hell-bent on ensuring that we do the same*. This is why we shouldn't be taken aback by the battle, nor ignorant of Satan's diabolical designs. For rarely does he demand that we worship Him directly; his usual strategy is to tempt us to exchange 'the glory of the immortal God for images resembling mortal man and birds and animals and creeping things' (Romans 1:23). In other words, Satan is more than content for us to worship idols of one kind or another.[36]

---

[35] Richard Lints, *Identity and Idolatry: The Image of God and its Inversion* (Downers Grove: IVP, 2015), 85.

[36] The reason for this, as Scripture makes clear, is that idol worship is nothing less than a form of demon worship (1 Corinthians 10:19-20; Revelation 9:20).

3.4   The danger of idolatry

It is important, then, that we spend a few moments grappling with the danger of idolatry for God's people.[37] Essentially, an idol is an empty substitute for the true and living God. This is why the Bible frequently refers to the many and various gods of human concoction as 'false' (*sheqer*), 'worthlesss' (*haval*) and without 'breath' (*ruach*).[38] Furthermore, in its exposition of the dark history of idolatry, Scripture shows that virtually any and every aspect of the created order has been worshipped in place of the creator – e.g., angels (Colossians 2:18), demons (Revelation 9:20), the sun, the moon and the heavenly hosts (Deuteronomy 17:3) and images in various shapes and sizes (Psalm 97:7), made of all kinds of materials (Deuteronomy 29:17). In addition to this, we learn that any source of alternative trust or security – whether it be human beings (Psalm 118:8), noble princes (Psalm 146:3), military might (Psalm 20:7), social stability (Psalm 30:6) or material prosperity (Psalm 49:6) – is implicitly, if not explicitly, idolatrous. Indeed, Paul goes so far as to say that all 'covetousness is idolatry' (Colossians 3:5), for the desire to find a tangible source of strength or a visible basis for hope stems from a fundamental failure to trust in the Lord.

The relevance of these insights is that *just as we will necessarily offer gifts and sacrifices to the primary object of our worship, so we will inevitably give our praise to our operational 'god' or 'gods'.* This is why an inability or unwillingness to wholeheartedly praise the Lord (the one true God) is invariably an indication that we have given our ultimate allegiance to an idol of some kind. It is not without point that Jesus warned, 'You cannot serve both God and mammon' (Matthew 6:24).

Perhaps an illustration will help. In my Australian context, I have often been told that Aussie men don't sing and are quite uncomfortable with exuberant praise or expressions of emotion. Doubtless, there is some truth to this – at least for the Anglos among us and at least when compared to men of some other cultures. But if I happen to attend a

---

[37] It is not my purpose to survey all that Scripture has to say on the nature of idolatry. For a thorough and insightful treatment see Gregory K Beale, *We Become What We Worship: A Biblical Theology of Idolatry* (Downers Grove: IVP, 2008).

[38] See, for example, 2 Kings 17:15; Psalm 31:6; Jeremiah 2:5; 10:14; 14:22; 18:5; 51:17.

World Cup Rugby match (and assuming the Wallabies are winning) what do I see and hear? Men singing their hearts out, sometimes with tears in their eyes; men clapping and cheering with joy on their faces; men leaping into the air with arms raised and filling the air with shouts of praise. Indeed, more emotional and exuberant worship is hard to find!

Now don't misunderstand me: I'm not criticizing them. I've sometimes been one of them. Nor do I think this kind of enthusiastic enjoyment is inherently problematic. It's not necessarily. A problem is revealed, however, when those who claim to know the mercies of God through our Lord Jesus Christ behave this way at a sports match, but then, when they gather with God's people the following day, could not be more half-hearted in their praise of the One who bore their sins, conquered death on their behalf and lives and reigns at God's right hand for His church.

How can this be? The answer may lie (partly) in a church culture that has normalized, if not spiritualized, apathy. It may also lie (partly) in a failure of leadership to release and encourage God's people to do what is actually in their hearts to do. But perhaps mostly (and most commonly) what is being revealed is a disturbing conflict between our *theoretical* God (the God we claim to worship) and our *operational* 'god' (the 'god' we actually worship). Our hypocrisy gives us away, our idolatry has been unmasked.

Of course, there are numerous other ways to expose real or potential idols – e.g., by asking what we dream about, get excited about, are dependent upon, addicted to, save our money for, spend our money on, give our time to, and so forth. But who and what we sing to and sing about, as well as how fervently we do so, is as good a litmus test as any. Therefore, wrote Calvin, 'it is not without reason that the Holy Spirit exhorts us so carefully by the holy Scriptures to rejoice in God and that our whole joy be directed there as to its true end. For he knows how we are inclined to rejoice in vanity. So completely does our nature draw us and lead us to seek after every means of foolish and vicious enjoyment'.[39]

We'll have more to say on this point later. For now it is enough to recognize that *idolatry is a guaranteed extinguisher of God-honouring praise and, all too often, a (if not the) major reason for the 'praise-less-*

---

[39] John Calvin, 'The Form of Prayers and Songs of the Church, 1542: Letter to the Reader' (trans. Ford Lewis Battles), *CTJ* 15.2 (November 1980), 163.

ness' of God's people. The danger of idolatry, then, is a real one. Little wonder the apostle John concluded his first letter with these words to Christians: 'Dear children, keep yourselves from idols' (1 John 5:21).[40]

3.5 Quenching the Spirit

But the evil one has other tricks up his sleeve. *Another of his all too common strategies is to instil in us a range of needless inhibitions* – ways of thinking and behaving that may seem very natural and reasonable to us, but make it feel very unnatural or inappropriate to praise God fully and freely.[41] These inhibitions may be personal, cultural, traditional or even theological. But behind them all lie problematic presuppositions; i.e., false beliefs that help us maintain and justify our unresponsiveness.

For example, I may have convinced myself that it is simply not part of my personality or my culture to praise God in an expressive and heartfelt way.[42] So I don't. And I assure myself (and others) that it would be hypocritical if I did. Or I may believe that because God is sovereign and self-existing (as the Bible assures us He is), passionate praise is not something He really desires. Or I may think that displaying emotion, exuberance or enthusiasm in our praise is a sign of immaturity and instability, rather than integrity and authenticity. Or I may have been told that it is self-centred and exhibitionist to lift my hands or move my body in praise of God. So I conclude that if I truly care about others, then I

---

[40] The New Testament contains numerous warnings to believers to resist (or repent of succumbing to) the lure of idolatry in all its many and various forms (e.g., 1 Corinthians 10:14; 2 Corinthians 6:16; Galatians 5:20; Colossians 3:5; 1 Peter 4:3; Revelation 2:14, 20).

[41] Lest I be misunderstood, I am not for a moment denying that there are legitimate and appropriate inhibitions that God's people ought to display, nor the importance of exercising self-control in the service of others. The call to praise God fully and freely is not a call for us to become extraverted exhibitionists who are insensitive to the needs of others!

[42] Interestingly, Scripture repeatedly calls upon God's people to praise or thank Him 'with a whole heart' (ESV) or 'with all my heart' (NIV) (e.g., Psalms 9:1; 86:12; 111:1; 138:1; cf. Ephesians 5:19). While such a response will, no doubt, look different in different people, it clearly constitutes a call both to personal integration and to holding nothing back in our response to God's majesty and mercies.

won't do anything that might distract them or make them feel uncomfortable.

Of course, it must be said that there is a grain of truth in each of these lines of logic. For example, we are all different – culturally, physically and emotionally – and it is not God's purpose that we are all the same. Likewise, if we think that our praise adds something to God, then we've badly misunderstood His divine nature. And, yes, it is certainly possible to be self-absorbed in our singing, and therefore to fail to serve and encourage those around us. Yet all too often these are not the real reasons why God's people are cautious and hesitant in their praise. Indeed, when probed, such responses are frequently revealed to be matters of convenience or cowardice; ways of letting ourselves off the hook; excuses for denying God His praise.

Why? What would move us in this direction? Almost invariably the answer is fear – fear of looking foolish, or fear of what others might think or say of us, or fear of how they might label us or what they might do to us! As reasonable as such concerns might be, this kind of 'fear of man' is deadly, for it turns confessors into concealers. We see a telling instance of this in John 12 where we're told that many of the Jewish authorities believed in Jesus, 'but for fear of the Pharisees they would not confess it' (v 42). John thus delivers the stinging diagnosis: 'for they loved the glory that comes from man more than the glory that comes from God' (v 43).

The danger here is again a real one and also a perennial one. Proverbs 29:25 states it plainly: 'The fear of man lays a snare, but whoever trusts in the LORD is safe'. What, then, happens to our praises when the fear of others overrides our trust in the Lord? Instead of praising Him with a whole heart, we remain detached; instead of displaying some appropriate exuberance, we 'play it cool'; instead of exulting with thankfulness, we muzzle our gratitude and suppress our joy. In short, when we are ruled by the 'fear of man' we all too easily quench the Spirit! The net result is that God is denied the praise He rightly deserves, and others are robbed of the proclamation they need to hear.

In the chapter to follow, we will explore a number of ways to remedy this tendency and 'the problem of praise paralysis' (as I like to call it) that is often produced by it.

Conclusion

In this chapter I have been content to do three things: *first*, to argue a case (albeit briefly) for the relevance of the Psalter to new covenant congregational worship; *second*, to unpack the key features of divine praise as these are revealed in the Psalter; and, *third*, to identify some of the chief obstacles that often prevent God's people from giving Him the praise He deserves, demands and desires. Doubtless, a number of other potential obstacles could have been examined – some theological (e.g., various misunderstandings of God), others practical (e.g., poor song choice). Some of these will get picked up in the following chapter as we turn from problem to solution, asking how we might overcome such obstacles and how we can ensure, in practice, that we truly praise the triune God.

But it's important to realise that the 'praise problems' we've identified in this chapter are far from new. God's people have battled them since time immemorial. As we've already noted, when Isaac Watts penned the *Preface to Hymns and Spiritual Songs* in 1707, similar failings amongst his contemporaries fuelled his concern:

> While we sing the praises of our God in his church, we are employed in that part of worship which of all others is the nearest a-kin to heaven: and 'tis pity that this of all others should be performed the worst upon earth. The gospel brings us nearer to the heavenly state than all the former dispensations of God amongst men: And in these very last days of the gospel we are brought almost within sight of the kingdom of our Lord; yet we are very much unacquainted with the songs of the *New Jerusalem*, and unpracticed in the work of praise.[43]

Let us, then, consider how we might become practiced in the work of praise.

---

[43] Watts, 'Preface' to *Hymns and Spiritual Songs*, iii.

6. Singing as Praise II:
Strategies and Practice

O God, whom to know is to live, whom to serve is to reign, and whom to praise is the health and joy of the soul; with my lips and my heart, and with all the might I have, do I praise, bless and adore three; through thy Son Jesus Christ our Lord.[1]

Having diagnosed something of the problems of praise and the obstacles that often prevent us from praising God fully and freely, we now turn to offering some solutions. Given that it is common for God's people to wrestle with the kind of temptations and fears outlined in the previous chapter (albeit in different ways and to differing degrees), the question to be answered is this: *How would God have us engage in the battle for biblical praise?*

1. From Prison to Praise

In his million-selling autobiographical account, *Prison to Praise*, U.S. Army chaplain, Merlin Carothers, tells the story of his (claimed) discovery of the key to unlocking the power of God in Christian lives. This key, Carothers suggested, is found in 1 Thessalonians 5:16-18: 'Rejoice evermore. Pray without ceasing. In every thing give thanks: for this is the will of God in Christ Jesus concerning you' (KJV). Carothers' claim is as bold as it is striking: 'Miracles, power, and victory will all be a part of what God does in our lives when we learn to rejoice in all things'.[2]

However, Carothers does not argue that the daily application of 1 Thessalonians 5:16-18 will always be easy or even something we want to do. To the contrary, he admits that praise is 'not something we do because we feel good; rather it is an act of obedience'.[3] It may even be the case that

---

[1] This prayer, translated from Latin, is Augustinian in origin, although probably not written by Augustine himself. Cited in Peter Toon, 'Freedom as a Christian – ancient and modern', *Virtue Online: The Voice for Global Orthodox Anglicanism* (n.d.): http://www.virtueonline.org/freedom-christian-ancient-and-modern-peter-toon.

[2] Merlin R Carothers, *Prison to Praise* (London: Hodder & Stoughton, 1970), 67.

[3] Carothers, *Prison to Praise*, 80.

'praise is done in sheer teeth-gritting willpower; yet when we persist in it, somehow the power of God is released into us and into the situation'.[4] The reason for this 'release' is that when we learn to praise God in the midst of trial, it helps us see God really is in total control of absolutely everything. It was this conviction that enabled Carothers to see his troubles as gifts and so as reason for praise.

Notwithstanding the triumphalism of Carothers' thesis, its decided lean towards a 'power of positive thinking' approach to the Christian life and a number of other worrying features,[5] there is an important theological truth that lies at the heart of *Prison to Praise*. That truth is that our heavenly Father is truly sovereign, thoroughly good and, therefore, worthy of our trust and thanks at all times and in all circumstances.[6] We do, then, have ample reason to 'rejoice in the Lord *always*' (Philippians 4:4) and to 'give thanks *in all circumstances*' (1 Thessalonians 5:17).

Rather than engage further with the strengths and weaknesses of Carothers' influential book, the aim of this chapter is, *first*, to supplement his basic insight with three biblically grounded strategies designed to help God's people overcome 'the problem of praise paralysis' and so to grow in our ability to truly praise the living God. Then, *second*, we will look more closely at the issue of implementation, asking what it might mean to put praise into practice in church life.

---

[4] Carothers, *Prison to Praise*, 80.

[5] For example, an understanding of the baptism of the Spirit as a post-conversion experience, repeated claims of regular dialogue with God, and an account of a curious vision in which Jesus held Carothers' feet, put His head on his knees and said: 'I don't want to use you. I want you to use Me!' (Carothers, *Prison to Praise*, 49).

[6] Nevertheless, Carothers may also be criticised for not adequately distinguishing between giving thanks *in* all circumstances and giving thanks *for* all circumstances. While he is not wanting to blur the distinction between good and evil circumstances, but simply to affirm that God remains sovereign over the latter and uses them both for His glory and for our good, this failure is potentially confusing (if not harmful) at a pastoral level. As we have seen, Scripture affirms that there is a time to mourn over our circumstances, as there is a call to weep with those who weep.

2.   Three Strategic Solutions

2.1   God truly deserves our praise

The first of the strategies implied by Scripture is for us to call to mind the fact that *God truly deserves our praise*. Both the Psalter and the book of Revelation are of immense help to us here. Listen, for example, to the logic and force of the following verses:

I will give to the LORD
    the thanks (Heb. *yada*) due to his righteousness,
    and I will sing praise (Heb. *zamar*)
    to the name of the Lord, the Most High.

Psalm 7:17

I will sing (Heb. *shir*) to the LORD,
    because he has dealt bountifully with me.

Psalm 13:6

I call upon the LORD,
    who is worthy to be praised (Heb. *halal*),
    and I am saved from my enemies.

Psalm 18:3

Because your steadfast love is better than life,
    my lips will praise (Heb. *shavach*) you.

Psalm 63:3

At midnight I rise to praise (Heb. *yada*) you,
    because of your righteous rules.

Psalm 119:62

Praise (Heb. *halal*) the LORD!
For it is good to sing praises (Heb. *zamar*) to our God;
    for it is pleasant (Heb. *na'im*),[7]

---

[7] The Hebrew word *na'im* could possibly be translated 'He is beautiful' (so ESV footnote) or 'He is lovely'. This is certainly a thought expressed elsewhere in the Psalter (e.g., 27:4) and one that so captivated C S Lewis that it elicited a whole chapter from his pen (See C S Lewis, *Reflections on the Psalms* [London: Harper Collins, 1958], 38-45). In context, however, it is more likely that it is the praise that is being described as beautiful (So Allan Harman, *Psalms: Volume 2: Psalms*

and a song of praise (Heb. *tehila*) is fitting.

Psalm 147:1

Worthy (Gk. *axios*) are you, our Lord and God,
    to receive glory (Gk. *doxa*)
    and honor (Gk. *timē*) and power (Gk. *dunamis*),
for you created all things,
    and by your will they existed and were created'.

Revelation 4:11

Worthy (Gk. *axios*) are you to take the scroll
    and to open its seals,
for you were slain, and by your blood
    you ransomed people for God
    from every tribe and language and people and nation ...

Revelation 5:9

Scripture is clear that the triune God, who is our creator and redeemer, saviour and sanctifier, deserves every bit of praise we can muster. It is simply not possible to over-praise Him! Praise is His due – it is what He deserves because of who He is and what He has done. Therefore, it is entirely fitting that we should bless the Lord *at all times* and that His praise should be *continually in our mouths* (Psalm 34:1). As the *BCP* Lord's Supper service expresses it, 'It is very meet, right, and our bounden duty, that we should at all times and in all places give thanks unto thee, O Lord, holy Father, almighty, everlasting God, through Jesus Christ thine only Son our Lord'.

Here, then, is the first way in which Scripture helps us to overcome our praise problems: by reminding us of who God is, what He has done and the fact that He is infinitely worthy of our constant, heartfelt and full-throated praise. Correspondingly, *our first strategy must be to remind ourselves and each other of these things, so that we regularly grasp them afresh and ever celebrate them anew.*

73-150 [Fearn: Mentor, 2011], 999, n 1). Nevertheless, it is difficult to disagree with Donald M Williams (*The Preacher's Commentary: Psalms 73-150* [Nashville: Thomas Nelson, 1989], 516) when he writes: 'To be caught up in a congregation of worshipers, to express our full human capacity to praise God, and to be in the midst of those doing the same is to experience some of God's beauty'.

What this reveals is that genuine praise of God will only ever be a consequence of a genuine knowledge of God. We, therefore, need to be alert to a common mistake made by many well-intentioned churches. The mistake is to substitute the pursuit of excellence for the pursuit of God. We are not, of course, here dealing with an either-or. But it is vital to realise that having a better sound system, more impressive music, more skilful song-leaders and more energised singing is not itself a guarantee that God will be glorified. Doubtless, all of these things have their proper place and may well help us in various ways. Scripture also encourages us to serve and 'play skilfully' (Psalm 33:3) and to praise beautifully (Psalm 147:1). But the nerve centre of God-honouring praise lies elsewhere. Carson explains why:

> Although there are things that can be done to enhance corporate worship, there is a profound sense in which excellent worship cannot be attained merely by pursuing excellent worship. In the same way that, according to Jesus, you cannot find yourself until you lose yourself, so also you cannot find excellent corporate worship until you stop trying to find excellent corporate worship and pursue God Himself. ... If you wish to deepen the worship of the people of God, above all deepen their grasp of His ineffable majesty in His person and in all His works.[8]

My point, then, is this: it is only as we grasp *who He is* (the God of all power and majesty, glory and grace) and comprehend *what He has done* (particularly in giving up His own Son and the pouring out of His own Spirit to make us His children) that we will see that God is truly worthy of all praise and so be inwardly moved to outwardly offer Him the praise He deserves.

2.2   God repeatedly demands our praise

The second scriptural strategy for combating 'praise paralysis' is to take seriously the fact that *God repeatedly demands our praise*. That is, praising God in song is not an optional element in our response to His majesty and mercies. It is a divine imperative. Of course, as we've noted previously, many scriptural commands function as gracious invitations or life-giving encouragements, not as threats or impositions. Furthermore, if the glory and grace of God don't draw forth our praise,

---

[8] Carson, 'Worship Under the Word', 30-31.

then little else will. Nonetheless, C S Lewis was right: 'God does not only "demand" praise as the supremely beautiful and all-satisfying Object. He does apparently command it as lawgiver'.[9] Lambert agrees, expanding on the point as follows:

> Praise is everywhere represented in the Bible as a duty no less than a natural impulse and a delight. To fail in this duty is to withhold from God's [sic] glory that belongs to Him (Ps 50:23; Ro 1:20f); it is to shut one's eyes to the signs of His presence (Isa 40:26 ff), to be forgetful of His mercies (Dt 6:12), and unthankful for His kindness (Lu 6:35). If we are not to fall into these sins, but are to give to God the honor and glory and gratitude we owe Him, we must earnestly cultivate the spirit and habit of praise.[10]

So how do we 'cultivate the spirit and habit of praise'? The Bible's answer is wonderfully straightforward: by faithfully listening to the scriptural commands (and there are many)[11] and gladly doing what they call us to do. Hear, for example, the call of Psalm 47:

> [1] Clap your hands, all peoples!
>   Shout to God with loud songs of joy! ...
> [6] Sing praises to God, sing praises!
>   Sing praises to our King, sing praises!
> [7] For God is the King of all the earth; sing praises with a psalm!

Or that of Psalm 66:

> [1] Shout for joy to God, all the earth;
> [2] sing the glory of his name;
>   give to him glorious praise!
> [3] Say to God, 'How awesome are your deeds!
>   So great is your power
>   that your enemies come cringing to you.'

---

[9] Lewis, *Reflections on the Psalms*, 79.

[10] Lambert, 'Praise'.

[11] For example, Exodus 15:21; 1 Chronicles 16:9, 23; Psalms 5:11; 9:11; 30:4; 33:3; 47:1, 6-7; 66:2; 68:4, 32; 81:1-2; 95:1-2; 96:1-2; 98:1, 4-5; 100:2; 105:2; 107:22; 135:3; 147:1, 7; 149:1, 5 Isaiah 12:5-6; 23:16; 27:2; 42:10; 44:23; 49:13: 54:1; Jeremiah 20:13; 31:7; Zephaniah 3:14; Zechariah 2:10; James 5:13.

Or that of Psalm 100:

> [1] Shout for joy to the Lord, all the earth.
> [2] Worship the Lord with gladness;
> come before him with joyful songs.

Or Revelation 19:5:

> Praise our God, all you his servants,
> you who fear him, small and great.

These are not suggestions; they are commands! But what liberating, life-giving commands. As Derek Kidner writes: 'While it must always be a "whole offering", never self-regarding, the very act of responding articulately to God's pure glory and goodness is enlivening and emancipating'.[12] This is what we were made for and saved for. To engage in such praise, therefore, is to know something of the truth contained in *The Second Collect, for Peace* found in the *BCP*'s Order for Morning Prayer: God's 'service is perfect freedom'.[13] For God's commandments are not burdensome (1 John 5:3). This includes His commandments to praise.

That said, the biblical calls to praise are demanding – they involve not just singing, but clapping, shouting, dancing, rejoicing and exulting. Clearly, obeying such calls requires the sustained, exuberant engagement of our whole selves. What's more, we are even called to 'Shout to God with *loud* songs of joy' and 'praise him with *loud* clashing cymbals' (Psalms 47:1; 150:5). Such commands can only be obeyed by a serious expense of energy. This, in turn, can only be done

> by arousing the soul from its slothfulness and sluggishness (Psalm 57:8; 103:1), by fixing the heart upon God (Psalm 57:7; 108:1), by meditation on His works and ways (Psalm 77:11ff), by recounting His benefits (Psalm 103:2), above all, for those to whom He has

---

[12] Derek Kidner, *Psalms 73-150* (Leicester: IVP, 1975), 485.
[13] The origin of this expression goes back to St Augustine, *The Greatness of the Soul*, Ch 34, §78. See Joseph M Colleran (trans. and annot.), *St. Augustine: The Greatness of the Soul, The Teacher* (New York: The Newman Press, 1978), 13-112.

spoken in His Son, by dwelling upon His unspeakable gift (2 Cor 9:15; compare Rom 8:31 ff; 1 Jn 3:1).[14]

God's commands are truly loving commands. We are called to praise not only for His glory but also for our good. Praise is a gracious gift whereby we become more and more like the object of our praise – God himself. But lest we be in any doubt: called we are, commanded we are, and called and commanded repeatedly. Consequently, the *second strategy* that Scripture gives us in order to overcome the many and various obstacles to praising God *is to regularly remind both ourselves and each other of both the seriousness and goodness of this demand.*

2.3 *God deeply desires our praise*

The third and final strategy that arises from Scripture is for us to call to mind that *God deeply desires our praise.* This is clear from numerous biblical statements. It is why, for example, the Lord described the nation of Israel as 'the people whom I formed for myself that they might declare my praise' (Isaiah 43:21). It is why Paul described the church of Jesus Christ as those who have been chosen 'for the praise of his glory' (Ephesians 1:12, 14). Praise, then, is God's demand because praise is God's desire.

It is worth clarifying, however, that God does not ultimately need our praise – neither ontologically (to supplement some deficiency in His being), nor psychologically (to supplement some deficiency in His person). He is entirely self-sufficient in His divine nature and relationally fulfilled in His own triune existence. Consequently, as Paul says, 'he is not served by human hands, as if he needed anything. Rather, he himself gives everyone life and breath and everything else' (Acts 17:25). Psalm 50 makes the point even more bluntly:

> [9] I have no need of a bull from your stall
>   or of goats from your pens,
> [10] for every animal of the forest is mine,
>   and the cattle on a thousand hills.
> [11] I know every bird in the mountains,
>   and the insects in the fields are mine.
> [12] If I were hungry I would not tell you,

---

[14] Lambert, 'Praise'.

for the world is mine, and all that is in it.
[13] Do I eat the flesh of bulls or drink the blood of goats?

The living God, then, has no need of our sacrifices, any more than His existence is dependent on ours. But that is not to say that He is indifferent to our response to Him. On the contrary, because we have been made for the praise of His glory, we are structured for sacrifice. Therefore, we misunderstand the stinging words of Psalm 50 (above) if we interpret them in such a way. Indeed, in their salvation-historical context, their aim was not to bring the old covenant sacrificial system to an end – not at that point. [15] Rather their purpose was to highlight the proper response to God's atoning grace, symbolised by the sacrificial system; a response without which all of the sacrifices were meaningless. [16] The central component of this response, as the very next verses of Psalm 50 make clear, is thankfulness – thankfulness that works itself out in prayerful obedience:

[14] Offer to God a sacrifice of thanksgiving (*todah*),[17]
    fulfill your vows to the Most High,
[15] and call on me in the day of trouble;
    I will deliver you, and you will honor me.

Here, then, is the key to why the Old Testament animal sacrifices could be described as 'a pleasing aroma to the LORD' (e.g., Leviticus 1:9, 13, 17, etc). Thankfulness (or what some call 'declarative praise'), with or without a physical offering, is the response that God ultimately desires from His

---

[15] John Goldingay, *Psalms: Volume 2: Psalm 42-89* (Grand Rapids: Baker, 2007), 116.

[16] This touches on a very important point of biblical (and especially Old Testament) theology: sacrifice is, first and foremost, God's gift to His people. This is the emphasis of Leviticus 17:11 where the sacrificial system was first introduced: 'I have given it to you ...' Thus, all the Old Testament sacrifices, rightly understood, recalled, rather than procured the grace of God; they were the fruit rather than the root of His mercy. P T Forsyth puts it like this: 'The positive truth is that the sacrifice is the result of God's grace and not its cause. It is given *by* God before it is given to Him' (*The Cruciality of the Cross* [London: Hodder & Stoughton, 1909], 185).

[17] The Hebrew noun *todah* (usually translated 'thanksgiving') is derived from the hiphil of the verb *yadah* (normally translated 'praise'). Consequently, the line between praise and thanksgiving is a fine one and either Hebrew term can be translated, quite legitimately, by either English word.

people. This is why Psalm 50 ends with the Lord saying, 'the one who offers thanksgiving as his sacrifice glorifies me' (v 23).

Moving to the New Testament, it should not surprise us to find that the spiritual sacrifices required of God's new covenant people are described in similar language.

> [15] Through Jesus, therefore, let us continually offer to God a sacrifice of praise – the fruit of lips that openly profess his name. [16] And do not forget to do good and to share with others, for with such sacrifices God is pleased. (Hebrews 13:15-16)

God, then, is both honoured and delighted when His people freely offer sacrifices of praise and thanksgiving in response to His great mercies. Of course, now that Christ has fulfilled and abrogated the old covenant sacrificial system, no further animal sacrifices need to be offered. Full atonement for sins has been made once and for all (Heb 10:1-18). But the responsive sacrifice of praise remains. It is God's abiding desire. As Geoffrey Wainwright has put it: 'Although God does not need us to be God, our praise brings the purpose of God to completion, and so is our duty'.[18]

The flipside of this is that God is rightly jealous for His praise. Indeed, He will not share it with another, nor will He play 'second fiddle' to anything else, as He says through the prophet Isaiah:

> I am the LORD; that is my name;
>   my glory I give to no other,
>   nor my praise to carved idols.

> *Isaiah 42:8*

This statement is, quite transparently, an application of both the first commandment – 'you shall have no other gods before me' (Exodus 20:3) – and the second commandment – 'You shall not make for yourself a carved image or ... bow down to them or serve them' (Exodus 20:4-5). It also picks up on the stated reason for both commandments – 'for I the LORD your God am a jealous God' (Exodus 20:5). Because idolatry is an expression both of liable falsehood (for idols are empty and accomplish

---

[18] Geoffrey Wainwright, 'The Praise of God in the Theological Reflection of the Church', *Interpretation* 39.1 (January, 1985), 40.

nothing) and culpable ingratitude (for God alone gives life and breath to everything), it is an utter insult to Him. It is 'a bringing of the gods we make before the God who made us'.[19] God, therefore, is justly provoked to anger by our idols (Deuteronomy 32:21).

As well as displeasing God and incurring His righteous wrath, idolatry dehumanises us. This tragic truth is simply an outworking (albeit in the negative) of a basic biblical principle: *what you revere you resemble, either for ruin or restoration*.[20] The reason for this, as Richard Lints has argued, is that human identity 'is rooted in what it reflects'. Consequently, if the living God is reflected, then the result is 'worship, honour, completion, and satisfaction'. But if an idol is reflected, the result is 'perversion, corruption, consumption, and possession'.[21] This is why Scripture repeatedly describes idols as 'vain' or 'worthless' (Psalms 31:6, 96:5; 97:7; Jon 2:8) and why it says of Israel: 'They went after false idols and became false' (2 Kings 17:15; Jeremiah 2:5). In short, those who make idols become like them, as do all who trust in them (Psalms 115:8; 135:18). As Isaiah again declares:

> They are turned back and utterly put to shame,
>   who trust in carved idols,
>   who say to metal images, 'You are our gods.'
>
> *Isaiah 42:17*

The best prophylactic against idolatry, then, is whole-hearted praise of the living God. For, as Rolf Jacobson observes, 'praise not only evokes a world, it also undoes, it deconstructs all other worlds'.[22] Why so? Because when 'we affirm our praise to God, we also dismiss other gods as illegitimate and irrelevant'.[23] The positive side of this is that we are never more truly ourselves than when we are 'lost in wonder, love and praise' (to use Charles Wesley's phrase), glorifying the one in whose image we were made and into whose likeness we are being restored.

---

[19] These words come from a sermon by Edmund Steimle, cited in James L Mays, *The Lord Reigns: A Theological Handbook to the Psalms* (Louisville: Westminster John Knox Press, 1994), 66,
[20] Beale, *We Become What We Worship*, 11 (emphasis his).
[21] Lints, *Identity and Idolatry*, 29.
[22] Jacobson, 'The Costly Loss of Praise', 378.
[23] Barker, 'Praise and Praxis', 9.

All of this underscores the fact that, far from being self-centred or narcissistic, God's desire for our praise cannot be separated from His desire to share Himself with us and for us to become like Him. For it is by giving Him glory that we come to share His glory.[24] Nevertheless, the central point must not be lost from view: *irrespective of the incalculable good that praise does for us, God seeks from us the praise that is rightfully His.* Not surprisingly, receiving what is rightfully His is His passionate desire, for our glorious creator and gracious redeemer 'is a consuming fire, a jealous God' (Deuteronomy 4:24).

Our third strategy, then, for overcoming 'the problem of praise paralysis' *is to regularly call to mind that God not only deserves and demands our praise, but deeply desires it as well.* So then, since we have every reason to bless the Lord at all times, even in seasons of suffering and distress, 'let us be thankful, and so worship God acceptably with reverence and awe' (Hebrews 12:28).

3.   How, then, Shall We Sing Praise?

We come finally to the practical question: How shall we sing praise? Let me answer this question in four parts.

3.1   In Spirit and truth

First, we will sing praise 'in Spirit and truth'. The simple reason for this is that, according to Jesus and as a consequence of His coming into the world, all true worship of the Father must be of this kind – worship 'in Spirit and truth' (John 4:24). What this means, as we saw in chapter two, is that the true worship of the new covenant will be guided by the Holy Spirit ('the Spirit of Truth') into a saving knowledge of the truth about God. And that means it will focus attention on the one who has revealed that truth to us and embodies that truth in himself: Jesus Christ, in whom 'the whole fullness of deity dwells bodily' (Colossians 2:9). Otherwise put, singing praise 'in Spirit and truth' will mean that our praise is Bible-based, gospel-centred and Christ-focussed. It will, therefore, reflect the balance and burden of the Bible, majoring on the major themes of the Bible and concentrating attention on the things of 'first importance': that 'Christ died for our sins according to the Scriptures, that he was buried,

---

[24] As C S Lewis writes: 'it is in the process of being worshipped that God communicates His presence to men' (*Reflections on the Psalms,* 79).

that he was raised on the third day according to the Scriptures, and that he appeared ...' (1 Corinthians 15:3-5).[25] In short, the central focus of Scripture will determine the central focus of our praise.

At a recent music ministry conference, a young church musician asked me why we sing so many songs about Jesus' death and resurrection. My answer was along the lines we've just seen: because these are matters of 'first importance', they are gospel central truths! That doesn't mean we won't ever sing about other things, for Scripture gives us much else to sing about. It is a simple recognition of the fact that the saving grace of God has been fully and finally revealed in the atoning work of Jesus Christ. So whatever else we sing about, the zenith of our praise will be concentrated there. Such an understanding is reflected in the words of *BCP*'s 'General Thanksgiving', where we bless the 'Father of all mercies ... for our creation, preservation, and all the blessings of this life; but above all, for [His] inestimable love in the redemption of the world by our Lord Jesus Christ'.

It matters little, then, whether our songs of praise are *descriptive* (praising God's general attributes and actions) or *declarative* (praising Him for a specific act of kindness), for, as Claus Westermann points out, declarative praise inevitably 'passes over into descriptive praise' and 'descriptive praise lives on declarative praise'.[26] This parallels what we've already seen in regard to the adoration and advertising aspects of praise, which likewise cannot finally be separated and necessarily entail each other. For whatever the precise form or direction of praise, what matters most is the *truth* of praise – the truth about who God is and what He has done.

---

[25] In context, Paul's phrase 'of first importance' (Gk. *en protois*) clearly means more than the things 'that were first spoken'. As verses 1-2 make clear, the gospel truths that he passed on are the truths 'in which you stand and by which you are being saved'. In other words, these are the things that matter most, which is (no doubt) why they would also have been spoken first. Furthermore, as Anthony Thiselton points out, the fact that Paul 'received' (v 1) and 'handed on' (v 3) this form of gospel tradition means that it effectively constitutes 'an early *creed which declares the absolute fundamentals of the Christian faith and on which Christian identity* (and the experience of salvation) *is built*'. See Anthony C Thiselton, *The First Epistle to the Corinthians* (Grand Rapids: Eerdmans, 2000), 1186 (emphasis his).

[26] Claus Westermann, *Praise and Lament in the Psalms* (trans. K R Crim and R N Soulen. Atlanta: John Knox Press, 1981), 117 and 133.

Indeed, so important is the truth of our praise that 'God's reputation is at stake when his people speak or sing about him to one another'.[27] This highlights the perpetual need for our praises to be harnessed to God's self-revelation.[28] This is one of the reasons why, along with expressions of praise and exhortations to praise, a clear articulation of the *reasons* for praise should never be absent from our singing.[29] We see this pattern exemplified repeatedly both in the Psalms and in the songs of the heavenly hosts in the book of Revelation:

> Blessed be the LORD,
>> *for* he has wondrously shown his steadfast love to me
>> when I was in a besieged city.
>
> *Psalm 31:21*

> Oh sing to the Lord a new song,
>> *for* he has done marvelous things!
> His right hand and his holy arm
>> have worked salvation for him.
>
> *Psalm 98:1*

> Praise the LORD!
> Oh give thanks to the LORD, *for* he is good,
>> *for* his steadfast love endures forever!
>
> *Psalm 106:1*

---

[27] Peterson, *Encountering God Together*, 113-114.

[28] All true praise of God, at every point in salvation-history, has been determined by God's self-revelation, and participates in the proclamation of that revelation. It is for this reason that the psalmists not only spoke of the Lord being 'enthroned upon the praises of Israel' (Psalm 22:3) but of seeing Him in the sanctuary (Psalm 63:2). In every other Ancient Near East temple, this latter expression would have made perfect sense, for all contained some visible representation of a local deity. But no such image was to be found in Israel's temple. There its place was taken by the revelation of God's name in the proclamation of His praise. It was in this sense (and this sense only) that the Lord was seen by faithful worshippers. See further Mays, *The Lord Reigns*, 65-66.

[29] This is not to say that every song must have identical proportions or follow the same formula. The Psalms are certainly not stylised in this way. The point applies more broadly to our collections and selections of songs for corporate worship.

Oh give thanks to the Lord, *for* he is good;
  for his steadfast love endures forever!

Psalm 118:1

Worthy are you, our Lord and God,
  to receive glory and honor and power,
for you created all things,
  and by your will they existed and were created.

Revelation 4:11

9 Worthy are you to take the scroll and to open its seals,
  for you were slain,
  and by your blood you ransomed people for God
  from every tribe and language and people and nation,
10 and you have made them a kingdom and priests to our God,
  and they shall reign on the earth.

Revelation 5:9-10

3 Great and amazing are your deeds,
  O Lord God the Almighty!
Just and true are your ways,
  O King of the nations!
4 Who will not fear, O Lord, and glorify your name?
For you alone are holy.
All nations will come and worship you,
  for your righteous acts have been revealed.

Revelation 15:3-4

Declaring God's glorious attributes because of His gracious actions – supremely revealed in the saving work His Son and the sanctifying work of His Spirit: this is the pattern and heart of scriptural praise. If we are to sing praise in Spirit and truth we will reflect this heart and cleave closely to this pattern.

3.2   With a thankful heart

Second, we will sing praise with a thankful heart. Praise and thanksgiving, as we've seen, are very closely related ideas in Scripture. So much so that 'one cannot live without the other'.[30] In fact, often the same

---

30 Marvin E Tate, *Psalm 51-100* (Waco: Word, 1990), 66.

Hebrew words can be translated by either English word. What is particularly noteworthy is the connection between thanksgiving and song. The following verses from the Psalms, where *yada* (give thanks) is paired up with *zamar* (sing praise), illustrate the point:

> Sing praises (*zamar*) to the LORD, O you his saints,
>   and give thanks (*yadah*) to his holy name.
>
> *Psalm 30:4*

> I will give thanks (*yadah*) to you, O LORD,
>   among the peoples;
> I will sing praises (*zamar*) to you among the nations.
>
> *Psalms 57:9; 108:3*

> It is good to give thanks (*yadah*) to the LORD,
>   to sing praises (*zamar*) to your name, O Most High
>
> *Psalm 92:1*

> I give you thanks (*yadah*), O LORD, with my whole heart;
>   before the gods I sing your praise (*zamar*)
>
> *Psalm 138:1*

This connection is not only a feature of Old Testament praise, it is also a major feature of Paul's exhortation in Colossians 3:15-17:

> [15] And let the peace of Christ rule in your hearts, to which indeed you were called in one body. And *be thankful (eucharistoi)*. [16] Let the word of Christ dwell in you richly, teaching and admonishing one another in all wisdom, singing psalms and hymns and spiritual songs, *with thankfulness (en chariti)* in your hearts to God. [17] And whatever you do, in word or deed, do everything in the name of the Lord Jesus, *giving thanks (eucharistountēs)* to God the Father through him.

Here we see that there are two essentials for God-honouring singing. The *first* is that we must sing *the Word of Christ*. I won't elaborate on this point here, as we'll return to it later. The *second* 'essential' is that we ought to *sing with accompanying thankfulness*. As Douglas Moo comments: 'more than attitude is called for here. Gratitude in the heart (v 16) must come to expression in actual, verbal giving of thanks to the

Father "through" Christ'.[31] The significance of thanksgiving for the apostle is clear from the fact that he mentions it three times in as many verses. This highlights a theme that recurs throughout the letter to the Colossians (see also 1:11; 2:7; 4:2). The 'take home' point is this: gratitude is 'an important component of Christian obedience and, at the same time, an important source of that obedience'.[32]

We will have more to say about thanksgiving later – particularly when we consider its relationship to prayer. Here we simply need to see that *the cultivation of a spirit of praise will inevitably go together with the development of a thankful heart*. On this point, at least, Merlin Carothers was right to remind us to 'give thanks in all circumstances, for this is the will of God in Christ Jesus for you' (1 Thessalonians 5:18). While praise may be more than thanksgiving, it is certainly not less.[33] We will, therefore, sing praise with a thankful heart.

3.3   With a fervent spirit

Third, we will sing praise with a fervent spirit. My language here comes from Romans 12:11-12: 'Do not be slothful in zeal, be fervent in spirit, serve the Lord. Rejoice in hope, be patient in tribulation, be constant in prayer'. Paul, of course, is not here talking about singing. These are general exhortations that relate to Christian living. But they can, quite appropriately, be applied to our singing, as they can to any and every facet of Christian obedience. Indeed, such an application is supported by two features of Paul's instruction in Colossians 3:16.

The first is his inclusion of the word 'richly' (Gk. *plusiōs*) at the end of the opening phrase ('Let the word of Christ dwell in you *richly*'). As we'll say more about this word in a later chapter, suffice it to say here that Paul's inclusion of it highlights the responsibility of believers to consciously feed on 'the word of Christ' in our songs so that we might be deeply nourished by it – both individually and corporately.[34]

---

[31] Douglas J Moo, *The Letters to the Colossians and to Philemon* (Grand Rapids: Eerdmans, 2008), 291.
[32] Moo, *The Letters to the Colossians and to Philemon*, 291.
[33] In fact, in Westermann's view (*Praise and Lament in the Psalms*, 25), 'praise is a stronger, more lively, broader concept which includes our 'thanks' in it'.
[34] Paul Foster, *Colossians* (London/New York: Bloomsbury/T & T Clark), 360.

The second feature of Paul's instruction that emphasises the need for spiritual fervency is in the final phrase of Colossians 3:16: 'with thankfulness *in your hearts* (*en tais kardiais humōn*) to God'. Far from being a reference to inward, silent worship, singing with the 'heart', as in the Old Testament (e.g., Psalms 9:1; 86:12; 111:1; 138:1), refers to singing with the whole of one's being – i.e., 'with all that is within me' (Psalm 103:1). What this means is that the 'entire man should be filled with songs of praise'.[35] Unsurprisingly, Paul uses an almost identical expression in Ephesians 5:19, when he urges his readers to 'make melody *with your heart* (*en kardia humōn*) to the Lord'. In both texts, the God-directedness of such whole-hearted praise is unambiguous.

Many of our evangelical forebears understood and articulated this need to sing to the Lord with intentional spiritual fervor only too well. John Wesley's famous exhortation, found in the 'Preface' of *Sacred Melody* (1761), is a case in point:

> Let not a slight degree of weakness or weariness hinder you. If it is a cross to you, take it up, and you will find it a blessing ... Sing lustily and with good courage. Beware of singing as if you were half dead, or half asleep; but lift up your voice with strength. Be no more afraid of your voice now, nor more ashamed of its being heard, than when you sung the songs of Satan.[36]

Our point could be developed further were we to look more closely at a number of other Hebrew words associated with praise – e.g., *'alatz* (usually translated 'exult'), which means 'to jump for joy' or 'to 'leap in the air'; *giyl* (usually translated 'joy'), which carries the idea of 'spinning around with excitement'; *simcha* (usually translated 'gladness'), which often refers to a state of exceeding gleefulness. Such a study would, no doubt, reinforce what we've already seen: 'Psalmic praise is *joyful*. It voices an enthusiastic exuberance over the presence and steadfast love of

---

[35] Eduard Lohse, *Colossians and Philemon: A Commentary on the Epistles to the Colossians and to Philemon* (Philadelphia: Fortress, 1965), 151.

[36] John Wesley, 'Directions' III-IV. These originally appeared on the final page of *Select Hymns with Tunes Annext: Designed Chiefly for the Use of the People Called Methodists* (London, 1761).

God that ought to embarrass the faint passion of our usual congregational singing'.[37]

But the main point should now be clear: *God's people need to learn to give themselves to praise*. This, of course, should only ever be a grace-motivated and Spirit-enabled response: that is, a response that is in view of God's mercies revealed in Christ and inspired by the Spirit He has given us. But for our part it still takes effort, energy and a decision of the will – ultimately, a decision to be ruled by the fear of the Lord, rather than the fear of others.

So then, out of reverence for Christ, let us sing the Lord's praise with a fervent spirit. For Bonhoeffer was right:

> The more we sing, the more joy will we derive from it, but, above all, the more devotion and discipline and joy we put into our singing, the richer will be the blessing that will come to the whole life of the fellowship from singing together.[38]

3.4 To encourage others

Fourth, while we are not to be governed by the fear of others, it is essential that we learn to praise God in ways that genuinely encourage others. This does not mean that we can never have moments of unselfconscious delight in our praise. But it does mean that we should never be oblivious or insensitive to the needs of our brothers and sisters. For, as we saw in Colossians 3:16, one of the purposes of singing the Word of Christ is to teach and admonish *one another*. This concern for other-person-edification explains why Paul comes down hard on uninterpreted tongue-speaking in church (see 1 Corinthians 14). Unless there is intelligibility in our speaking (and likewise our singing), there can be no meaningful instruction and consequently no real benefit to others. It is essential, then, that we prioritise truth and clarity in our praise, and be ruthless with our repertoire to replace any song or hymn that is either untrue or unclear.

As chapters nine and ten will be devoted to the subject of 'Singing as Preaching', we won't now delve further into the didactic dimension of congregational song. But it is worth stressing the point that directly

---

[37] Mays, *The Lord Reigns*, 70.
[38] Dietrich Bonhoeffer, *Life Together* (London: SCM, 1954), 51.

engaging with God and deliberately encouraging others are not an either-or. Indeed, it is God's will that our praise be *both* God-focussed *and* other-focussed at one and the same time. Admittedly, we can sometimes feel (if not create) a certain tension here. As we noted in the previous chapter, some of our inhibitions are rooted in a concern that if our praise is too exuberant others will be distracted. Nor is this an entirely unwarranted concern, for God desires that we glorify Him only in ways that build others up (1 Corinthians 14:19).

What, then, is the way forward? The *first part* of the solution involves distinguishing between a Christ-like concern for others and a slavish fear of my neighbour – a fear that is ultimately self-serving, not other-serving or God-honouring. The *second part* of the solution involves recognising the importance of the both-and mentioned above. That is, if we are truly committed to encouraging others in the way we praise, then we need to realise that this is unlikely to happen if we are disengaged and unaffected in our singing.

The antidote to being enslaved by the fear of others, then, is not to be impervious to their needs or unconcerned about how our singing impacts them. To the contrary, we will want to minister to those needs and impact our neighbours for their good, so they might all the more join their voice with ours as we sing the Word of Christ together. It is not without reason that Colossians 3:16 is immediately preceded by the exhortation: 'And let the peace of Christ rule in your hearts, to which indeed you were called in one body' (v 15). Our goal, therefore, is not to sing as disparate (and perhaps competing) individuals, but as a peacefully united and harmonious family. To this end, some of John Wesley's exhortations in the 'Preface' to *Sacred Melody* are especially helpful and pointedly practical. For example:

> V. Sing modestly. Do not bawl, so as to be heard above or distinct from the rest of the congregation, that you may not destroy the harmony; but strive to unite your voices together, so as to make one clear melodious sound.

> VI. Sing in time. Whatever time is sung be sure to keep with it. Do not run before nor stay behind it; but attend close to the leading voices, and move therewith as exactly as you can; and take care not to sing too slow. This drawling way naturally steals on all who are

lazy; and it is high time to drive it out from us, and sing all our tunes just as quick as we did at first.

Yet the priority of Godwardness remains. So Wesley concludes:

> VII. Above all sing spiritually. Have an eye to God in every word you sing. Aim at pleasing him more than yourself, or any other creature. In order to do this attend strictly to the sense of what you sing, and see that your heart is not carried away with the sound, but offered to God continually; so shall your singing be such as the Lord will approve here, and reward you when he cometh in the clouds of heaven.

Conclusion

We began this chapter by drawing attention to Paul's exhortation in 1 Thessalonians 5:16-18: 'Rejoice always, pray without ceasing, give thanks in all circumstances; for this is the will of God in Christ Jesus for you'. We then explored three biblically grounded strategies for helping God's people overcome 'the problem of praise paralysis', and saw the importance of regularly calling to mind the fact that the triune God deserves, demands and desires our praise. In so doing, we saw something of why we need the Psalms – not just to inform our pattern of praise but to be employed in our gatherings. For the Psalms, as Calvin rightly saw, are uniquely able to 'incite us to lift up our hearts to God and move us to an ardour in invoking and exalting with praises the glory of his Name'.[39]

In the second half of the chapter, we gave our attention to how we might put praise into practice in church life, noting the need to praise in Spirit and truth, with a thankful heart, with a fervent spirit and in ways that encourage others. In terms of practical implementation, it is not my purpose to be overly prescriptive as this can breed a box-ticking mentality and an insensitivity to context. Every situation is unique and so making wise decisions requires wisdom, prayer, consultation and a certain principled pragmatism. Getting the theological principles clear is, therefore, critical. Ministry must be driven by theology. The patterns and teaching of Scripture must inform and direct not only *what* we sing but

---

[39] John Calvin, 'Articles Concerning the Organisation of the Church and of Worship at Geneva (1537)', in J K S Reid (ed. & trans.), *Calvin: Theological Treatises* (London: SCM, 1954), 53.

also *how* we sing. Consequently, hard questions will sometimes need to be asked not just of the songs in our repertoire but also of our attitudes, motivations, and corporate praise habits.

God's people ought to be committed to praising Him in song not so much because we enjoy the experience of singing (although most of us do), or because we have access to an abundance of wonderful songs (although many of us have), but because we know something of the greatness and goodness of God Himself and so know that a song of praise is fitting (Psalm 147:1). We should likewise know that our creator and redeemer has made us and saved us for the magnification of His glory and grace. If so, indwelt by His Word and filled with His Spirit, we will long to give Him all that He rightly deserves, demands and desires. We are not our own: we are a people purchased for praise – bought by the blood of the Son of God Himself. Praise, then, is 'meet, right and our bounden duty', as it will also be our eternal delight.

> Therefore with Angels and Archangels, and with all the company of heaven, we laud and magnify thy glorious Name; evermore praising thee, and saying, Holy, holy, holy, Lord God of hosts, heaven and earth are full of thy glory: Glory be to thee, O Lord most High. *Amen.*[40]

---

[40] Taken from the *BCP*'s 'The Order of the Administration of the Lord's Supper, or Holy Communion'. According to the rubric, it may be either sung or said.

7. SINGING AS PRAYER I: NATURE AND VALUE

By day the LORD directs his love, at night his song is with me
– a prayer to the God of my life.

Psalm 42:8

Deliver me from bloodguiltiness, O God,
O God of my salvation,
and my tongue will sing aloud of your righteousness.

Psalm 51:14

About midnight Paul and Silas were praying and singing
hymns to God, and the prisoners were listening to them.

Acts 16:25

What am I to do? I will pray with my spirit, but I will pray with
my mind also; I will sing praise with my spirit, but I will sing
with my mind also.

1 Corinthians 14:15

Is anyone among you suffering? Let him pray. Is anyone
cheerful? Let him sing praise.

James 5:13

It is an all-too-little-considered fact that there is a profound relationship between praying and singing in Scripture. But what kind of relationship? Sometimes it is one of *connection* – i.e., *when* my prayer is answered, *then* I will sing your praise (e.g., Psalm 51:14). Sometimes it is one of *contrast* – i.e., if *suffering*, one should pray, if *joyful*, one should sing (e.g., James 5:13). Sometimes it is one of *combination* – i.e., we should *pray and sing* with both mind and spirit (e.g., 1 Corinthians 14:15). All of these relationships, and especially their implications for Christian discipleship and church life, would be well worth pondering and exploring further.

The main focus of this and the following chapter, however, is on a fourth relationship: one that is even closer and, perhaps, more surprising too. For sometimes the connection between prayer and song is one of *concurrence* and *identicality* – i.e., prayer and song not only take place *at the same time* (concurrence), but *as the same action* (identicality). This is what we see in Acts 16:25. In fact, the precise relationship between Paul and Silas' praying and singing is obscured by most English translations.[1] More literally, the verse reads: 'Paul and Silas were praying, singing hymns to God' (Gk. *proseuchomenoi humnoun ton theon*). That is, their prayers were not accompanied by hymns, but took the form of hymns.[2] This does not mean that there was no praise in their singing. Indeed, as Peterson speculates, they 'could have been using any one of a number of the Psalms, which combine such prayer and praise (e.g., Psalms 140-143)'.[3] Whatever the songs sung by Paul and Silas, the point is clear: singing is not only something we can do *along with praying*, but is also *a way of praying*. It is this phenomenon of sung prayer that I want to explore.

1. Singing as a Form of Prayer

1.1. What is prayer?

Before going any further, we need to ask: What is prayer?

The answer to Question 178 of the *Westminster Shorter Catechism* (1647) provides us with a helpful starting point:

> Prayer is an offering up of our desires unto God for things agreeable to his will, in the name of Christ, by the help of his Spirit; with confession of our sins, and thankful acknowledgment of his mercies.

This statement has a number of strengths. The *first* is that it succinctly captures the Bible's understanding of prayer: to pray is to *ask* God to meet our needs according to His will. Its *second* strength is that it reflects the Trinitarian nature of prayer as revealed in the New Testament: to pray is

---

[1] Exceptions include the Berean Literal Bible, Douay-Rheims Bible, Darby Bible Translation and Young's Literal Translation.

[2] See Eckhard J Schnabel, *Acts* (Grand Rapids: Zondervan, 2012), 689; Ernst Haenchen, *The Acts of the Apostles: A Commentary* (trans. Bernard Noble and Gerald Shinn; Philadelphia: The Westminster Press, 1971), 497; Michael F Sadler, *The Acts of the Apostles* (London: Bell, 1906), 312.

[3] David G Peterson, *The Acts of the Apostles* (Grand Rapids: Eerdmans, 2009), 468.

to call upon *God* (the Father), through *Christ* (the Son), by *the Spirit*. The *third* strength is that it distinguishes between prayer and other kinds of divine address (e.g., confession and thanksgiving).

This last point underscores the first: to pray is to request, plead, beseech, supplicate, petition, call or cry out, even beg. It is asking language. What this means is that confession and thanksgiving are not themselves prayer, but accompaniments to prayer. This is why the *Catechism* speaks of prayer being made '*with* confession of our sins, and thankful acknowledgment of his mercies'. This, of course, does not make confession and thanksgiving any less important. Indeed, to pray without them would be unusual, to say the least. It is simply to clarify that confession is confession, thanksgiving is thanksgiving, but prayer is asking.

Although such an understanding of prayer seems to have eluded many contemporary Christians, it was not always so. More than a century ago, Edwyn Bevan put it this way:

> Prayer is by the very definition of the term petitionary: what it means is asking that something we desire may take place. It is not [...] the whole of worship. Worship includes, besides prayer, acts of adoration and thanksgiving, and acts of acceptance of the Divine Will. Prayer is just the petitionary part of worship. To speak of 'petitionary prayer' is a redundant phrase; the adjective is not wanted.[4]

Countless biblical texts bear out the truth of Bevan's judgement. For example, the opening verses of Psalm 17 (which is titled, 'A Prayer of David') reveal the petitionary character of prayer:

> [1] Hear a just cause, O Lord; attend to my cry!
>   Give ear to my prayer from lips free of deceit!
> [2] From your presence let my vindication come!
>   Let your eyes behold the right!

---

4 Edwyn Bevan, 'Petition: Some Theoretical Difficulties', in H Anson, et al (eds.), *Concerning Prayer: Its Nature, its Difficulties and its Value* (London: McMillan & Co., 1916), 194.

So does 'the Lord's prayer' (Matthew 6:9-13), which is introduced with the words: 'This then is how you should pray' (v 9), and then contains a series of requests – *may* your name be hallowed, *may* your kingdom come, *may* your will be done on earth, and so on. The same is true of Jesus' 'high-priestly prayer' (John 17), which also consists of supplications and intercessions. Paul's numerous 'prayer reports' follow the same pattern (e.g., Romans 1:9-10; Ephesians 1:15ff; Philippians 1:9-11; Colossians 1:9-12), as do his various 'prayer requests' (e.g., Romans 15:30-32; Ephesians 6:19; Colossians 4:3-4). The point is further emphasised by the Bible's language of 'asking in prayer' (e.g., Matthew 21:22; Mark 11:24; Romans 1:10; Colossians 1:9) and, most notably, by the piling together of three New Testament 'prayer synonyms' in Philippians 4:6:

> Do not be anxious about anything, but in everything by prayer (*proseuchē*) and supplication (*deēsei*) with thanksgiving (*eucharistias*), let your requests (*aitēmata*) be made known to God.[5]

In short, *to pray, according to Scripture, is to present our petitions before God, our heavenly Father.*

But petitions for what? The fact is that often 'we do not know what to pray for as we ought' (Romans 8:26). This is why Scripture gives us considerable liberty in asking for anything we think we need, knowing that 'the Spirit intercedes for the saints according to the will of God' (Romans 8:27) and that God will only give good gifts to His children (Matthew 7:11). And yet these assurances do not absolve us of our responsibility to petition God 'for things agreeable to his will'. In practice, this means we need to learn to pray in line with what God has revealed in His Word. Otherwise put, *prayer to God* ought to be shaped and informed by the *promises of God.* Indeed, biblical prayer, as Gary Millar insists, is

---

[5] It is not clear whether any distinction in meaning can be drawn between Paul's use of 'prayer' and 'supplication' in this context (So Gordon D Fee, *Paul's Letter to the Philippians* [Grand Rapids: Eerdmans, 1995], 409). Grotius' suggestion that the difference is between *precatio* (asking to obtain good) and *deprecatio* (asking to avert evil) is unlikely and Calvin's suggestion that the distinction is between *precatio* (general prayer) and *rogatio* (particular prayer), while more plausible, is uncertain. See R C Trench, *Synonyms of the New Testament* (London: Kegan, Paul, Trench, Trübner, 1880), 188-189.

nothing less than 'calling upon God to deliver on his promises'.[6] It is wise, then, to model our prayers on the prayers of Scripture, most especially (but not exclusively) the prayer that Jesus taught in answer to His disciples' request, 'Lord, teach us to pray, as John taught his disciples' (Luke 11:1). This is the best way to ensure that the concerns of His kingdom govern our petitions.[7]

Acknowledging the petitionary character of prayer, however, does not completely preclude the broadening of the language of prayer to include other ways in which we might speak to our heavenly Father. In fact, Scripture itself (very occasionally) displays this broader usage (e.g., 1 Samuel 2:1 and Daniel 9:20).[8] It is in this 'umbrella' fashion that the language of prayer often functions in popular piety, devotional literature and systematic theology. Nevertheless, it is vitally important that the primacy of petition not be obscured. Donald Bloesch explains why:

> In the Bible petition and intercession are primary, though adoration, thanksgiving, and confession also have a role. Yet the petitionary element is present in all these forms of prayer. Biblical prayer is crying to God out of the depths; it is the pouring out of the soul before God (cf. 1 Sam. 1:15; Pss. 88:1-2; 130:1-2; 142:1-2; Lam. 2:19; Matt. 7:7-8; Phil. 4:6; Heb. 5:7). It often takes the form of importunity, passionate pleading to God, even wrestling with God.[9]

---

[6] J Gary Millar, *Calling on the Name of the Lord: A Biblical Theology of Prayer* (Downers Grove: IVP, 2016), 155.

[7] For brief but helpful expositions of the Lord's prayer, see Graeme Goldsworthy, *Prayer and the Knowledge of God: What the Whole Bible Teaches* (Leicester: IVP, 2003), 85-105; Timothy Keller, *Prayer: Experiencing Awe and Intimacy with God* (London: Hodder & Stoughton, 2014), 108-119; N T Wright, *Simply Good News: Why the Gospel Is News and What Makes It Good* (New York: HarperCollins, 2015), 153-171.

[8] It is also the case that a number of the 'prayer psalms, which have titles referring to prayer, not only ask for things, but also are intermingled with expressions of trust (Pss 17:15; 102:28), praise (Pss 86:7-10; 90:1-6), innocence (Pss 17:2-5; 86:2), and vows (Ps 86:12-13)'. See Kyu Nam Jung, 'Prayer in the Psalms', in D A Carson (ed.), *Teach Us To Pray: Prayer in the Bible and the World* (Exeter: Paternoster, 1990), 36.

[9] Donald G Bloesch, 'Prayer', in Walter A Elwell (ed.), *Evangelical Dictionary of Theology* (Grand Rapids: Baker Academic, 2001), 947. Such an understanding provides a gentle, but necessary, corrective to the influential ACTS model of

An additional reason why we must not lose sight of the petitionary heart of all prayer is that, in biblical understanding, *to ask is to honour*. That is, humbly calling upon God to do for us what we cannot do for ourselves is an expression of trust and, in that sense, an act of worship. For petition, as Stanley Grenz writes, 'discloses the true state of affairs. It reminds the believer that God is the source of all good, and that human beings are utterly dependent and stand in need of everything'.[10]

1.2. Singing our petitions

If prayer is essentially petitionary in character, and if prayers can be sung, then it follows that one of the ways of offering up 'our desires unto God for things agreeable to his will' is by singing them. This is more than just a truism, given that anything that can be said can also be sung; it's an observation from Scripture.

The Psalter, once again, is our prime example here, as a large proportion of its content consists of prayers (either in part or in whole). This is made explicit in the titles of a number of psalms. For example, Psalms 17 and 86 are both called 'A Prayer of David' and Psalm 142, 'A Maskil of David, when he was in the Cave. A Prayer'. Psalm 90 is similarly labelled, 'A Prayer of Moses, the man of God', and Psalm 102, 'A Prayer of one who is afflicted, when he is faint and pours out his complaint before the Lord'. It is also apparent from the language of prayer (the key Hebrew terms are

prayer (i.e., that prayer = Adoration, Confession, Thanksgiving and Supplication). While this model has been helpful in reminding us of a number of key things God calls us to do, the language of prayer in Scripture does not equal all of those things, only the last. Furthermore, the model is a little too suggestive of a rigid sequence (whereas Scripture is more flexible) and potentially lends itself to the view that the first three are a necessary prelude to the fourth (i.e., in order to ask things of our heavenly Father we first need to spend time adoring, confessing and thanking Him). Again, without diminishing the value of adoration, confession and thanksgiving, or their necessity as accompaniments to prayer, the biblical pattern is more varied. In fact, in the view of Graham Cole, the ACTS model is also to be faulted for missing an 'L' – lament. See Graham Cole, 'Lament: A Missing Practice', *The Gospel Coalition Australia* (September 22, 2016): https://australia.thegospelcoalition.org/article/lament-a-missing-practice.
[10] Stanley J Grenz, *Prayer: The Cry of the Kingdom* (Peabody: Hendrickson, 1988), 37.

tefilla and *palaḷ* that appears frequently throughout the Psalter,[11] and from the petitionary character of many psalms.[12] Finally, Psalm 72:20 concludes book II of the Psalter with the words: 'The prayers of David, the son of Jesse, are ended',[13] suggesting 'the word *prayers* was the earliest collective term for the Psalms'.[14]

As to the singing of these prayers, we have already noted that there is a plethora of evidence (both intra- and extra-biblical) that a large number of the Psalms were sung in the temple – some by the Levitical choir only, but many by the people as well. At their point of composition, some may well have been written as reflections or meditations, and only later turned into songs. But many were written as songs. This is clear from the content of those psalms in which we find exhortations to sing (e.g., Psalms 9:11; 30:4; 68:4) or calls to join the psalmist in singing (e.g., Psalms 34:3; 95:1-2; 118:24). It is also clear from a number of psalm titles. For example, Psalm 7 has the title: *A Shiggaion*[15] *of David, which he sang to the Lord concerning the words of Cush, a Benjaminite.* So what does David's song say?

> [1] O Lord my God, in you do I take refuge;
>   save me from all my pursuers and deliver me,
> [2] lest like a lion they tear my soul apart,
>   rending it in pieces, with none to deliver.

This, then, is a prayer for deliverance, for rescue, for salvation. But more than that, it is a prayer for vindication, for judgement, for justice. So David continues:

---

[11] Psalms 4, 5, 6, 17, 32, 35, 39, 42, 54, 55, 61, 65, 66, 69, 72, 80, 84, 86, 88, 90, 102, 109, 116, 118, 122, 141, 142 and 143.

[12] E.g., Psalms 3-8, 9-10, 12-13, 16-18, etc.

[13] The Psalter is structured into five 'books' – Book 1: Psalms 1-41; Book 2: Psalms 42-72; Book 3: Psalms 73-89; Book 4: Psalms 90-106; Book 5: Psalms 107-150.

[14] Derek Kidner, *Psalms 1-72* (Leicester: IVP, 1973), 257.

[15] 'Shiggaion' is generally thought to be a musical or liturgical term, possibly calling for 'an animated musical beat'. See Nancy L deClaissé-Walford, Rolf A Jacobson and Beth LaNeel Tanner, *The Book of Psalms* (Eerdmans: Grand Rapids, 2014), 111, n 6.

⁶ Arise, O Lord, in your anger;
   lift yourself up against the fury of my enemies;
   awake for me; you have appointed a judgement ...

⁹ Oh, let the evil of the wicked come to an end,
   and may you establish the righteous –
   you who test the minds and hearts, O righteous God!

Here, then, is one example of a sung prayer; a song that petitions God – in this case by pleading for the salvation of His servants and for vengeance on their enemies, who are also His enemies. Do we ever think to sing this kind of prayer? David did. And those who sing the Psalter do. But what about the rest of us?

1.3.   Paul's encouragements to sing the Psalms

As we saw in the first half of this book, new covenant Christians are not called to replicate everything that went on in Israel's temple. In fact, there are some things we must not repeat. The sacrificial system, outlined in the book of Leviticus, for example, is now defunct. Not only could the blood of goats and bulls never take away sins (Hebrews 10:11), but Christ has offered a single sacrifice for sins and in so doing 'has perfected for all time those who are being sanctified' (Hebrews 10:12-14). In other word, full atonement has been made once and for all. Consequently, 'there is no longer any offering for sin' (Hebrews 10:18). Therefore, any attempt to reinstall such sacrifices or to regard a particular Christian activity (e.g., prayer, singing, giving to the needy or the Lord's Supper) as some kind of replacement of them, must be regarded an act of unbelief, if not blasphemy.

As we saw in chapter four, this does not mean that the notion of sacrifice has been banished from the new covenant (see Hebrews 13:15). Nor does it mean that everything that was done in the temple is irrelevant to followers of Christ or that there is no overlap between temple activities and Christian assemblies. In fact, the apostle Paul commands Christians to devote themselves to 'the public reading of Scripture, to exhortation, to teaching' (1 Timothy 4:13) – just as the Israelites did in the temple. He also urges that 'supplications, prayers, intercessions, and thanksgivings be made for all people' (1 Timothy 2:1) – just as they were in the temple. He further encourages the singing of 'psalms and hymns and spiritual songs' (Ephesians 5:19; Colossians 3:16) – just as took place in the temple.

None of this means that Christians should *only sing the Psalms*. As we noted in chapter five, the case for 'exclusive psalmody' is not strong. This is not to deny the oft cited fact that in the LXX 'the Greek words *psalmois*, *humnois*, *odais* translate the Hebrew words *mizmorim, tehillim, shirim* and that these are the terms used in the Book of Psalms and of the various contents of the Book of Psalms'.[16] The problem, however, is that the New Testament's use of *psalmois*, *humnois* and *odais* is too fluid and varied to establish that when Paul uses the three terms together in Ephesians 5:19 and Colossians 3:16 he is using them *all* to refer to the Psalter.[17]

Having said that, the evidence favours seeing Paul's first term (*psalmois*) as, at least, including the Psalter.[18] For, as Ralph Martin points out, 'Christian song did not break forth upon the world which had been hitherto dumb and in which hymns were unknown. The church was cradled in Judaism, and borrowed many of its forms of worship from the Temple and synagogue'.[19] Paul's three terms, then, would seem to cover the whole spectrum of Christian congregational song – from the *canonical Psalms* (at one end) to *spontaneous songs* (at the other).[20] This means that the Psalter, while not the only part of the church's hymn/prayer-book, ought to be regarded a key part – indeed, it is the divinely inspired part! This is certainly how it was understood in the early

---

[16] Hugh Cartwright, 'Does the Bible tell us what to sing?' (14 February 2000): www.fpchurch.org.uk/about-us/how-we-worship/exclusive-psalmody/does-the-bible-tell-us-what-to-sing.

[17] See further Robert S Smith, 'Psalms, Hymns and Spiritual Songs: What are They and Why Sing Them?', *CASE* 23 (2010), 26-29.

[18] For every other use of *psalmos* in the New Testament, with the possible exception of 1 Corinthians 14:26, clearly refers to the Psalter. Interestingly, John Calvin (*Sermons on Ephesians* [Edinburgh: Banner of Truth, 1973], 552-553), takes the view that Paul's three terms 'scarcely differ from one another, and therefore there is no need to seek entertainment for ourselves in setting forth any subtle distinction among them'.

[19] Ralph P Martin, *Worship in the Early Church* (Grand Rapids: Eerdmans, 1974), 40.

[20] Martin takes a different view, arguing that the adjective 'spiritual', which comes at the end of Paul's phrase, applies to 'psalms' and 'hymns' also. This enables him to conclude that all three of Paul's terms refer to compositions 'which were spontaneously "inspired" and created for the occasion' (*Worship in the Early Church*, 43). Most recent commentators, however, are far from convinced. See, for example, Moo, *The Letters to the Colossians and to Philemon*, 290.

church, at least by the second century.[21] Consequently, we should not only take seriously the apostolic exhortations to sing the Psalms (as well as other songs that convey the Word of Christ), but also realise what such exhortations imply: that it is God's will for us, at least on occasion, to sing our prayers.[22]

I am not here arguing that the Psalms must *only ever be sung* – i.e., that they should never simply be read, pondered, recited or even chanted. Just because something can be sung, doesn't mean it must be sung. But it is instructive that the Psalms *were sung* (not just by the people of Israel but also by Jesus and His disciples), that they *have been sung* (down through the ages in a variety of different ways), and that this practice has been a source of immense spiritual blessing to many. Little wonder that John Chrysostom, once remarked:

> Learn to sing psalms, and thou shalt see the delightfulness of the employment. For they who sing psalms are filled with the Holy Spirit, as they who sing satanic songs are filled with an unclean spirit.[23]

In some form or another, then, the followers of Jesus ought to sing the Psalms. There may be practical difficulties that need to be overcome, but that is not an excuse to neglect the practice altogether. And if we do, then what singing the Psalms will inevitably mean is that, at least on occasion, we will be singing our prayers. This raises the question: What is the particular value of *singing* prayers?

---

[21] It may well have been so earlier, but the evidence prior to this time, as Edward Foley notes, is 'fragmentary and ambiguous'. Consequently, it is impossible 'to ascertain any set pattern for employing psalms within Christian worship of the first century' (Edward Foley, *Foundations of Christian Music: The Music of Pre-Constantinian Christianity* [Collegeville: The Liturgical Press, 1996], 96).

[22] It also needs to be said that in singing the canonical psalms, even those that are addressed explicitly and exclusively to God, we are simultaneous singing the Word of God which is addressed to us.

[23] John Chrysostom, 'Homily XIX. Ephesians V. 15, 16, 17', in Philip Schaff (ed.), *Nicene and Post-Nicene Fathers: Chrysostom: Homilies on Galatians, Ephesians, Philippians, Colossians, Thessalonians, Timothy, Titus, and Philemon* (Peabody: Hendrickson, 1999), 138.

2. The Value of Singing Prayers

2.1. *Singing enables us to express and enrich our unity*

There are a number of distinct benefits to singing prayers.[24] The first is that it gives us a way of praying together with one mind and one voice and, in so doing, expressing the unity that is ours in Christ. There is an old German proverb that says 'the one who speaks with me is my fellow human; the one who sings with me is my brother'.[25] Consequently, 'offering up of our desires unto God' in song is one fulfilment of Paul's 'wish-prayer' for unity in Romans 15:

> [5] May the God of endurance and encouragement grant you to live in such harmony with one another, in accord with Christ Jesus, [6] that together you may with one voice glorify the God and Father of our Lord Jesus Christ. (Romans 15:5-6)

True unity, of course, can only ever be unity in 'the word of truth, the gospel of salvation' (Ephesians 1:13). This is why God desires us to all 'attain to the unity of the faith and of the knowledge of the Son of God' (Ephesians 4:13), and why taking up the sword of the Spirit (i.e., the Word of God) is a necessary prerequisite to 'praying at all times in the Spirit, with all prayer and supplication' (Ephesians 6:17-18). In the *BCP*, these truths are captured and combined in the collect of Saint Simon and Saint Jude, Apostles:

> O almighty God, who hast built thy Church upon the foundation of the Apostles and Prophets, Jesus Christ himself being the head corner-stone; Grant us so to be joined together in unity of spirit by

---

[24] These benefits are not, of course, unique to sung prayer; they also apply to sung praise and sung proclamation. To a lesser degree, they also apply to spoken liturgy.

[25] In German, 'Wer spricht mit mir ist mein Mitmensch; wer singt mit mir ist mein Bruder'. I am indebted to Mark Noll for this proverb. See Mark A Noll, 'Praise the Lord: Song, culture, divine bounty, and issues of harmonization', *Books & Culture* (November/December 2007):
http://www.booksandculture.com/articles/2007/novdec/9.14.html.

their doctrine, that we may be made an holy temple acceptable unto thee; through Jesus Christ our Lord. Amen.[26]

This concern for *unity in the apostles' teaching* not only highlights the need for our prayers to shaped by Scripture, but also the value of sung prayer. How so? Because 'in singing together', as Bonhoeffer observed, 'it is possible to speak and pray the same Word at the same time', thereby enabling us to 'unite in the Word'.[27]

So what kind of corporate song best expresses such unity in God's Word? Bonhoeffer was convinced that anything other than 'the purity of unison singing' risks giving 'musical art an autonomy of its own apart from the words'.[28] Doubtless, such a risk exists and ought to be minimised. But as it does not necessarily follow, to bind ourselves to monophony is needlessly restrictive, if not theologically one-sided. For the 'unity of the Body of Christ is not a bland, undifferentiated uniformity, but a rich and manifold concord'.[29] Likewise, there is no inherent competition between the one voice of the body and the many voices of its members, or displacement of the parts by the whole. Rather, as 'we sing together, different sounds – your voice, and mine – occupy the same time and the same space, without obstructing or negating one another'.[30] This is in keeping with the work of the Spirit: for the Spirit creates both unity and diversity, making us one body in Christ and yet giving us different gifts that perform different functions in that one body (1 Corinthians 12:7-13).[31]

---

[26] As we saw at the end of the introductory chapter to this book, it is also captured in the *BCP*'s prayer for 'the whole state of Christ's Church militant here in earth' (found in 'The Order of the Administration of the Lord's Supper, or Holy Communion') in which the Lord is asked 'to inspire continually the Universal Church with the spirit of truth, unity, and concord', so that 'all they who do confess thy holy Name may agree in the truth of thy holy Word, and live in unity, and godly love'.

[27] Bonhoeffer, *Life Together*, 49.

[28] Bonhoeffer, *Life Together*, 49-50. Although Bonhoeffer claims that this is a matter of spiritual discernment, his arguments are, essentially, practical.

[29] Steven R Guthrie, 'Singing in the Body and in the Spirit', *JETS* 46.4 (December 2003), 645.

[30] Guthrie, 'Singing in the Body and in the Spirit', 643.

[31] It may also be seen as a reflection (albeit a partial and dim one) of the divine relationships in the Trinity – where the three distinct persons do not displace one another, but mutually indwell one another to such an extent that they are one God.

In terms of song style, then, provided the content of the prayer is both biblical in substance and meaningfully communicated, the doors are wide open to a range of musical forms and likewise to singing that is antiphonal, responsorial, monophonic or polyphonic.[32]

As well as *expressing* our unity, singing our prayers together also gives us a way of *enriching* that unity. This is, no doubt, largely a result of corporately voicing our shared concerns. But it is also, in part, because all congregational singing helps to develop a sense of belonging or group solidarity. The neurochemical explanation for this is that communal singing increases the oxytocin (the 'bonding hormone') levels of the participants, creating an experience of intense social connection.[33]

For Christians, however, the benefit is more than biological. When God's children petition Him together in song, the spiritual bonds between us are profoundly enhanced. For sung prayer "transports' us not only to God, but connects us to the people with whom we are worshiping'.[34] More than that, such singing, according to the apostle, is one of the means by which the church is filled with the Spirit (Ephesians 5:19-21)[35] and thereby enabled to maintain 'the unity of the Spirit in the bond of peace' (Ephesians 4:3). Indeed, as Steven Guthrie notes, there is 'an analogy of form between the sound of people singing together and the unity to which

---

[32] For those who are unfamiliar with these terms, in responsorial singing, a soloist or choir sings a series of verses, each one followed by a response from either the choir or the congregation. In antiphonal singing, verses (or lines) are sung alternately by soloist and choir, or by soloist and congregation, or by choir and congregation, or by half of the congregation followed by the other half. Monophonic means having a single melody line. Polyphonic means in two or more parts, each with its own melody.

[33] See, for example, J R Keeler, E A Roth, B L Neuser, J M Spitsbergen, D J M Waters and J-M Vianney, 'The neurochemistry and social flow of singing: bonding and oxytocin', *Frontiers in Human Neuroscience* (23 September 2015): http://dx.doi.org/10.3389/fnhum.2015.00518.

[34] Alison Werner Hoenen, 'How Can I Keep from Singing? An Appeal to Christians to Sing the Faith', *Journal of Lutheran Ethics* (10/01/2010): http://www.elca.org/JLE/Articles/254#_edn20.

[35] For the arguments in favour of the 'means reading' of Paul's participles, see Timothy G Gombis, 'Being the Fullness of God in Christ by the Spirit: Ephesians 5:18 in its Epistolary Setting', *TynB* 53.2 (2002), 268-270; Robert S Smith, 'Music, Singing and Emotions: Exploring the Connections', *Themelios* 37.3 (2012), 473-474.

the church aspires'.[36] For this reason, music and song are not only 'a particularly apt vehicle for worship', but are 'uniquely equipped to provide an aural image of this kind of community, in which union is not unanimity, nor multiplicity a cacophony'.[37]

Furthermore, if we are singing historic prayers or prayers sung universally, then singing our prayers together also expresses and enriches our unity at larger level: it 'reminds one that all individual Christians are part of a great body of believers stretching through time and space'.[38] Again, Bonhoeffer captures the point well:

> Thus all singing together that is right must serve to widen our spiritual horizon, make us see our little company as a member of the great Christian Church on earth, and help us willingly and gladly to join our singing, be it feeble or good, to the song of the Church.[39]

We should not minimise the importance of this unity with both the *church militant* (on earth) and the *church triumphant* (in heaven). It is both helpful and humbling to be reminded that we are part of the communion of saints from every period of history and every part of the world. Singing traditional prayers is not the only way to be made aware of this, but I agree with Charles Taliaferro that 'set prayers (either spoken or in the form of hymns) that can be memorized by Christians could meet the need for authentic solidarity over the ages'.[40] This, needless to say, has been one of the great boons that the *BCP* (and other reformed liturgies) has brought to the people of God.

For these reasons, *corporate sung prayer cannot help but build and strengthen the assemblies of God's people*: it expresses the fellowship we enjoy as Christ's followers, as it also enriches the unity of the Spirit we are called to maintain. We neglect such a gift to our detriment.

---

[36] Guthrie, 'Singing in the Body and in the Spirit', 644.

[37] Guthrie, 'Singing in the Body and in the Spirit', 644-645.

[38] Charles Taliaferro, 'Evil and Prayer: Set Prayers and Other Special Weapons', in C Meister and J K Dew Jr. (eds.), *God and Evil: The Case for God in a World Filled with Pain* (Downers Grove: IVP, 2013), 157.

[39] Bonhoeffer, *Life Together*, 51.

[40] Taliaferro, 'Evil and Prayer', 158.

2.2. *Singing helps us to express and evoke appropriate emotions*

But what does *singing*, in particular, add? Why not simply *say* our prayers together?

The unique value of singing our prayers (and indeed of music and song in general) is that it helps us engage emotionally with the truths we are saying or the requests we are praying. Lyricist, Yip Harburg – who, amongst other things, penned the words for the songs in *The Wizard of Oz* – expressed the point succinctly and memorably: 'Words make you think a thought; music makes you feel a feeling; a song makes you feel a thought'. Singing, thus, plays a critical role in helping us to bridge the 'cognitive' and the 'affective' aspects of our humanity.

Part of the reason for this is that music is an inherently emotional medium. One way of understanding the connection between music and emotion is in terms of what philosopher Stephen Davies calls 'appearance emotionalism'.[41] What he means is that music can, for example, sound sad in the same way that, say, a weeping willow looks sad. In Davies' words: 'The resemblance that counts most for music's expressiveness [...] is between music's temporally unfolding dynamic structure and configurations of human behaviour associated with the expression of emotion'.[42] Jeremy Begbie describes the same phenomenon in terms of 'representative concentration',[43] explaining that 'in music, emotionally significant bodily movements are embodied in a concentrated (musical) form, in such a way that the music can represent us and concentrate us emotionally as we are drawn into its life'.[44] In this way, music has the capacity to 'enable *a more concentrated emotional engagement with the object or objects with which we are dealing*'.[45] However we best account for and articulate the inherent emotionality of music, in practical terms it is generally recognized that minor keys, heavy textures and slow tempos

---

[41] Stephen Davies, 'Artistic Expression and the Hard Case of Pure Music', in M Kieren (ed), *Contemporary Debates in Aesthetics and the Philosophy of Art* (Oxford: Blackwell, 2006), 179-191.

[42] Davies, 'Artistic Expression and the Hard Case of Pure Music', 181.

[43] Jeremy S Begbie, 'Faithful Feelings: Music and Emotions in Worship', in Jeremy S Begbie and Steven R Guthrie (eds.), *Resonant Witness: Conversations between Music and Theology* (Grand Rapids: Eerdmans, 2011), 349.

[44] Begbie, 'Faithful Feelings', 352.

[45] Begbie, 'Faithful Feelings', 350 (emphasis his).

normally express and evoke grief, just as major keys, light textures and fast tempos normally express and evoke joy.

When the human voice is brought into the equation, and meaningful words are added to the mix, the power of music is further increased as our affective and cognitive capacities are bridged. That is, by singing words, especially words of truth, singers (and listeners too) are helped to 'feel a thought' in a way that speaking those same words can rarely achieve. The physiological reality behind this phenomenon, as a number of neuroimaging studies have shown, is that while the majority of sensorimotor processes for singing and speaking are the same, singing engages parts of our brain that speech alone does not.[46] This is why singing is a unique activity not only for expressing genuine emotion, but also for evoking appropriate emotion. *The very activity of singing truth assists us to access and process the emotional reality of that truth.*

Biblical evidence of this phenomenon is found, in a particularly striking way, in the lament psalms. This is a point that was long ago noted by Athanasius: 'Whatever your particular need or trouble, from this same book you can select a form of words to fit it, not so that you hear and then pass on, but learn the way to remedy your ill'.[47] Similarly, and speaking of the Psalter as a whole, Calvin remarked that 'there is not an emotion of which any one can be conscious that is not here represented as in a mirror'.[48]

Furthermore, while the tunes to which the psalms were originally sung have long since disappeared from the musical memory of God's people, the fact that they were sung speaks of an awareness of the God-given capacity of singing to aid us in the honest articulation of sorrow, the effective processing of pain and the awakening of hope in God. Psalm 142

---

[46] See, for example, E Özdemir, A Norton & G Schlaug, 'Shared and Distinct Neural Correlates of Singing and Speaking', *Neuroimage* 33 (2006), 633.

[47] Athanasius, 'A Letter to Marcellinus, Our Holy Father, Bishop of Alexandria, On the Interpretation of the Psalms', in Robert G Gregg (trans.), *Athanasius: The Life of Antony and the Letter to Marcellinus* (Mahway: Paulist Press, 1980), 103.

[48] John Calvin, 'The Author's Preface' (1557), in *A Commentary on the Book of Psalms – Volume 1: Translated from the original Latin, and collated with the author's French version, by The Rev James Anderson* (Calvin Translation Society, 1845–1849; repr. Grand Rapids: Baker, 1979): http://www.ccel.org/ccel/calvin/calcom08.vi.html.

bears this out. The title describes it as 'a *maskil* (i.e., 'song') of David',[49] and also as 'a prayer' (Heb. *tefilla*). It begins with a plea for mercy (v 1), followed by an explanation of David's 'trouble' (vv 2-4) and a further cry to the Lord (v 5), before coming to the main petition in v 6 ('Deliver me from my persecutors for they are too strong for me!'). A parallel request follows in v 7a ('Bring me out of prison'), which also reveals the ultimate purpose of David's prayer ('that I may give thanks to your name!'). It concludes with a bold statement of confidence in v 7b: 'The righteous *will* surround me, for you *will* deal bountifully with me'.

This kind of progression is typical of many biblical laments. They begin in the depths, or move there very quickly, as God is addressed from a place of undisguised desperation. This feature is crucial, for 'the psalms of lament do not dismiss or deny or seek to avoid sorrow. On the contrary, they allow a grieving person to move more fully into the valley of the shadow; knowing on different levels, that no matter what, God is indeed present in the sorrow'.[50] But rarely do they conclude in the valley.[51] For singing of the reality of God's presence, power and promises not only provides comfort in the valley but shows the way out or points to the mountain beyond. Otherwise put, the singing of lament not only helps in the processing of pain but, by arousing faith and hope, ultimately brings us to a point of praise.

Little wonder, then, that the lament psalms (or 'petitionary praise psalms', as Westermann calls them) typically move from pleading to praising. For, as Westermann goes on to explain, '[t]he goal of the transition which we have observed in the structure of the Psalm of lament is the praise of God.

---

[49] Although the precise meaning of this term is uncertain, it is generally understood to be a musical term and most likely refers to 'an artistic or teaching song'. See deClaissé-Walford, et al, *The Book of Psalms*, 399.
[50] Logan C Jones, 'The Psalms of Lament and the Transformation of Sorrow', *The Journal of Pastoral Care & Counselling* 61.1-2 (Spring-Summer, 2007), 47.
[51] I say 'rarely', because there are two exceptions: Psalm 44 and Psalm 88. Yet even these psalms, despite their lack of resolution, are not without hope. Psalm 44 ends with the petition: 'Redeem us for the sake of your steadfast love!' (v 26), and Psalm 88 begins with the words: 'O Lord, God of my salvation, I cry out day and night before you. Let my prayer come before you; incline your ear to my cry' (vv 1-2).

This is indicated primarily by the fact that the Psalm of lament concludes with a vow of praise'.[52]

Although the *singing* of lament is not *essential* to this transition, it greatly assists it. Indeed, the ability 'to give structure to emotionally charged experiences is what makes music such a powerful aid to the process of mourning'.[53] The same could be said of singing and joy; that is, music's ability 'to give structure to emotionally charged experiences' also makes it a powerful aid to rejoicing. It is for these reasons that Luther penned these oft quoted words:

> Next to the Word of God, music deserves the highest praise. She is a mistress and governess of those human emotions ... which control men or more often overwhelm them ... Whether you wish to comfort the sad, to subdue frivolity, to encourage the despairing, to humble the proud, to calm the passionate or to appease those full of hate ... what more effective means than music could you find.[54]

Calvin likewise claimed that 'among the other things which are appropriate to recreate man and give him desire, music is either the first or one of the chief ones, and we must deem it to be a gift of God intended for this use'.[55]

God's people have long been aware of the power of music to express and evoke appropriate emotions, and of the way in which, when it is conjoined with the truth of God's Word, it can help bring us to both spiritual and emotional maturity. In fact, writes Begbie, 'music is particularly well suited to being a vehicle of emotional renewal in worship, a potent instrument through which the Holy Spirit can begin to remake and

---

[52] Westermann, *Praise and Lament in the Psalms*, 267. Such vows can be found in Psalms 5:11-12; 7:17; 13:5-6; 22:22ff.; 26:12; 31:7; etc. Actual declarations of praise are also common (e.g., Psalms 28:6; 31:21; 35:9-10; 36:5-9; etc).
[53] Elaine J Ramshaw, 'Singing at Funerals and Memorial Services', *Currents in Theology and Mission* 35.3 (June 2008), 206.
[54] Martin Luther, 'Preface to Georg Rhau's Symphonoiae iucundae, 1538', in *Liturgy and Hymns* (eds. Ulrich S Leupold and Helmut T Lehmann; trans. Ulrich S Leupold; vol. 53 of *Luther's Works*, American Edition, eds. Jaroslav Pelikan and Helmut T Lehmann; Philadelphia: Fortress, 1965), 323.
[55] John Calvin, 'Letter to the Reader', 164.

transform us in the likeness of Christ, the one true worshipper'.[56] It's difficult to think of a greater incentive for us, at least on occasion, to sing our prayers.

3. Incentives and Obstacles to Singing the Psalms

There are several further aspects of sung prayer that we will discuss in the next chapter. But before concluding this one, I want to add some further reasons why churches should seek to develop, or perhaps rediscover, the practice of singing the Psalter. At the same time, I also want to acknowledge some of the inherent difficulties with this practice and offer suggestions as to how they might be overcome.

3.1. The unique benefits of singing the Psalms

'The Psalter occupies a unique place in the Holy Scripture', writes Bonhoeffer. 'It is God's Word and, with a few exceptions, the prayer of men as well'.[57] This makes psalm singing an immensely powerful practice. We are not only singing genuinely human prayers but praying divinely inspired words! Such 'dual authorship' is, of course, a feature of every part of Holy Scripture, for all Scripture is God's Word through human words (2 Timothy 3:16; 2 Peter 1:21). But the point is that the Psalms are not just divinely inspired human words, but divinely inspired human words *addressed to God*. And while there are numerous other prayers found in Scripture, the uniqueness of these prayers is that they were compiled to be used by God's people in their corporate worship.

Not surprisingly, singing the Psalms has a number of unique benefits. *First*, it develops us *communally*. If, as we have argued, petitioning God together in song strengthens the spiritual bonds between us, then singing the Psalms achieves this in ways that few other songs and prayers can. Why so? Because they push us beyond ourselves, enabling us to pray in ways we otherwise might not. So, writes Bonhoeffer,

> It does not depend, therefore, on whether the Psalms express adequately that which we feel at a given moment in our heart. If we are to pray aright, perhaps it is quite necessary that we pray contrary

---

[56] Begbie, 'Faithful Feelings', 353.
[57] Bonhoeffer, *Life Together*, 34.

to our own heart. Not what we want to pray is important, but what God wants us to pray.[58]

In so doing, 'the psalms teach us to pray as a fellowship. The Body of Christ is praying, and as an individual one acknowledges that his prayer is only a minute fragment of the whole prayer of the Church. He learns to pray the prayer of the Body of Christ. And that lifts him above his personal concerns and allows him to pray selflessly'.[59] The net result is a deepening of relationships through the fostering of empathy. For this reason, the singing of the Psalms can help us to develop *communally*.

Second, psalm singing also matures us *spiritually*. Why? Because '*the psalter as a whole provides us with the most detailed and sustained treatment of how God's people can, should and must call on him*'.[60] So how, according to the Psalms, ought we to call upon God in prayer? In any and every state (regardless of how raw), without pretence about ourselves, our sins or our circumstances, and without holding back. Indeed, it is precisely because the Psalms express the whole gamut of emotions that Calvin described them as 'An Anatomy of all Parts of the Soul'.[61] Nor was he the first to speak this way. In the fourth century, Ambrose of Milan made a similar observation about the Psalter:

> All with eyes to see can discover in it a complete gymnasium for the soul, a stadium for all the virtues, equipped for every kind of exercise; it is for each to choose the kind he judges best to help him gain the prize.[62]

The book of Psalms, then, 'powerfully teaches us to seek the Lord in all our varied conditions'.[63] It does so by helping us pray both in a *truly human way* and in *divinely inspired words*. Therefore, writes Bonhoeffer, 'whoever has begun to pray the Psalter seriously and regularly will soon give a vacation to other little devotional prayers and say: "Ah, there is not

[58] Dietrich Bonhoeffer, *Psalms: The Prayerbook of the Bible* (Minneapolis: Augsburg, 1974), 14-15.
[59] Bonhoeffer, *Life Together*, 38-39.
[60] Millar, *Calling on the Name of the Lord*, 140 (emphasis his).
[61] Calvin, 'The Author's Preface' (1557), in *A Commentary on the Book of Psalms – Volume 1*.
[62] Ambrose, *Commentary on Psalm* 1:4, 8.
[63] Kyu Nam Jung, 'Prayer in the Psalms', 57.

the juice, the strength, the passion, the fire which I find in the Psalter. It tastes too cold and too hard" (Luther)'.[64] For this reason, psalm singing can help us to mature *spiritually* in ways that few other songs and prayers can.

3.2. *Understanding our connection to the Psalms*

If singing the Psalter is so beneficial, why don't more churches do it? Part of the answer is because there are some inherent difficulties in singing the Psalms. For example, although 'there is every indication that the whole collection was taken over quite early as public property',[65] many psalms do not read like the prayers of ordinary Israelites, let alone contemporary Christians. The chief reason for this is that *the prayers and praises of the book of Psalms are not, first and foremost, those of the average believer*. In fact, if there's one thing that has emerged from the last 30 years of scholarship on the Psalms, it is that the Psalter, in both substance and shape, is designed to reflect the historic progression of Israelite kingship in light of the promise made to David (Psalm 2:7; cf. 2 Samuel 7).[66] What this means is that the 'I' of the Psalms is very often the 'I' of the Lord's anointed, God's Messiah. As such, 'David's prayer *cannot possibly* be our prayers'.[67]

When rightly understood, however, this difficulty actually provides the key to the Psalter's connection to us. For the promises made to David, like everything written in 'the book of David', are ultimately fulfilled by great David's greater son, Jesus Christ (Luke 24:44). It is He who shares these promises and prayers with us – those who have received His Spirit and so are joint heirs with Him (Romans 8:14-17). This is vital to understand. For if we want to pray or sing the Psalms, writes Bonhoeffer, 'we must not

---

[64] Bonhoeffer, *Life Together*, 25.

[65] Goldsworthy, *Prayer and the Knowledge of God*, 130.

[66] On the purpose and shape of the Psalter and the structural significance of the kingship theme, see Gerald H Wilson, *The Editing of the Hebrew Psalter* (Chico: Scholars Press, 1985); Andrew E Hill and John H Walton, *A Survey of the Old Testament* (Grand Rapids: Zondervan, 2000), 346-351; Mark D Futato, *Interpreting the Psalms: An Exegetical Handbook* (Grand Rapids: Kregel, 2007), 57-116; James Hely Hutchinson, 'The Psalter as a Book', in Andrew G Shead (ed.), *Stirred by a Noble Theme: The Book of Psalms in the Life of the Church* (Nottingham: Apollos, 2013), 23-45.

[67] Millar, *Calling on the Name of the Lord*, 142 (emphasis his).

ask first what they have to do with us, but what they have to do with Jesus Christ'.[68] Elsewhere he adds:

> A psalm that we cannot utter as a prayer, that makes us falter and horrifies us, is a hint to us that here Someone else is praying, not we; that the One who is here protesting his innocence, who is invoking God's judgment, who has come to such infinite depths of suffering, is none other than Jesus Christ. He it is who is praying here, and not only here but in the whole Psalter.[69]

In one sense, then, we don't relate directly to the Psalms. 'All the details of the individual psalms need to be refracted through their fulfilment in Christ'.[70] Otherwise put, the prayers of the Psalms 'are first the prayers of the Messiah, which, in the kindness of God, become the prayers of the Messiah's people as he draws them into relationship with him'.[71] So the Psalms are indeed ours – just as they were Israel's; for even in the Old Testament, God's Messiah was never thought about independently of 'all who take refuge in him' (Psalm 2:12). But for new covenant believers our relationship to our king is even more profound. We are both 'in Christ' and indwelt by His Spirit. This means we have every reason to make Jesus' psalms ours, particularly as we sing them with Him and back to Him – whether in prayer or in praise. So, asks Bonhoeffer:

> Who prays the Psalms? David (Solomon, Asaph, etc.) prays, Christ prays, we pray. We – that is, first of all the entire community in which alone the vast richness of the Psalter can be prayed, but also finally every individual insofar as he participates in Christ and his community and prays their prayer. David, Christ, the church, I myself, and wherever we consider all of this together we recognize the wonderful way in which God teaches us to pray.[72]

3.3. The practical challenge of singing the Psalms

The other obvious challenge of psalm singing is *practical*. How should they be sung? Are we obliged to sing entire psalms? Are we meant to work

---

[68] Bonhoeffer, *Psalms*, 14.
[69] Bonhoeffer, *Life Together*, 35.
[70] Goldsworthy, *Prayer and the Knowledge of God*, 139.
[71] Millar, *Calling on the Name of the Lord*, 143.
[72] Bonhoeffer, *Psalms*, 21.

our way sequentially through the whole Psalter? My own view is that are no one-size-fits-all answers to these questions. Rather *spiritual wisdom is required in order to discern how best to use the Psalms in order to most effectively glorify God and edify His people.* To that end we should make full use of our new covenant freedom to explore and experiment with different ways of singing the Psalter. Nor do we need to 'reinvent the wheel'. Christians have been singing the Psalms for centuries in a variety of ways and numerous resources exist to help us.[73]

In general terms, there are two basic approaches to psalm singing. Either the words of a particular translation need to be massaged to fit a pre-existing tune, or a tune needs to be written or chosen to fit a particular translation. Neither task is simple. And if the latter path is taken, textual adjustment is usually unavoidable. This is not a problem, theologically speaking, as there are multiple ways of faithfully translating Scripture, and all translations engage in some mixture of 'formal equivalence' (i.e., word for word) and 'functional equivalence' (i.e., thought for thought) approaches. What matters most is that the sense of the psalm is accurately, clearly and naturally conveyed.[74] Here, for example, is how *Sing Psalms* (the 2003 production of the Free Church of Scotland Psalmody and Praise Committee) renders the opening verses of Psalm 4:

---

[73] For a discussion and list of contemporary resources see John D Witvliet, *The Biblical Psalms in Christian Worship: A Brief Introduction and Guide to Resources* (Grand Rapids: Eerdmans, 2007), 116-120. For review of a range of recent recordings see Greg Scheer, 'Singing the Psalm in Modern Worship', *Reformed Worship* 85 (June 2007):
http://www.reformedworship.org/article/june-2007/singing-psalms-modern-worship.

[74] It is generally acknowledged that a good translation has four features: accuracy, clarity, naturalness, and acceptability. Luther thought similarly. Writing about his own German translation of the Psalter, he argued that the translator 'must see to it – once he understands the Hebrew author – that he concentrates on the sense of the text, asking himself, 'Pray tell, what do the Germans say in such a situation?' Once he has the German words to serve the purpose, let him drop the Hebrew words and express the meaning freely in the best German he knows'. See Martin Luther, 'Defense of the Translation of the Psalms', in *Word and Sacrament I* (eds. E Theodore Bachmann and Helmut T Lehmann; trans. Jeremiah J Schindel; vol. 35 of *Luther's Works*, American Edition, eds. Jaroslav Pelikan and Helmut T Lehmann; Philadelphia: Fortress, 1960), 213-214.

1 O hear my cry, my righteous God.
    Relieve me; I'm distressed.
  Display your mercy to me now,
    and answer my request.

2 The glory of my name, O men,
    how long will you despise?
  How long will you delude yourselves,
    still searching after lies?

3 Know that the LORD has set apart
    the godly as his own;
  The LORD will hear me when I call
    and my request make known.[75]

It is also vital that the music employed matches the content of the psalm, that it 'bear a gravity and majesty fitting to the subject and also to be appropriate to sing in the church'.[76] For example, adding a cheerful tune to a lament psalm would be emotionally jarring, whereas adding a mournful (yet hopeful) tune would increase both its cognitive and affective impact. For when well-chosen or well-written, the 'music is by no means a superfluous addition to the words that might equally well convey consolation simply by being read. On the contrary, the music enacts the consolation of which the text speaks'.[77]

There are a number of ways that Christians have sung (and continue to sing) the Psalms with great benefit. (I have outlined the main historic and contemporary approaches in Appendix 2, so won't elaborate on them here.) Most churches today also have easy access to the numerous books and websites that provide information and resources for those who would like to learn more about the history and methods of psalm singing or to (re)introduce or improve their practice of it.

---

[75] A free pdf of *Sing Psalms* can be found here:
https://freechurch.org/assets/documents/2014/Sing_Psalms_words.pdf.
[76] John Calvin, 'Letter to the Reader', 165.
[77] Francis Watson, 'Theology and Music', *SJT* 51.4 (1998), 451. Watson's remarks are made with reference to Handel's Messiah. However, they are equally applicable, if not more so, to the singing of the Psalter.

As we'll see in the next chapter, there are plenty of other prayers that God's people can and should sing. But I share Calvin's view, that 'when we have searched here and there, we will not find better songs nor ones more appropriate for this purpose than the Psalms of David, which the Holy Spirit has spoken to him and made. Therefore, when we sing them, we are certain that God has put the words in our mouth as if they themselves sang in us to exalt his glory'.[78] This does not mean psalm singing will always be easy. Indeed, there is merit in approaching it as a spiritual discipline. But like every discipline, if we persevere in it, it will yield great rewards.

Conclusion

The purpose of this chapter has been to awaken readers to both the reality and possibilities of praying together in song. To that end we began by clarifying the nature of prayer, then explored the value of sung prayer and, finally, outlined some of the blessings and obstacles to singing the Psalms. Corporate prayer is, of course, a thoroughly biblical phenomenon (e.g., Psalm 118:25; Acts 1:24; 4:24ff) and the Psalter provides us with a rich treasury of prayers that can be (and have been) sung congregationally. So even though the arguments for 'exclusive psalmody' are unconvincing, Christian churches have good reasons to adopt of a practice of 'inclusive psalmody' – i.e., by including, if not prioritising, the Psalms in our sung repertoire.

If I have convinced you of this, and particularly if yours is a non-psalm-singing church, then it is important that you do something. What you do will depend largely on your role in the congregation. Obviously, those who are pastors or music directors have the greatest scope to introduce changes. But others can have conversations, make suggestions and share resources (written or musical). My aim in urging some sort of action is not to start a revolution, but to aid a renaissance – a rebirth of 'effective psalmody'. On this point, and particularly having quoted from him so extensively in this chapter, it is only fitting that we allow Bonhoeffer the final word:

> The Psalter filled the life of early Christianity. But more important than all of this is that Jesus died on the cross with words from the Psalms on his lips. Whenever the Psalter is abandoned, an

---

[78] John Calvin, 'Letter to the Reader', 164.

incomparable treasure is lost to the Christian church. With its
recovery will come unexpected power.[79]

---

[79] Bonhoeffer, *Psalms*, 26.

8. Singing as Prayer II:
Questions and Implications

As to public prayers, there are two kinds: the one consists of words alone; the other includes music. And this is no recent invention. For since the very beginning of the church it has been this way, as we may learn from history books. Nor does St. Paul himself speak only of prayer by word of mouth, but also of singing. And in truth, we know from experience that song has a great power and strength to move and inflame the hearts of men to invoke and praise God with a heart more vehement and ardent.[1]

These words, taken from Calvin's 'Preface' to *The Geneva Psalter* (1543), effectively sum up the main points of our previous chapter. In this chapter, I wish to explore three further questions: What other prayers might we sing? What things should accompany sung prayer? What are the practical implications?

1.   What Other Prayers Might We Sing?

1.1.   Praying the Word of God

As we have seen, prayer involves calling upon God, by His Spirit and in the name of Christ, and petitioning Him to meet our needs and (even more importantly) fulfil His gracious promises and accomplish His sovereign purposes. This can be done silently and privately, as it can also be done verbally and publicly. What is more, it can be done not only in speech but also in song.

Whenever, wherever and however we pray to God, if we are to ask 'for things agreeable to his will' (as the *Westminster Shorter Catechism* rightly encourages us to do) *our prayers will need to be governed and guided by the Word of God*. This is always the case, but particularly so in

---

[1] John Calvin, 'Preface' to *The Geneva Psalter* (1543): https://www.ccel.org/ccel/ccel/eee/files/calvinps.htm.

corporate prayer[2] – whether spoken or sung – which not only calls for agreement ('Amen'!) but has a subsidiary teaching function as well. It also highlights one of the great advantages of using the Psalter in congregational worship; for in praying the Psalms, we can be in no doubt that we are praying the Word of God.

However, we have already established that Scripture does not commit us to 'exclusive psalmody'. In fact, one of the arguments against it is that, although the Psalms clearly testify of Christ (Luke 24:44), they do so obliquely, presenting Him 'in the shadows'. Frame, therefore, suggests that 'to limit one's praise to the Psalms is to praise God without the name of Jesus on one's lips'.[3] It was for this reason that Isaac Watts believed the Psalms needed to be 'imitated in the language of the New Testament;'[4] that is, Christianised. Perhaps so. But if additional songs and prayers are needed, then the Bible has plenty more to offer – most of which have been (and continue to be) set to music for choral and congregational use.

So, then, as with the Psalms, a similar case could be made for plundering the plethora of musical and liturgical resources, based on such songs and prayers, so that we might fruitfully sing these other parts of Scripture.

However, the fact remains that we are not committed by Scripture to sing only Scripture. Nor is this an entailment of the doctrine of *sola Scriptura* (Scripture alone). Rather, '*Sola Scriptura* is the doctrine that Scripture, and only Scripture, has the final word on everything, all our doctrine and all our life'.[5] What this means, as the Westminster Confession puts it, is that Scripture is the 'supreme judge by which all controversies of religion are to be determined, and all decrees of councils, opinions of ancient writers, doctrines of men, and private spirits, are to be examined, and in whose sentence we are to rest'.[6] *Sola Scriptura*, then, is not to be confused with *nuda Scriptura* (bare Scripture).

---

[2] It is, of course, important in personal prayer too. But here, there is more scope for fumbling, groaning and readily confessing that we do not always know what to pray for.
[3] Frame, *Worship in Spirit and Truth*, 125.
[4] See Appendix 2 for a fuller discussion of Watt's modified Psalter of 1719.
[5] John M Frame, 'Appendix 2: Sola Scriptura in Theological Method', Frame, *Contemporary Worship Music*, 177.
[6] The Westminster Confession of Faith (1646), I.X.

In fact, if we applied this latter notion to the practice of preaching, all sermons would be reduced to Bible readings. The Reformers clearly did not think this way.[7] Nor did the New Testament writers. The apostle's call is to sing 'the word of Christ' (Colossians 3:16); that is, 'the message of the gospel with its central focus on Christ'.[8] The key to faithfully singing this Word, like the key to faithfully preaching it, is *the clear communication of the meaning of Scripture* – whether in direct scriptural language or in songs of 'mere human composure' (as extra-scriptural songs have sometimes, somewhat disparagingly, been called).[9] In other words, our responsibility is to always sing the *truth of Scripture*, whether or not we sing the actual *text of Scripture*.

In light of this, even our approach to the Psalms (and other biblical songs and prayers) need not be a wooden one. Of course, if the truth be told, every metrical version of the Psalter necessarily engages in paraphrase (despite the claims of translators to the contrary). It cannot be otherwise. For no translation of the Bible, no matter how 'literal', can preserve the *inspired form* of the original text. The aim, rather, is to faithfully convey the *inspired meaning* of the original text.[10] The German maxim – *so frei wie nötig, so treu wie möglich* ('as free as necessary, as faithful as possible') – captures the translator's aim. Furthermore, there are also ways, as John Witvliet suggests, 'of using the Psalms as a guide to structure extemporaneous prayer' or 'as the basis for improvising our own prayers'.[11] We have lots of options.

The simple point is this: there are more scriptural prayers that can be sung than those found in the Psalms and, while our prayers must always

---

[7] Scott M Manetsch, 'Is the Reformation Over? John Calvin, Roman Catholicism, and Contemporary Ecumenical Conversations', *Themelios* 36.2 (2011), 199–200.

[8] Fee, God's Empowering Presence, 650.

[9] See, for example, the 1673 'Preface' to *The Psalms of David in Metre* (i.e., The Scottish Psalter). In fairness, the 'Preface' does concede that 'spiritual songs of mere human composure may have their use'. But it is clear that compared to 'David's Psalms' they are deemed to have little value.

[10] For an informed and enlightening discussion of these issues, see Allan Chapple, 'The English Standard Version: A Review Article', *RTR* 62.2 (Aug, 2003), 76-78.

[11] Witvliet, *The Biblical Psalms in Christian Worship*, 121.

be true to Scripture, there are more ways of praying the Word of God than by singing only Scripture.

1.2. Praying 'in the Spirit'

Such an approach is reinforced by the apostle Paul's call for Christians to pray 'in the Spirit, with all prayer and supplication' (Ephesians 6:18). In context, this exhortation comes at the conclusion of a series of instructions, beginning with the call to put on 'the whole armor of God, that you may be able to stand against the schemes of the devil' (v 11). Whether prayer is understood as 'yet a further weapon in the warfare'[12] or, as is more likely, 'a major way in which believers appropriate the divine armor',[13] it is clear that 'Paul ties prayer to the previous pieces of armor and uses it to explain how one stands'.[14] This not only highlights the fact that the power of believers is to be found 'in the Lord and in the strength of his might' (v 10), but also their constant need 'to appeal to the 'captain' as they continue in the fight'.[15] Prayer, then, is essential for successful spiritual warfare.

Of particular relevance is the link between 'praying ... in the Spirit' (v 18) and 'the sword of the Spirit, which is the word of God' (v 17). In light of Paul's reference (in v 15) to 'the gospel of peace' (which in 1:13 is called 'the word of truth') and his request for prayer (in v 19) that divine help might be given him 'to proclaim the mystery of the gospel', Gordon Fee rightly concludes that 'Paul is not identifying the 'sword' with the book [i.e., the Bible], but with the proclamation of Christ, which in our case is indeed to be found in the book'.[16] What this means is that 'the 'word of God' that is the Spirit's sword is the faithful speaking forth of the gospel in the arena of darkness, so that men and women might hear and be delivered from Satan's grasp'.[17] Due to our insufficiency for such a task,

---

[12] Fee, *God's Empowering Presence*, 730.
[13] Lincoln, *Ephesians*, 452.
[14] Clinton E Arnold, *Ephesians* (Grand Rapids: Zondervan), 463.
[15] Fee, *God's Empowering Presence*, 730.
[16] Fee, *God's Empowering Presence*, 729.
[17] Fee, *God's Empowering Presence*, 729.

wielding the Spirit's sword cannot properly be done apart from Spirit-enabled prayer.[18]

Given that we are to pray in or by the Spirit 'at all times' and 'with all prayer and supplication', it's also important to realise that Paul cannot be referring to either wordless prayer or speaking in tongues. Rather, prayer 'in the Spirit' is prayer that draws upon the strength and direction of the Spirit, as all prayer should. Otherwise put, it is *'petition inspired by the Spirit'*.[19] But how does this inspiration come? No doubt there is a personal, subjective dimension to the Spirit's help.[20] But Paul's instruction is decidedly *corporate*. Moreover, his focus is on the objective reality of gospel truth (v 17), for given that the Spirit's sword is God's Word, 'the Spirit does not work apart from the word'.[21] Therefore, Peterson's conclusion is surely correct:

> The Spirit enables believers to pray in the light of the gospel, with the certainty that they have a loving Father who has their best interests at heart and can provide all they need to love and serve him, until they come at last to share in their inheritance with Christ in glory. Spirit-inspired prayer will be prayer based on the truths of the gospel.[22]

In practice, this returns us to Scripture. For where else do we find an objective and inspired written record of both the gospel, as well as instructions regarding to how to pray? And such instruction is sorely needed. For while we can be confident that 'the Spirit intercedes for the saints according to the will of God', even when 'we do not know what to pray for as we ought' (Romans 8:27), the fact remains that praying 'in the Spirit' will always mean seeking to pray 'in accordance with the revealed

---

[18] The dative case with the preposition (*en pneumati*) is best regarded as a 'dative of means', rather than a 'dative of sphere'. In other words, praying 'by the Spirit'. See Arnold, *Ephesians*, 464.

[19] David G Peterson, 'Prayer in Paul's Writings', in *Teach Us to Pray: Prayer in the Bible and the World* (ed. D A Carson. London: WEF, 1990), 98 (emphasis his).

[20] Arnold (*Ephesians*, 464) speaks of the Spirit standing by the side of believers 'to prompt them to pray, to direct them whom to pray for and how to pray, as well as to energize them in praying for themselves and others'.

[21] Goldsworthy, *Prayer and the Knowledge of God*, 81.

[22] Peterson, 'Prayer in Paul's Writings', 98.

will of God in the word of God'.[23] Such prayer – whether personal or congregational, whether spoken or sung – ought not be the exception, but the rule. We are to pray '*at all times* in the Spirit, with *all prayer and supplication*'.

1.3. Singing Bible-based prayer-songs

How, then, does this help us to decide what prayers to sing? By driving us back to the Scriptures to either turn its prayers into congregational prayer-songs or to test our inherited or freshly created prayer-songs by its teaching. If we are seeking to do the latter, then we need to be clear that

> Biblically shaped prayer does not simply ask God to meet our material needs, but begs him to sustain and mature us as disciples of Christ (Eph. 3:14-19; Col. 1:9-14; 1 Thess. 3:12-13). Spirit-directed prayer seeks wisdom from God so that we may fulfil his purpose for us and be fruitful in his service (Jas 1:4-8). Such prayer should characterize our individual lives and our gatherings as his people.[24]

If, however, we are looking for scriptural prayers that could be turned into songs, then Gary Millar has helpfully identified five prayers that the New Testament writers assure us God will always answer: (1) prayers for forgiveness (1 John 1:9); (2) prayers to know God better (Ephesians 1:15-22; 3:18-19); (3) prayers for wisdom – to know how to live for God (James 1:5-6); (4) prayers for strength to obey/love/live for God (Ephesians 1:15-22; 3:14-15); and (5) prayers for the spread of the gospel (Luke 10:2; Acts 5; Colossians 4).[25] To petition God about such matters in song is, undoubtedly, to pray in the Spirit.

Similarly, Carson has provided the church with a series of insightful and inspiring expositions of a number of Paul's prayers.[26] No doubt, a skilful songwriter could turn these prayers into effective congregational prayer-

---

[23] Peterson, 'Prayer in Paul's Writings', 98.

[24] Peterson, *Encountering God Together*, 95.

[25] Millar, *Calling on the Name of the Lord*, 239. The Scripture references are also Millar's.

[26] D A Carson, *A Call to Spiritual Reformation: Priorities from Paul and His Prayer* (Grand Rapids: Baker, 1992).

songs. Indeed, some attempts have already been made,[27] and more ought to be attempted. For any songs that can help us to pray these prayers, are songs that will help us to pray in the Spirit.

When it comes to the Lord's Prayer, the western church is amply supplied with a myriad of musical options and metrical versions – both ancient and modern. Luther, for example, expanded the prayer into the nine-verse congregational hymn, *Vater unser im Himmelreich* ('Our Father in Heaven').[28] Shorter versions of the prayer, however, that are both 'congregationally friendly' and cleave close to the biblical text, are not always easy to come by. In fact, many of the contemporary versions of the prayer have been designed for performance, not congregational singing. Perhaps surprisingly, one of the more usable is 'The Millennium Prayer' – Cliff Richard's 1999 charity single that went to number one on the UK charts! Its 'singability' has to do with the fact that the words are adapted from the King James' version and the tune is that of 'Auld Lang Syne'.

In terms of sung liturgy, the Church of England has a substantial heritage. For example, Robert Crowley's *The Psalter of Dauid* (1549) was not only the first complete English metrical psalter, as well as the first to include musical notation, but included English versions of a number of other biblical songs (e.g., the *Benedictus* or 'Song of Zechariah', the *Magnificat* or 'Song of Mary', and the *Nunc Dimittis* or 'Song of Simeon') and traditional prayers or creeds (e.g., the *Te Deum Laudamus* or 'Ambrosian Hymn', and the *Quicumque Vult* or 'Athanasian Creed'). In 1550, Thomas Merbecke provided musical settings for the first Edwardine Prayer book, *The Book of Common Praier Noted*. From 1662 onward, the *BCP* included Myles Coverdale's Psalter in its pages with the instruction that the appointed psalms could either be 'said or sung' in Anglican

---

[27] For example, Cathy Sampson and Rob Smith's 'His Love' (2004): CCLI #4358509, which is based on Ephesians 3:16-21. Or the chorus of Mark Altrogge's 'How High and How Wide' (1990): CCLI #435313, which is based on Ephesians 3:18.

[28] For the full text, both in German and English translation, and a fascinating discussion of other Lord's Prayer hymns of this period, see Robin A Leaver, *Luther's Liturgical Music: Principles and Implications* (Grand Rapids: Eerdmans, 2007), 128-134.

Chant.[29] The Litany (or General Supplication) was also either 'said or sung' after Morning Prayer, on Sundays, Wednesdays, and Fridays.

But what about the *BCP* 'Collects' – those short prayers (many the work of Cranmer) set for particular days or seasons? The introductory rubric in the 1662 *BCP* gives no option for these to be sung. But given that biblical prayers may be sung, why not these 'prayers of human composure'? Could we not try setting some (at least) to music? I take Mark Ashton's point that if we are to be 'true to Cranmer' (i.e., to his desire for language to be intelligible and accessible) we ought not simply repeat the Collects unchanged.[30] But the modifications, in many cases, need only be minor and, in fact, have already been made in numerous Prayer Book revisions.[31]

Again, I'll leave this as a challenge for songwriters to take up. But that it can be done successfully has been well illustrated by a team of songwriters from Sovereign Grace Music. Each of the 12 songs on the 2006 album, *Valley of Vision*, was inspired by a prayer contained in *The Valley of Vision: A Collection of Puritan Prayers and Devotions*.[32] For example, Bob Kauflin's 'Let Your Kingdom Come' was based on the prayer 'God's Cause', [33] and his 'O Great God' on the prayer 'Regeneration'.[34] Both of these songs, plus a number of others from the album, have performed a much needed service for many congregations, enabling us to pray together for the progress of the gospel ('Let Your Kingdom Come') and our own progress in holiness ('O Great God').

What all of this highlights is the fact that *churches are already singing some wonderful, Bible-based prayer-hymns.* In fact, they have been for centuries – like Robert Robertson's 'Come Thou Fount', or Bianco da Siena's 'Come Down O Love Divine',[35] or William Williams' 'Guide Me

---

[29] See Appendix 2 for an explanation of Anglican Chant.

[30] Ashton, 'Following in Cranmer's Footsteps', 93.

[31] See, for example, the modernised versions of a number of *BCP* Collects in *An Australian Prayer Book* (Sydney: Anglican Information Office, 1978).

[32] Arthur Bennett (ed.), *The Valley of Vision: A Collection of Puritan Prayers & Devotions* (Edinburgh: Banner of Truth, 1975).

[33] © 2006 Sovereign Grace Praise. CCLI #4804046. For 'God's Cause', see Bennett (ed.), *The Valley of Vision*, 175.

[34] © 2006 Sovereign Grace Praise. CCLI #4804015. For 'Regeneration', see Bennett (ed.), *The Valley of Vision*, 47.

[35] Translated into English by Richard Frederick Littledale, Jr in 1867.

O Thou Great Jehovah', or Kate Wilkinson's 'May the Mind of Christ My Saviour', or John Greenleaf Whittier's 'Dear Lord and Father of Mankind', or Frances Havergal's 'Take My Life', or Charles' Wesley's 'Love Divine All Loves Excelling'! These are just some of the better-known prayer-hymns that have been and continue to be a blessing to English speaking churches around the world.

By way of contrast, a quick glance at the 'CCLI Top 100' reveals that only a small number of prayers are regularly being sung.[36] This is not to say that people aren't writing contemporary prayer-songs or that no churches are singing them. But if the 'CCLI Top 100' is any indication of the balance of what is being sung in many congregations, then it reflects neither the balance of our evangelical past, nor that of the biblical Psalter. If we are to sing 'in the Spirit', it is important not only that every song conveys some aspect(s) of the *truth* of the Bible, but that our broader repertoire reflects the overall *balance* of the Bible. We'll return to these priorities in our last chapter.

2.   What Should Accompany Sung Prayer?

We turn now to consider some of the more obvious things that should accompany prayer. As we noted at the beginning of the previous chapter, prayer (strictly speaking) is neither adoration, nor confession, nor thanksgiving. Prayer is essentially petitionary – i.e., asking. But, of course, if we are to petition the Lord biblically, our prayers will inevitably be accompanied by 'confession of our sins, and thankful acknowledgment of his mercies' (to use again the language of the *Westminster Shorter Catechism*). Likewise, if we are to sing our prayers biblically, then our prayer-songs will be similarly accompanied. It is necessary, then, to explore briefly the relationship between (i) prayer and confession of sin and (ii) prayer and thanksgiving to God.

---

[36] A themes analysis of the 'Top 100' shows there to be 7, but a quick look at the lyrics reveals that two of these are not, in fact, prayers. So that takes the number down to 5. However, Stuart Townend and Keith Getty's 'Speak O Lord' and Bob Kaulfin's 'Let Your Kingdom Come', which are both in the 'Top 100', don't appear in the list, but clearly should. So that takes the number back up to 7.

2.1. Prayer and confession of sin

The relationship between prayer and confession of sin is a natural one in Scripture. Edmund Clowney explains why: 'Since prayer is offered by sinful people, God's Lordship demands that we confess the holiness of God and penitently plead for forgiveness of sin'.[37] We see this play out in Daniel's great prayer of intercession:

> [3] Then I turned my face to the Lord God, seeking him by prayer and pleas for mercy with fasting and sackcloth and ashes. [4] I prayed to the LORD my God and made confession, saying, 'O LORD, the great and awesome God, who keeps covenant and steadfast love with those who love him and keep his commandments, [5] we have sinned and done wrong and acted wickedly and rebelled, turning aside from your commandments and rules. (Daniel 9:3-5)

As was the case in Daniel's day, there are times when God's people are guilty of grievous sin and, therefore, need to engage in very specific confession. But because 'we all stumble in many ways' (James 3:2) and are in daily danger of being 'hardened by the deceitfulness of sin' (Heb 3:13), general confession of our sins ought also to be a regular part of 'the normal Christian life'. The biblical reason for this is twofold:

> If we say we have no sin, we deceive ourselves, and the truth is not in us. If we confess our sins, he is faithful and just to forgive us our sins and to cleanse us from all unrighteousness. (1 John 1:8-9)

Cranmer well understood this and so began the 'Orders' for both Morning and Evening Prayer with a range of appropriate Scripture sentences (concluding with 1 John 1:8-9), followed by this exhortation:

> Dearly beloved brethren, the Scripture moveth us, in sundry places, to acknowledge and confess our manifold sins and wickedness; and that we should not dissemble nor cloak them before the face of Almighty God our heavenly Father; but confess them with an humble, lowly, penitent, and obedient heart; to the end that we may

---

[37] Edmund P Clowney, 'A Biblical Theology of Prayer', in D A Carson (ed.), *Teach Us to Pray: Prayer in the Bible and the World* (Exeter: Paternoster, 1990), 150.

obtain forgiveness of the same, by his infinite goodness and mercy.[38]

This is then followed by a frank confession of sin:

Almighty and most merciful Father; We have erred, and strayed from thy ways like lost sheep. We have followed too much the devices and desires of our own hearts. We have offended against thy holy laws. We have left undone those things which we ought to have done; And we have done those things which we ought not to have done; And there is no health in us.

It then moves to petition – for mercy, restoration and sanctification:

But thou, O Lord, have mercy upon us, miserable offenders. Spare thou them, O God, who confess their faults. Restore thou them that are penitent; According to thy promises declared unto mankind in Christ Jesu our Lord. And grant, O most merciful Father, for his sake; That we may hereafter live a godly, righteous, and sober life, To the glory of thy holy Name. Amen.

Finally, it is followed by a prayer of absolution, the set Collect and the Lord's Prayer.

The reason for Cranmer's order was entirely biblical: he wanted to convey our absolute need for divine mercy; that justification is by grace alone, through faith alone, in Christ alone. This is God's way of salvation and His free gift to all who 'truly repent, and unfeignedly believe his holy Gospel'.[39] As Mark Lindsay puts it: 'what Cranmer's genius offered most of all was not so much a set of restrictive rubrics for prayer, but a way of teaching the people about God in the midst of their prayers to God'.[40]

---

[38] This is the version that appears in the 1662 *BCP*. While the English is older in Cranmer's 1552 *BCP*, the substance of both the exhortation and the confession to follow is identical.

[39] From 'The Absolution' as it appears in the 1662 *BCP*.

[40] Mark R Lindsay, 'Thomas Cranmer and the Book of Common Prayer: Theological Education, Liturgy and the Embodiment of Prosper's Dictum', *Colloquium* 47.2 (November 2015), 207.

Central to a true knowledge of God is the fact that He is, as Jesus calls Him, the 'Holy Father' (John 17:11). This is why true prayer is a gift that belongs only to the children of God, and so must always and only be understood in a filial context.[41] Yet, at the same time, it must also be remembered that our heavenly Father is holy and will judge each of us impartially (1 Peter 1:14-17). Therefore, prayer and confession necessarily go together for God's children. For when it comes to presenting our requests before God, the very first thing we should seek is the forgiveness we daily need. This presupposes, and so should naturally be preceded by, a forthright confession of our sins, said 'with a pure heart, and humble voice, unto the throne of the heavenly grace'.[42]

But could not such a prayer be sung? Again, while there is no rubric in the *BCP* suggesting as much, it no doubt could be, and probably has been. Of course, Scripture provides us with a series of 'penitential psalms' that could be sung instead of, or in addition to, a set prayer of confession (e.g., Psalms 32; 38; 51; 130). Alternatively, there are a number of modern songs based on these psalms that could perform this function (e.g., Brown Bannister's 'Create in Me a Clean Heart'[43]). There are also numerous 'confession-hymns' found in the confession or repentance sections of most hymnbooks (e.g., Charles Wesley's 'O Jesus Full of Truth and Grace'), as well as contemporary 'confession-songs' (e.g., Dale Bischof and Pat Sczebel's 'Have Mercy On Me'[44] or D A Carson and Sandra McCracken's 'I Am Ashamed'[45]). The options for sung confession, therefore, are many.

2.2. Prayer and thanksgiving to God

As with petition and confession, the link between prayer and thanksgiving is also a natural one. The *practical reason* for this is because it is (or ought to be) virtually impossible to petition God without some appreciation of what He has already given or some anticipation of what He has promised to provide (Philippians 4:19). The *theological reason* has

---

[41] Goldsworthy, *Prayer and the Knowledge of God*, 44ff.

[42] From the exhortation as it appears in the 1662 *BCP*.

[43] © 1982, Bases Loaded Music. CCLI #3113130

[44] © 2011, Sovereign Grace Praise. CCLI #6167705.

[45] © 2016, Drink Your Tea Music. Both a lead sheet and MP3, as well as an article about the song, are freely available from The Gospel Coalition: https://www.thegospelcoalition.org/article/lets-sing-the-beauty-of-confession.

to do with the twin reality of human dependency and divine lordship. As David Pao writes: 'When God is acknowledged as the Lord of all, thanksgiving becomes a humbling act admitting the dependency of human existence'.[46]

Prayer and thanksgiving, then, belong together, and Scripture is replete with examples of their interrelationship. In a number of psalms, for instance, giving thanks to God is presented as the ultimate purpose of His people's cry for salvation and restoration. For example:

> Save us, O LORD our God,
>   and gather us from among the nations,
> that we may give thanks to your holy name
>   and glory in your praise.
>
> *Psalm 106:47*[47]

More typically, however, prayer and thanksgiving are conjoined. We see this in Daniel's response to King Darius' decree that anyone who makes petition to any god or man for thirty days, other than the king, shall be cast into the den of lions (Daniel 6:7). For on hearing of this, Daniel 'got down on his knees three times a day and *prayed and gave thanks* before his God, as he had done previously' (v 10). And we have seen it already in Philippians 4:6 where Paul writes: 'in everything by prayer and supplication with thanksgiving, let your requests be made known to God'.[48] In fact, the combination of prayer and thanksgiving appears so frequently in Paul's writings that the 'two cannot be separated in the Pauline model of prayer'.[49]

---

[46] David W Pao, *Thanksgiving: An Investigation of a Pauline Theme* (Downers Grove: IVP, 2002), 35.

[47] See also 1 Chronicles 16:35; Psalms 118:19; 142:7.

[48] See also 1 Timothy 2:1 for a similar combination of petitionary terms, as well as a conjoining of prayer with thanksgiving: 'First of all, then, I urge that supplications, prayers, intercessions, and thanksgivings be made for all people'.

[49] Pao, *Thanksgiving*, 37. This is particularly apparent in the 'thanksgiving paragraphs' that introduce many of Paul's letters (e.g., Romans 1:8-10; Ephesians 1:16; Philippians 1:3-4; Colossians 1:3; 1 Thessalonians 1:2; 2 Timothy 1:3; Philemon 4).

I trust by now that it hardly needs to be said that just as we can speak words of thanksgiving to God, we can also sing them. And, what's more, it is entirely biblical that we do so, as the following psalms illustrate:

> The LORD is my strength and my shield;
>> in him my heart trusts, and I am helped;
> my heart exults,
>> and with my song I give thanks to him.
>
> *Psalm 28:7*

> [11] You have turned for me my mourning into dancing;
>> you have loosed my sackcloth and clothed me with gladness,
> [12] that my glory may sing your praise and not be silent.
>> O LORD my God, I will give thanks to you forever!
>
> *Psalm 30:11-12*

> [2] Give thanks to the LORD with the lyre;
>> make melody to him with the harp of ten strings!
> [3] Sing to him a new song;
>> play skillfully on the strings, with loud shouts.
>
> *Psalm 33:2-3*

It is also worth noting that both sung prayer and sung thanksgiving are called for by Paul's exhortation to sing 'psalms [which, as we have seen, includes prayers] and hymns and spiritual songs, *with thankfulness in your hearts to God*' (Colossians 3:16). It's similarly entailed in the exhortation of Ephesians 5, where 'addressing another in psalms, hymns and spiritual songs' (v 19a) is inseparable from both 'singing and making melody to the Lord with all your heart' (v 19b) and from '*giving thanks always and for everything* to God the Father in the name of our Lord Jesus Christ' (v 20).

So what songs of thanksgiving should accompany our prayers? Once again, we have a range of psalms at our disposal (e.g., Psalms 100; 107; 118; 136; 138) and various liturgical thanksgivings that either have been or could be set to music. Furthermore, many older hymns (e.g., Martin Rinckart's 'Now thank we all our God'[50] or Nahum Tate and Nicolas Brady's 'O render thanks to God above'[51]) and numerous contemporary

---

[50] Written in 1636. Translated by Catherine Winkworth (1827-1878).
[51] Written in 1696.

songs (e.g., Steve Stewart's 'Father I thank you'[52] or Pat Sczebel's 'Jesus, thank you'[53]) are dominated by explicit expressions of thanksgiving. Furthermore, when we realise that thanksgiving and praise not only belong together in Scripture but are so deeply intertwined 'that one cannot really sift out one from the other',[54] then our options multiply. Another way of asking our question is this: What praises should be sung with our prayers? Any song of praise that expresses gratitude to God is a worthy candidate.

The simple point is this: If we follow Scripture's lead, we will take conscious steps to combine sung prayer with sung thanksgiving. We will likewise learn to give thanks in all circumstances with a depth of gratitude appropriate for those who are by nature children of wrath, but now, because of God's great love and mercy, have been made alive together with Christ, and adopted as His beloved children (Ephesians 2:3-5; 5:1).

2.3. Prayer and the body

Before leaving the subject of 'things that accompany prayer', we need to address the relationship between prayer and the body. The simple reason for this is that we all do something (if not several things) with our bodies whenever we pray.[55] Some of us close our eyes; others of us lift our eyes toward heaven. Some of us raise our hands; others of us clasp our hands together. Some of us lift up our heads; others of us bow our heads. Some of us stand; others of us sit. Some of us prostrate ourselves; others of us, like Daniel, kneel down (Daniel 6:10).

Most of these gestures and postures are seen repeatedly in Scripture. This is clear from the following verses, all taken from the Psalms, where either prayer or blessing or worship are accompanied by some consonant bodily action:

---

[52] © 1980, Universal Music. CCLI #47323.

[53] © 2003, Integrity's Hosanna! Music. CCLI #4475341.

[54] Miller Jr., 'Enthroned on the Praises of Israel', 10.

[55] Just as we do when we praise and preach. In fact, I could have easily raised this issue in our discussion of praise (where I alluded to it), as I could also in our discussion of preaching. However, it is natural to raise it at this point, as Scripture has much to say about the postures and gestures that often accompanied the prayers of God's people in biblical times.

Hear the voice of my *pleas* for mercy,
when I *cry* to you for help,
when I *lift up my hands* toward your most holy sanctuary.

Psalm 28:2

But I, when they were sick – I wore sackcloth;
I afflicted myself with fasting;
I *prayed* with *head bowed on my chest.*

Psalm 35:13

So I will *bless* you as long as I live;
in your name I will *lift up my hands.*

Psalm 63:4

Oh come, let us *worship and bow down*;
let us *kneel* before the LORD, our Maker! (Psalm 95:6)

Lift up your hands to the holy place
and *bless* the LORD!

Psalm 134:2

Let my *prayer* be counted as incense before you,
And the *lifting up of my hands* as the evening sacrifice!

Psalm 141:2

As has often been pointed out, not every biblical description is meant to be imitated, nor are all biblical prescriptions binding on all people, at all times and in all places. Luther, therefore, had good reason to write:

> It is of little importance whether you stand, kneel, or prostrate yourself; for the postures of the body are neither forbidden nor commanded as necessary. The same applies to other things: raising the head and eyes heavenward, folding the hands, striking the breast. Only do not despise these things, because Scripture and Christ Himself praise them.[56]

---

[56] Cited in Ewald M Plass (ed.), *What Luther Says: A Practical In-Home Anthology for the Active Christian* (St. Louis: Concordia Publishing House, 1959), #3474, 1087.

It is also important to remind ourselves that the Bible privileges inner attitudes over outward actions, as the latter not only vary, but can also be hypocritical. As the author of 1 Samuel reminds us: 'For the LORD sees not as man sees: man looks on the outward appearance, but the LORD looks on the heart' (1 Samuel 16:7). C S Lewis, therefore, struck the right balance when he wrote: 'The body ought to pray as well as the soul. Body and soul are all the better for it. Bless the body'. But then he continued: 'The relevant point is that kneeling does matter, but other things matter more. A concentrated mind and a sitting body makes for better prayer than a kneeling body and a mind half asleep'.[57]

Nevertheless, what the descriptions and prescriptions in the Psalms reveal is that such bodily actions are natural ways of expressing with our 'outer person' what is (or ought to be) true of our 'inner person'. As Calvin writes, 'just as the lifting up of the hands is a symbol of confidence and longing, so in order to show our humility, we fall down on our knees'.[58] In technical terms, what Calvin is talking about and what we see modelled in the Psalms is authentic psychosomatic unity. Such personal integration will, no doubt, express itself differently in different people, in different cultures and on different occasions. That understood, Thomas Staubli and Silvia Schroer are right: 'Those who pray the psalms present themselves before God in their concrete corporeality; their prayer is an expression of longing for integral, whole humanity before Yhwh'.[59] Furthermore, the pattern we have seen in the Psalter is repeated elsewhere in both Old and New Testaments. For example:

> And [Hannah] said, 'Oh, my lord! As you live, my lord, I am the woman who was *standing* here in your presence, *praying* to the LORD.
>
> *1 Samuel 1:26*

---

[57] C S Lewis, *Letters to Malcolm Chiefly on Prayer: Reflections on the Intimate Dialogue Between Man and God* (London: Collins, 1966), 19.

[58] John Calvin in David W Torrance and Thomas F Torrance (eds.), *Calvin's Commentaries: The Acts of the Apostles: 14-28* (trans. John W Fraser. Grand Rapids: Eerdmans, 1973), 190.

[59] Thomas Staubli and Silvia Schroer, *Body Symbolism in the Bible* (Collegeville: The Liturgical Press, 2001), 29.

Now as Solomon finished offering all this *prayer and plea* to the
LORD, he arose from before the altar of the LORD, where he had
knelt with hands outstretched toward heaven.

1 Kings 8:54

And Ezra blessed the LORD, the great God, and all the people
answered, 'Amen, Amen,' *lifting up their hands.* And they *bowed
their heads and worshiped the LORD with their faces to the
ground.*

Nehemiah 8:6

And whenever you *stand praying*, forgive, if you have anything
against anyone, so that your Father also who is in heaven may
forgive you your trespasses.'

Mark 11:25

And going a little farther, [Jesus] '*fell on the ground and prayed* that,
if it were possible, the hour might pass from him.'

Mark 14:35

But Peter put them all outside, and *knelt down and prayed*; and
turning to the body he said, 'Tabitha, arise.'

Acts 9:40

[14] For this reason I *bow my knees* before the Father, [15] from whom
every family in heaven and on earth is named, [16] that according to
the riches of his glory he may grant you to be strengthened with
power through his Spirit in your inner being, [17] so that Christ may
dwell in your hearts through faith.

Ephesians 3:14-17

I desire then that in every place the men should *pray, lifting holy
hands* without anger or quarreling.

1 Timothy 2:8

In view of such texts, it is curious that many evangelicals have become
somewhat allergic to the slightest sign of bodily engagement – whether
in prayer or praise – by other members of the congregation. There are, of
course, historic reasons for such nervousness and genuine dangers in

both 'emotionalism' and 'experientialism'.[60] Nevertheless, our forefathers in the faith were not guilty of the over-reactions characteristic of some today. Note, for instance, what Calvin had to say about lifting hands in prayer:

[T]his custom has been practiced in worship during all ages, for it is natural for us to look upwards when we seek God, and the habit has been so strong that even idolaters, though they fashion gods in images of wood and stone, yet keep this custom and lift up their hands to heaven; we should learn therefore that this practice is in keeping with true godliness, provided that the truth it represents also accompanies it.[61]

Here, as Calvin comments on Paul's instruction in 1 Timothy 2:8, he warmly commends the biblical practice of lifting hands in prayer. What's more, he does this despite the fact that idolaters also do it. In other words, rather than rejecting the practice (because of its misuse), Calvin wishes to affirm it (because of its 'accordance with true godliness'). There is an important lesson here – one which Cranmer clearly understood, as the 'Preface' to the *BCP* makes clear: *when a good (and especially biblical) practice is misunderstood and/or misused, the better solution is always to retain and reform it, rather than to demonise and discard it.*

Furthermore, both Luther and Calvin were also aware that what we do with our outer person has a bearing on our inner person. As Luther put it: 'Although it is true that prayer can take place in the heart without any words or gestures, *yet such things help* in stirring up and enkindling the

---

[60] The historical reasons can be found in the debates between the Reformers and the Anabaptists, the Puritans and the Quakers, calvinistic Anglicans and perfectionist Wesleyans, Evangelicals and Pentecostals, Reformed Christianity and Charismatic Christianity. The fundamental danger of both 'emotionalism' and 'experientialism' is not that there is anything wrong with either gospel-inspired emotion or gospel-generated experience. Rather it is that Scripture is subordinated to human emotion and human experience – if not in theory, then in practice.
[61] John Calvin in David W Torrance and Thomas F Torrance (eds.), *Calvin's Commentaries: The Second Epistle of Paul the Apostle to the Corinthians and the Epistles of Timothy, Titus and Philemon* (trans. T A Smail. Grand Rapids: Eerdmans, 1964), 214.

spirit even more'.[62] This is because the relationship between mind and body is a 'two-way street'; for not only do our thoughts and feelings impact our actions, but what we do with our bodies also has a profound influence on what we think and feel, as it does on the thoughts and feelings of others. Here is Calvin again:

> The inward attitude certainly holds first place in prayer, but outward signs, kneeling, uncovering the head, lifting up the hands, have a twofold use. The first is that we may employ all our members for the glory and worship of God; secondly, that we are, so to speak, jolted out of our laziness by this help. There is also a third use in solemn and public prayer, because in this way the sons of God profess their piety, and they inflame each other with reverence of God.[63]

Our discussion may seem to have wandered a long way from the subject of singing. But not so. The various bodily actions that can accompany and assist spoken prayer, can also (and perhaps even more naturally) accompany and assist sung prayer. For music has a range of effects on the body, many of them involuntary, which in turn impact both our thoughts and feelings.[64] It is, therefore, even more natural for our bodies to be engaged when we sing our prayers (and, similarly, our praises) in one way or another. Indeed, it's impossible to do nothing with one's body. The question, however, is whether my body is fighting my soul or assisting it; whether my actions are contradicting my words or affirming them.

This hit home for me in a recent visit to a church. During the service, we sang Stuart Townend and Dustin Kensrue's song, 'Rejoice'.[65] Each time

---

[62] Martin Luther, 'The Sermon on the Mount', in *The Sermon on the Mount (Sermons) and the Magnificat* (ed. Jaroslav Pelikan; vol. 21 of *Luther's Works*, American Edition, eds. Jaroslav Pelikan and Helmut T Lehmann; Philadelphia: Fortress, 1968), 139 (emphasis mine).

[63] John Calvin in *Calvin's Commentaries: The Acts of the Apostles: 14-28*, 190.

[64] See Appendix 3 for a fuller discussion of the complex interrelationship between music, mind, body and emotions.

[65] CCLI #7004663. Dustin Kensrue & Stuart Townend. © 2013 Townend Songs (Admin. by CopyCare Pacific Pty. Ltd.). Dead Bird Theology (Admin. by Music Services, Inc.). We Are Younger We Are Faster Music (Admin. by Music Services, Inc.).

we sang the chorus, we exhorted each other, 'Come and lift your hands and raise your voice'. Voices were certainly raised (at least to a point). But as I looked around the room, not a single hand was raised. This begged a range of questions in my mind: Did anyone else feel the contradiction? Did some people want to lift their hands, but felt they couldn't? Was there an unspoken rule that they shouldn't? If so, who imposed this and why and how?

This anecdote raises two issues worth exploring briefly. The *first* concerns authenticity. God is a god of reality. He desires His people to be genuine and sees straight through our hypocrisy. Furthermore, He has wired us all differently – both personally and culturally. Our bodies are different, our minds work differently and our emotions function in uniquely differing ways. Consequently, it would be 'unreal' to expect any two of His children, let alone a whole congregation, to respond in exactly the same way at every level. The mature believer, therefore, will not be disturbed or threatened by such differences, but will welcome and appreciate them. Likewise, the wise pastor will instruct his flock about such matters, presenting the scriptural norms (in all their variety), encouraging authenticity (in all its diversity) and not insisting on strict uniformity (as if we were all meant to be carbon copies of each other).

The *second* issue is other-person-centredness. The reality is that not every believer is mature, nor every pastor wise, and in most churches there is, what Zac Hicks calls, 'an unspoken spectrum of propriety when it comes to how physically demonstrative people are in worship'.[66] For this reason, problems can easily arise 'when individuals stick out too far beyond the community's unspoken boundaries'.[67] How should such 'problems' be addressed? If my goal is to edify others, then I will seek to subordinate my (legitimate) desire for personal authenticity to 'the common good' (1 Corinthians 12:7). We are not called to be 'expressive individuals', but to use our freedom for each other's edification. As John Bell writes: 'Public worship is not private devotion, and ministers and musicians have to be clear that encouraging this kind of individualism is the enemy of

---

[66] Zac Hicks, *The Worship Pastor: A Call to Ministry for Worship Leaders and Teams* (Grand Rapids: Zondervan, 2016), 27.
[67] Hicks, *The Worship Pastor*, 27.

corporate liturgy and community singing'. [68] In light of these considerations, Hicks' conclusion is both balanced and wise:

> It's my belief that we should encourage full-bodied physicality in worship and that we should stretch our congregations to increase those expressive boundaries over time. Still, a pastor will detect that worship's communal nature is in jeopardy when people are (I believe selfishly) insisting that their expressive freedom in worship trumps others' discomfort around them.[69]

One caveat is in order, however. Sometimes discomforting others may, in fact, be the best way to serve them. It may (in Calvin's words above) help us to be 'jolted out of our laziness' or 'inflame each other with reverence of God'. In short, it does not follow that the best way for you to serve others is by singing 'as if you were half dead, or half asleep' (to, once again, cite John Wesley's memorable words).

So what am I suggesting? Let me sum it up in four points:

(i) *We should not be embarrassed by the fact that we each have a body.* Our bodies, despite all their present weaknesses and imperfections, are good gifts from a gracious God. Indeed, God is so committed to our bodies, that He is determined to raise them up at the last day. Therefore, we need to learn to thank Him for our bodies, not be ashamed of them, and glorify Him with them even now.

(ii) *We should not be surprised when the things we think or feel express themselves in and through our bodies* – whether in smiles or tears, whether by lifting hands or bowing knees. All of that is very normal and very healthy. We should be even less surprised when such responses accompany our singing or, conversely, when music and song enhance or evoke such feeling and actions.

---

[68] John L Bell, *The Singing Thing: A Case for Congregational Singing* (Glasgow: Wild Goose Publications, 2000), 129. I must confess that I have taken Bell's words slightly out of context, as he is addressing a different problem: that of individuals distancing themselves from one another by spreading themselves out all over the building, rather than sitting in reasonable proximity to each other. However, his insight applies equally to the subject at hand.

[69] Hicks, *The Worship Pastor*, 27.

(iii) *We should not be afraid to explore the helpfulness of using different bodily postures or gestures in prayer* (and likewise in praise) – whether we are speaking or singing. Try doing something – even if only in private! The goal, however, is naturalness and authenticity, not a new kind of uniformity. Keep in mind that what is most helpful will, inevitably, be different for different people.

(iv) *We should not forget that God is most glorified when others are most edified.* Therefore, when we are meeting, praying and singing together, our priority must be to serve others, not ourselves. This may sometimes mean reining ourselves in and other times letting ourselves out. Either way, our aim will be the same: to ensure that our actions effectively encourage our brothers and sisters.

I have given particular attention to this issue because in seeking to distance ourselves from the follies of the charismatic movement, many Reformed evangelicals have surrendered a valuable part of our spiritual heritage. David and Tim Bayly put the point strongly: 'somehow, somewhere, we lost our way and now think we're honoring Scripture and our spiritual fathers when in fact we're directly contradicting them'.[70] We would do well, then, to reflect on the biblical relationship between prayer, praise, emotional and bodily engagement, remembering that neither Scripture's descriptions nor its prescriptions are meant to be constrictions. Rather, they are meant to liberate us to do what is 'meet and right' for redeemed sinners to do: love the Lord our God with heart, soul, mind and strength, engaging Him with our intellects, emotions and bodies both for His glory and each other's (and indeed our own) good.

3.   What Are the Practical Implications?

Before concluding, I want to spell out – albeit briefly – three practical implications of the main point of this and the preceding chapter: the fact that *we can and do and should not only say our prayers but sing them also.*

---

[70] David Bayly and Tim Bayly, 'John Calvin: Lifting hands helps "jolt us out of our laziness" in worship ...' (June 12, 2009): http://baylyblog.com/blog/2009/06/john-calvin-lifting-hands-helps-jolt-us-out-our-laziness-worship.

3.1. Greater understanding

The *first* of these implications is that we ought to be more aware that as we sing together we are also, very often, engaged in 'common prayer'. Pastors would do well to point this out so that, both personally and corporately, we might better understand what we are, in fact, doing and be more focussed in sung-petition. Cranmer clearly understood this need, which was why in the Preface to Henry VIII's 'Primer Book' (1545), which was prepared under his direction, these words (which we cited in chapter one but are worth repeating) appear:

> Now prayer is used or made with right and perfect understanding, if we sing with our spirit, and sing with our mind or understanding; so that the deep contemplation or ravishing of the mind follow the pithiness of the words, and the guiding of reason go before: lest when the spirit doth pray, the mind take no fruit at all, and the party that understandeth not the pith or effectualness of the talk, that he frankly maketh with God, may be as an harp or pipe, having a sound, but not understanding the noise that itself hath made.[71]

We should not be surprised, then, if next Sunday the service leader or song leader introduces a particular song by saying, 'Let us lift our voices in prayer to our heavenly Father as we sing our next song together'. For often that is exactly what we're doing.

3.2. Greater authenticity

Second, the obvious advantage of greater understanding of what we are doing is that it encourages greater authenticity in both our singing and praying. That is, if we realise that we are praying when we're singing, then we're more likely to mean the things we're praying. This is vital for Christian growth; for as P T Forsyth long ago observed:

> Prayer alone prevents our receiving God's grace in vain ... We come out with a courage and a humanity we had not when we went in, even though our old earth remove, and our familiar hills are cast

---

[71] Cranmer, 'A Preface made by the King's most excellent Majesty unto his Primer Book' (1545), 497.

into the depth of the sea. The true Church is thus co-extensive with the community of true prayer'.[72]

So, once again, don't be surprised if the service leader or song leader takes a moment or two to introduce a prayer-song, so that you better attend to what you're about to pray, and so pray with mind, heart and body more fully engaged.

3.3. Greater creativity

The *third* implication of the fact that songs can be prayers and prayers can be sung is that our times of singing and our times of praying are clearly not neatly partitioned off from each other. They may appear as if they are on the 'Run Sheet' or 'Service Plan', but the reality is otherwise. Once we recognise this, it opens up all sorts of new possibilities for deliberately intertwining the two, perhaps interspersing spoken prayers with sung prayers or vice versa, or singing certain prayers on some occasions, and saying them on others. This, as we have already noted, is an option suggested by the rubrics in the *BCP* for both the appointed psalms and the Litany.

There is clearly scope here, at least for those who plan our gatherings, to be highly creative and to explore ways of doing things other than the way they've usually been done. The aim is not novelty for novelty's sake, but to assist God's children to pray together in ways that are more intentional, meaningful, heartfelt and engaged.

Conclusion

In 1855, upon receiving news that his mother was gravely ill, Joseph Scriven wrote a poem to comfort her, giving it the title, 'Pray Without Ceasing'. It contained these memorable lines at the end of its first stanza:

O what grace we often forfeit,
O what needless pain we bear,

---

[72] P T Forsyth, *The Soul of Prayer* (London: Independent Press, 1949), 48.

> All because we do not carry
> Everything to God in prayer![73]

Interestingly, Scriven's now famous 'prayer-song' is not itself a prayer, but a song about prayer or, more accurately, a 'call to prayer'. We need songs that perform this thoroughly scriptural service; songs that call us to be perpetual petitioners, 'praying at all times in the Spirit, with all prayer and supplication' (Ephesians 6:17-18). In other words, we not only need songs that *enable* us to pray, but also songs that *encourage* us to pray.

But pray we must. This can take many forms: we can *think* our prayers, *groan* our prayers, *speak* our prayers, *sob* our prayers and *sing* our prayers. We can also pray alone or pray with others. It's this latter practice, and the particular value of singing our prayers together, that has been our concern in this and the preceding chapter. I hope you're now convinced, if you weren't already, of the value of this ancient practice and can begin to see some new possibilities – either to implement or suggest.

In theory, any prayer can be sung. In practice, some prayers will be more conducive to singing than others and what proves suitable in some settings, may not work in all. So whether we use or adapt historic liturgy, older prayer-hymns or contemporary prayer-songs, we will almost certainly need to experiment, discovering by trial and error what is most edifying for the saints we are seeking to serve.

In all of this, we would be foolish to neglect the Bible's own prayers, particularly those found in the book of Psalms. As we have seen, the advantages of singing the Psalter are many. It is 'a practice that combines the reading of Scripture and praying. Through the Psalter God has given us entry into the universe's eternal song of praise, and to take up the Psalms is to join that congregation. This means that the song the church sings is a fully earthly song of a pilgrim people and a groaning cosmos. But it is also an eternal song, being bound to the Word of revelation in Jesus Christ'.[74] In addition to this, very 'few contemporary songs deal with suffering, testing, loneliness, persecution or deliverance from

---

[73] In 1868, the poem was set to music by Charles Crozat Converse, and given the (now familiar) title: 'What a Friend we have in Jesus'.

[74] Brian Brock, *Singing the Ethos of God: On the Place of Christian Ethics in Scripture* (Grand Rapids: Eerdmans, 2007), 357.

sickness and death, as many psalms do'.[75] The Psalms, therefore, teach us how to pray in faith.

Of course, similar things could be said of other biblical prayers. Indeed, the Lord's Prayer is unparalleled for its sheer God-centred clarity. For this reason, it presents us with something of a 'template' and, regardless of whether we sing it or speak it, highlights a range of questions that are worth asking of any of our prayer-songs. For example:

- Do they reflect a kingdom focus or overriding concern for 'God's Cause'?
- Do they express a desire that God's purposes for his world are fulfilled?
- Do they drive us to acknowledge our sins and seek God's forgiveness?
- Do they help us to resist temptation and seek deliverance from evil?[76]

How we pray matters – not least because our prayers shape us profoundly. The same applies to sung-prayer. It is a powerful teacher. Therefore, to the fifth century motto of Prosper of Aquitaine, *lex orandi, lex credendi* ('the law of praying [establishes] the law of believing'), we can add the obvious corollary: *lex cantandi, lex credendi* ('the law of singing [establishes] the law of believing'). In this sense, Mark Noll is surely correct: 'We are what we sing!'[77]

Whatever prayers we decide to sing and in whatever form we decide to sing them, our aim should be clear and consistent: 'the offering up of our desires unto God for things agreeable to his will, in the name of Christ, by the help of his Spirit; with confession of our sins, and thankful acknowledgment of his mercies'.[78]

---

75 Peterson, *Encountering God Together*, 102.
76 This list is adapted from Peterson, *Encountering God Together*, 95-96.
77 See Mark A Noll, 'We Are What We Sing: Our classic hymns reveal evangelicalism at its best', *Christianity Today* (June 12, 1999): http://www.christianitytoday.com/ct/1999/july12/9t8037.html.
78 Answer to Question 178 in the *Westminster Shorter Catechism* (1647).

9. SINGING AS PREACHING I:
OLD COVENANT SOUNDINGS

1.   Worship and Edification

Why do Christians gather together? And why do we usually spend time singing when we do? The traditional Reformed answer to these questions, as we saw in chapter two, is that we gather for divine worship and sing together as a way of praising God and praying to Him. However, as we also saw, over the last 20 or so years, a different answer to these questions has emerged. According to this answer, we don't gather for worship (or, at least, not uniquely or primarily), rather we gather for edification – that is, to build one another up. Our singing, too, has the same purpose: we address and instruct *one another* in psalms and hymns and spiritual songs (Ephesians 5:19; Colossians 3:16).

This revisionist answer has been immensely helpful, for it has highlighted a vital aspect of New Testament teaching – the *horizontal dimension* of both our gatherings and our singing, and the consequent need for everything we do when we gather together to *build up others* (1 Corinthians 14:26).

And yet, as so often happens in the pendulum swings of theological discussion, the 'revisionist case' has sometimes been presented as if the answer has to be an either/or – *either* worship *or* edification. This is regrettable, for as I argued in Part I of this book, a stronger case can be made for a both-and answer – i.e., we gather *both* for worship *and* for edification. Or, if we think it best to give the language of 'worship' a rest, we could equally say that we gather *both* to glorify God *and* to edify others.[1] This was the preferred terminology of C S Lewis, who was also clear about the fact that 'nothing should be done or sung or said in church which does not aim directly or indirectly either at glorifying God or

---

[1] Or, alternatively, we could equally say that we gather to *love* God and to *love* His people, or to *serve* God and to *serve* His people, or to *engage* with God and to *encourage* His people, etc.

edifying the people or both'.[2] In practice, this means we need to ask two questions of everything we do when we come together: (i) Does it glorify God? (ii) Does it edify others? The answer must be 'Yes' to both questions.

Wherever we decide to settle on matters of terminology (or whether, as I would suggest, we employ a range of equally biblical ways of speaking), the reason for this both-and understanding is, as we saw in chapter four, because there is a 'three-way movement' within our church gatherings: from *God to us* (movement 1), from *us to God* (movement 2), and from *us to each other* (movement 3). Everything we do together will participate in one or more of these 'movements'. For example, if our songs faithfully communicate God's Word, then they participate in movement 1; if they form part of our response to God, they participate in movement 2; and to the extent that they enable us to instruct and encourage each other, they participate in movement 3. And if they do all three things (as many songs do), then they participate in all three movements at once.

In the preceding chapters, we've focussed on the upward-vertical function that singing so regularly performs – i.e., as a way of directly addressing God, whether in praise or in prayer (movement 2). In this chapter and the one following, we turn our attention to the outward-horizontal or ministry function of our singing – i.e., as a way of directly addressing one another or, otherwise put, as a form of preaching (movement 3).[3] This, of course, presupposes that our singing participates in the downward-vertical ministry of God's Word to us (movement 1), which, in turn, highlights the need for our songs to convey God's truth with clarity – a point to which we will return!

The purpose of this chapter is to examine what the Old Testament reveals about the connections between music, singing and the preaching of God's Word. In the next chapter, we will turn to the New Testament before, finally (in Part Three), exploring some points of historical insight and contemporary application.

---

[2] C S Lewis, 'On Church Music', in Walter Hooper (ed.), *Christian Reflections* (London: Geoffrey Bles, 1967), 94.
[3] I am using the language of preaching in a fairly general sense to refer to the many and various ways that God's people (individually and collectively) communicate God's truth to each other and to the world.

2. Singing and Preaching in the Old Testament

2.1. Music, song and prophecy

One of the more intriguing features of Old Testament revelation is the connection it draws between music, song and prophecy.[4] The first hints of this connection appear immediately after Israel's dramatic rescue from the hand of the Egyptians (Exodus 14:21-31). With the Israelites safe on the far side of the sea and the Egyptians lying dead on the seashore,

> Miriam the prophetess, the sister of Aaron, took a tambourine in her hand, and all the women went out after her with tambourines and dancing. And Miriam sang to them:
>
> 'Sing to the Lord, for he has triumphed gloriously;
> the horse and his rider he has thrown into the sea.'
>
> *Exodus 15:20-21*

Commentators have pondered why Miriam is here described as a prophetess. While certainty is difficult, the most likely reason is because she performs the prophetic function of declaring divine victory and publicly exhorting others to join in divine praise.[5] This conclusion is further supported by the fact that Miriam's exhortation is a clear adaptation of the opening lines of the song of 15:1-18. This song, sung by none other than the prophet Moses (Deuteronomy 34:10), 'celebrates Yahweh present with his people and doing for them as no other god anywhere and at any time can be present to do'.[6] Furthermore, it is a song that contains a promise of what God will yet do for Israel (v 17). It is thus a mixture of forth-telling and fore-telling and, on both counts, may appropriately be designated as 'prophecy'.[7]

---

[4] Parts of the following section has been adapted from Robert S Smith, 'Belting Out the Blues as Believers: The Importance of Singing Lament', *Themelios* 42.1 (2017), 98-100.

[5] So Ronald W Pierce, 'The Feminine Voice of God: Women as Prophets in the Bible', *Priscilla Papers* 21:1 (Winter 2007), 4-5.

[6] John I Durham, *Exodus* (Waco: Word, 1987), 210. Durham also rightly notes that the song 'is a kind of summary of the theological base of the whole Book of Exodus'.

[7] In light of this, it is interesting to note that the climactic oracle of Moses' prophetic ministry also took the form of a song. This time, however, it was a song

In the book of Judges, a similar link between prophecy and song emerges from the fact that Deborah, who (like Miriam) is also described as 'a prophetess' (Judges 4:4), is the co-author of another song celebrating 'the righteous triumphs of the LORD' (5:11). [8] That this prophetic song is primarily Deborah's oracle is suggested by the order of names in 5:1 ('Then sang Deborah and Barak') and confirmed by the summons in 5:12: 'Awake, awake, Deborah! / Awake, awake, break out in a song!'

Further evidence that prophecy often took a musical form emerges in the early monarchical period. Saul, for example, is told that he will meet 'a procession of prophets coming down from the high place with lyres, timbrels, pipes and harps being played before them, and they will be prophesying' (1 Samuel 10:5). He is then informed that the Spirit of the Lord will descend upon him and he too will prophesy (v 6). Much later in the period of the monarchy, when Elisha is called upon to prophesy (2 Kings 3:11-19), his response is 'bring me a musician. And when the musician played, the hand of the Lord came on him' (v 15).

Reflecting on this connection, and the power it seems to accord to the gift of music, Luther once remarked:

> The Holy Ghost himself honors [music] as an instrument for his proper work when in his Holy Scriptures he asserts that through her his gifts were instilled in the prophets, namely, the inclination to all virtues, as can be seen in Elisha [II Kings 3:15]. On the other hand, she serves to cast out Satan, the instigator of all sins, as is shown in Saul, the king of Israel [I Samuel 16:23].[9]

In addition to these more informal associations between music, song and prophecy is David's appointment of 'some of the sons of Asaph, Heman and Jeduthun for the ministry of prophesying, accompanied by harps,

---

of warning issued to the people of Israel as they prepared to enter the promised land (Deuteronomy 32:1-43).

[8] Samuel A Meier, *Themes and Transformations in Old Testament Prophecy* (Downers Grove: IVP, 2009), 83. For expositions of the songs of both Exodus 15 and Judges 5, along with explorations of their implications for congregational singing, see Mike Raiter and Rob Smith, *Songs of the Saints: Enriching our singing by learning from the songs of Scripture* (Sydney: Matthias Media, 2017), 27-57.

[9] Luther, 'Preface to Georg Rhau's Symphonoiae iucundae, 1538', 323.

lyres and cymbals' (1 Chronicles 25:1). The musical mode of their prophetic ministry is again stressed in verse 3 where we're told that they 'prophesied, using the harp in thanking (Heb. *yadah*) and praising (Heb. *hallel*) the Lord'.

A number of reasons have been suggested as to why these singers are described as prophets and their songs as prophecy. [10] Allen Ross highlights two of the most significant. *First*, as their inclusion in the canonical Psalter reveals, the psalms written, collected and sanctioned by Asaph (et al) 'were understood to be God's word to the people, that is, prophetic compositions'.[11] *Second*, not only was the elevated poetic form of their songs harmonious with the form of much divine prophecy but, as we've already seen, 'singing or rhythmic chanting was considered the most powerful form that prophecy could have and a form of prophecy itself'.[12]

In light of such an understanding, it is not surprising that sung prophecy continued in the later prophetic tradition and that examples abound in the writings of the canonical prophets of the Old Testament.[13] Isaiah's 'vineyard song' (Isaiah 5) is a notable case in point. Here, as Alec Motyer points out, 'Isaiah the singer is the minister of another's words'[14] – God's! In other words, Isaiah sings the Word of the Lord to the people of Israel in order to convict them of their crimes and convince them that their judgement is merited. What's more, the poetic *form* is vital to the didactic *content*.[15] This is highlighted by the powerful, rhetorical punch landed in the concluding verse of the song through a play on words:

> and he looked for *justice* (Heb. *mishpat*),
> but behold, *bloodshed* (Heb. *mishpach*);

---

[10] For example, Sara Japhet suggests that their prophesying was not being ascribed to 'isolated, unique phenomena, but to the permanent singing establishment, which is part of the cultic framework' (*I & II Chronicles: A Commentary* [Louisville: Westminster John Knox Press, 1993], 440–41).

[11] Allen P Ross, *Recalling the Hope of Glory: Biblical Worship from the Garden to the New Creation* (Grand Rapids: Kregel, 2006), 257.

[12] Ross, *Recalling the Hope of Glory*, 257-58.

[13] For example, Isaiah 26:1-6, Ezekiel 19, Amos 5:2 and Habakkuk 3.

[14] J A Motyer, *The Prophecy of Isaiah* (Leicester: IVP, 1993), 68.

[15] C H Knights, 'Singing Prophets and Prophetic Songs – Isaiah's Song of the Vineyard', *ExpTim* 125.12 (Sep 2014), 602-603.

for *righteousness* (Heb. *tsedaqah*),
   but behold, *an outcry* (Heb. *tse'aqah*)!

Isaiah 5:7

It is also worth noting the three 'taunt songs' (Heb. *mashal*) found in the Old Testament prophetic writings: Isaiah 14:4-21; Micah 2:4; Habbakuk 2:6-20. As *taunt* songs, they all have the same goal: to 'shame the proud, highlight God's sovereignty, and convey the advance of His kingdom program'.[16] That is, they are declarative and educative. As taunt *songs*, they all exhibit a range of similar literary features: 'assonance, concise wording, third person grammar in a second person context, a theme of judgment, an interrogative, and the use of the root *msl* in the introduction'.[17] So again the *medium* is crucial to the *message*.

As we saw in Exodus 15, the biblical concept of prophecy encompasses not only *fore-telling* (prediction) but also *forth-telling* (proclamation).[18] This explains why it can function as a very natural rubric under which to gather all divinely inspired words, including the songs of Scripture. And, as we'll see when we come to the New Testament, it also explains why it can function as an appropriate descriptor for non-divinely-inspired human words – either spoken or sung – that faithfully impart God's Word.[19]

In sum, the lesson of this strand of Old Testament revelation is as follows: whether by singing the *texts* of Scripture or by singing the *truths* of Scripture, *singing is one very powerful way in which God's servants have prophesied in the past, and* (as we'll see in the following chapter) *can prophesy in the present.*

---

[16] Mark A Hassler, 'Isaiah 14 and Habakkuk 2: Two Taunt Songs Against the Same Tyrant?', *MSJ* 26.2 (Fall 2015), 222.
[17] William D Barrick, 'The Eschatological Significance of Leviticus 26', *MSJ* 16.1 (Spring 2005), 103.
[18] Walter C Kaiser Jr. and Moisés Silva, *An Introduction to Biblical Hermeneutics: The Search for Meaning* (Grand Rapids: Zondervan, 2007), 139.
[19] For this reason, I toyed with titling this chapter, 'Singing and Prophecy'. But, as we're about to see, proclamation is, arguably, an even more expansive category.

2.2. Music, singing and proclamation

This naturally leads to a related strand of Old Testament teaching: the connection between music, singing and proclamation. As we saw in chapter five, it's impossible to separate (what we called) *the two faces of praise* – i.e., praise as *divine adoration* and praise as *public declaration*. The reason for this is that when our praise of God is directed to others He is present to receive it, and when our praise is directed to Him it is always done in the hearing of others – if not always in the earthly realm, then certainly in the heavenly realms!

Nevertheless, given that the two faces of praise remain distinct, Scripture presents this dual directionality not merely as something *inevitable*, but as something that ought to be *intentional*. In other words, singing that praises *God to God* and singing that proclaims *God to others* are meant to go together. This is clear from the numerous exhortations and promissory declarations found throughout the Psalms. For example:

> Sing praises (Heb. *zamar*) to the LORD,
>> who sits enthroned in Zion!
> Tell (Heb. *nagad*) among the peoples his deeds!
>
>> *Psalm 9:11*

> I will tell (Heb. *safar*) of your name to my brothers;
>> in the midst of the congregation
>> I will praise (Heb. *halal*) you:
>
>> *Psalm 22:22*

> But I will declare (Heb. *nagad*) it forever;
>> I will sing praises (Heb. *zamar*) to the God of Jacob.
>
>> *Psalm 75:9*

> ² Sing (Heb. *shir*) to the LORD, bless his name;
>> tell (Heb. *basar*) of his salvation from day to day.
> ³ Declare (Heb. *safar*) his glory among the nations,
>> his marvelous works among all the peoples!
>
>> *Psalm 96:2-3*

> Sing (Heb. *shir*) to him, sing praises (Heb. *zamar*) to him;
>> tell (Heb. *sicha*) of all his wondrous works!
>
>> *Psalm 105:2*

²¹ ... that they may declare (Heb. *safar*) in Zion
    the name of the Lord,
    and in Jerusalem his praise (Heb. *tehilla*),
²² when peoples gather together,
    and kingdoms, to worship (Heb. *'avad*) the Lord.

Psalm 102:21-22

The same connections are also found in the prophets. For example:

⁴ ... 'Give thanks (Heb. *yadah*) to the Lord,
    call (Heb. *qara*) upon his name,
make known (Heb. *yada*) his deeds among the peoples,
    proclaim (Heb. *zakhar*) that his name is exalted.
⁵ 'Sing praises (Heb. *zamar*) to the Lord,
    for he has done gloriously;
    let this be made known (Heb. *yada*) in all the earth.
⁶ Shout (Heb. *tzahal*), and sing for joy (Heb. *ranan*),
    O inhabitant of Zion,
    for great in your midst is the Holy One of Israel'.

Isaiah 12:4-6

For thus says the Lord:
 'Sing aloud (Heb. *ranan*) with gladness for Jacob,
    and raise shouts (Heb. *tzahal*) for the chief of the nations;
proclaim (Heb. *shama*), give praise (Heb. *halal*), and say,
    'O Lord, save your people, the remnant of Israel.'

Jeremiah 31:7

¹⁰ Sing and rejoice, O daughter of Zion, for behold, I come and I will dwell in your midst, declares the Lord. ¹¹ And many nations shall join themselves to the Lord in that day, and shall be my people.

Zechariah 2:10-11

What is clear from these examples, is that singing, praising and proclaiming (on the one hand) and the salvation of Israel and the nations (on the other) are profoundly interconnected.[20] In this sense, *singing praise may rightly be described as a form of mission.*[21]

We see this with particular clarity in Isaiah 42:1-17. As the first of Isaiah's 'Servant Songs', the passage begins by introducing us to the Lord's servant who, in the power of the Spirit, has come to 'bring forth justice to the nations' (v 1). Although his manner will be gentle and humble (vv 2-3), and 'there is more than a hint that his mission will involve him in personal suffering',[22] we are nonetheless assured that he will 'not grow faint or be discouraged till he has established justice in the earth' (v 4a). The servant is thus presented as the judge and saviour of the world. This is why 'the coastlands wait for his law' (v 4b).

In the second stanza (vv 5-9), the servant is further described as 'a covenant for the people, a light to the nations' (v 6). His task is, likewise, further specified: to open blinded eyes and release prisoners from their captivity (v 7). The identity of the servant, the nature of his sufferings and how he will accomplish his mission are further clarified in later 'songs' (e.g., 49:1-6 and 52:13-53:12). What is clear at this point is that the 'new things' to be accomplished by him (v 9) will, in fact, be the work of Him who will not give His glory to another or His praise to carved idols – the Lord himself (v 8).

In the third stanza (vv 10-17), we see that the 'new things' now declared 'furnish the impulse and materials of 'a new song', such as has never been heard in the heathen world before'.[23] The saving work of the servant thus unleashes an avalanche of sung praise that begins with the people of Israel but extends to the nations (cf. Isaiah 49:6). This explains the global

---

[20] It is important to clarify that while singing has various God-given 'powers' (i.e., emotive, communicative, unitive, etc), it has no inherent *saving* power. Rather it is both a celebration and communication of God's saving power. So while singing may assist the publication of God's mighty acts, salvation (like power) belongs only to the Lord (Psalms 3:8; 62:11; Jonah 2:9).

[21] As Elmer Martens writes: '*Mission*, understood from within the OT, means making available the good news of God, as Israel knew it, to peoples outside of Israel'. See Elmer A Martens, 'Impulses to Mission in Isaiah: An Intertextual Exploration', *Bulletin for Biblical Research* 17.2 (2007), 216.

[22] Barry G Webb, *The Message of Isaiah* (Leicester: IVP, 1996), 172.

[23] Franz Delitzsch, *Isaiah: Commentary on the Old Testament: Volume 7* (trans. James Martin; Peabody: Hendrickson, 2006), 419.

nature of the summons to sing (vv 10-13). As Westermann puts it: 'the prophet here proclaims as binding that God's final saving act towards his people is to take place in full view of the entire world of men and of nature, and that it looks for the response not merely of the faithful, but of all men and of nature'.[24]

What is significant, for our purposes, is that while this salvation will be accomplished solely by the servant for the people, *the people are to be involved in the publication of the message of salvation as they sing the 'new song' inspired and called forth by the servant's saving work.* When this prospect is linked with the vision of 2:1-4, it is clear that the singing of praise is not merely to accompany the law going forth from Zion, but that it is one of the ways that the word of the Lord will go forth from Jerusalem so that the nations might be taught His ways (2:3).[25]

In sum, the lesson of this strand of Old Testament revelation is as follows: *singing is one very powerful way in which God's servants have proclaimed (and likewise can proclaim) His wondrous deeds both to themselves and among the peoples.*

2.3. Music, singing and instruction

The inseparable link between evangelism and education naturally leads to a third strand of Old Testament revelation: the connections between music, singing and *instruction*. While many parts of the Old Testament illustrate these connections, the Psalter does so in a way that is unique among the biblical books. Luther explains why:

> In other books we are taught by both precept and example what we ought to do. This book not only teaches but also gives the *means*

---

[24] Claus Westermann, *Isaiah 40-66* (London: SCM, 1966), 104.

[25] To this understanding Samuel Whitefield adds the following comment: 'We should understand this instruction as an expansion of the ministry of singing in the temple in Jerusalem. At the time Isaiah prophesied, there was already a regimen of night and day singing that had been put in place by King David (1 Chronicles 15:16, 27; 2 Chronicles 35:15; Nehemiah 12:45-46). Isaiah's prophecy has a clear message: night and day singing in Jerusalem is not enough. It has to fill the nations. It has to go beyond what David set in place'. Samuel Whitefield, 'The Role of Prophetic Singers in God's Plan to Redeem the Nations', *Samuel Whitefield* (October 6, 2016): https://samuelwhitefield.com/1986/the-role-of-prophetic-singers-in-gods-plan-to-redeem-the-nations.

and method by which we may keep the precept and follow the example. For ... what is the Psalter but prayer and praise to God, that is, a book of hymns?[26]

Tellingly, Luther's words reveal that the Psalter is not only prayer and praise, but also *torah* (i.e., law or instruction or teaching); indeed, it is an exceedingly rich source of both theology and ethics for God's people.[27]

As has often been observed, 'the Psalter presents itself as a second Torah, divided into five books like the Pentateuch, and it invites its readers to meditate on them day and night, just as Joshua was told to mediate on the law of Moses (Ps. 1:2; Josh. 1:8)'.[28] In other words, *the Psalter has a clear and carefully crafted didactic purpose.*[29] As Timothy Pierce notes, 'instruction plays a key role in the intention of the arrangement of the book as a whole. Indeed, instruction serves a significant purpose in the structures, function and forms of the book of Psalms, individually and collectively'.[30]

Furthermore, the language and content of the very first psalm, along with the other '*torah* psalms' (19 and 119), as well as the strategic placement of a series of 'wisdom psalms' (e.g., 37, 49, 73, 112, 127, 128 and 133), suggests that the theological aim and the editorial shape of the Psalter has

---

[26] Martin Luther, 'Preface' to *Works on the First Twenty-Two Psalms, 1519 to 1521*, in *Select Psalms III* (trans. Jaroslav Pelikan; vol. 14 of *Luther's Works*, American Edition, eds. Jaroslav Pelikan and Daniel E Poellot; St Louis: Concordia, 1958), 286.

[27] See, for example, David G Firth, 'The Teaching of the Psalms', in David G Firth and Philip S Johnston (eds.), *Interpreting the Psalms: Issues and Approaches* (Downers Grove: IVP, 2005), 159-174; Gordon J Wenham, 'The Ethics of the Psalms', idem, 175-194.

[28] Gordon J Wenham, *Psalms as Torah: Reading Biblical Song Ethically* (Grand Rapids: Baker, 2012), 7.

[29] For further insights into the structural indicators contained within the Psalter, as well as the theological implications of its final shape, see Gerard H Wilson, 'The Structure of the Psalter', in David G Firth and Philip S Johnston (eds.), *Interpreting the Psalms: Issues and Approaches* (Downers Grove: IVP, 2005), 229-246.

[30] Timothy M Pierce, *Enthroned on Our Praise: An Old Testament Theology of Worship* (Nashville: B&H Academic, 2008), 233.

been strongly influenced by the wisdom tradition.[31] Consequently, the language of law, teaching, wisdom, counsel and meditation appears regularly, so much so that the collection as a whole has been well-described as 'a guidebook along the path of blessing'.[32]

Psalm 32 is as an obvious 'case in point'. It is described as 'A *maskil* of David' – a musical or liturgical term that is generally understood to identify it as a teaching song.[33] *That* it is designed to instruct is clear from verse 8:

> I will *instruct* (Heb. *sakhal*) you
> and *teach* (Heb. *yara*) you in the way you should go;
> I will *counsel* (Heb. *ya'atz*) you with my eye upon you.
>
> *Psalm 32:8*

What it is designed to teach is expressed *negatively* in verse 9 – 'Be not like a horse or a mule, without understanding' and *positively* in verse 6 – 'Therefore let everyone who is godly offer prayer to you at a time when you may be found'. The purpose of such prayer, as David's self-testimony reveals (vv 3-5), is to come to know the 'blessing' (Heb. *'esher*) of sins forgiven (vv 1-2). And, lest we miss the obvious, not only does this instruction take the form of a song, but the end point of heeding it is itself praise:

> Be glad (Heb. *samach*) in the Lord,
> and rejoice (Heb. *giyl*), O righteous,
> and shout for joy (Heb. *ranan*),
> all you upright in heart!
>
> *Psalm 32:11*

More broadly, the instructional dimension of the Psalter may be seen as having two foci: instruction for *blessedness* and instruction for

---

[31] Gerald H Wilson, 'Shaping the Psalter: A Consideration of Editorial Linkage in the Book of Psalms', in J Clinton McCann (ed.), *The Shape and Shaping of the Psalter* (Sheffield: JSOT, 1993), 72-82.

[32] Brevard S Childs, *Introduction to the Old Testament as Scripture* (Philadelphia: Fortress, 1979), 513.

[33] This is supported by the fact that the Hebrew root of *maskil* (i.e., *sakhal*) means 'to have insight' or 'to teach'.

righteousness.[34] The two are, of course, profoundly related; for, as Psalm 1 reveals, the goal of blessedness is reached via the path of righteousness. How so? Because the righteous are characterised by their delight in, meditation on and obedience to 'the law of the LORD' (v 1). It is this response to divine wisdom that is the cause of their fruitfulness, perseverance and prosperity (v 2); i.e., their blessedness.

But, as Calvin was all too aware, the demand for such a response also creates a potential problem: it 'excludes from the hope of happiness all who do not worship God perfectly'.[35] Calvin, of course, was also alert to the Psalter's own solution to this problem; a solution which, as we've seen, is flagged in Psalm 32:

> When uprightness is demanded of the children of God, they do not lose the gracious remission of their sins, in which their salvation alone consists. While, then, the servants of God are happy, they still need to take refuge in his mercy, because their uprightness is not complete. In this manner are they who faithfully observe the law of God said to be truly happy; and thus is fulfilled that which is declared in Psalm 32:2, 'Blessed are they to whom God imputeth not sins'.[36]

Furthermore, when 'law' (Heb. *torah*) is understood not simply as *commandment* but, more comprehensively, as *instruction*, the 'problem' is not only put into perspective, but the solution is seen to have been present all along. For obeying 'the instruction of the LORD' (Psalm 1:1) includes obeying His call to confess our transgressions to Him (Psalm 32:5), as it does the call to believe the promise that 'steadfast love surrounds the one who trusts in the LORD' (Psalm 32:10). In other words, the 'righteous' of the Psalms are, first and foremost, righteous by faith and their obedience (imperfect as it is) is, only and ever, an obedience born of faith. This explains why exhortations to trust in the Lord are

---

[34] This is a modification of the helpful suggestion of Futato (*Interpreting the Psalms*, 63), who speaks in terms of 'instruction for happiness and instruction for holiness'.

[35] John Calvin, *Commentary on the Book of Psalms* (trans. Henry Beveridge; Grand Rapids: Baker, 1979), 317.

[36] Calvin, *Commentary on the Book of Psalms*, 317.

central to the teaching of the Psalter (e.g., Psalms 4:5; 37:3; 40:4; 62:8; 115:9).

However, all such instructions only truly make sense when understood in the light of the message that lies at the heart of the Psalter; a message encapsulated in the second half of the book's introduction: Psalm 2. The thematic importance of Psalm 2 is vital to understand, for while 'Psalm 1 orients the reader to receive the whole collection as instruction, Psalm 2 makes explicit the essential content of the instruction – the Lord reigns!'[37] This, then, becomes a recurring theme throughout the Psalter, linking up with the related themes of kingship, enthronement, provision, protection, judgement and mission (e.g., Psalms 9:7-11; 10:16; 24:8-10; 29:10-11; 47:2, 8-9; 93:1; 95:3; 96:10; 97:1; 99:1).[38] Consequently, the 'introduction to the Psalter is anything but an invitation to pedantry, legalism, or self-righteousness. On the contrary, it is an invitation to be *open to God's instruction* and to the reality of *God's* reign in the world'.[39]

More than this, Psalm 2 goes on to reveal that 'as King, our God reigns through his "anointed one"',[40] which – as Psalm 18:50 makes clear – is a reference to the rule of 'David and his offspring' (cf. the promise of 2 Samuel 7). But what is immediately apparent is that this reign of the Davidic Messiah is a hotly contested one: 'The kings of the earth set themselves, and the rulers take counsel together, against the Lord and against his Anointed' (v 2). More than that, this contest sets the stage for the general 'plotline' of the Psalter, as it tracks the fortunes of the Israelite monarchy from David's experience of persecution in the days of Saul (Book I), through the ups and downs of his reign (Book II), from Solomon's reign to the time of the exile (Book III), to a reaffirmation of divine kingship (Book IV), to the hope of redeemed existence under a new messianic king (Book V).[41] Psalm 2 anticipates this final outcome, assuring all who sing and hear its message that the Lord will give the

---

[37] J Clinton McCann, Jr., 'Psalms', in *New Interpreter's Bible in Twelve Volumes: Volume IV: 1 & 2 Maccabees; Introduction to Hebrew Poetry; Job; Psalms* (Nashville: Abingdon, 1996), 688.
[38] See further Mays, *The Lord Reigns*, 12-22.
[39] J Clinton McCann, Jr., *A Theological Introduction to the Book of Psalms: The Psalms as Torah* (Nashville: Abingdon Press, 1993), 27 (emphasis his).
[40] Futato, *Interpreting the Psalms*, 74.
[41] See the discussion in Hill and Walton, *A Survey of the Old Testament*, 346-351.

nations to His Son and that he will rule them with a rod of iron (vv 7-9). Hence its closing exhortation – 'Kiss the Son' (v 12a) – and its closing benediction – 'Blessed are all who take refuge in him' (v 12d).

If the Psalms have been well described as 'the Bible in miniature', then Psalm 2 may similarly be described as 'the Psalter in miniature'. How, then, might we sum up its message? Mark Futato puts it this way:

> The message of Psalm 2, and the book of Psalms, is that our God is in control, in spite of what circumstantial evidence might indicate. The book of Psalms called ancient Israelites, and calls us, to live a life of faith in the reign of God – to believe that a truly happy life is possible not just for 'us' but for '*all* who take refuge in him' (Psalm 2:12).[42]

It is the progression from suffering to glory, characteristic of the historic journey of the kings (and so people) of Israel, that best accounts for the Psalter's macro-structural movement from lament to praise. Of course, the final doxological outcome of this journey is not only found within numerous individual psalms (e.g., Psalms 3-7), but is anticipated at the end of each 'Book' in a burst of divine blessing and praise (i.e., 41:13; 72:18-19; 89:52; 106:48). In the larger frame, however, praise psalms dominate the latter 'books' and Book V concludes with a five-fold canon of undiluted praise psalms (Psalms 146-150). None of this accidental. Rather, 'the concentration of clusters of purer praise psalms in the fourth and fifth books (Psalms 93-100; 111-118; 145-150) forms part of the overall message of the Psalter. Far from being "all summons and no reason", Ps. 150 presupposes the context of the whole collection'.[43] This leads James Hely Hutchinson to the stunning conclusion that '*praise in the Psalter arises particularly from a circumstance-defying belief that Yahweh's covenant promises will come to realization – through the arrival of the Davidic king*'.[44]

To the extent that our songs are our teachers, the 150 songs that comprise the Psalter are a *tour de force* of divinely inspired instruction. The nutshell version of that instruction is this: '*We find blessing in God's*

---

[42] Futato, *Interpreting the Psalms*, 76.
[43] Hely Hutchinson, 'The Psalms and Praise', 96.
[44] Hely Hutchinson, 'The Psalms and Praise', 97.

righteous king, which leads to a life of praise.[45] Of course, the words 'leads to' are important here. For, as we've seen, the path of praise is peppered with seasons of lament. But praise is the end point – an end point that colours every part of the journey. This why the entire Psalter bears the name *Tehillim* (Praises). 'By its movement, conclusion, and title the book in its shape defines all its contents, the prayers and instruction, as the praise of the LORD'.[46] The message that *the blessedness found in God's righteous king leads to a life of praise* is instruction that God's children (now as then) need to hear, sing, and sing repeatedly, both to themselves and to each other. It is therefore worth asking how consistently and successfully our current mix of congregational songs communicates this message.

In sum, the lesson of this strand of Old Testament revelation is as follows: *singing is one very powerful way in which God's servants have instructed (and likewise can continue to instruct) one another in the ways of the Lord.*

2.4. Music, singing and recollection[47]

A further way in which music and song assist in the ministry of God's Word is by aiding its recollection. The reason for this is simple: *we remember what we sing*. Again, we see this repeatedly in the Psalter, not only in the praise and thanksgiving psalms, where God's gracious character and saving acts are called to mind (e.g., 105:5; 143:5), but also in various lament psalms (e.g., 42:6; 137:6) – as we will illustrate below.

Music's capacity to both form and evoke memories is well-recognised, not only in common experience but also across a range of scientific disciplines.[48] Both personal and corporate memories are embedded in

---

[45] Dan Wu, 'The Role of Lament in the Shape of the Psalter', in G Geoffrey Harper & Kit Barker (eds.), *Finding Lost Words: The Church's Right to Lament* (Eugene: Wipf & Stock, 2017), 140 (emphasis his).

[46] Mays, *The Lord Reigns*, 62. See further Appendix 1 of this book.

[47] This section has also been adapted from Smith, 'Belting Out the Blues as Believers', 100-102.

[48] Not surprisingly, an increasing number of psychological and neurological studies are seeking to better understand the connection; e.g., Christopher Bergland, 'Why Do the Songs from Your Past Evoke Such Vivid Memories?', *Psychology Today* (11 December, 2013): http://tinyurl.com/hh2h5vc; P Janata,

and by music, so much so that when the past is unrecoverable by other means, it can often be regained by playing or listening to familiar music. When the human voice is brought into the equation and truthful and meaningful words are articulated in song, the effect is significantly intensified. For the fact of the matter is that words add meaning and communicate with a clarity that music alone cannot. This is not because the music is unimportant or dispensable. To the contrary, the 'remembrance of the words is carried and prompted by the melody and sometimes the harmonic and rhythmic elements'. [49] Moreover, because emotions are known to enhance memory processes and music evokes strong emotions, music plays a key role in controlling and modulating various cognitive functions. [50] So meaningful words and memorable music work powerfully together.

Not surprisingly, music and song played a vital role in Israel's life of faith, but particularly in her seasons of distress. Why so? Because singing of God's mercies in days past – e.g., when they 'groaned in their slavery and cried out' (Exodus 2:23) – was a way of putting the present into perspective and awakening hope for the future. Otherwise put, the Israelites understood the power of song to articulate grief in a way that assists its resolution. Therefore, writes Brueggemann, 'Israel enacted and trusted liturgical practices that made the transformation of pain vivid, powerful, and credible. It did its singing and praying and praising in ways that shaped pain into hope, and grief into possibility'. [51]

Of course, it is not simply the act of singing (as therapeutic as this can be) that transforms pain into possibility. Rather it is the recollection of saving truth. That is, *the key to productive lament is faithful remembrance of divine grace*. Psalm 77 illustrates the point. Its title ('For the director of music. For Jeduthun. Of Asaph. A psalm') tells us plainly that it is a song. The repeated use of a series of related verbs – 'remember' (Heb. *zakhar*), 'meditate' (Heb. *sicha*), 'ponder' (Heb. *hagah*), 'consider' (Heb. *chashav*) and 'seek' (Heb. *darash*) – tell us that it is a song with a focus on

---

'The Neural Architecture of Music-Evoked Autobiographical Memories', *Cerebral Cortex* 19 (2009), 2579-594.

[49] Don E Saliers, *Worship as Theology: Foretaste of Glory Divine* (Nashville: Abingdon, 1994), 161.

[50] Lutz Jäncke, 'Music, Memory and Emotion', *Journal of Biology* 7.6 (2008): https://jbiol.biomedcentral.com/articles/10.1186/jbiol82.

[51] Brueggemann, *Israel's Praise*, 136.

remembering. But it is the structure or journey of the song that is of greatest interest.

The first nine verses contain the lament of one who is in such distress that he can neither sleep nor speak (v 4). In fact, at this point Asaph's memories only provoke his pain: 'I remembered you, God, and I groaned; I meditated, and my spirit grew faint' (v 3). Even his 'song in the night' (v 6),[52] rather than consoling him, only serves to produce a series of troubling doubts and painful questions (vv 7-9). But then, in verse 10, Asaph decides to think back to 'the years when the Most High stretched out his right hand'; that is, to the Lord's deliverance of Israel at the time of the Exodus:

> I will remember (Heb. *zakhar*) the deeds of the LORD;
>   yes, I will remember your miracles of long ago.
> I will ponder (Heb. *hagah*) all your works
>   and meditate (Heb. *sicha*) on all your mighty deeds.
>
> *Psalm 77:11–12*

So what happens as a result of Asaph's determination to 'remember the deeds of the LORD'? Not only is his mind taken off the hopelessness of Israel's present plight, but the 'memory of hurt resolved contextualizes present hurt, as yet unresolved'.[53] In other words, it is as he meditates on his knowledge of God's ways and words that his fear is directly addressed, and his doubt is effectively resolved. In fact, so much so that by the end of the psalm 'the pervasive "I" has disappeared, and the objective facts of the faith have captured all his attention and all of ours'.[54]

Psalm 77, then, not only celebrates in musical form the power of recalling God's truth, but it then embeds this lesson in a song of remembrance that instructs all who sing it in the knowledge of God and His ways. It thus serves to remind us that, whatever our present afflictions, *faithful recollection of God's redeeming grace in the past can grant us a new perspective on the present and awaken our hope for the future.*[55] This is

---

[52] This, presumably, refers to happier days when he could sing the praises of Yahweh freely. See Kidner, *Psalms 73–150*, 278.

[53] Brueggemann, *Israel's Praise*, 138.

[54] Kidner, *Psalms 73–150*, 277.

[55] According to James Harrichand, 'it is within the prayer of lament that Israel recalls its covenant relationship with God, which then gives rise to Israel's hope'.

the gift that Asaph offers to all who will sing his psalm. As Elmer Leslie writes:

> The psalmist's purpose is clear. Through this brilliant ending to his psalm he will say to worshiping Israel in its hour of deep dejection that the God of Israel's ancient and glorious past is still leading His people through waters that threaten to engulf them and will still provide 'shepherds' like unto Moses and Aaron.[56]

The combination of lament and recollection, then, has proved effective – not because it has removed the source of Asaph's original distress, but because it has enabled a renewed trust in the Lord in the midst of continuing trial.

Furthermore, the musical form of the psalm is far from incidental in achieving this end.[57] Gordon Wenham is right: 'Memorization of texts, especially if they are set to music, inevitably makes them more influential. They become part of the memorizer. Those who have learned a song sing it themselves, and the song expresses their own feelings'.[58] This is not only because memories and emotions are profoundly intertwined, but because music taps both the emotional and memory centres of the brain at once.[59] Furthermore, when recollection of 'the deeds of the LORD' (or what G Ernest Wright refers to as 'confessional recital of his acts, together with the teaching accompanying these acts')[60] is added to the mix, and

---

See James J S Harrichand, 'Recovering the Language of Lament for the Western Evangelical Church: A Survey of the Psalms of Lament and their Appropriation within Pastoral Theology', *MJTM* 16 (2014–2015), 107.

[56] Elmer A Leslie, *The Psalms: Translated and Interpreted in the Light of Hebrew Life and Worship* (New York: Abingdon-Cokesbury Press, 1949), 240.

[57] In fact, one recent neuropsychological study on those who have sustained brain injuries found that music was 'more efficient at evoking autobiographical memories than verbal prompts'. See A Baird and S Samson, 'Music evoked autobiographical memory after severe acquired brain injury: Preliminary findings from a case series', *Neuropsychological Rehabilitation: An International Journal* 24 (2014), 125.

[58] Wenham, *Psalms as Torah*, 204.

[59] C S Pereiral, J Teixeira, P Figueiredo, J Xavier, S L Castro and E Brattico, 'Music and Emotions in the Brain: Familiarity Matters', *PLoS ONE* 6.11 (November 2011): http://www.ncbi.nlm.nih.gov/pmc/articles/PMC3217963.

[60] See G Ernest Wright, *God Who Acts: Biblical Theology as Recital* (London: SCM, 1952), 85.

then articulated in corporate song, the combination is an extremely potent one. Bruggemann spells out the result: 'The ones who sing and recite can remember when it was not like it is now, and can hope for when it will again not be like it is now'.[61] Elihu, then, had good reason to exhort:

> Remember to extol his work,
> of which men have sung.
>
> *Job 36:24*

In sum, the lesson of this strand of Old Testament revelation is as follows: *singing is one very powerful way in which God's servants have (and therefore can) remember the living Word of the living God.*

2.5. *Music, singing and exhortation*

This brings us, finally, to the relationship between music, singing and exhortation. The Psalter, yet again, is replete with numerous calls to the people of God to, for instance, 'worship (Heb. *chawah*) the LORD' (e.g., Psalm 29:2), 'love (Heb. *'ahav*) the LORD' (e.g., Psalm 31:23), 'magnify (Heb. *gadal*) the LORD' (e.g., Psalm 34:3), 'fear (Heb. *yare*) the LORD' (e.g., Psalm 34:9), 'exalt (Heb. *rum*) the LORD' (Psalm 99:5), 'extol (Heb. *shavach*) the LORD' (e.g., Psalm 117:1), and especially to 'bless (Heb. *barakh*) the LORD' (e.g., Psalm 103:1-2, 20-22) or 'praise (Heb. *halal*) the LORD' (e.g., Psalm 147:1, 12, 20). Many other lines of exhortation could be added but, for our purpose, these last two deserve a brief comment – not least because they further illustrate a point we noted back in chapter five: the interrelationship between (horizontal) exhortation and (vertical) adoration.

While 'blessing' normally means 'imparting vital power to another',[62] blessing the Lord 'serves more as a recognition of His already evident claim to strength and glory'.[63] Consequently, exhorting either oneself or others to bless the Lord amounts to 'a call to praise Him based on the memory of who He has been in the past and who He will continue to be in the future'.[64] Psalm 103 perfectly illustrates the point – so much so that

---

[61] Brueggemann, *Israel's Praise*, 149.

[62] Claus Westermann, *Blessing in the Bible and the Life of the Church*, trans K Crim (Philadelphia: Fortress, 1978), 19.

[63] Pierce, *Enthroned on Our Praise*, 242.

[64] James L Mays, *Psalms* (Louisville: John Knox, 1994), 326.

James Mays describes it as 'a liturgical "not forgetting" of all the LORD's dealings'. This explains the seven-fold exhortation to 'bless', which 'introduces two lines at the beginning and the four lines at the end to emphasize the psalm's function as a rehearsal of declarations that exalt the LORD'.[65] Thus, the 'benefits' (v 2) with which David has been blessed not only reveal the *reason* why he calls upon himself and others to bless the Lord, but dictate both the *form* and *content* of his psalm of blessing.[66]

While Psalm 103 contains no reference to singing, it clearly has been and can be sung and, taken as a whole, reads like an exposition, if not a demonstration, of Psalm 96:2: 'Sing to the Lord, bless his name; tell of his salvation from day to day'. Furthermore, in terms of its editorial placement in the Psalter, it is clearly linked with Psalm 104, which not only contains the same blessing formula at its beginning and end but concludes with a call to 'praise (Heb. *halal*) the LORD' (v 35). This, in turn, links Psalms 103-104 with the two 'history psalms' which follow, Psalms 105-106, both of which contain various references to singing, were sung as the ark was brought into Jerusalem (1 Chronicles 16:8-33) and end with an identical call to 'praise (Heb. *halal*) the LORD' (105:45; 106:48).[67]

This leads us to our second, even briefer, comment. For such calls are often seen as *exclamations of praise* when, in fact, they are *exhortations to praise*! Now, in one sense, calling others to bless and praise God is an act of personal adoration. For not only is it part of the 'advertising aspect' of praise, but 'praising God alone has never been the apex of worship, for joy seeks company, and those who are most driven to His praise find themselves calling in their neighbors to join them'.[68] Nonetheless, strictly speaking, *hallelujah* (usually translated 'Praise the LORD') is a plural imperative (*halelu* = you *all* must praise, plus a shortened form of Yahweh, *yah*). In other words, it is a corporate command. Not surprisingly, the hallelujah command is 'the crescendo of the book of

---

[65] Mays, *Psalms*, 326.

[66] Otherwise put, inside the *inclusio* of imperatives to 'bless the LORD' (i.e., vv 1 and 20-22), the body of the psalm is one long series 'recollecting, remembering, reminding' (Mays, *Psalms*, 326).

[67] Psalm 106 also begins with this call.

[68] Pierce, *Enthroned on Our Praise*, 242.

Psalms since the last five psalms are dominated by the word and concept'.[69]

What all this means is that we can (and should) exhort fellow believers to praise by singing to them and then praise God by singing with them. This is exactly what Psalm 149 exhorts and envisages:

> [1] Praise (Heb. *halal*) the LORD!
> Sing (Heb. *shir*) to the LORD a new song,
>   his praise (Heb. *tehillah*) in the assembly of the godly!
> [2] Let Israel be glad (Heb. *samach*) in his Maker;
>   let the children of Zion rejoice (Heb. *gil*) in their King!
> [3] Let them praise (Heb. *halal*) his name with dancing,
>   making melody (Heb. *zamar*) to him with tambourine and lyre!

Psalm 150, then brings the Psalter to a fitting conclusion, urging that the Lord be praised both on earth and in heaven (v 1) and for both His deeds and His character (v 2). The psalmist then calls for an array of movements and musical instruments to be brought into play. Indeed, 'every kind of instrument, solemn or gay, percussive or melodic, gentle or strident, is rallied here to the praise of God'.[70]

> [3] Praise him with trumpet sound;
>   praise him with lute and harp!
> [4] Praise him with tambourine and dance;
>   praise him with strings and pipe!
> [5] Praise him with sounding cymbals;
>   praise him with loud clashing cymbals!

Finally, the progression from the *where* of praise to the *why* of praise and to the *how* of praise, comes to the ultimate hortatory crescendo as the psalm homes in on the *who* of praise – both who is to *give* it and who is to *receive* it: 'Let everything that has breath praise the LORD' (Psalm 150:6). In other words, the final exhortation of the final hallelujah psalm is not only an enactment of praise, but it is aimed at producing an endless stream of songs of praise in every place and from every facet of the created

---

[69] Pierce, *Enthroned on Our Praise*, 242.
[70] Kidner, *Psalms 73-150*, 491.

order (cf. Psalm 148), but most especially 'the children of Zion' in 'the assembly of the godly' (Psalm 149:1-2).

In sum, the 'take home' lesson of this strand of Old Testament revelation is this: *singing is one very powerful way in which God's servants have (and therefore can) exhort one another to bless and praise the Lord our God.*

3.   What Are the Implications?

In 1952, G Ernest Wright drew attention to what he described as 'a widespread revival of Marcionism in the modern Church'. His claim was that in actual practice (although not, of course, by official dogma) 'the Protestant Church has tended to emend radically the official canon of Scripture'.[71] It was certainly the view of some at the time that studying the Old Testament was 'like eating a large crab; it turns out to be mostly shell, with very little meat in it'.[72] Thankfully, the discipline of biblical studies has come a long way since the post-war period.[73] Developments in the field of biblical theology (a discipline which 'seeks to uncover and articulate the unity of all the biblical texts taken together'[74]) have also been enormously helpful in integrating the teaching of the testaments.[75] Even so, a range of problems continue to bedevil evangelical Old Testament scholarship[76] and, at the level of church membership, too many Christians all too easily lose sight of the fact that 'whatever was written in former days was written for our instruction' (Romans 15:4).

---

[71] Wright, *God Who Acts*, 16.
[72] Comment cited in Godfrey E Phillips, *The Old Testament in the World Church* (London: Lutterworth Press, 1942), 23.
[73] See David W Baker and Bill T Arnold (eds.), *The Face of Old Testament Studies: A Survey of Contemporary Approaches* (Grand Rapids: Apollos/Baker, 1999).
[74] D A Carson, 'Systematic Theology and Biblical Theology', in T Desmond Alexander and Brian S Rosner (eds.), *New Dictionary of Biblical Theology* (Leicester: IVP, 2000) 100.
[75] See the various works by Graeme Goldsworthy: e.g., *The Goldsworthy Trilogy* (Carlisle: Paternoster, 2000); *According to Plan* (Leicester: IVP, 1991); and *Preaching the Whole Bible as Christian Scripture: The Application of Biblical Theology to Preaching* (Leicester: IVP, 2000).
[76] See, for example, those raised by Todd S Beall, 'Evangelicalism, Inerrancy, and Current Old Testament Scholarship', *DBSJ* 18 (2013), 67-81.

While our brief survey of a handful of strands of Old Testament teaching has been far from exhaustive, what it has revealed is that there is a long and rich history to the relationship between music, song and the communication of God's Word. Once again, the Psalter has proved to be particularly illuminating in this regard. Not only does it repeatedly exemplify the phenomenon of the 'sermon in song' but it also reveals that prophecy, proclamation, instruction, recollection and exhortation have always been inseparable from divine praise and integral to divine worship.[77]

This observation has three important implications for the gatherings of God's new covenant people.

3.1. The vertical and the horizontal

The *first* has to do with *the necessity of integrating the vertical and the horizontal, both in theory and in practice.* That is, acts of divine glorification need to be *other instructive*, just as acts of instruction need to be *God glorifying.* We may sometimes be more conscious of one dimension than the other and the words we're singing may highlight one 'audience' more than the other. But whatever the focus of the particular psalm, hymn or song, both audiences (God and others) need to be kept in mind. For *if we are addressing God, we're doing so in the presence of one another and if we're addressing one another, we're doing so in the presence of God.* As Timothy Pierce writes:

> Focusing on instruction does not mean the abandonment of praise and thanksgiving. In fact, there needs to be more of an inclusion of both these elements in preaching. Evangelical preachers often seem oblivious to the fact that the presence of both was abundant in the teaching of the biblical saints (Dan 2:23; Hab 3:3; 1 Cor 1:4; Phil 1:3; 1 Thess 5:23-24; Heb 1:1-4). Focusing on instruction simply advocates that everything done in worship should teach something.[78]

---

[77] Pierce, *Enthroned on Our Praise*, 238.
[78] Pierce, *Enthroned on Our Praise*, 239.

3.2.   Singing and spiritual formation

The *second* implication has to do with *the role of singing in spiritual formation* (i.e., theological, ethical and devotional development). As with all public confession or corporate liturgy, articulating beliefs and advocating behaviours in speech or in song challenges the speaker/singer to embrace, own and internalise their words in a way that hearing alone does not. Gordon Wenham explains why:

> If we praise a certain type of behavior in our prayers, we are telling God that this is how we intend to behave. On the other hand, if in prayer we denounce certain acts and pray for God to punish them, we are in effect inviting God to judge us if we do the same. This makes the ethics of liturgy uniquely powerful. It makes a stronger claim on the believer than either law, wisdom, or story, which are simply subject to passive reception: one can listen to a proverb or a story and then take it or leave it, but if you pray ethically, you commit yourself to a path of action.[79]

Of course, the challenge is not only to the speaker/singer but to the hearer too – who may also be a fellow speaker/singer. Here's where declaration, instruction and exhortation all overlap and are practically inseparable. For when biblical truth 'is sung or recited in public worship, other worshippers are aware of their fellows and whether they are joining in saying or singing the psalm or prayer. This public dimension thus creates a strong social pressure to conform to the beliefs or values of the text being recited'.[80] This 'pressure' may not be appreciated by all and some may prefer to ponder rather than participate. But the pressure can also be helpful – both as a challenge to the resistant and as an encouragement to the receptive.

> This makes the ethics embedded in liturgy – whether it be the Lord's Prayer, a psalm, or a worship song – particularly potent. In the act of reciting a psalm, a worshipper is making a public commitment to its sentiments. ... Liturgy does not simply invite assent; it demands it.'[81]

---

[79] Wenham, *Psalms as Torah*, 57.
[80] Wenham, *Psalms as Torah*, 204-205.
[81] Wenham, *Psalms as Torah*, 205.

3.3.   The theological content of our songs

The *third* implication – which we will explore further in the next chapter – has to do with *the importance of the theological content of our songs*. One of the great strengths of psalm singing is that, for obvious reasons, the words sung cannot be faulted for their truthfulness. (Whether they pass the edification test, however, will depend on how well they've been versified, what tunes are put to them and how effectively they're used.) But, as we've argued in previous chapters, there's no valid reason to restrict ourselves to the Psalter or even to songs taken directly from Scripture. Singing the *truth* of Scripture (even more than the *text* of Scripture) is the key to faithfully singing God's Word. This in turn means that *the theological content of our songs is paramount.* Consequently:

> Music leaders, writers, and performers need to become better versed in theology. It is not enough to be able to construct a tune and lyrics that are aesthetically pleasing and emotionally evocative. Music must be immersed in proper theology precisely because it has a power to instruct and evoke in a manner that few mediums can ... For the writer or leader who has had only a passing introduction to the content and theology of worship, there is a great danger of presenting content that is less than ideal.[82]

Conclusion

Clearly, then, there is much to be learned from a study of the relationship between Word and song in the Hebrew Scriptures. If God's new covenant people are going to be led wisely and served well, the theology and wisdom of the Old Testament needs to be carefully pondered and thoughtfully applied to our gatherings. Of course, for the fullness of biblical wisdom to be appreciated, the insights and perspective of the New Testament also need to be brought to bear. So before we delve further into the realm of practical application, our next task is to complete the canonical picture by seeing what the Lord Jesus and His apostles add to what we've seen so far.

---

[82] Pierce, *Enthroned on Our Praise*, 239.

10. Singing as Preaching II: New Covenant Explorations

The New Testament era was birthed in outbursts of praise and thanksgiving. Think, for instance, of the 'songs' of Mary (the *Magnificat*, Luke 1:46-55), Zechariah (the *Benedictus*, Luke 1:68-79), Simeon (the *Nunc dimittis*, Luke 2:29-32) and, of course, that of the angels (*Gloria in excelsis Deo*, Luke 2:14).[1] While it is not certain how many of these 'songs' were sung (as opposed to being declared) at their point of origin, they certainly have been sung many times since! Moreover, not only is it entirely natural that the dawning of a new covenant should produce a whole host of 'new songs', but 'all the antecedents of the Church's appearance in the world of the first century would lead us also to expect that the early Church will be a hymn-singing community'.[2] And so it was. With the coming of the Messiah, the inbreaking of His kingdom, His saving death and victorious resurrection, the sending of His Spirit, and the gifts of forgiveness, adoption and eternal life, there was all the more reason to heed the psalmist's summons: 'Oh sing to the LORD a new song, for he has done marvellous things!' (Psalm 98:1).

Building on the findings of the previous chapter, our particular interest in this one is to explore the preaching function of congregational song in the New Testament. Once this task is completed, in our next chapter we will probe more deeply into the practical implications of this teaching for contemporary church life by identifying three 'keys' to ongoing musical reformation and expounding these with reference to a range of biblical principles and historical insights.

1.   Jesus' Pattern of Ministry

Even a cursory reading of the Gospels shows that preaching and teaching were a key part of the ministry of the Lord Jesus. Both Matthew and Mark record that from the moment John the Baptist was imprisoned, 'Jesus

---

[1] The italicised titles (e.g., *Magnificat*, etc), come from the Latin translations of the opening words of these 'songs', and are the traditional ecclesiastical names for the liturgical canticles based on them.

[2] Martin, *Worship in the Early Church*, 39.

began to preach (Gk. *kērussō*), saying, 'Repent, for the kingdom of heaven is at hand" (Matthew 4:17; cf. Mark 1:14-15). Consequently, Jesus 'went throughout all Galilee, teaching (Gk. *didaskō*) in their synagogues and proclaiming (Gk. *kērussō*) the gospel of the kingdom and healing every disease and every affliction among the people' (Matthew 4:23; cf. 9:35; Mark 1:39). This focus on preaching and teaching (usually, but not always, accompanied by miraculous deeds) continued to be His pattern throughout His earthly ministry (e.g. Matthew 11:1). Indeed, in Luke 4:43 Jesus explicitly affirms that He was 'sent for this purpose'. Peter Adam is, therefore, right: 'The kingdom comes, in part, by Jesus' preaching'.[3]

Nowhere, however, do the Gospels record that Jesus preached to the crowds by singing! This is not really surprising. *Where intelligibility of message is the primary goal, the spoken Word will be the primary means.*[4] There is, however, one recorded instance of Jesus teaching and encouraging His disciples by way of song. On the night of His betrayal, at the conclusion of the last Passover meal He would eat with the twelve before His death and resurrection, Matthew records: 'And when they had sung a hymn, they went out to the Mount of Olives' (Matthew 26:30; cf. Mark 14:26). So what was the 'hymn' that Jesus and His disciples sang? Carson answers as follows:

> The 'hymn' normally sung was the last part of the *Hallel* (Pss 114-118 or 115-118). It was sung antiphonally: Jesus as the leader would sing the lines, and his followers would respond with 'Hallelujah!' Parts of it must have been deeply moving to the disciples when after the Resurrection they remembered that Jesus sang words pledging that he would keep his vows (Ps 116:12-13), ultimately triumph despite rejection (Ps 118), and call all nations to praise Yahweh and his covenant (Ps 117).[5]

The significance of these observations should be clear: as Jesus sang to and with His disciples, He was instructing them in the nature of the work He was about to accomplish – even though it would not be until 'he

---

[3] Peter Adam, *Speaking God's Words: A Practical Theology of Preaching* (Leicester: IVP, 1996), 45.

[4] See Walter R Wietzke, *The Primacy of the Spoken Word: Redemptive Proclamation in a Complex World* (Minneapolis: Augsburg Fortress Press, 1988), 35-54.

[5] D A Carson, 'Matthew', 539.

opened their minds to understand the Scriptures' (Luke 24:45) that they would receive the full benefit of that instruction.

2.   The Place of Song in Paul's Churches

While there are no other recorded instances of Jesus and His disciples singing, it is not to be doubted that there were numerous other occasions on which they did so – e.g., in temple, synagogue, wedding and festival contexts. When we come to Paul's epistles, however, it is clear that 'hymns had a special significance in the meetings for worship of the earliest Christian mission communities, and were an essential part of that worship'.[6] In order to appreciate the didactic role of singing in Paul's churches, three passages warrant brief exploration.

2.1.   1 Corinthians 14:26

What then, brothers? When you come together, each one has a hymn (Gk. *psalmos*), a lesson, a revelation, a tongue, or an interpretation. Let all things be done for building up (Gk. *oikodomē*).

New Testament scholars continue to debate the nature of the 'hymn' to which Paul here refers. On the one hand, Anthony Thiselton sees it as a 'strong possibility that, grounded in biblical tradition, the earliest hymns were probably from the Psalms of the OT'.[7] Martin Hengel, on the other, asserts that the *psalmos* 'will hardly have been an Old Testament 'psalm' learnt off by heart; it will have been a new composition, inspired by the Spirit'.[8] While not ruling out this possibility, Roy Ciampa and Brian Rosner suggest that the 'assumption that any Spirit-inspired utterance must be spontaneous may owe more to the modern

---

[6] Martin Hengel, *Between Jesus and Paul: Studies in the Earliest History of Christianity* (trans. John Bowden; London: SCM, 1983), 81.

[7] Anthony C Thiselton, *The First Epistle to the Corinthians* (Grand Rapids: Eerdmans, 2000), 1135.

[8] Hengel, *Between Jesus and Paul*, 79. Gordon Fee (*God's Empowering Presence*, 690) supports this view of Paul's list of 'contributions', arguing that 'since the last three are Spirit-inspired utterances, and therefore spontaneous, it is likely that the first two are to be understood in that way as well'. It is not certain, however, that any of these items is necessarily spontaneous.

charismatic/Pentecostal traditions and experience than to the biblical evidence'.[9]

The simple fact is that we do not know whether Paul was thinking of 'a fresh composition or a known composition (from the Psalms); something for all to sing or for only one; something accompanied by an instrument or unaccompanied; or a vehicle to exhort, instruct, or uplift others'.[10] Nor do we need to know. What we need to know is what we do know: *whatever type of 'hymn' Paul may have had in mind or whatever type of song anyone might bring to sing, all things must be done 'for building up'.*

The need for everything that takes place in the Christian assembly to achieve this end, has been Paul's driving concern right throughout this chapter of 1 Corinthians (see vv 3, 4, 5, 12, 17; cf. 8:1; 10:23). By 'building up' (Gk. *oikodomē*) or edification he plainly means building up *others,* something that cannot be achieved apart from *intelligible instruction.* This is why he encourages the Corinthians to pursue the gift of prophecy (i.e., intelligible, other-edifying speech and song) and discourages the public use of uninterpreted tongues (i.e., unintelligible, self-edifying speech and song). We see this clearly in v 4: 'The one who speaks in a tongue *builds up himself,* but the one who prophesies *builds up the church'.* Likewise, in the verdict of v 5: 'The one who prophesies is greater than the one who speaks in tongues, unless someone interprets, *so that the church may be built up'.* It also explains Paul's determination in v 19: 'Nevertheless, in church I would rather speak five words with my mind *in order to instruct others,* than ten thousand words in a tongue'.

Furthermore, Paul is not only concerned for the *building up of insiders* but also for the *building in of outsiders.* So vv 23-25:

> [23] If, therefore, the whole church comes together and all speak in tongues, and outsiders or unbelievers enter, will they not say that you are out of your minds? [24] But if all prophesy, and an unbeliever or outsider enters, he is convicted by all, he is called to account by

---

[9] Roy E Ciampa and Brian S Rosner. *The First Letter to the Corinthians* (Grand Rapids: Eerdmans, 2010), 709.
[10] David E Garland, *1 Corinthians* (Grand Rapids: Baker Academic, 2003), 657-658.

all, [25] the secrets of his heart are disclosed, and so, falling on his face, he will worship God and declare that God is really among you.

The key point for our present discussion is this: *any 'hymn' that does not have the capacity to edify others has no place being sung in the assemblies of God's people.* Such a song may encourage the individual singer (and so may have a place in private devotion), but if it is unintelligible to others then it will not build the church and ought not be sung in the gathering.[11]

As we have seen at various points in the preceding chapters, this does not mean that praise of God or prayer to God is really just a means to another end; namely, the encouragement or evangelisation of others.[12] No. God is to be praised for His own sake; worshipped because of who He is and what He has done. What it does mean is that the *way* we praise or pray to God in the presence of others matters acutely.[13] The right way is the 'more excellent way' (1 Corinthians 12:31), the way of love. And love will mean that our choice of songs, as well as the way we play and sing them, will be aimed at the 'upbuilding and encouragement and consolation' of others (1 Corinthians 14:3). Otherwise put, our songs must function as intelligible prophecy, not as unintelligible tongues.

2.2. *Ephesians 5:18-21*

[18] And do not get drunk with wine, for that is debauchery, but be filled with the Spirit, [19] addressing one another in psalms and hymns and spiritual songs, singing and making melody to the Lord with your heart, [20] giving thanks always and for everything to God

---

[11] As Frame (*Contemporary Worship Music*, 19) rightly points out, 'intelligibility, to some extent, implies contemporaneity'. This, of course, can be pushed too far. For, as Frame also notes, traditional music and even lyrical archaisms can still communicate quite effectively. Nevertheless, priority should be given to the language of our day and the music of our time.

[12] Peterson, *Engaging with God*, 221.

[13] As Claire S Smith (*Pauline Communities as 'Scholastic Communities': A Study of the Vocabulary of 'Teaching' in 1 Corinthians, 1 and 2 Timothy and Titus* [Tübingen: Mohr Siebeck, 2012]) writes: 'The importance of educational outcomes from all speech in the public community setting is clearly indicated by the necessity for even Godward speech to have didactic benefit for those present' (259).

the Father in the name of our Lord Jesus Christ, [21] submitting to one another out of reverence for Christ.

A full exegesis of these verses is neither possible nor necessary here. Instead, I will briefly recap the discussion in chapter seven about the Paul's three song terms, then engage in a longer exploration of the relationship between the command in v 18 ('be filled with/by the Spirit')[14] and the five participles in vv 19-21 ('addressing', 'singing', 'making melody', 'giving thanks' and 'submitting') and, finally, make a comment about the ministry function of song in this passage.

Regarding, Paul's three terms, 'psalms, hymns and spiritual songs', author and composer, Jack Hayford, has memorably distinguished them in the following fashion:

- In *psalms*, we declare His *Word* in song; ...
- In *hymns*, we announce His *works* in song; ...
- In *spiritual songs*, we welcome His *will* in song; ...[15]

This is wonderfully neat and has the added appeal of alliteration. But it is highly unlikely that Paul would have defined his terms in this way. Not only should every psalm, hymn or spiritual song do all three of these things (to one degree or another) but, from a lexical point of view, 'it is difficult to draw any hard and fast distinctions among the three categories of psalms, hymns, and spiritual songs'.[16] This is not to say that they are synonymous. More likely, they are meant to cover the whole gamut of congregational song – from the canonical psalms to spontaneous compositions.[17]

Regarding the relationship between the command in v 18 and the five participles in vv 19-21, it is commonly argued that the latter are best

---

[14] Paul's language suggests that the Spirit is the *instrument* of filling rather than the *content* of the filling. For the grammatical arguments that lead to this conclusion, see Harold W Hoehner, *Ephesians: An Exegetical Commentary* (Grand Rapids: Baker, 2002), 703.

[15] Jack Hayford, *Worship His Majesty* (Waco: Word, 1987), 152.

[16] Andrew T Lincoln, *Ephesians* (Waco: Word, 1990), 345.

[17] Certainly, the fluidity of the New Testament's use of the terms tells against the view that Paul intends them *all* to refer to the Psalter. See further Raiter and Smith, *Songs of the Saints*, 118-122.

understood as 'result participles'.[18] If this is correct, Paul is making the point that when a person or church is filled by the Spirit, these are the kinds of actions that will result. There is much to commend this interpretation (both grammatically and theologically) and its implication – that 'addressing one another in psalms and hymns and spiritual songs' and 'singing and making melody to the Lord with your heart' are key marks of the Spirit-filled church – has a considerable amount of historical support.

However, in my judgement, a stronger case can be made for understanding the participles in vv 19-21 as 'means participles'; that is, Paul is saying that these are the means by which he expects his readers to carry out his command to 'be filled by the Spirit'.[19] To see the strength of this interpretation we need to place the command of v 18 in its broader context.

Back in chapter 3, Paul makes mention of his prayer that through the Spirit's empowerment, Christ might so dwell in his readers' hearts that they 'may be filled with all the fullness of God' (3:16-19). In chapter 4 he spoke of the fact that the church has been divinely supplied with the necessary gifts to grow into 'the measure of the stature of the fullness of Christ' (4:13). As it is the Spirit who is in the process of building the church into the 'dwelling place of God' in Christ (2:21-22), all believers have a responsibility not simply to avoid grieving the Spirit (4:30), but to

---

[18] See, for example, Ernest Best, *Ephesians* (London: T&T Clark, 1998), 510; Bryan Chapell, *Ephesians* (Phillipsburg: P&R Publishing, 2009), 263; Glenn H Graham, *An Exegetical Summary of Ephesians* (Dallas: Summer Institute of Linguistics, 1997), 469; Hoehner, *Ephesians*, 706; Lincoln, *Ephesians*, 345; Benjamin L Merkle, *Exegetical Guide to the Greek New Testament: Ephesians* (Nashville: B&H Academic, 2016), 175.

[19] So, for example, Arnold, *Ephesians*, 351-352. Grammatically, either 'means' or 'result' is possible. Curiously, Daniel B Wallace (*Greek Grammar Beyond the Basics* [Grand Rapids: Zondervan, 1996]) rejects a 'means' reading on theological grounds. He believes 'it would be almost inconceivable to see this text suggesting that the way in which one is to be Spirit-filled is by a five-step, partially mechanical formula!' (639). But this is not only a caricature of the 'means' reading (for the participles are neither a formula nor are they mechanical) but fails to explain why the 'means reading' is more inconceivable than his own 'measurement reading'; i.e., that the participles provide 'the way in which one measures his/her success in fulfilling the command of 5:18' (639).

actively participate in bringing the body of Christ to 'mature manhood' (4:13, cf. v 16).

The command to 'be filled by the Spirit' (5:18) needs to be understood in this context and in line with this larger purpose. Moreover, because the one Spirit has created one body (4:4), the command is necessarily corporate ('you *all* be filled'); it is not simply a matter of private practice or personal piety. In terms of concrete outworking, it entails not only a call to God's people to 'maintain the unity of the Spirit' (4:3), but to 'be so "full of God" by his Spirit that our worship and our homes give full evidence of the Spirit's presence'.[20] So, like the command to 'walk by the Spirit' (Galatians 5:16), being 'filled by the Spirit' is not a matter of 'letting go and letting God', but a matter of *active obedience to the will of God* (5:17).

How, then, does the apostle see this command being carried out? Thankfully, we're not left to guess; the following participles spell out the 'means of grace' by which the Spirit continually fills the church. As Timothy Gombis writes: 'The church is to be the temple of God, the fullness of Christ by the Spirit *by* being the community that speaks God's word to one another, sings praises to the Lord, renders thanksgiving to God for all things in the name of the Lord Jesus Christ, and lives in relationships characterized by mutual submission'.[21]

The unavoidable conclusion, then, is that singing 'psalms, hymns and spiritual songs' is the apostolically mandated means by which gathered believers simultaneously address one another (thereby edifying the church), make melody to the Lord (thereby praising Christ), and are filled by the Spirit with the fullness of God. That such singing will also be the result of such filling is not only logical but also the common experience of God's people. Indeed, as the history of revivals has often demonstrated, 'where the Spirit of God is there is also singing'.[22] Nevertheless, true as this might be, the 'means reading' of the participles of vv 19-21 makes better sense of Paul's thought in context; i.e., it is by engaging in the activities of 'addressing', 'singing', 'making melody', 'giving thanks' and

---

[20] Fee, *God's Empowering Presence*, 722.
[21] Gombis, 'Being the Fullness of God in Christ by the Spirit', 271 (emphasis his).
[22] Fee, *God's Empowering Presence*, 656. It could even be argued that Paul's thought contains a certain circularity – i.e., singing leads to Spirit-filling which leads to singing and so on.

'submitting' that Paul envisages believers being filled by the Spirit. Why and how this comes about is something that will become even clearer as we explore the parallel statement in Colossians 3:16.

But lest we miss the key point (at least, in terms of our concern in this chapter): *singing, for Paul, was a powerful means of horizontal address and mutual encouragement; a vital form of corporate Word ministry.* This ministry is mutual and reciprocal. For when Paul writes, 'speaking to yourselves (Gk. *lalountes heautois*) in psalms, hymns and spiritual songs' (KJV), he is not instructing each person to sing only to him or herself, but for *all to sing to all*.[23] This does not necessarily imply that this was only to be done in formal 'public worship' settings, although these are the most obvious contexts for such a ministry. The key point is simply the educational one: *addressing one another in song is a way of instructing one another in the truth.*[24]

2.3. *Colossians 3:15-17*

> [15] And let the peace of Christ rule in your hearts, to which indeed you were called in one body. And be thankful. [16] Let the word of Christ dwell in you richly, teaching and admonishing one another in all wisdom, singing psalms and hymns and spiritual songs, with thankfulness in your hearts to God. [17] And whatever you do, in word or deed, do everything in the name of the Lord Jesus, giving thanks to God the Father through him.

Once again, I will not attempt anything close to a full exposition of these verses. Instead, I'll focus on the main features of relevance to our chapter's primary concern. The first of these is that, like Ephesians 5, the context envisaged is a corporate one. Not only is there reference to 'one body' (v 15) and 'one another' (v 16),[25] but the expressions '*your* hearts',

---

[23] In other words, the reflexive pronoun (*heautois*) is functioning reciprocally not self-referentially. See Merkle, *Ephesians*, 175.

[24] Although, in Ephesians 5:19, Paul uses the more general term, 'speaking', rather than the teaching terms employed in Colossians 3:16, there is little doubt that his meaning is the same. See Hengel, *Between Jesus and Paul*, 79 and Lincoln, *Ephesians*, 345.

[25] As in Ephesians 5:19, the reflexive pronoun, *heautous*, is reciprocal, and so has the sense of (and may be translated as) 'one another' rather than 'yourselves'.

'in *you*', and '*you* do' are all plural, and the main verbs and participles – e.g., 'be thankful', 'teaching', 'admonishing', 'singing', 'giving thanks' – are plural as well. In short, 'Paul is reflecting on the Christian community;' [26] its unity, harmony, corporate thankfulness and, in particular, its mutual ministry responsibilities and activities.

Paul's primary concern is that 'the word of Christ' (i.e., 'the gospel and all the teachings and doctrines of and about Jesus'[27]) might dwell richly in and among the members of Christ's body. This further underscores the corporate nature of congregational song (for 'in you' does not only mean 'in *each* of you', but 'among you *all*'),[28] as well as the crucial fact that 'Christ is the ground and content of Christian song'. [29] That is, if Christians 'sing about God, it is especially what God has done through Christ; if about the Holy Spirit, it is the Holy Spirit as the gift of Christ; if about instruction of one another, it is the life in Christ'.[30] In short, 'Paul is urging the community as a whole to put the message about Christ at the center of its corporate experience'. [31]

But how is this to happen? As with Ephesians 5, we are not left to guess. It will happen as believers teach and admonish one another in all wisdom. But what form is this teaching and admonition to take? No doubt, it could (and did) take various forms – from public instruction to private conversation. But Paul's thought here is that it takes place by means of psalms, hymns and spiritual songs; that is, through corporate singing of the Word of Christ.[32]

See Murray J Harris, *Exegetical Guide to the Greek New Testament: Colossians and Philemon* (Nashville: B&H Academic, 2010), 146.

[26] Fee, *God's Empowering Presence*, 649.

[27] Michael D Raiter, *Colossians & Philemon: Growing Strong in Christ* (Grand Rapids: Discovery House, 2015), 46.

[28] Moo, *Colossians*, 286.

[29] Everett Ferguson, *The Church of Christ: A Biblical Ecclesiology for Today* (Grand Rapids: Eerdmans, 1997), 269.

[30] Ferguson, *The Church of Christ*, 269.

[31] Moo, *Colossians*, 286.

[32] So NIV (2011) which renders the verse: 'Let the message of Christ dwell among you richly as you teach and admonish one another with all wisdom through psalms, hymns, and songs from the Spirit, singing to God with gratitude in your hearts'.

Curiously, not all commentators are agreed that this is Paul's meaning. For example, on the basis of evidence gleaned from some bilingual manuscripts and early commentaries, Paul Foster suggests that the syntax of Colossians 3:16 is comprised of three clauses:[33]

a. Let the Word of Christ dwell in you richly,
b. teaching and admonishing each other in all wisdom,
c. singing psalms, hymns, spiritual songs, with thankfulness in your hearts to God.

This leads him to conclude that 'the various forms of lyrical praise should not be understood as the mode for teaching and admonishing one another as mentioned in the previous clause, any more than Paul's acts of teaching and admonishing in Col. 1:28 should be thought of as being sung'.[34]

While Foster's understanding of the structure of Paul's verse is uncontroversial, it is difficult to see how it necessitates his conclusion. Simply identifying the three clauses, does not itself explain the relationship between them. In the Greek text, they are transparently linked. The participles (teaching, admonishing, singing) in clauses 'b' and 'c', all connect to main verb ('Let ... dwell in') in clause 'a'. The question, then, is whether clauses 'b' and 'c' speak of two distinct modes by which the 'word of Christ' is to indwell the church – i.e., by teaching and admonishing (on the one hand) and by singing psalms, etc (on the other) – or whether clause 'c' modifies clause 'b' – i.e., 'Paul wants the community to teach and admonish each other *by means of* various kinds of songs'.[35] The HCSB appears to opt for the former interpretation, and so inserts an 'and' between clauses 'b' and 'c'. But there is no conjunction in the Greek text and so no justification for inserting one in English. Moo's verdict, therefore, is difficult to gainsay: 'Our text ... identifies 'psalms, hymns and songs from the Spirit' as the way in which believers teach and admonish each other'.[36]

Such an understanding does not imply that singing is the only means of teaching and admonishing. Songs do not replace the functions of

---

[33] Paul Foster, *Colossians* (London: Bloomsbury, 2016), 358-359.
[34] Foster, *Colossians*, 361.
[35] Moo, *Colossians*, 288 (emphasis mine).
[36] Moo, *Colossians*, 289.

prophets and teachers, any more than they do away with the need for apostolic instruction. And, obviously, one can address others without singing to them. Paul is simply drawing attention to the most potent way in which *mutual and simultaneous* teaching and admonition take place in the Christian assembly – as we sing the Word of Christ together and to one another. Paul's point, then, is not that singing is *one of the means* by which mutual instruction can be given (true as that might be), but that it is *the primary means* by which this can be done *corporately and reciprocally.*[37]

For this reason, it is highly unlikely that Paul had solo singing in mind.[38] Antiphonal or responsorial singing is more possible, as this was used in the Hebrew synagogues of the first century, and there is some evidence of it in the writings of both Pliny the Younger and Ignatius.[39] But for the reasons we've given, it is most likely that he is envisaging full congregational participation.

Paul's first concern, however, is to highlight the God-given potency of 'psalms, hymns and spiritual songs' to enable a rich indwelling of the life-giving 'word of Christ'. This, of course, can only have taken place by means of 'songs that were biblically grounded and theologically substantive, songs that both communicated truth and called for heartfelt consecration, repentance, and devotion to the Lord'.[40] His larger point, then, is that *the corporate singing of such songs is a powerful and productive form of one another 'Word ministry'.*

This explains why Paul (as we saw in Ephesians 5:18-21) regards singing as a means of being filled by the Spirit. For to be indwelt by the Word of Christ is not a different experience from being 'filled by the Spirit'.

---

[37] Spoken liturgy would, of course, accomplish a similar goal. But, for the reasons outlined in earlier chapters, sung liturgy (which is what hymns are) has additional potency.

[38] Not that he would have objected to it. If the Word of Christ can be spoken or read by one person to others, it can also be sung by one person to others.

[39] Ralph P Martin, *Carmen Christi: Philippians ii. 5-11 in Recent Interpretation and in the Setting of Early Christian Worship* (Cambridge: CUP, 1967), 3-4; Egon Wellesz, *A History of Byzantine Music and Hymnography* (Oxford: OUP, 1949), 26-28, 35.

[40] Sam Storms, 'Singing Truth (3:16)', *Sam Storms* (n.d.): https://www.samstorms.org/all-articles/post/singing-truth--3:16-.

Christ's person cannot be detached from His Word, nor is He separate from His Spirit. Indeed, the Word is 'the sword of the Spirit' (Ephesians 6:17) and it is by the Spirit that Christ himself dwells in our hearts through faith (Ephesians 3:17). Therefore, as we sing the Word of Christ to one another, 'with gratitude in our hearts to God', we are not only instructed and made wise, but we have a greater experience as a community of what it means to be filled full in Christ, in whom 'the whole fullness of deity dwells bodily' (Colossians 2:9-10).

Finally, it is worth pondering Paul's addition of the word 'richly' (Gk. *plusiōs*) at the end of the phrase: 'Let the Word of Christ dwell in you *richly*'. The reason for it – highlighted by the present, active, imperative form of the verb 'to dwell' – is that *believers have a responsibility to ensure that they sing Christ's Word in such a way that it deeply enriches them.* There is, of course, an inherent richness to the Word of Christ, but this objective reality needs to be met by a conscious and enthusiastic reception on the part of believers, so that it might indwell us (both personally and corporately) in a truly beneficial way. [41]

There is an implicit warning here. For it is evidently possible for Christ's Word to indwell us poorly, superficially or ineffectually. How might this happen? Not only by singing songs that are untrue (and so not His Word at all) or unclear (and so not understood by those who sing them), but also by singing in a faithless or perfunctory way – that is, without any genuine intellectual or emotional engagement or a heartfelt desire to glorify God and edify others. Just as it is incumbent upon those who write and choose our songs that they are rich in the Word of Christ, so it is incumbent upon all of us who sing them that they dwell in us richly.

Luther clearly understood this, believing that the primary purpose of the hymn was 'to preach the word of God, and thus be the word of God, preached to the gathered assembly by those singing it to each other'. [42] Not surprisingly, most of Luther's hymns (e.g., 'To Shepherds as They Watched by Night', 'A Mighty Fortress Is Our God', 'Christ Jesus Lay in Death's Strong Bands'), and most classical Lutheran chorales, are 'sermons in song'. Luther also held that the purpose of the hymn was

---

[41] James D G Dunn, *The Epistles to the Colossians and to Philemon* (Grand Rapids: Eerdmans, 1996), 237.
[42] Gracia Grindal, 'The Rhetoric of Martin Luther's Hymns: Hymnody Then and Now', *Word & World* 26.2 (Spring 2006), 179.

larger than the edification (or building *up*) of those who are already believers; it had potential to edify (or build *in*) not-yet believers too! Luther thus contended that those who truly believe the gospel should 'gladly and willingly sing and speak about it so that others also may come and hear it'.[43]

Like Ephesians 5:18-21, Paul's teaching in Colossians 3:15-17 leaves us in no doubt that *corporate singing of the Word of Christ is essential for the life, health and growth of the church of Christ.* It is a potent form of 'Word ministry', and so an important mode of gospel proclamation, theological education and ethical instruction. 'In this regard, it is significant that much of what is taken to be hymnic in the Pauline corpus has a strong didactic and paraenetic function (e.g., Phil 2:6-11; Col 1:15-20; 1 Tim 3:16)'.[44] Congregational singing is also a mutual ministry; one in which all members of the body of Christ are to be engaged. It is therefore profoundly unifying for the church, and one of the ways in which the peace of Christ exercises its rule in our hearts (Colossians 3:15).

3.   The Hymns of the Apocalypse[45]

When we come to the Book of Revelation, the first thing to note is that it is, quite literally, hymn-laden.[46] Fifteen hymns or hymn fragments are commonly recognised (4:8; 4:9-11; 5:9-10; 5:12; 5:13; 7:10; 7:11-12; 11:15; 11:16-18; 12:10-12; 15:2-4; 16:5-7; 19:1-4; 19:5; 19:6-8), and some scholars have identified even more.[47] While there is some debate about how many

---

[43] Martin Luther, 'Preface to the *Babst Hymnal, 1545*', in *Liturgy and Hymns* (eds. Ulrich S Leupold and Helmut T Lehmann; trans. Paul Zeller Strodach; vol. 53 of *Luther's Works*, American Edition, eds. Jaroslav Pelikan and Helmut T Lehmann; Philadelphia: Fortress, 1965), 333.

[44] Lincoln, *Ephesians*, 345. For a helpful survey of hymnic material in Paul, see Ralph P Martin, 'Hymns, Hymn Fragments, Songs, Spiritual Songs', in Gerald F Hawthorne, Ralph P Martin, Daniel G Reid, *Dictionary of Paul and His Letter* (Leicester: IVP, 1993), 419-423.

[45] The following section is a condensed version of Robert S Smith, 'Songs of the Seer: The Purpose of Revelation's Hymns', *Themelios* 43.2 (2018), 193-204.

[46] Although it is the term 'song' (Gk. *ōdē*) that is used throughout John's prophecy, the designation 'hymn' is also equally fitting. See Craig R Koester, *Revelation: A New Translation with Introduction and Commentary* (New Haven & London: Yale University Press, 2014), 127.

[47] For example, 1:6, 13:4 and 18:1-24. A further reference to singing 'a new song' is found in 14:3, but nothing of the song's content is given.

of the hymns are depicted as being sung – given that some are described as simply being 'said' (e.g., 4:8, 11) and others as exclaimed with a 'loud voice' (e.g., 5:12-13), there is a strong case to be made that most of them were 'said by singing'.[48] But whatever the precise number of songs, Craig Koester's verdict is difficult to gainsay: 'Music plays a larger role in the book of Revelation than in any other book of the New Testament, and few books in all of Scripture have spawned more hymns sung in Christian worship today'.[49]

Over the last half century, much attention has been given to the sources or origins of the songs of Revelation. Where exactly did all of these hymns come from? What accounts for their form and content? These are interesting questions to explore, for it is clear that John is providing us with more than 'mere transcriptions' of what he saw and heard.[50] His numerous allusions to Old Testament texts within the songs are evidence of this (e.g., Isaiah 6:3 in 4:8b and Daniel 12:7 in 4:9b).[51] However, affirming that various factors have influenced John's presentation of the heavenly hymns, does not mean that they have simply been taken over from the liturgy of the early churches.[52] Rather, it is clear that the 'praises offered in heaven establish the focus for worship on earth'.[53] That is,

---

[48] While only two of the songs of Revelation are explicitly described as being sung (5:9-10 and 15:2-4), several observations suggest that they are far from alone. First, Revelation 5:9 reveals that what the living creatures and the twenty-four elders *say*, they say by *singing*. Second, the description of the song of 5:9 as a '*new* song', suggests an earlier song. The obvious candidate is the parallel 'song' in 4:9-11 – with its identical opening ('Worthy are you ...') and, more than likely, the 'song' of 4:8 also. Third, both of these observations open up the real possibility that other (perhaps all?) of the book's 'songs' were, similarly, *said by singing*.

[49] Craig R Koester, 'The Distant Triumph Song: Music and the Book of Revelation', *Word & World* 12.3 (Summer, 1992), 243.

[50] Steven Grabiner, *Revelation's Hymns: Commentary on the Cosmic Conflict* (London/New York: T&T Clark, 2015), 6.

[51] See also the discussion of Revelation 15:2-4 and its relation to the song of Moses in Exodus 15 in Richard J Bauckham, *The Climax of Prophecy: Studies on the Book of Revelation* (London: T & T Clark, 1993), 296ff.

[52] *Pace* Larry W Hurtado, *One God, One Lord: Early Christian Devotion and Ancient Jewish Monotheism* (Philadelphia: Fortress, 1988), 103; Martin, *Worship in the Early Church*, 45; Edgar Krentz, 'The Early Dark Ages of the Church', *Concordia Theological Monthly* 41 (1970), 67-85.

[53] Koester, *Revelation*, 129.

instead of reflecting earthly patterns in his portrayal of heaven, 'John wrote to encourage his readers to *reflect the pattern of the heavenly assembly in their life on earth*.'[54]

3.1.   The function of the songs

This leads us to probe more deeply into the function of the songs.[55] In light of the fact that the proper worship of God is, arguably, the ultimate issue and aim of the book (19:10; 22:9), and given that 'an aggressive programme of Caesar-worship' was being 'forced upon the population of the Roman Empire in the latter part of the first century',[56] there is merit to the claim that 'John's depiction of the ceremonial in the heavenly throne room has been significantly influenced in its conceptualization by popular images of Roman imperial court ceremonial'.[57] But rather than simply echoing various aspects of that ceremonial, John has heightened and expanded their cosmic significance.[58] 'The result', writes David Aune, 'is that the sovereignty of God and the Lamb have been elevated so far above all pretensions and claims of earthly rulers that the latter, upon comparison, become only pale, even diabolical imitations of the transcendent majesty of the King of kings and Lord of lords'.[59]

So what does all this mean for Revelation's songs and what might it tell us about their place and importance? It is noteworthy that the heavenly worship scenes, and the hymns that are so central to them, 'always occur at critical junctures in the book and provide commentary on the significance of the action'.[60] They thus perform the function of

---

[54] Peterson, 'Worship in the New Testament', 89-90 (emphasis his).

[55] For a detailed and insightful treatment of the book's main songs, particularly in light of their relationship to the cosmic conflict theme, the leitmotif of John's prophecy, see Grabiner, *Revelation's Hymns*, chapters 5-7.

[56] Peterson, 'Worship in the New Testament', 85. For a brief but useful discussion of the dating of the book, and a persuasive argument in favour of a Domitianic date (e.g., 95–96AD), see D A Carson and Douglas J Moo, *An Introduction to the New Testament* (Leicester: Apollos, 2005), 707-712.

[57] David E Aune, 'The Influence of Roman Imperial Court Ceremonial on the Apocalypse of John', *BR* 18 (1983), 22.

[58] Aune, 'The Influence of Roman Imperial Court Ceremonial on the Apocalypse of John', 22.

[59] Aune, 'The Influence of Roman Imperial Court Ceremonial on the Apocalypse of John', 22.

[60] Grant Osborne, *Revelation* (Grand Rapids: Baker, 2002), 47.

interpreting the narrative sections of the prophecy. Consequently, 'all the major events of the book are accompanied by heavenly hymns'.[61] The five hymns found in chapters 4-5, in particular, not only 'stand at the beginning of the vision section, functioning as an impressive portal into the rest of the apocalypse, but they set the tone for the following chapters (6-21)'.[62] The hymns, more broadly, have also been shown to connect both to each other and to the larger narrative theme of cosmic conflict.[63]

But the songs do more than simply create connections, set tone and convey understanding. They also model celebration and, by so doing, teach a pattern of responding to tribulation that feeds 'the patient endurance' (1:9; 2:2, 19; 3:10; 13:10; 14:12) required of all those who will conquer. Otherwise put, by confirming ultimate reality and the certainty of divine victory, the songs inspire confidence, engender hope and impart strength. In fact, as Steven Grabiner has ably demonstrated, 'the hymns are sung with the accusing voice of Satan in the background', and thereby play a key role in both the refutation of those accusations and the vindication of God and His people.[64] Therefore, if John's aim was to assist beleaguered believers 'to maintain their faith in Christ and resist every temptation to idolatry and apostasy, the hymnic material, with its focus on the sovereignty of God and the victory of the Lamb, must have provided the original recipients with every encouragement to do just that'.[65]

Furthermore, the very image of the Lamb, standing 'as though it had been slain' (5:6), and the repeated mentions of His blood (1:5; 7:14; 12:11), speak powerfully 'to the 'walking wounded' who suffer under Roman oppression'.[66] Indeed, in chapter 17, the great harlot (an image of Rome) is depicted as being 'drunk with the blood of the saints, the blood of the

---

[61] Josephine M Ford, 'The Christological Function of the Hymns in the Apocalypse of John', *Andrews University Seminary Studies*, 36 (1998), 211.

[62] Gottfried Schimanowski, "Connecting Heaven and Earth': The Function of the Hymns in Revelation 4-5', in Ra'anan S. Boustan and Annette Yoshiko Reed, *Heavenly Realms and Earthly Realities in Late Antique Religions* (Cambridge: CUP, 2004), 67.

[63] Grabiner, *Revelation's Hymns*, 218-219, 223-224.

[64] Grabiner, *Revelation's Hymns*, 225.

[65] Peterson, *Engaging with God*, 277.

[66] Luke A Powery, 'Painful Praise: Exploring the Public Proclamation of the Hymns of Revelation', *Theology Today* 70.1 (2013), 72.

martyrs of Jesus' (17:6). In light of this, the honour and praise that is given to the once slain Lamb, precisely because of His sacrifice, links up with the encouragement given to believers to love not their lives even unto death, but instead to overcome by 'the blood of the Lamb and by the word of their testimony' (12:11).

Along with these powerful encouragements, the songs contain both implicit and explicit warnings. For example, the songs of exclusive devotion to the Holy One who sits on the throne (e.g., chapter 4) remind believers 'not to assimilate comfortably into the idolatry of the surrounding culture'.[67] Likewise, by hearing that all wisdom, wealth, glory and power belong to the Lamb (e.g., chapter 5), believers are tacitly warned 'not to let the prosperous times lull them into a state of spiritual torpor'.[68] The message is clear, and has already been sounded in the letters to the seven churches: only those who confess Jesus' name before others will have their names confessed by Jesus before His Father and before His angels (3:5).

It is also important to note that the warnings contained in the heavenly hymns are not only given to believers (the prophecy's *primary audience*), but also to unbelievers (its *secondary audience*). We see this, for example, in the 'eternal gospel' which is proclaimed 'to those who dwell on earth, to every nation and tribe and language and people' (14:6). The proclamation is uncompromising: 'Fear God and give him glory, because the hour of his judgement has come, and worship him who made heaven and earth, the sea and the springs of water' (14:7). In short, the call to worship and the threat of judgement go hand in hand.

Of particular interest is the way in which the theme of judgement is expounded in a number of the songs. For example:

> The nations raged,
>> but your wrath came,

---

[67] Koester, 'The Distant Triumph Song', 245. For further discussion of the importance of the throne motif to the book's hymns, the pastoral implications that flow from the connection, and the praise offered to Him who sits on the throne and to the Lamb, see Laszlo Gallusz, *The Throne Motif in the Book of Revelation* (London: Bloomsbury T&T Clark, 2014), 111-113, 153-158, 230-232, 333-334.

[68] Powery, 'Painful Praise', 72.

and time for the dead to be judged,
and for rewarding your servants, the prophets and saints
and those who fear your name,
both small and great —
and for destroying the destroyers of the earth.' (11:18)

5 ... 'Just are you, O Holy One, who is and who was,
for you brought these judgements.
6 For they have shed the blood of saints and prophets,
and you have given them blood to drink.
It is what they deserve!' (16:5-6)

1 ... 'Hallelujah!
Salvation and glory and power belong to our God,
2 for his judgements are true and just;
for he has judged the great prostitute
who corrupted the earth with her immorality,
and has avenged on her the blood of his servants.' (19:1-2)

The songs of Revelation, then, not only contain promises of salvation for God's servants but threats of destruction for His (and His people's) enemies. This is why the songs unashamedly celebrate the doom of all who worship the beast and its image, and rejoice in the justice of Babylon's demise. This response is summed up in the shout of the heavenly multitude: 'Hallelujah! The smoke from her goes up for ever and ever' (19:3).

The pastoral purpose of these musical foreshadowings of the future is to fortify believers against compromise and embolden them in their worship and witness. Inasmuch as they simultaneously warn a rebellious world that Jesus Christ is nothing less than 'the ruler of the kings of earth' (1:5) and the one who will 'repay each one for what he has done' (22:12), they may also be described as having both an evangelistic purpose and a political purpose. That is, the hymns of Revelation not only function as calls to worship and encouragements to the church, but as 'coded musical weapons that struggle against and seek to undermine the ruling empire of its day'.[69] My near namesake, Robert H Smith, puts it well:

---

[69] Powery, 'Painful Praise', 71.

The Seer is possessed by a burning desire to show Christians that hymns and doxologies and obeisance are to be made only to God and the Lamb and never to the emperor or his agents. So the hymns of Revelation have not simply evolved gradually and peacefully out of temple and synagogue patterns. They are weapons in John's warfare against Rome and its claims.[70]

3.2. The theology of the songs

Given that the hymns are clearly pedagogical, what more can be said about their theological content? What are some of their more notable themes? In answer to this question, four brief observations will have to suffice.

The *first* is revealed by what Paul Barnett has described as the 'two-beat rhythm' of many of the book's songs. In chapter 4, for example, the first beat of this rhythm is 'the evangelical proclamation of the four creatures that *holy, holy, holy* is the Lord God Almighty. ... The second beat is the worshipful response of the twenty-four elders representing the redeemed people of God'.[71] Moreover, this two-beat pattern is not only a feature of the elders' *actions* but applies equally to their *words*. As Barnett writes:

> They begin by declaring God to be worthy to receive glory, honour and power. Then, in reverse order, they state the evangelical truth that is the basis for their worship of God. It is because (Greek: *hoti* = for) by his will God *created all things* that they declare God to be *worthy of glory, honour and power.*[72]

This first observation leads naturally to a *second*. This relationship between the two 'beats', highlights the theological order of things: revelation comes first, response comes second. In other words, creaturely praise and adoration is generated by divine reality and activity. Consequently, God is praised *because* He is holy, *because* He is eternal, *because* He is creator (4:8, 11). Similarly, the Lamb is deemed worthy *because* He was slain, *because* His blood has purchased persons for God,

---

[70] Robert H Smith, '"Worthy is the Lamb" and Other Songs of Revelation', *Currents in Theology and Mission* 25.6 (Dec 1998), 504.
[71] Paul W Barnett, *Apocalypse Then and Now: Reading Revelation Today* (South Sydney: Aquila Press, 2004), 70 (emphasis his).
[72] Barnett, *Apocalypse Then and Now,* 70-71 (emphasis his).

because He has now 'made them a kingdom and priests to our God, and they shall reign on the earth' (5:9-10).

This second observation leads naturally to a *third*. The songs not only teach us that we should respond to God's being and doing, they expound His nature, character and works. So, for example, in chapter 4, the Lord God Almighty is described as 'thrice-holy' (cf. Isaiah 6) and as the one who transcends time and history. Furthermore, this is theology with a clear pastoral purpose. As Greg Beale notes:

> The titles show that the intention of this crucial vision is to give the supra-historical perspective of 'the one who is, was, and is coming', which is to enable the suffering readers to perceive his eternal purpose and so motivate them to persevere faithfully through tribulation.[73]

This, then, is an important vision for suffering Christians to see, particularly in light of (what Leon Morris calls) 'the troubled state of the little church'.[74] The songs, likewise, are equally important for fearful believers to hear, if not to sing themselves. For they remind the church that 'God has not abandoned the world, and it is indeed His world. He made all things and made them for His own purpose'. Evil may be a reality, but it is not ultimate and not in control: 'the divine purpose still stands'.[75]

This third observation naturally extends to a *fourth*. For more remarkable still is the fact that the divine attributes and glorious ascriptions applied to God in chapter 4 are then extended to Jesus in chapter 5. This is underscored by the fact that just as the one who sits on the throne is 'worthy' (4:11), so the one to whom He gives the scroll is also 'worthy' (5:9). Indeed, 'the parallels between 4:9-11 and 5:8-12 make it clear that Christ is being adored on absolutely equal terms with God the Creator!'[76]

---

[73] Gregory K Beale, *The Book of Revelation: A Commentary on the Greek Text* (Grand Rapids: Eerdmans, 1999), 333.
[74] Leon L Morris, *The Book of Revelation: An Introduction and Commentary* (Leicester: IVP, 1987), 92.
[75] Morris, *The Book of Revelation*, 92.
[76] Peterson, 'Worship in the New Testament' in Worship', 88.

Little wonder that the final song of chapter 5 ends by combining the two songs into one:

> To him who sits on the throne and to the Lamb
> be blessing and honor and glory and might for ever and ever!
> (5:13b)

The Christological title, 'the Lamb', also deserves further comment, as it is without doubt 'the central feature of the christology' of the book, occurring some 29 times (six times in the songs). [77] Of particular note is the two-fold fact that it is 'only the Lamb who is capable of opening the book of visions (5:9), which shows a christology containing a revelatory element, and only he can open the seals of the scroll of destiny, which points to a christology full of sovereignty'.[78] Jesus is, therefore, not only 'the slain Lamb' but also 'the eschatological Ram' – the one who is 'Lord of lords and King of kings' (17:14).[79]

Alongside these clear affirmations of the divinity of Jesus' person is the grateful and joyful acknowledgement of His saving work – a work that could not have been accomplished apart from His full humanity.[80] In this sense, the Apocalypse can be said to locate Jesus *both* on the side of Deity *and* on the side of the creatures. But the reason for His incarnation is equally clear: substitutionary-sacrifice. For it is not His life that atones but

---

[77] Donald Guthrie, 'The Christology of Revelation', in Joel B Green and Max Turner (eds.), *Jesus of Nazareth: Lord and Christ: Essays on the Historical Jesus and New Testament Christology* (Grand Rapids: Eerdmans, 1994), 400.

[78] Guthrie, 'The Christology of Revelation', 401.

[79] Of course, He can only be the latter because He was the former; He is victorious through sacrifice, He conquers because He suffered. See further Osborne, *Revelation*, 35.

[80] Curiously, the Apocalypse has been accused of providing 'little evidence ... for an incarnational Christology' (so Guthrie, 'The Christology of Revelation', 403). In point of fact, Jesus' humanity is everywhere presupposed, if not explicitly affirmed. For example, His birth is affirmed in 12:1-5, as is His descent from David in 5:5 and 22:16, and His identity with 'the Son of Man' in 1:13 and 14:14. Furthermore, His choosing of 12 apostles is affirmed in 21:14 and references to words spoken during His 'state of humiliation' are recorded in 3:3 and 16:15. Most importantly, the reality of His death is a major theme of the book (1:5, 18; 2:8; 5:9; 7:14; 12:11). See further M Eugene Boring, 'Narrative Christology in the Apocalypse', *CBQ* 54 (1992), 702-723.

His death – the shedding of His blood. Thus, right from the opening chapter, He is presented as the one 'who has freed us from our sins *by his blood*' (1:5). Believers are therefore defined as those who have 'washed their robes and made them white in *the blood of the Lamb*' (7:14; cf. 12:11). So while the Apocalypse contains only a vague reference to the historical particulars of the event of the cross (11:8), Donald Guthrie is right to remark that 'its shadow is everywhere present'.[81]

Given that the cross is the key to the Lamb's victory, it is not surprising that the theme of redemption is particularly prominent in the songs (e.g., 5:9-10, 12; 7:10; 12:10-11; 19:1). Nor is it surprising that the first song sung in praise of the Lamb is described as a 'new song' (5:9). As Morris writes: 'The Lamb's saving work has created a new situation and this elicits a new outburst of praise. No song meant for another situation quite fits this'.[82] But there is more to it than this. The word 'new' (Gk. *kainos*) occurs a total of nine times in the Apocalypse (2:17; 3:12[x2]; 5:9; 14:3; 21:1[x2], 2, 5). In each other instance it relates to some aspect of the world to come. The 'new song' thus celebrates the fulfilment of the new covenant and 'the foundation for the eschatological renewal of creation by the Messiah who has been appointed by God'.[83] Robert Mounce puts it this way: 'The song of the Lamb is a new song because the covenant established through his death is a new covenant. It is not simply new in point of time, but more important, it is new and distinctive in quality'.[84] This, then, is a song that will go on forever, for the redemption it proclaims is eternal! It is for this reason that 'Revelation may be claimed to be the capstone of NT Christology'.[85]

---

[81] Guthrie, 'The Christology of Revelation', 402.

[82] Morris, *The Book of Revelation*, 98-99.

[83] Hengel, *Between Jesus and Paul*, 83

[84] Robert H Mounce, *The Book of Revelation* (Grand Rapids: Eerdmans, 1998), 147.

[85] Guthrie, 'The Christology of Revelation', 409. While the same cannot be said for New Testament Pneumatology, there is no reason to regard the Apocalypse as anti-trinitarian. See Jan A du Rand, '"... Let Him Hear What the Spirit Says ...": The Functional Role and Theological Meaning of The Spirit in The Book of Revelation', *Ex Auditu* 12 (1996), 43-58; Louis A Brighton, 'Christological Trinitarian Theology in the Book of Revelation', *Concordia Journal* 34.4 (2008), 292-297; Hee Youl Lee, *A Dynamic Reading of the Holy Spirit in Revelation:*

3.3.   Heeding the hymns of the Apocalypse

The revelation of Jesus Christ was given to John to encourage true worship of the living God in the interadvent period – a period marked by tension, temptation, suffering, persecution and martyrdom. As one who shares with his readers 'the tribulation and the kingdom and the patient endurance that are in Jesus' (1:9), John's prophecy is delivered into a context of intense conflict – a conflict he knows first-hand. The songs, which form such a significant part of the book, speak into this conflict and minister to those caught up in it. This explains why they have not only been a rich source of inspiration for church liturgy and Christian hymnody, but a profound encouragement to believers, especially those experiencing opposition. It also highlights their importance for us in the west today, where religious freedom is daily being sacrificed in the name of erotic freedom, and where those who follow the Lamb are coming under increasing pressure to bow at the altar of the sexual revolution. We need to heed the call of these songs!

This is entirely in line with the purpose of the prophecy. For while the book's hymns are transparently doxological, they are also richly pedagogical and pointedly pastoral. That is, they are designed both to glorify God and to instruct and strengthen His people. Moreover, as the hymns define and declare the character of God, they not only 'shape the identities of those who worship him', but 'shape the way worshipers see their place in a world where they live with competing claims upon their loyalties, while fostering their hope in God's kingdom'.[86] Therefore, the more we listen to them and make them our own, the more they summon and assist us 'to enter into healthier relations to Creator and creation, to Redeemer and all the redeemed. And in the singing, we also begin to move at least tentatively toward exiting from our multiple idolatries and abuses of the things of creation'.[87]

In addition to this, the songs have much to teach us about the nature, content and purpose of praise, as well as 'the importance of singing God's praise in a way that is truly honouring to him and helpful to his people'.[88]

A Theological Reflection of the Functional Role of the Holy Spirit in the Narrative (Eugene: Wipf & Stock, 2014), 68-129.
[86] Koester, *Revelation*, 130.
[87] Smith, 'Worthy is the Lamb', 506.
[88] Peterson, *Engaging with God*, 278.

Indeed, in light of the deadness and/or shallowness of much contemporary praise, they raise a series of questions (some quite pointed) about both our praise practices and, particularly, our song choices. For example:

- Do they major on praising God for his character and his mighty acts in history on our behalf?
- Do they draw us to the great truths of the gospel?
- Is the choice of songs too narrowly focussed on only one aspect of the gospel?
- How well does the language we use reflect the power and meaning of the language used in biblical forms of praise?
- Do our hymns and songs help us to rejoice in God's gracious and powerful rule, acknowledge its blessings and look forward to its consummation in the new creation?
- Do they challenge us to take a firm stand against every manifestation of evil and to bear faithful witness to the truth of the gospel in our society? [89]

While this present age persists, and the Dragon continues to make war on 'those who keep the commandments of God and hold to the testimony of Jesus' (12:17), we need the songs of the book of Revelation – to hear and sing them, be taught and fortified by them, and to echo their themes and concerns in our own musical compositions. But their purpose is not for this life only. They are a foretaste of our eternal future, as Jonathan Edwards rightly saw:

> So far therefore as we sing this song on earth, so much shall we have the prelibations of heaven ... And this will make our public assemblies some image of heaven, and will make our sabbath days and thanksgiving days some resemblance of that eternal sabbath and thanksgiving that is solemnized by that innumerable company of angels and spirits of just men made perfect.[90]

---

[89] Peterson, *Encountering God Together*, 124-125.
[90] Jonathan Edwards, 'They Sang a New Song (Rev 14:3a)', in Harry S Stout (ed.), *Sermons and Discourses, 1739-1742; WJE Online Vol. 22* (New Haven: Jonathan Edwards Centre at Yale University, 2008), 241.

Conclusion

The particular aim of this chapter has been to expound the kerygmatic and didactic (or 'Word ministry') dimension of corporate singing in the New Testament. What we have seen is that congregational song is one of the ways in which the Word of God is preached by the people of God to both insiders and outsiders alike. It is both a way of evangelising the lost and encouraging the found, and therefore a key means by which the church is built in both quantity and quality.

In the final Part of this book, we will probe more deeply into the practical implications of such an understanding for contemporary church life. But in light of all that we have seen, we dare not underestimate the power of the song in the gospel purposes of God. Of course, singing is not the only or primary way in which God's will is being accomplished in this world, so it is clearly not of the *esse* (being) of the church. But as it is a means of being filled by God's Spirit, indwelt by Christ's Word, strengthened in suffering and prepared for glory, it is certainly of the *bene esse* (well-being) of the church. Edward Bickersteth summarises the main reasons why:

> The privilege of singing is as great as the duty is clear. It tends to store the memory with the precious truths of God's word, and thus assists in maintaining spirituality of mind and constant communion with our God. It greatly helps the poor to acquire the knowledge of the things of Christ. It furnishes constant subjects of devout meditation. The heart is prepared for and supported under trials, and many a vital and precious truth is received and expressed in a hymn, which the unhealthy moral atmosphere of the world would otherwise quench and suppress. What holy feelings, what heavenly desires, what sublime joys, what nearness to God and all holy things, have experienced Christians thus enjoyed![91]

---

[91] Edward Bickersteth, *Christian Psalmody, A Collection of Above 900 Psalms, Hymns and Spiritual Songs Selected and Arranged for Public, Social, Family and Private Worship* (London: S Staughton, 1839), v.

PART THREE:
HELPING GOD'S PEOPLE CHANGE

At the time when divine truth lay buried under this vast and dense cloud of darkness – when religion was sullied by so many impious superstitions – when by horrid blasphemies the worship of God was corrupted, and His glory laid prostrate – when by a multitude of perverse opinions, the benefit of redemption was frustrated, and men, intoxicated with a fatal confidence in works, sought salvation anywhere rather than in Christ – when the administration of the Sacraments was partly maimed and torn asunder, partly adulterated by the admixture of numerous fictions, and partly profaned by traffickings for gain – when the government of the Church had degenerated into mere confusion and devastation – when those who sat in the seat of pastors first did most vital injury to the Church by the dissoluteness of their lives, and, secondly, exercised a cruel and most noxious tyranny over souls, by every kind of error, leading men like sheep to the slaughter; – then Luther arose, and after him others, who with united counsels sought out means and methods by which religion might be purged from all these defilements, the doctrine of godliness restored to its integrity, and the Church raised out of its calamitous into somewhat of a tolerable condition. The same course we are still pursuing in the present day.[1]

So wrote John Calvin in 1543 to 'the most invincible Emperor Charles V', and to 'the most illustrious Princes and other Orders', as they prepared for 'A Diet of the Empire' to be held at the Imperial city of Spires. Calvin's purpose was to set out the principal reasons for the Protestant

---

[1] John Calvin, *The Necessity of Reforming the Church* (1543): https://www.monergism.com/thethreshold/sdg/calvin_necessityreform.html.

Reformation and, in so doing, 'to show how just and necessary the causes were which forced us to the changes for which we are blamed'.[2]

It is Calvin's last sentence (of the words quoted) to which I want to draw attention: 'The same course we are still pursuing in the present day'. Obviously, the 'present day' for Calvin was a few years shy of the midpoint of the sixteenth century. But the work that Calvin made his own in his day is the work that we must make our own in our day. For the task of reformation continues and, in fact, is bequeathed afresh to each new generation.

The purpose of these final two chapters (as well as the four appendices to follow) is to help distil the lessons of the preceding chapters, chart the path ahead, and identify the keys to the musical reformation of the church in our 'present day'.

---

[2] Calvin, *The Necessity of Reforming the Church.*

11. Three Keys to Musical Reformation

I couldn't believe he actually said it. But he did. After leading us so helpfully in prayer, the service leader then uttered these puzzling words: 'In order to stretch our legs and help us concentrate better during the sermon, we're going to stand and sing ...' We did indeed stretch our legs and, no doubt, getting our blood circulating and exercising our lungs helped us to concentrate during the sermon that followed. But were these the only reasons, or even the main reasons, why we sang 'the hymn before the sermon'?

As we've seen throughout this book, the Bible gives us numerous reasons to sing. But, interestingly, stretching our legs before the sermon is not among them. We sing to praise, we sing to pray, we sing to preach. In fact, as we've seen in the last two chapters, inasmuch as we are singing the Word of Christ, our singing is part of the sermon or, perhaps better, an additional sermon. Either way, it is a sermon we *all* preach, to each other as well as to ourselves. And the fact is – and it's a humbling one for those of us who are preachers! – the songs we sing are often remembered long after our sermons have been forgotten. Warren Wiersbe, therefore, has good reason to write:

> I am convinced that congregations learn more theology (good and bad) from the songs they sing than from the sermons they hear. Many sermons are doctrinally sound and contain a fair amount of biblical information, but they lack that necessary emotional content that gets hold of the listener's heart. Music, however, reaches the mind and the heart at the same time. It has power to touch and move the emotions, and for that reason can become a wonderful tool in the hands of the Spirit or a terrible weapon in the hands of the Adversary.[1]

As we dig more deeply into the issues of ongoing reformation and practical implementation, we need to ask how we engage in congregational singing so that it accomplishes its God-intended

---

[1] Warren Wiersbe, *Real Worship: Playground, Battleground, or Holy Ground?* (Grand Rapids: Baker, 2000), 137.

purposes. What steps do we need to take to ensure that it truly glorifies God and effectively edifies His people – rather than being used by 'the Adversary' to divide and destroy? Let me suggest three keys.

1. Educating Christian Pastors

The *first key* is to *educate Christian pastors as to the value and importance of church music (in general) and congregational singing (in particular)*. My appeal here is not only to theological lecturers and ministry trainers but also to pastors themselves. For all of us who have been appointed to oversight in the church have a life-long responsibility to engage in ongoing theological and ministerial self-development, and that includes growing in our understanding of the theology and practice of church music ministry.

Luther had very strong views on this subject, as the following words reveal:

> I always love music; who so has skill in this art, is of a good temperament, fitted for all things. We must teach music in schools; a schoolmaster ought to have skill in music, or I would not regard him. Neither should we ordain young men as preachers, unless they have been well exercised in music.[2]

Luther was not being frivolous. Nor did he hold such a view because he was a musical aficionado. He understood that 'music has a theological reason for being: it is a gift of God, which comes from the "sphere of miraculous audible things", just like the word of God. Music is unique in that it can carry words. Since words carry the word of God, music and the word of God are closely related'.[3] In his 1538 'Preface to Georg Rhau's Symphonoiae Iucundae', Luther expresses his thinking in this way:

> Thus it was not without reason that the fathers and prophets wanted nothing else to be associated as closely with the Word of God as music ... After all, the gift of language combined with the gift of song was only given to man to let him know that he should

---

[2] Martin Luther, *The Table Talk of Martin Luther* (trans. and ed. William Hazlitt; London: H G Bohn, 1857), 340.
[3] Paul Westermeyer, *Te Deum: The Church and Music* (Minneapolis: Augsburg Fortress, 1998), 144-145.

praise God with both word and music, namely, by proclaiming [God's word] through music and by providing sweet melodies with words.[4]

Consequently, and in typically humourous fashion, Luther claimed that anyone 'who gives this some thought and yet does not regard [music] as a marvelous creation of God, must be a clodhopper indeed and does not deserve to be called a human being; he should be permitted to hear nothing but the braying of asses and the grunting of hogs'.[5] Doubtless, Luther was being playfully provocative, but behind his rhetoric lies the serious theological conviction that God is 'praised and honored and we are made better and stronger in faith when his holy Word is impressed on our hearts by sweet music'.[6] Nor was this theory only for Luther; he had seen it play out in practice. In fact, there is strong evidence that, despite beginning in 1517, the Reformation in Germany only really took hold 'after 1523, when the hymns first began to appear'.[7] It is hardly surprising, then, that Luther came to the conclusion that 'next to the word of God, music deserves the highest praise'.[8]

In support of such a view, both common human experience and a range of human sciences highlight the capacity of music and song to assist cognition and aid recollection. For example, there is mounting neuroscientific evidence of the way in which 'songs enhance cognitive processing by involving the brain in sequencing of information, short-term as well as long term memory storage, and motor learning as individuals respond to auditory cues'.[9] This evidence confirms what is common human experience. As Wenham writes: 'Everyone finds poetry

---

[4] Luther, 'Preface to Georg Rhau's Symphonoiae Iucundae, 1538', 323-324.
[5] This is Walter Buszin's translation of a sentence in Luther's, 'Preface to Georg Rhau's Symphonoiae Iucundae'. It appears in Walter A Buszin, 'Luther on Music', *The Musical Quarterly* 32:1 (1946), 85.
[6] Martin Luther, 'Preface to the Burial Hymns, 1542', in *Liturgy and Hymns* (eds. Ulrich S Leupold and Helmut T Lehmann; trans. Paul Zeller Strodach; vol. 53 of *Luther's Works*, American Edition, eds. Jaroslav Pelikan and Helmut T Lehmann; Philadelphia: Fortress, 1965), 328.
[7] Robin A Leaver, *The Whole Church Sings: Congregational Singing in Luther's Wittenberg* (Grand Rapids: Eerdmans, 2017), 7.
[8] Luther, 'Preface to Georg Rhau's Symphonoiae Iucundae, 1538', 323.
[9] Dale B Taylor, *Biomedical Foundations for Music as Therapy* (Saint Louis: MMB Music, 1997), 41.

easier to memorise than prose. Its rhythm and symmetries, repetitions and rhymes, combine to assist the memory'.[10] Adding music to poetry only tends to deepen and accelerate this process. Consequently, if 'poetry is more memorable than prose, songs are more memorable than poems'.[11]

If we map onto this phenomenon the well-known connections between music and the imagination, as well as, what some call, 'embodied music cognition' (i.e., the interrelationship between music, song and our mental and physical systems),[12] then we have additional evidence of the capacity of songs to implant the Word of Christ deeply within us. James Smith puts it this way:

> Singing is a mode of expression that seems to reside in our imagination more than other forms of discourse. Partly because of cadence and rhyme, partly because of the rhythms of music, song seems to get implanted in us as a mode of bodily memory. Music gets 'in' us in ways that other forms of discourse rarely do. A song gets absorbed into our imagination in a way that mere texts rarely do. Indeed, a song can come back to haunt us almost, catching us off guard or welling up within our memories because of situations or contexts that we find ourselves in, then perhaps spilling over into our mouths till we find ourselves humming a tune or quietly singing. The song can invoke a time and a place, even the smells and tastes of a moment. The song seems to have a privileged channel to our imagination, to our *kardia* [heart], because it involves our body in a unique way ... Perhaps it is *by* hymns, songs, and choruses that the word of Christ 'dwells in us richly' and we are filled with the Holy Spirit.[13]

As we have seen, there is no 'perhaps' about it. This is precisely Paul's teaching in Colossians 3 and Ephesians 5. Therefore, if we want Christ's sheep to be richly nourished by Christ's Word, then we'd better make sure

---

[10] Wenham, *Psalms as Torah*, 50.
[11] Wenham, *Psalms as Torah*, 50.
[12] Jakub Ryszard Matyja, 'Music-animated body', *Avant. The Journal of the Philosophical-Interdisciplinary Vanguard* 2.1 (2011), 205-209.
[13] James K A Smith, *Desiring the Kingdom: Worship, Worldview, and Cultural Formation* (Grand Rapids: Baker Academic, 2009), 171.

they sing it. Wise shepherds of the flock will appreciate these things and minister accordingly.

2.   Equipping Church Musicians

The *second key* to musical reformation is to *equip church musicians to be wise and effective servants of the sung Word.* It should go without saying that all who are involved in church music ministry need some degree of teaching and training (including those who look after sound and projection). But those who have been entrusted with various leadership responsibilities – e.g., team-directing, song-choosing, music-arranging or song-leading – need additional assistance and encouragement. Of course, it's sometimes true that those who lead church music have not only sought out training, but also done more reading and thinking about these issues than their pastors! Perhaps this is understandable, given their interests and responsibilities. But this does not absolve pastors from pursing the first of our keys, nor from providing local support and supervision. Ministerial delegation is one thing; pastoral abdication quite another.

Furthermore, pastors should not underestimate the degree to which many a church musician is tossed to and fro by the ever-changing trends of popular music and the not-always-well-thought-through attempts of some Christian artists to mimic them. There is also what John Bell calls 'The fallout from a performance culture', which risks turning church musicians into entertainers and congregations into spectators. [14] For all these reasons and more, wise direction from (and humble submission to) those in pastoral authority is vital for church music ministry to thrive. In short, as well as entrusting music ministry to suitably able members of the body, pastors need to equip and encourage them in an ongoing way. The ministry of the Word in song is too important for it to be otherwise.

So what is it that church musicians need to know? The place to begin is with *their 'job description'.* How might that be expressed? Here's my

---

[14] Bell, *The Singing Thing,* 113-120. On this point, see also the helpful challenge of Ed Stetzer, 'Worship Leaders Are Not Rock Stars: Instead of performing music, we should be leading worship', *Christianity Today* (March, 2015): http://www.christianitytoday.com/edstetzer/2015/march/worship-leaders-are-not-rock-stars.html.

'tweaked version' of the definition provided by Bob Kauflin in his book, *Worship Matters.*[15]

> *A faithful church musician*
> *humbly magnifies the greatness of God in Jesus Christ*
> *through the power of the Holy Spirit*
> *by skilfully combining God's Word with music,*
> *thereby enabling the gathered church*
> *to praise and pray to the living God,*
> *to proclaim the gospel to a needy world,*
> *to teach and admonish one another,*
> *to cherish God's presence together,*
> *and to live for God's glory.*[16]

As useful as it would be to do so, it is not my purpose here to unpack each line of this definition. Kauflin does this more than successfully in his book. What we will do instead is explore three implications that are embedded in it and flow from it.

2.1. The need for a 'service mindset'

The *first* of these is *the need for a 'service mindset'*; that is, for church musicians to be committed to humble, self-effacing service of both God and others. Therefore, as the above definition makes clear, the *first objective* of every church musician ought to be the magnification of the greatness of God in Jesus Christ by the power of the Holy Spirit. Then, as a necessary outworking of this, the *second objective* ought to be to enable the church to praise Him, pray to Him and preach His Word in song. As we have elaborated on these objectives in earlier chapters, as well as the

---

[15] Bob Kauflin, *Worship Matters: Leading Others to Encounter the Greatness of God* (Wheaton: Crossway, 2008), 55.

[16] The adjustments I have made are these: (1) I have substituted 'church musician' for 'worship leader'; (2) I have inserted the word 'humbly' before 'magnifies'; (3) I have added the line: 'to praise and pray to the living God'; (4) I have substituted 'enabling' for 'motivating'; (5) I have added 'to a needy world' after 'proclaim the gospel'; (6) I have added the line 'to teach and admonish one another'; (7) I have added the word 'together' after 'God's presence'. None of these changes and additions signal any disagreement with Kauflin's definition (although I do think 'worship leader' is a potentially confusing label), and all are, in fact, implicit in it.

various dangers, toils and snares that threaten them, I will not expound them further here.

What does need to be said, however, is that servant-hearted ministry is not the antithesis of clear-minded leadership. For the Word to be ministered effectively in song, the body of Christ needs encouragement and direction. Obviously, the type or style of leadership required may vary from church to church, gathering to gathering, or even song to song. Sometimes *directive leadership* is needed (e.g., if a congregation is unfocussed or a song needs explaining or is not well-known), other times more *supportive leadership* is most appropriate (e.g., if a congregation is eager to sing and knows the songs well). Effective musical leadership will, therefore, be both discerning and flexible. What's more, if it is understood that *the church is the choir* (not the audience) and that *the goal is for the church to sing* (not to be sung to), then this will determine the kind of assistance song-leaders need to provide.[17] Their consistent aim will be to *help the congregation to sing the Word of Christ.*

This is not to suggest that the ideal form of leadership is necessarily passive or 'from behind'. Even the most mature believers need direction and encouragement to engage heart, soul, mind and strength in the service of the sung Word. This is why John Wesley, for example, instructed Methodist ministers to interject during congregational hymn singing with questions like, 'Now do you know what you said last? Did it suit your case? Did you sing it as to God, with the spirit and understanding also?'[18] Obviously, the helpfulness of such coaxing needs to be gauged by its effects. What should not be in doubt is the need for insightful and proactive musical leadership.

This applies to the musical accompaniment just as much as to the song leading. My 'golden rule' for all church musicians (whatever their instrument) is this: *play in such a way that you best serve the song, that the song might best serve the people, that the people might best serve the Lord and each other.* This is why Kauflin's definition speaks of 'skilfully

---

[17] These issues are discussed at greater length in Raiter and Smith, *Songs of the Saints*, 202-204.

[18] Taken from the Manuscript Minutes of the Bristol Methodist Conference, 'Thursday, May 15th, 1746', found in Henry D Rack (ed.), *The Works of John Wesley: Volume 10: The Methodist Societies: The Minutes of Conference* (Nashville: Abingdon, 2011), 182.

combining God's Word with music', and where the biblical injunction to 'play skilfully' (Psalm 33:3) reveals its importance. Considerable skill is needed to play in such a way that people find it easy to sing and easy to take in the words they're singing and sharing without frustration or distraction.

But the greatest need of all is for good judgement. This is underscored by Paul's call to minister the Word of Christ by 'teaching and admonishing one another *in all wisdom*' (Colossians 3:16). This, as Moo explains, means engaging in sung Word ministry 'in appropriate ways, governed by insight into the situation and the people being addressed'.[19] This, in turn, means that obstacles to effective sung Word ministry will be identified and removed. So, for example, if a congregation isn't singing, despite the musicians' skilful playing, the reason will first need to be discerned. John Bell highlights some common causes of congregational 'songlessness':

> It may be because the physical line-up of musicians reminds them of a concert where they listen rather than of a community where they join in. Or it may be because they haven't been taught the songs; or because the songs are from the performance rather than the participatory category, and the musicians have not recognised that there is a difference.[20]

Of course, it may be none of these reasons or a complex of factors. Wisdom is therefore required to work out what is going wrong and how to make it right. Bell's last point, however, leads naturally to a second implication of our definition.

2.2.   The importance of selecting suitable songs

The *second* implication is *the importance of selecting suitable songs*. Obviously, if the Word of God is going to be sung, the songs need to contain and communicate that Word. This is non-negotiable. But often there is more to suitability than truthfulness. What works well for one congregation or occasion may not work well for another. So, again, discernment is needed in order to choose wisely and well.

---

[19] Moo, *Colossians*, 289.
[20] Bell, *The Singing Thing*, 120.

As someone who has been selecting congregational songs for over 30 years, I can assure readers that choosing appropriate songs for a church gathering is no easy task. Even when working with a strong pool of songs, a range of considerations need to be taken into account. For example:

- What is the purpose of the gathering?
- What is the theme of the sermon?
- What songs/hymns does the congregation know?
- What has been sung recently?
- What songs/hymns are the musicians capable of playing effectively?
- How many songs/hymns are required?
- Where should they be placed?

A range of formal and aesthetic factors also need to be checked:

- Are they all the same type of song (e.g., hymns of praise)?
- Are all the songs/hymns in the same key?
- Are they all the same tempo?
- Are they all the same mood?
- Are they all in the first-person singular?
- Are they all in the first-person plural?
- Do they all follow the same structure?

While these issues are not determinative, and sometimes there may be reason to focus things very narrowly, usually a mixture of these features is helpful.

When it comes to general guiding principles, thankfully we are not the first Christians to have wrestled with these matters and there is much wisdom to be gleaned from those who've gone before us. For example, the *Minutes of the Methodist Conference* for 15 May, 1746, record John Wesley's response to the question: 'How shall we guard more effectually against formality in public singing?' His answer is instructive:

1. By the careful choice of hymns proper for the congregation. 2. In general try choosing hymns of praise or prayer, rather than descriptive of particular states. 3. By not singing too much, seldom

a whole hymn at once, seldom more than 5 or 6 verses at a time. 4. By suiting the tune to the hymns.[21]

What is of particular help here is Wesley's call for 'careful' and 'proper' choices, his advice not to over-sing, his concern for a good fit between text and tune, and his desire that expressions of objective truth ('hymns of praise or prayer') outweigh expressions of subjective feeling ('descriptive of particular states'). This last point should not be heard as a criticism of hymns that express elements of personal response or songs that are cast in the first-person singular – as these were notable features of many of the Wesley brothers' hymns.[22] His concern is for biblical balance and appropriate reverence.[23]

Charles Spurgeon's description of the work of the preacher can also be applied to the work of those who choose and lead our songs: 'To know truth as it should be known, to love it as it should be loved, and then to proclaim it in the right spirit, and in its proper proportions'.[24] How, then, might such balance and reverence be achieved in our congregational singing? Four things are needed.

(i) We need to establish and maintain the right order of priorities. This means allowing the *objective realities* of divine revelation (as revealed in

---

[21] The Minutes of the Bristol Methodist Conference, 'Thursday, May 15th, 1746', 182.

[22] Think, for instance, of some of the titles/first lines of Charles Wesley's better-known compositions: 'And can it be that *I* should gain an interest in the Saviour's blood?' or 'O for a thousand tongues to sing *my* great redeemer's praise' or 'Jesus, lover of *my* soul, let *me* to Thy bosom fly'.

[23] However, it is interesting to note that in later life John Wesley frowned on any hint of overfamiliarity with God – especially the use of amatory or intimate language in preaching or prayers. As he revealed in his 1789 sermon, 'On Knowing Christ After the Flesh', he particularly disliked the word 'dear' (e.g., 'dear Lord' or 'dear Saviour), and was even critical of Charles (who had died the year before), for using such expressions in his hymns. His concern was that such language 'has a direct tendency to abate that tender reverence due to the Lord [our] governor'. See Albert Outler (ed.), *The Works of John Wesley: Volume 4: Sermons IV: 115-151* (Nashville: Abingdon, 1987), 102. See also the larger discussion in Steven Darsey, 'John Wesley as Hymn and Tune Editor', *The Hymn* 47.1 (January 1996), 18-19.

[24] Charles Haddon Spurgeon, *An All-Round Ministry* (Edinburgh: The Banner of Truth Trust, 1960), 8.

Scripture) to generate and shape our *subjective response* to that revelation (as articulated in our songs). This was Wesley's concern, and it's one we should share. This does mean that every song has to have the same proportions. That could hardly be said of the biblical psalms. No, different songs are needed to do different jobs – some teach us what God has done for us, others instruct us as to what we should to do in response. Many do both. [25] Nevertheless, a church's over-all repertoire should be monitored (and, if needs be, adjusted) to make sure that God's revelation determines our response to Him. If not, we predispose ourselves to the error of the medieval church, where 'divine service was performed as a work whereby God's grace and salvation might be won'.[26]

(ii) We need to make sure that the dominant themes of Scripture are the dominant themes of our songs. As Isaac Watts saw clearly, this requires taking care that 'greatest Part of them are suited to the General State of the Gospel, and the most common Affairs of Christians'.[27] Once again, this does not mean that every song has to fit within a narrow thematic range. Indeed, across a calendar year or two, there is merit in striving for the kind of biblical breadth reflected in John Wesley's *A Collection of Hymns for the Use of the People Called Methodists* (1780). This is a hymnal in which few, if any, major doctrinal heads are left unexplored and which was intended by Wesley to be 'a little body of experimental and practical divinity;'[28] i.e., a systematic and pastoral theology in song. Nevertheless, as we pursue appropriate biblical breadth, we will also

---

[25] In his discussion of different hymn forms, Peter Ward notes: 'Analysing individual hymns can be problematic because more than one of these forms may be present at the same time. A lengthy song may switch from objective to reflexive modes as the hymn reaches its climax' (*Selling Worship*, 207).

[26] Martin Luther, 'Concerning the Order of Public Worship, 1523', in *Liturgy and Hymns* (eds. Ulrich S Leupold and Helmut T Lehmann; trans. Paul Zeller Strodach; vol. 53 of *Luther's Works*, American Edition, eds. Jaroslav Pelikan and Helmut T Lehmann; Philadelphia: Fortress, 1965), 11.

[27] Watts, 'Preface', to *Hymns and Spiritual Songs*, v.

[28] John Wesley, 'Preface' (*Oct. 20*, 1799) in *A Collection of Hymns for the Use of the People Called Methodists* (London: John Mason, 1780), 4. As an illustration of the hymnal's breadth, the 'Index of Scriptural Allusions' in the latest critical edition of the *Collection* contains some 2,500 entries drawn from every biblical book, excepting Nahum and Philemon!

ensure that the things of 'first importance' remain at the centre of our singing.

(iii) As noted above, a mixture of different song types is usually to be preferred. Hymnologist, Lionel Adey, differentiates between 'objective hymns' – which praise God, plead for mercy or convey teaching, 'subjective hymns' – which contain 'a core of objective assertions', but usually focus on their implications and are often in the first person, and 'reflexive hymns' – which focus on the actions of worshippers.[29] All of these have their place, albeit in descending order of importance. Different songs also do different jobs, and no song can do everything. Some songs are calls to worship, others are confessions of sin. Some songs proclaim the gospel, others tease out its ethical implications. Some songs praise God for His creative work, others for His redemptive activity. The great value of variety is that 'one hymn's individual piety will be balanced by another's social conscience, and I can entrust myself to the viewpoint of the hymn I'm singing now, confident that it will be enriched, corrected, and supplemented by the next hymn I sing and by the hymns I sing next Sunday'.[30]

(iv) We do well to keep the past and the present in, what Marva Dawn calls, 'a dialectical tension of tradition and reformation'.[31] This means striving for cultural contemporaneity without squandering our musical heritage.[32] It has been well said that 'an appreciation of the devotional treasure of the ages bequeathed to us in the legacy of the historic worship of the church helps us resist the rampant chronological snobbery of our own age'.[33] In short, new does not always equal better. At the same time, we need to be wary of perpetuating 'tradition that has grown stale',[34] and similarly aware of our missional responsibility to communicate clearly

---

[29] Lionel Adey, *Hymns and Christian 'Myth'* (Vancouver: University of British Columbia, 1986), 7.

[30] Brian Wren, *Praying Twice: The Music and Words of Congregational Song* (Louisville: Westminster John Knox Press), 365.

[31] Dawn, *Reaching Out Without Dumbing Down*, 93.

[32] These things are further discussed in Raiter and Smith, *Songs of the Saints*, 208-212.

[33] J Ligon Duncan III, 'Foundations for Biblically Directed Worship', in Philip Graham Ryken, Derek W H Thomas, and J Ligon Duncan III (eds.), *God: A Vision for Reforming Worship* (Phillipsburg: P&R, 2003), 61.

[34] Dawn, *Reaching Out Without Dumbing Down*, 93.

with our culture. This, then, pushes us toward contemporaneity, but not in such a way that we are forced to sever our connections with the past.[35] While the ideal mix of past and present will depend on context, the solution is bound to be of the 'both-and', rather than the 'either-or', variety.[36]

There are also a number of obvious criteria that make for a suitable congregational song. Kent Hughes puts it this way: 'Whatever the genre of music, it must meet three criteria: text, tune, and fit'.[37] To expand, the words must be true and clear, the music must be singable and memorable, and the two must work naturally and effectively together. Rather than say more about these criteria here, I have discussed them at length in Appendix 4. The practical point, however, is that song-selectors need to see themselves as what Hicks calls 'theological dieticians', and so develop good 'criteria for food selection'.[38] Hicks' own list is as follows:

- Is it singable?
- Does the music complement the lyrics?
- Is it theologically precise?
- Is it logically coherent?
- Is it aimed Godward?
- Is it in line with the gospel?

To this we could easily add the following:

- Is it aimed otherward?
- Is it comprehensible?
- Does it fit the occasion?

In fairness to Hicks, he is more than alert to these additional questions. In fact, as to the last, he helpfully paints the following scenario: You have found 'a wonderful, upbeat, joyful song ready to introduce to your congregation'. And yet 'a recent national event spurred on by racial unrest has your congregation feeling the weight of suffering and injustice'. What

---

[35] Frame, *Contemporary Worship Music*, 19.
[36] Frame, *Contemporary Worship Music*, 41.
[37] R Kent Hughes, 'Free Church Worship: The Challenge of Freedom', in D A Carson (ed.), *Worship by the Book*. (Grand Rapids: Zondervan, 2002), 169.
[38] Hicks, *The Worship Pastor*, 74.

then should you do? Hicks' answer is simple: leave it for another day. For '[t]hough the song passes your criteria with flying colors, your congregation is not in a place to receive it'.[39] This is wise advice and highlights the point with which we began this section: suitable song-choice decisions will always be made not only with reference to sound selection criteria, but with a sensitivity to context.

2.3. The relationship between the various forms of word ministry

The *third* implication is *the need to understand the relationship between the various forms of word ministry*. Notwithstanding all that we have seen and said about the value and importance of singing the Word of Christ, the New Testament is clear that the sung Word should neither replace nor eclipse the spoken Word in the regular gatherings of the congregation. Paul's instruction to Timothy implicitly makes this point: 'Until I come, devote yourself to the public reading of Scripture, to exhortation, to teaching' (1 Timothy 4:13). *The spoken Word, therefore, is primary; the sung Word secondary.* This primacy is reflected in the fact that God has prioritised the giving of ministers of the spoken Word to His church (Acts 13:1; 1 Corinthians 12:28; Ephesians 4:11). For this reason, congregational singing ought never to become 'the tail that wags the dog'. It is not to dominate, let alone squeeze out, the preached word; it is to function as its handmaid and complement, its servant and supplement.

Luther understood this. For while it has been claimed that he won more converts through his hymns than he did through his sermons,[40] he was in no doubt that 'the preaching and teaching of God's Word is the most important part of divine service'.[41] Consequently, Luther had no interest in elevating the sung Word over the preached Word. Moreover, passages like Ephesians 4:11 convinced him that there are ministries of the Word that the people as a whole cannot perform, 'but must entrust or have them

---

[39] Hicks, *The Worship Pastor*, 74-75.

[40] Donald P Hustad, *Jubilate II: Church Music in Worship and Renewal* (Carol Stream: Hope Publishing, 1993), 188. The claim appears to date back to a remark made in 1620 by the German Jesuit, Adam Contzen.

[41] Martin Luther, 'The German Mass and Order of Service, 1526', in *Liturgy and Hymns* (eds. Ulrich S Leupold and Helmut T Lehmann; trans. Augustus Steimle; vol. 53 of *Luther's Works*, American Edition, eds. Jaroslav Pelikan and Helmut T Lehmann; Philadelphia: Fortress, 1965), 68.

entrusted to one person'.[42] He thus had a high view of pastoral office and saw the preaching of God's Word as its key task – a task that 'stands at the heart of the community into which God incorporates individual believers'. [43] Without taking anything away from his view of congregational singing as the *'viva vox evangelii*, the living voice of the Gospel',[44] Luther believed that

A Christian congregation should never gather together without the preaching of God's Word and prayer, no matter how briefly ... Therefore, when God's Word is not preached, one had better neither sing nor read, or even come together.[45]

Not surprisingly, in Luther's estimation, 'the most important reform needed in the worship of the church of his day was to re-establish the centrality of the reading and preaching of the Word in public worship'.[46] Why so? Because in his rich theology of the Word, in all its various forms – oral, written and sacramental, 'preaching stands at the center of the Christian life. There in the sermon, in the move from law to gospel, the fundamental struggle of the Christian is played out every time the preacher ascends the pulpit'.[47] For Luther, then, the preaching of God's Word has a necessary primacy over all other forms of Word-ministry, including the sung Word.

---

[42] Martin Luther, 'On the Councils and the Church, 1539', in *Church and Ministry III* (eds. Eric W Gritsch and Helmut T Lehmann; trans. Charles M Jacobs; vol. 41 of *Luther's Works*, American Edition, eds. Jaroslav Pelikan and Helmut T Lehmann; Philadelphia: Fortress, 1966), 154.

[43] Robert Kolb and Charles P Arand, *The Genius of Luther's Theology: A Wittenberg Way of Thinking for the Contemporary Church* (Grand Rapids: Baker Academic, 2008), 180.

[44] Carl F Schalk, *Luther on Music: Paradigms of Praise* (St Louis: Concordia, 1988), 30.

[45] Luther, 'Concerning the Order of Public Worship, 1523', 11. The ecclesiology behind this understanding is succinctly expressed in the *Augsburg Confession*: 'The church is the gathering of all believers, in which the gospel is purely preached and the holy sacraments are properly administered' (7:1).

[46] Hughes Oliphant Old, *The Reading and Preaching of the Scriptures in the Worship of the Christian Church: Volume 4: The Age of the Reformation* (Grand Rapids: Eerdmans, 2002), 39.

[47] Carl Trueman, *Luther on the Christian Life: Cross and Freedom* (Wheaton: Crossway, 2015), 97.

The history of revivals also bears out the wisdom of Luther's understanding and priorities. While there are exceptions to the claim that the church 'can never sing its way into revival',[48] the fact remains that whenever church leaders have attempted to revive their people primarily by means of song alone, they have soon found that 'without proper teaching, preaching, and praying, they will have less and less authentically to sing about'.[49] This fact has led authors Henry Blackaby, Richard Blackaby and Claude King to distinguish between Word-centred and experience-centred revivals. They explain the difference as follows:

> Word-centered revivals are generally led by pastors and are anchored in preaching. Experience-centered revivals are led by laypeople who participate through sharing their testimonies and singing. While both are legitimate forms of revival, Word-centered revivals are less vulnerable to abuse and extravagance, and as a result they tend to last longer.[50]

None of this should be seen as a disparagement of the place of singing. Indeed, the importance of song to the history of revivals parallels its importance in Luther's theology and ministry. Furthermore, as we have seen repeatedly in this and the previous chapter, singing is a biblically mandated way of preaching the Word of God.

But because it is not the primary way, the relationship between the *said Word* and the *sung Word* is critical to understand and the priority of the former vital to maintain. This does not mean that every song sung in a service has to tie tightly to the sermon (although that is often a good way

---

[48] Brian Edwards, *Revival! A People Saturated with God* (Durham: Evangelical Press, 1994), 31. For example, it was the singing of William Williams' 'O'er the gloomy hills of darkness' and other hymns taken from his collection, *Songs of those upon the Sea of Glass* (1762), that led to the Welsh revival of 1763. See further D Martyn Lloyd-Jones, *Singing to the Lord* (Bridgend: Bryntirion Press, 2003), 23-24.

[49] Henry Blackaby, Richard Blackaby and Claude King, *Fresh Encounters: God's Pattern for Spiritual Awakening* (Nashville: B&H Publishing, 2009), 206.

[50] Blackaby, Blackaby and King, *Fresh Encounters*, 206. They cite the Welsh revival of 1904 as a case in point, suggesting that because Evan Roberts did not sufficiently emphasise preaching during the services, 'the meetings consisting of much singing and testifying, were open to abuses that eventually quenched the Spirit's work' (206).

of doing things). Nor does it mean that if there is a total of 30 minutes of singing, then there must always be at least 40 minutes of sermon (although time is usually a good measure of priorities). What it does mean is that the singing of God's Word will be sensitive to and supportive of the reading and preaching of God's Word. Wise church musicians will understand this and will conduct all aspects of their music ministry accordingly.

3.   Encouraging Christian Congregations

The third key to ensuring that our singing glorifies God and edifies His people is *to regularly encourage congregations to give themselves wholeheartedly to the ministry of song.* Needless to say, if our singing is to be truly congregational, then the participation of every member is essential. But why is this important? As Luther understood, it is 'a necessary consequence of the doctrine of the royal priesthood of all believers'.[51]

Luther's thought was thoroughly biblical in this regard and may be summarised in the following five points.

(i) According to 1 Peter 2:4-5, 'all who have the faith that Christ is a priest for them in heaven before God ... are true priests ... Therefore all Christian men are priests, all women priestesses, be they young or old, master or servant, mistress or maid, learned or unlearned. Here there is no difference, unless faith be unequal'.[52]

(ii) According to 1 Peter 2:9, one of the reasons believers have been incorporated into this new royal priesthood is so that 'you may proclaim the excellencies of him who called you out of darkness into his marvelous light'. This, for Luther, had 'an obvious connection with the role of music and worship as praise and proclamation'.[53]

---

[51] Schalk, *Luther on Music*, 42.
[52] Martin Luther, 'Treatise on the New Testament', in *Word and Sacrament I* (eds. E Theodore Bachmann and Helmut T Lehmann; trans. Jeremiah J Schindel; vol. 35 of *Luther's Works*, American Edition, eds. Jaroslav Pelikan and Helmut T Lehmann; Philadelphia: Fortress, 1960), 101.
[53] Schalk, *Luther on Music*, 42.

(iii) Given that the new priesthood is corporate and the verb in 1 Peter 2:9 plural (i.e., '*you* [all] may proclaim'), Luther believed it was necessary that 'all pray and sing and give thanks together; here there is nothing that one possesses or does for himself alone; but what each one has also belongs to the other'.[54]

(iv) While Luther maintained a place for a choir, its purpose was to sing with the congregation, not instead of it. This, however, could take various forms. Antiphonal singing was certainly envisaged in his 1529 publication of *The Latin Litany Corrected* and *The German Litany*, where the choir is designated 'the first choir' and the congregation 'the second choir'. As Robin Leaver remarks: 'Congregation and choir sang the hymns together, almost certainly in alternation stanza by stanza'.[55]

(v) Luther's preference was for hymns to be sung by 'the whole choir'.[56] By this he meant 'the totality of the gathered community at worship, choir and congregation singing together'.[57] Behind this lay the conviction that God 'wants to hear the throngs and not me or you alone, or a single isolated Pharisee'. So, he advises, 'sing with the congregation and you will sing well. Even if your singing is not melodious, it will be swallowed up by the crowd'.[58]

The English reformers saw things similarly. As is well-known, a major motivation behind the liturgical reformation and Cranmer's production of the 1552 *BCP* was a desire to have church 'ceremonies' in the language of the people. As Cranmer stated it: 'Saint Paul would have such language

---

[54] Martin Luther, 'Sermon at the Dedication of the Castle Church, Torgau, 1544', in *Sermons I* (eds. John W Doberstein and Helmut T Lehmann; trans. John W Doberstein; vol. 51 of *Luther's Works*, American Edition, eds. Jaroslav Pelikan and Helmut T Lehmann; Philadelphia: Fortress, 1959), 333.

[55] Leaver, *The Whole Church Sings*, 116.

[56] This language is found at numerous points in Luther's 'The German Mass and Order of Service, 1526'. For example, Luther writes: 'After the Epistle a German hymn, either "Now Let Us Pray to the Holy Ghost" or any other, is sung by the whole choir' (74).

[57] Leaver, *The Whole Church Sings*, 150.

[58] Martin Luther, 'An Exposition of the Lord's Prayer for Simple Laymen, 1519', *Devotional Writings I* (eds. Martin O Deitrich and Helmut T Lehmann; trans. Martin H Bertram; vol. 42 of *Luther's Works*, American Edition, eds. Jaroslav Pelikan and Helmut T Lehmann; Philadelphia: Fortress, 1969), 60.

spoken to the people in the Church, as they might understand, and have profit by hearing the same'.[59] Of course, intelligibility did more than make comprehension possible, it allowed for 'common prayer'; i.e., corporate participation by the people. While the English reformers were not of one mind about the value of congregational singing, they were uniform in their conviction that corporate worship 'is not the preserve of a priest functioning in isolation from the people. Nor are the people intended to be uncomprehending spectators or mere attenders. They are there *to worship*, and they should therefore be able to participate intelligently in the service'.[60]

Two centuries later, John Wesley evinced a similar passion for (what Horton Davies calls) 'a more democratic type of worship'.[61] That is, Wesley shared the reformers' concern for *corporateness*. He was, therefore, adamant that the whole congregation must sing, not just a trained choir. This was one of the reasons he loathed choral anthems, as these gave a small group a monopoly on the praise and robbed the congregation of an opportunity to proclaim Christ's Word in song.[62] Wesley also understood the power of songs to teach. He thus 'sought to exploit the potential of corporate song as a memorable means of concisely

---

[59] 'The Preface', *The Boke of common prayer, and administracion of the Sacramentes, and other rites and Ceremonies in the Churche of Englande*, 1552.
[60] Philip Edgcumbe Hughes, *Theology of the English Reformers* (London: Hodder & Stoughton, 1965), 146-147 (emphasis his). Consequently, after Mary took the throne in 1553, returning all services to Latin, Nicholas Ridley lamented from his prison cell that now 'the people neither can tell how to pray, nor what to pray for; and how can they join their hearts and voices together, when they understand no more what the voice signifieth, than a brute beast?' See Nicholas Ridley, 'Letter VIII (Coverdale)', in Henry Christmas (ed.), *The Works of Nicholas Ridley D. D.: Sometime Lord Bishop of London: Martyr 1555* (Eugene: Wipf & Stock, 2008), 350.
[61] Horton Davies, *Worship and Theology in England: From Watts and Wesley to Maurice, 1690-1850* (Book 2, Section III, 1961: Grand Rapids: Eerdmans, 1996), 201.
[62] In his journal entry for Tuesday, August 9, 1768, Wesley writes of a church service at which he preached in Neath, saying that he was 'disgusted at the *manner* of singing'. What he meant, as he goes on to explain, was that 'twelve or fourteen persons kept it to themselves and quite shut out the congregation'. See Richard P Heitzenrater and W Reginald Ward (eds.), *The Works of John Wesley: Volume 22: Journals and Diaries* (Nashville: Abingdon, 1983), 152 (emphasis his).

conveying a theological message to his followers and likely converts through the marriage of words and music'.[63]

These anecdotes reveal that our evangelical forebears understood the meaning and implications of Ephesians 5:19 and Colossians 3:16 only too well. All of God's people are to sing the Word of Christ to one another. As Harold Best has written: 'A congregation is just as responsible to sing the gospel as the preachers are to preach it. These two tasks (singing and preaching) jointly undertaken to their fullest, then reduce themselves to one common act'.[64] Such an understanding does not obliterate the distinction between preaching the Word and singing the Word, nor does it undermine the precedence of the former. It simply reminds us that distinction does not mean separation, any more than order of priority entails a denial of unity. For the fact of the matter is that

> The Word goes forth among God's people in several ways, including their conversing with each other and consoling one another. The Word in the mouth of the called Servant of the Word, the pastor, is the same Word that the Holy Spirit places in the mouths of all believers. In their mouths it has the same power as it does in preaching and formal absolution. It forgives sins, defies evil, and bestows life and salvation.[65]

Conclusion

True Christianity is marked not only by *subscription* to a Reformed evangelical doctrine of Scripture, but even more importantly by *submission* to the living Word of God in Scripture. Consequently, as Robert Jenson writes: 'The churches most faithful to Scripture are not those that legislate the most honorific propositions about Scripture but those that most often and thoughtfully sing and listen to it'.[66]

The aim of this chapter has been to encourage such thoughtful singing and listening by expounding a number of keys to ongoing musical

---

[63] Martin V Clarke, *John Wesley and Methodist Music in the Eighteenth Century: Principles and Practice* (Doctoral thesis, Durham University, 2008), i.

[64] Harold Best, *Music Through the Eyes of Faith* (San Francisco: Harper, 1993), 192.

[65] Kolb and Arand, *The Genius of Luther's Theology*, 188.

[66] Robert W Jenson, *Systematic Theology II* (Oxford: OUP, 1999), 273.

reformation. What we have seen is that the ministries of the pulpit, the lectern and the music stand are all of a piece, and God's people need them all. This is not to say that songs sit on a par with sermons or that hymns can replace homilies. There is an evident priority given to the spoken Word in Scripture. The sung Word is to reinforce it and respond to it.

Nevertheless, the power of the sung Word should not be underestimated. As Bishop J C Ryle noted in his discussion of the hymnody of Augustus Toplady:

There is an elevating, stirring, soothing, spiritualizing, effect about a thoroughly good hymn, which nothing else can produce. It sticks in men's memories when texts are forgotten. ... The makers of good ballads are said to sway national opinion. The writers of good hymns, in like manner, are those who leave the deepest marks on the face of the church.[67]

In other words, our songs are our teachers. 'What the Church sings, therefore, is determinative of the faith which the singers hold'.[68] Furthermore, by them we teach and admonish both ourselves and each other, instructing and reminding one another of vital gospel truth and the appropriate response to them. Bob Kauflin illustrates this phenomenon with characteristic insight:

When we sing, 'Though the eye of sinful man thy glory may not see,' we're counselling each other that our sins have caused a separation between us and God that we can't close ourselves. The words 'You give and take away' teach us that whether God bring us to a place of abundance or lack, we can still bless the Lord. With the lyrics 'Because the sinless Savior died, my sinful soul is counted free' we're admonishing each other not to live in condemnation for sins that the Savior has already paid for. 'Riches I heed not, nor man's empty praise' instructs us in the futility of living for fleeting

[67] J C Ryle, *Christian Leaders of the 18th Century* (Carlisle: Banner of Truth, 1970), 382.
[68] Bell, *The Singing Thing*, 57.

wealth or the applause of others. Singing is meant to be an educational event.[69]

Little wonder, then, that the Scripture says: 'Let the word of Christ dwell in you richly, teaching and admonishing one another in all wisdom, singing psalms and hymns and spiritual songs, with thankfulness in your hearts to God' (Colossians 3:16).

---

[69] Bob Kauflin, *True Worshippers: Seeking What Matters to God* (Wheaton: Crossway, 2015), 105-106.

12. The Road Ahead

In March, 1560, the Church of England bishop, John Jewell, wrote the following to the Italian-born reformer, Peter Martyr Vermigli:

> Religion is now somewhat more established than it was. The people are everywhere exceedingly inclined to the better part. The practice of joining in church music has very much conduced this. ... You may now sometimes see at Paul's cross, after the service, six thousand persons, old and young, of both sexes, all singing together and praising God. This sadly annoys the mass-priests, and the devil. For they perceive that by these means the sacred discourses sink more deeply in the minds of men, and that their kingdom is weakened and shaken at almost every note.[1]

The devil and the mass-priests were right to be annoyed. As we have seen throughout this book, 'singing together and praising God' is one of the divinely appointed means by which we are indwelt by the Word of Christ and filled by the Spirit with the fullness of God. It is one of the ways He is establishing His kingdom and building His church. It is a powerful *means of grace*.

It is also a powerful *result of grace*. That is, singing is a natural (and often commanded) response to divine intervention, protection, presence and blessing. On this point, the testimony of the psalmists and the prophets is both unequivocal and overwhelming.[2] For example:

> The Lord is my strength and my song,
>   and he has become my salvation;
> this is my God, and I will praise him,
>   my father's God, and I will exalt him.
>
> *Exodus 15:2*

---

[1] Taken from Hastings Robinson (ed.), *The Zurich Letters, Comprising the Correspondence of Several English Bishops and Others, With Some of the Helvetian Reformers, During the Early Part of the Reign of Queen Elizabeth* (For the Parker Society; Cambridge: CUP, 1842), 71.
[2] For example, Psalms 13:6; 59:16; 71:23; 95:1; 101:1; 105:2; 145:7, Isaiah 26:19; 35:10; 38:20; 44:23; 51:11, Jeremiah 31:7, 12; 51:48, and Zephaniah 3:14-15.

Oh sing to the Lord a new song,
  for he has done marvelous things!
His right hand and his holy arm
  have worked salvation for him.

Psalm 98:1

Sing praises to the Lord, for he has done gloriously;
  let this be made known in all the earth.
Shout, and sing for joy, O inhabitant of Zion,
  for great in your midst is the Holy One of Israel.

Isaiah 12:4-5

Sing for joy, O heavens, and exult, O earth;
  break forth, O mountains, into singing!
For the Lord has comforted his people
  and will have compassion on his afflicted.

Isaiah 49:13

Sing and rejoice, O daughter of Zion,
  for behold, I come and I will dwell in your midst,
  declares the Lord.

Zechariah 2:10

This has always been the way of things in God's gracious economy. Where there is mercy, there you will find music. Where there is salvation, there you will find song. Where God is present, there you will hear God's praise. For example, in 1739, after George Whitefield had preached the gospel to immense crowds in Philadelphia and with great effect, Benjamin Franklin remarked how 'one could not walk through Philadelphia in the evening without hearing psalms sung in different families of the street'.[3]

Furthermore, Bishop Jewell was right: 'by these means the sacred discourses sink more deeply in the minds of men'. That is, singing the Word of Christ is a means of theological and spiritual formation; it imparts the knowledge of God. This is why Psalm 22:3 describes God as being 'enthroned on the praises' of His people. In light of all that we have

---

[3] Reported in Luke Tyreman, *The Life of the Rev. George Whitefield*, 2 vols (London: Hodder & Stoughton, 1876), Vol 1, 338.

seen about the way that singing preaches, the meaning of this enigmatic phrase should be now clear: because praise proclaims, it also reveals. Divine praise, therefore, has an iconic function. It is, as Karl Barth once put it, the 'little revelation on our side corresponding to God's great one'.[4] James Mays elaborates:

> The 'enthroned on the praises' points to what replaces the icon in Israel. The hymns of praise and the praise in the prayers render the character of God with a fullness and intentionality found nowhere else in scripture. Praise portrays the person of God by speaking of what Adonai has done and typically does, and evokes Adonai's character by a pattern of attributes ... The content of praise creates a *verbal* icon.[5]

This capacity of our hymns to reveal and exalt the living God is not only a feature of descriptive praise (which proclaim God's eternal attributes) and declarative praise (which proclaim God's saving acts), but of every type of song: summons, prayer, confession, lament, imprecation, even protest – for all of these contain elements of praise, as well as being forms of praise.[6] God is honoured and proclaimed in every variety of Word-based or gospel-inspired song. Because of this, His people are made strong in their singing and the devil's kingdom 'weakened and shaken at almost every note'. It is for good reason that the psalmist writes: 'Oh come, let us sing to the LORD' (Psalm 95:1).

*   *   *

For those who have got lost in the detail, *the argument of this book* can be summed up in two statements, which correspond to the book's two main parts:

> (1) The people of God are called to gather together *both* to glorify God *and* to edify one another.

> (2) The people of God are called to sing together as a way of *praising* God, *praying* to God, and *preaching* His Word.

---

[4] Barth, *Church Dogmatics, III/4*, 74.
[5] Mays, *The Lord Reigns*, 65-66.
[6] See Appendix 1 for a fuller discussion of the relationship of lament to praise.

These two statements (and the two corresponding parts of this book) are profoundly interrelated. Moreover, the elements within them are also intertwined. For while, superficially, it may appear that glorifying God and edifying others are two separate activities, in reality they are not – especially not when the church is gathered. True glorification of God will edify others, just as true edification of others will glorify God. It may likewise appear that praising and praying are ways of glorifying God, whereas preaching is a way of edifying others. But, once again, the reality is more complex. All three glorify and all three edify – albeit in different ways.

This does not mean that there are no distinctions to be made between praising, praying and preaching. There clearly are.[7] And God and His people are certainly not to be confused with one another! Rather, my aim in drawing attention to these interrelationships and points of overlap is simply to encourage us to see and celebrate the multidimensional nature of our gatherings and the singing that takes place within them. This, in turn, serves as a warning against the lure of reductionism (e.g., reducing church to a horizontal activity or reducing singing to a vertical act). We are dealing with both-ands, not either-ors. Therefore, what God has joined together, let no one separate!

The purpose of this book has been to encourage ongoing musical and liturgical reformation in our churches. This is in line the with reformers' dictum: *ecclesia reformata, ecclesia semper reformanda* (i.e., 'the reformed church is the church that is always reforming'). Indeed, we are bound to the task of personal and ecclesial reform 'until we all attain to the unity of the faith and of the knowledge of the Son of God, to mature manhood, to the measure of the stature of the fullness of Christ' (Ephesians 4:13). The task, of course, has many parts to it – spiritual, structural, relational, educational, missional, etc – and different churches may need to prioritise some aspects over others. But the musical and liturgical aspects dare not be neglected. They are too important and too formative.

I have pitched this book primarily at pastors and teachers not because we alone are tasked with identifying all problems and implementing all

---

[7] Even though, as we've seen, the 'advertising aspect' of praise is a form of preaching and (as I argue in Appendix 1) prayer can be a form of praise.

solutions, but because we have unique, God-given responsibilities that are not shared by the rest of the flock.[8] Pastors, musical and liturgical reform (like all other aspects of church growth) will not happen without you and can easily be sabotaged by you! Be shepherds of the flock. Lead them to greener pastures, rather than leaving them to their own devices.

Regrettably, I know of too many preachers who disappear for the first 15 minutes of their church gatherings, usually for a last minute read of their sermon and sometimes with the justification that they are not missing out on anything important. As a preacher, I know this temptation and acknowledge that very occasionally (read, 'rarely') there may be valid grounds to absent oneself from the beginning of the service. But normally it is a temptation you should resist, and if it has become an habitual practice, it is something of which you need to repent. Get over your anxiety, trust God and, if necessary, get up 30 minutes earlier. Free the flock by joining with them in their songs of praise and lead by example, modelling the kind of engagement that God requires and desires.

Whether or not the last paragraph has 'struck oil' with you, I urge you to grapple with the issues raised in this book, to search the Scriptures for yourselves, and to teach those under your care what God's Word says and how it applies. And please don't duck the difficult issues (e.g., emotional expression and bodily movement). These things rarely sort themselves out. Explore them with your congregation and decide together how best to conduct yourselves in God's household.[9] And in case you missed the memo in chapter eleven, work with your church musicians: feed them, encourage them, train them, support them and learn from them too – for they have often done a fair bit of reading and thinking about their ministry.

Consequently, *this book has also been written for them – for music directors, song-leaders and church musicians of every kind* (including those on the 'tech team'). Having met and talked with hundreds of church musicians across 30 years of music ministry training experience, I know that many of you are more than capable of wrestling your way through a book of this nature (so I hope you have) and some of you are as

---

[8] See further Robert S Smith, 'A "Second Reformation"!? "Office" and "Charisma" in the New Testament', *RTR* 58 (1999), 151-162.
[9] See the discussion in Appendix 3 for a fuller understanding of these issues.

theologically trained as your pastors (so you have no excuse if you haven't). Whoever you are, you too need to keep stretching yourself biblically and theologically, not just at the level of skill. However, I also know that for many of you, your most pressing questions are at the level of application and your most immediate need, therefore, is for wise counsel.

To that end, let me share with you, in summary-point form, some very good and godly advice found in two web articles. The *first* is by Scott Connell, professor of music and worship at Boyce College/Southern Baptist Theological Seminary in Louisville, Kentucky and worship pastor at First Southern Baptist Church in Floyds Knobs, Indiana. In his article, '10 Things I Did Not Do that Improved My Congregation's Singing',[10] Connell shares the following:

1. I did not turn down the lights.
2. I did not turn up the sound.
3. I did not try to sound like the Youtube video.
4. I did not try lengthy or frequent instrumental solos.
5. I did not try the newest worship songs.
6. I did not try to get rid of their old favorite songs.
7. I did not try to greatly expand the song library.
8. I did not try rhythmically challenging melodies.
9. I did not try too many songs in a worship service.
10. I did not have my band play on every verse and chorus.

The *second* is written by Jamie Brown, a recording artist in his own right and Director of Worship and Arts at Truro Anglican Church in Fairfax, VA. In a timely and salutary article, titled 'Is Evangelical Worship Headed for a HUGE Crash?',[11] Brown offers 14 'words of wisdom' to those who

---

[10] Scott Connell, '10 Things I Did Not Do that Improved My Congregation's Singing', *TGC: U.S. Edition* (March 16, 2017): https://www.thegospelcoalition.org/article/10-things-i-did-not-do-that-improved-my-congregations-singing.

[11] Jamie Brown, 'Is Evangelical Worship Headed for a HUGE Crash?', *Church Leaders* (November 9, 2017): https://churchleaders.com/worship/worship-articles/175020-jamie-brown-evangelical-worship-headed-for-a-huge-crash.html/2.

are engaged in church music ministry which, if followed, may well prevent the kind of 'crash' he fears is ahead for some of us:

1. Sing songs people know (or can learn easily).
2. Sing them in congregational keys.
3. Sing and celebrate the power, glory and salvation of God.
4. Serve your congregation. Saturate them with the Word of God.
5. Get your face off the big screen.
6. Use your original songs in extreme moderation.
7. Err on the side of including as many people as possible in what's going on.
8. Keep the lights up.
9. Stop talking so much.
10. Don't let loops/lights/visuals become your outlet for creativity at the expense of the centrality of the gospel.
11. Point to Jesus. Don't draw attention to yourself.
12. Don't sing songs with bad lyrics or weak theology.
13. Tailor your worship leading, and the songs you pick, to include the largest cross-section of your congregation that you can.
14. Lead pastorally.

Both articles are worth reading in full. There are also many others like them, as well as some highly recommended websites – like Bob Kauflin's,[12] Mike Cosper's[13] and *Magnify*[14] – and reliable blogsites – like *Doxology and Theology*.[15] So there is no lack of good guidance available from those working in the field, and the best of it will not only address aesthetic and pragmatic issues but take you into the theological underpinnings of sound ministry practice. Keep working at the theology!

But, in case you haven't noticed, *this book is also intended for a third audience: Christian congregations.* In fact, one of the points I have sought to make repeatedly throughout has to do with the importance of the

---

[12] Worship Matters: Resources for Music, Worship, & More from Bob Kauflin: http://worshipmatters.com.
[13] http://www.mikedcosper.com.
[14] https://magnify.org.au.
[15] The Doxology & Theology blog features posts by a range of authors and practitioners, including Matt Boswell, Aaron Ivey, Matthew Westerholm, Zac Hicks, Sandra McCracken and Jordan Kauflin: http://www.doxologyandtheology.com/blog.

congregation for congregational song (as obvious as that may sound). That is, when we come *together* to engage with God and *each other*, we should be aiming at *common* praise, *common* prayer, and (as far as our singing is concerned) *common* preaching. If we are *all* going to teach and admonish *one another* in psalms, hymns and spiritual songs (Colossians 3:16), then *the whole body* must be engaged and *each part* must do its work (Ephesians 4:16).

Cranmer came to see this clearly. In his 1552 revision of the 1549 Prayer Book (in which the role of the choir dominated), he systematically took things away from the choir and gave them to the congregation. For example, both 'Morning Prayer' and 'Evening Prayer' now began with a *general* confession which was 'to be sayd of the whole congregacion after the minister'. Similarly, the Creed and the Lord's Prayer were now to be said by all. In the revised Communion service, 'every reference to the choir is removed, and the people have been written into the service, as respondents to the newly inserted ten commandments'.[16]

This underscores one of the keys to the ongoing reformation of congregational song: it has to keep being given back to the people.[17] The tendency of 'natural religion' will always be to take it away, turning the body into a passive (and, all too often, disengaged) audience. Beware of the 'performance culture' and even more of musical priest-craft. Church is not a concert and, in Christ and by the Spirit, we all have immediate access to God (Ephesians 2:18) and a vital part to play in His service (Ephesians 4:16). Regardless of whether we are led by song-leaders or a group of people we call 'the choir', in reality the congregation is the choir! God desires to hear *all* our voices. Not surprisingly, the musical journey of the Bible begins and ends in the same way:

> Then *Moses and the people of Israel* sang this song to the Lord, saying,
> 'I will sing to the Lord, for he has triumphed gloriously;
> the horse and his rider he has thrown into the sea.' (Exodus 15:1)

---

[16] Shead, 'Is There a Musical Note in the Body?', 5-6.
[17] This, as we have seen, does not mean that there is no place for 'special music' – e.g., choral anthems or solo items. It simply means that these will play a minor role, rather than a major one.

Then I heard *every creature in heaven and on earth and under the*
earth and on the sea, and all that is in them, saying:
'To him who sits on the throne and to the Lamb
be praise and honor and glory and power,
for ever and ever!' (Revelation 5:13)

Of course, this ministry of song not only needs to be *given* to God's people
but *embraced* by them. For that to happen congregations need both
understanding and encouragement. This takes us back to the role of
pastors and song-leaders, and their duty to provide teaching and
exhortation. But to congregations themselves I say this: Even if you are
rarely encouraged to do so, pick up the ball and run with it!

¹ Make a joyful noise to the Lord, all the earth!
² Serve the Lord with gladness!
Come into his presence with singing!
³ Know that the Lord, he is God!
It is he who made us, and we are his;
we are his people, and the sheep of his pasture.
⁴ Enter his gates with thanksgiving,
and his courts with praise!
Give thanks to him; bless his name!
⁵ For the Lord is good;
his steadfast love endures forever,
and his faithfulness to all generations. (Psalm 100:1-5)

*   *   *

Every church gathering is a spiritually powerful and eternally significant
event. Within such gatherings, the ministry of God's people – including
their praising, praying and preaching of God's Word in song – is serious
business. It is one of the key means by which we worship God together
and edify each other. In order to bring this book to a close, and with the
priority of corporateness taken as read, I offer the following seven
summary points about when the singing of the saints will best serve
God's goals for our gatherings.

First, our music will only serve God's goals for it *when singing serves its*
proper end. Like every other aspect of creation, music and song are
neither self-generating nor self-serving. They are gifts of a generous

creator, given for His glory; they are from Him, through Him, and to Him. In a more particular sense, every psalm, hymn or spiritual song written by one (or more) of His redeemed has been prompted by His Spirit, elicited in response to His grace, and given so that His name might be honoured and His church built. Our singing, therefore, while natural and enjoyable, must never be an end in itself. If ever it seeks to be, it becomes idolatrous and self-consuming. And yet, because of our fallenness, we are dangerously prone to worship the *creature* instead of the *creator*, the *means* of worship rather than the *object* of worship. We need constant reminding, then, that our singing will only serve God's purpose, when it serves His glory. To quote Carson yet again: 'you cannot find excellent corporate worship until you stop trying to find excellent corporate worship and pursue God Himself'. [18]

Second, our music will only serve God's goals for it *when it is the servant of the Word of God*. This means that instrumental music (which does have its uses) will be of considerably less value than songs, which are able to convey the Word of God. Most importantly, as the primary channels through which God's Word comes to us are the reading and exposition of the Scriptures, the sung Word must never displace, dominate or detract from the read/taught Word. Nor should our singing be split-off from the other forms of the Word or thought of as belonging to a different category of ministry. In short, singing should support and supplement the read/preached Word, not rival it. When used wisely, music is a very beautiful servant, but (as too many churches have discovered), when used foolishly, it is a very destructive master! Finally, while spontaneity is important (see below), if our songs are going to serve God's Word effectively, careful and prayerful planning are usually required.

Third, our congregational singing will only serve God's goals for it *when the words of our songs are true, clear and helpfully expressed*.[19] That a song has a good tune is not enough. If some of the words are erroneous, incomprehensible or easily open to misunderstanding, then it is more of a hindrance than a help. *Truth* cannot be compromised, neither can *clarity* – for without clarity the truth will be obscured. Ideally, truth also needs to be *helpfully expressed*. By 'helpful' I mean poetically skilful and

---

[18] Carson, 'Worship Under the Word', 31.
[19] This point, and the one following, are explored at greater length in Appendix 4.

rhythmically accessible. I don't mean theologically impenetrable or emotionally unreal. The fact is that some congregational songs are unhelpful, and others heretical! This calls for discernment and (sometimes) tough decisions. It may also mean that some songs can only be sung with an explanation as to what they do (and don't) mean. Some song words can be freely changed (e.g., archaisms can be modernised and 'I' changed to 'we' or vice versa). But most require either the writer's and/or publisher's permission.

Fourth, our congregational singing will best serve God's goals for it when the music is *appropriate, singable and memorable*. That a song has good words is not always enough either. If the tune is unsingable or doesn't fit with the mood of the song, then the usefulness of the song will be severely limited. Many good hymns need better tunes found for them or new tunes written for them. Others may need to be simplified, rearranged or played in a more congregationally friendly tempo (see more under the next point). When good words and a good tune come together, then the song will be more satisfying to sing and its truth more easily grasped and remembered. Of course, singability is a somewhat subjective quality – as what is singable for one person or congregation may not be singable for another – and there are degrees of memorability. Nevertheless, there is a melodic range that works for most people,[20] and a degree of ease required for a song to be played successfully and sung effectively.

Fifth, our songs will best serve God's goals for them *when their accompaniment is skilfully and sensitively played*. One of the tensions in church ministry is between the desire to 'give everyone a go' and the wisdom of using the most able people up front. Each congregation needs to decide how best to manage this tension in terms of its history, its size and the gifts God has given to it. While we should avoid a utopian approach, some degree of competence is a prerequisite for effective service. Here is where humble realism must prevail. Different songs require different levels of competence. Some songs simply cannot be played by some musicians or by some combinations of musicians (for lack of the right instruments). This is not a problem. We are spoiled for

---

[20] For most men, this extends from two As below middle C to the D above middle C. For most women it extends from the A below Middle C to two Ds above middle C.

choice. Choose songs within your capabilities.[21] By 'sensitively played' I don't necessarily mean softly played (although many church bands, like many organists, drown out their congregations). I mean played in a way that enables people to sing easily and effectively.

Sixth, our congregational singing will best serve God's goals for it *when our musicians and song leaders are humble and dedicated servants of the Lord and His church*. As sinners saved by grace, arrogance and self-promotion are always improper for God's people. If these sins are found in those who lead us, they are often contagious – spreading throughout the body. Musical gifts have a way of tantalising the ego, causing many a musician to succumb to pride and glory-seeking. This danger needs to be monitored and addressed when necessary. The antidote to it is the humility that comes from privileging the interests of others and developing the mind of Christ (Philippians 2:4-5). As well as being humble servants, those who lead in our music also need to be committed, disciplined and punctual – not always traits that come easily to some musicians. Having made these points, I should add that the large majority of musicians with whom I have shared the pleasure of serving the saints have been all of these things in abundance.

Seventh, our congregational singing will best serve God's goals for it *when it is creatively employed in our gatherings*. It is to our loss that an understanding has developed that has restricted singing to our response to God and lost sight of the fact that it is also one of the ways that God speaks to us. It is also almost exclusively thought about in terms of praise, but not in terms of prayer or preaching. Once we rediscover the larger biblical picture and the way in which our songs participate in all three dimensions of our gatherings (God to us, us to God, and us to each other), then this is bound to open up new possibilities for deploying our songs more creatively. For example, given that some hymns are prayers, why not intersperse spoken prayers with sung prayers? Given that some of our songs are mini-sermons, why not sometimes sing an appropriate song

---

[21] There is always the option of singing to a pre-recorded track of some sort (as many churches do) or singing *a cappella* (i.e., unaccompanied). Of course, this again highlights the need for wise and appropriate choices, for not every song works *a cappella* and some congregations lack the confidence to sing without support.

mid-sermon? Conversely, why not intersperse songs with Scripture readings? There are multiple possibilities.

*   *   *

The ability to sing and make music is one of God's great gifts to humanity. Songs can lift our hearts, excite our minds, stir our emotions, engage our bodies and bind us together in ways that few other things can. As such, they are a natural and powerful vehicle for accomplishing God's work among us when we come together in Jesus' name. As we have seen, the purpose of our gatherings, as well as the singing that takes place within them, is not primarily to do what we could do on our own at home (spend time in *personal* devotion and *private* reflection), but to draw near to God *together*, to exhort and encourage *one another*, to build up *our brothers and sisters* in faith, hope and love, and to engage in the ministry of giving and receiving the Word of God *corporately*. Were he to see and hear us singing and serving together, Cranmer would, no doubt, be

> heartened, even excited, by the simple fact that we all join in, and that we do so with all our hearts. And although the music we enjoy, whether it be Pop, Rock, Jazz or Mozart, would be totally alien to him, he would have nothing but approval for the fact that the music we sing together is in the English of today and in the musical idioms and genres of today.[22]

Of course, it is not Cranmer we are seeking to please. It is the triune God of glory and grace. Therefore, the ongoing musical reformation of the church requires not so much an application of Cranmer's legacy as a continuous putting into practice of the divinely inspired scriptural exhortation:

> Let the word of Christ dwell in you richly, teaching and admonishing one another in all wisdom, singing psalms and hymns and spiritual songs, with thankfulness in your hearts to God. (Colossians 3:16).

So I say again, dearly beloved, come, let us sing!

---

[22] Shead, 'Is There a Musical Note in the Body?', 16.

APPENDIX I: THE RELATIONSHIP BETWEEN LAMENT AND PRAISE*

What is the precise relationship between lament and praise? Is one simply the antonym of the other? Does the presence of one mean the absence of the other? Or are they in some way interrelated? If so, how? Perhaps the most obvious correlation (or, at least, point of comparison) is that they both have a way of breaking forth into song. Paul Westermeyer maps out the parallels with poetic flare:

> *Joy* inevitably breaks into song. Speech alone cannot carry its hilarity. The physical equipment we use to laugh is the physical equipment we use to sing. From laughter to song is but a small step. To praise God, the highest form of joy is to make music ... The same can be said of *sorrow*, the opposite of joy. Sorrow also inevitably breaks into song. Speech alone cannot carry its moan. The physical equipment we use to cry is also the physical equipment we use to sing. From mourning to song is but a small step. To cry out to God in lament, the deepest form of sorrow, is to make music.[1]

While this parallel tells us much about the relationship between music and emotion, it does not immediately reveal the connection between praise and lament. This is a little harder to see. It is, therefore, commonplace for the two to be viewed as polar opposites. Of course, there is an important truth contained in such a view, for they are certainly juxtaposed in Scripture. The writer of Psalms 42-43, for example, laments the fact that he cannot praise and so longs for the day when he will be restored to praise and no longer have cause to lament. And yet, with this juxtaposition, there are profound connections between lament and praise that also need to be appreciated. In fact, there is even a case for regarding lament as a form of praise.

---

* This appendix is adapted from Smith, 'Belting Out the Blues as Believers', 108-110.
[1] Westermeyer, *Te Deum*, 28.

1.   Lament as the Pathway to Praise

The shape of the Psalter, as we noted in chapter seven, is governed by the historic progression of Israelite kingship in light of the promise made to David in 2 Samuel 7. After the introduction of Psalms 1-2, Book I begins with a series of laments, reflecting David's experience of persecution in the time of Saul (Psalms 3-7). Books II-IV take us from the reign of Solomon through the exile and to the ground for Israel's hope. Book V climaxes with a celebration of redeemed existence under a new Davidic king (Psalms 144-145), before concluding with an explosive catena of pure praise psalms (Psalms 146-150). Therefore, while lament may be seen as the first word of the Psalter, praise is most certainly the last. As Miller writes:

> To go through the Book of Psalms is to be led increasingly toward the praise of God as the final word ... The literary arrangement of the Psalter gives clear testimony to this reality as each book of the Psalter is concluded with doxology (Pss. 41:13; 72:18-19; 89:52; 106:48), and the Psalter as a whole ends in Psalm 150 with its fulsome call for everything to praise God every way that is possible.[2]

What is true at the macro level of the Psalter is also true at the micro level of many particular lament psalms: they begin with pleading but end with praising.[3] As Jones writes: 'a distinctive movement from plea to praise characterizes the lament psalm. This movement may be, at times, sharp and somewhat disjointed. It may be uneven. Nevertheless, this movement from plea to praise is essential in understanding the power of the psalms of lament'.[4] The power of which Jones speaks is the power of reality: the reality of our pitiful plight (on the one hand) and the reality of God's game-changing grace (on the other). As Jones puts it: 'The depth of pain expressed in the laments is all too real. Yet so too is the possibility that this pain can be transformed, will be transformed, into praise'.[5]

But what is the link between possibility and certainty? How is the singing of pain transformed into the singing of praise? According to Jones, we are never told: 'A mystery occurs in the movement between plea to praise,

---

[2] Miller Jr., '"Enthroned on the Praises of Israel"', 8.
[3] Psalm 88 being the most notable exception to this 'rule'.
[4] Jones, 'The Psalms of Lament and the Transformation of Sorrow', 48.
[5] Jones, 'The Psalms of Lament and the Transformation of Sorrow', 49.

from disorientation towards new orientation. There is no clear and certain answer as to what makes this movement possible. Nevertheless, it is a most remarkable transformation'. [6] Remarkable it certainly is, but perhaps not quite so impenetrable as Jones seems to think.

The transformation, as Westermann notes, lies in 'lament's function as an appeal'.[7] In other words, 'lament is supplication; it is the means by which suffering comes before the One who can take it away'.[8] What this reveals is that the movement from plea to praise is actually a reflex of the sufferer's movement toward God. This is why a change of mood often occurs within the lament psalm itself, even if it's only a change in outlook and not yet a change in situation.[9] Otherwise put, lamentation is turned into praise not only by *the experience of deliverance* but also by *the expectation of deliverance*. This is because the honest articulation of need opens the door to the faithful reception of provision, even if only in anticipation. As we have seen, the key lies in the way that lament arouses faith and hope, and so enables the sufferer 'to see the path leading to an alleviation of suffering'.[10]

A song of lament does not need to be autobiographical in order to have this effect. Singing the laments of other saints can be just as effective, if not more so, in helping us 'express our frustrations and remind us that in them all God is present and 'working for our good'. Then we may be free to join in a psalm of pure praise and thanksgiving'.[11] In fact, as we've seen, the lament psalms of Scripture are ultimately none other than the words of Him who 'in the days of his flesh offered up prayers and petitions with fervent cries and tears to the one who could save him from death' (Heb 5:7).[12] It is He who has given them back to us that we might

---

[6] Jones, 'The Psalms of Lament and the Transformation of Sorrow', 52-53.

[7] Westermann, *Praise and Lament in the Psalms*, 267. Indeed, writes Westermann, 'Lamentation has no meaning in and of itself. That it functions as an appeal is evident in its structure. [...] The lament appeals to the one who can remove suffering' (266).

[8] Westermann, *Praise and Lament in the Psalms*, 273.

[9] Westermann, *Praise and Lament in the Psalms*, 267.

[10] Westermann, *Praise and Lament in the Psalms*, 267.

[11] Donald P Hustad, 'The Psalms as Worship Expressions: Personal and Congregational', *Review & Expositor* 81 (Summer 1984), 423.

[12] See the discussion in Richard P Belcher Jr, *The Messiah and the Psalms: Preaching Christ from all the Psalm* (Fearn: Mentor, 2006), 199-200.

sing them before His 'throne of grace, that we might receive mercy and find grace in our time of need' (Heb 4:16). Little wonder, then, that the psalms of lament typically end with a vow of praise.[13] For true lament is none other than the divinely established pathway to praise. Perhaps this is the key to the meaning of the enigmatic words of 'The Teacher': 'Sorrow is better than laughter, for by sadness of face the heart is made glad' (Eccl 7:3).

2. Lament as Praising in the Dark

To sing lament, however, is not merely to *begin a journey toward praise*, it is itself to *set foot on the path of praise*. After all, the whole Psalter is labelled *tehillim* (praises); the laments as much as every other 'type'. As Shead and Cameron write: 'Whatever a given psalm looks like – lament, instruction, thanksgiving, and so on – the act of taking it upon our lips becomes an act of praise'.[14] This can be seen in the way the lament psalms 'express a fundamental trust in God in the midst of tribulation'.[15] Hence my description of lament above as 'praising in the dark'! But even more than that, the laments 'open us to the greatness of a God who not only can hear, but also can handle our pain, our self-pity, our blame, and our fear'.[16] They, thus, propel us toward 'new and unforeseen breakthroughs in understanding who God is and how God can be trusted'.[17] In this way real lament leads to growth in faith and in the knowledge of God and thus serves to increase His praise.

In the larger frame, and this side of the consummation, praise and lament work together and need one another to keep the one honest and the other focussed. For, on the one hand, praise 'can retain its authenticity and naturalness only in polarity with lamentation'.[18] Yet on the other hand,

---

[13] Westermann, *Praise and Lament in the Psalms*, 267.

[14] Andrew G Shead and Andrew J Cameron, 'Singing with the Messiah in a Foreign Land', in Andrew G Shead (ed.), *Stirred by a Noble Theme: The Book of Psalms in the Life of the Church* (Apollos: Nottingham, 2013), 170.

[15] Michael Jinkins, *In the House of the Lord: Inhabiting the Psalms of Lament* (Collegeville: Liturgical Press, 1989), 40.

[16] Jinkins, *In the House of the Lord*, 39.

[17] Jinkins, *In the House of the Lord*, 40.

[18] Westermann, *Praise and Lament in the Psalms*, 267. Allen Verhey speaks similarly: 'Hope that cannot lament denies the awful reality and the continuing

and as we learn from the content of the Psalter itself, 'Israel also mixes lament with praise, because they know beyond doubting that in God's unchanging, unfailing love they will be saved in the end'.[19] The same is true for the Christian church: lament we must, but only ever in hope! For 'the spine of lament is hope: not the vacuous optimism that "things will get better", which in the short run is usually a lie, but the deep and irrepressible conviction, in the teeth of present evidence, that God has not severed the umbilical cord that has always bound us to the Lord'.[20] It is this conviction that enables believers to sing their griefs before the throne of grace, confident that He will never leave or forsake us (Hebrews 13:6).

Such singing is not only an act of faith and an expression of hope but may also be seen as a form of praise – albeit praising in the dark. But the darkness will not last. Its end has been appointed. For while 'weeping may tarry for the night, joy comes in the morning (Psalm 30:5). Indeed, a Day is coming when there will be no more mourning, nor crying, nor pain anymore, for the former things will have passed away and God himself will wipe away every tear from our eyes (Revelation 21:4). On that Day, all the laments of this present age will give way to unqualified, uninhibited and uninterrupted praise of 'the God and Father of our Lord Jesus Christ, the Father of mercies and God of all comfort' (2 Corinthians 1:3). Come, Lord Jesus!

---

power of death and sin' (*The Christian Art of Dying: Learning from Jesus* [Grand Rapids: Eerdmans, 2011], 269).

[19] Bruce K Waltke, J M Houston and E Moore, *The Psalms as Christian Lament: A Historical Commentary.* (Grand Rapids: Eerdmans, 2014), 10.

[20] C Clifton Black, 'The Persistence of the Wounds', in Sally Brown and Patrick D Miller (eds.), *Lament: Reclaiming Practices in Pulpit, Pew, and Public Square* (Louisville: Westminster John Knox Press, 2005), 54.

Appendix II: Approaches to Psalm Singing

As we saw in chapters seven and eight, the singing of the Psalter is 'a practice that combines the reading of Scripture and praying. Through the Psalter God has given us entry into the universe's eternal song of praise, and to take up the Psalms is to join that congregation. This means that the song the church sings is a fully earthly song of a pilgrim people and a groaning cosmos. But it is also an eternal song, being bound to the Word of revelation in Jesus Christ'.[1] Christian people, then, have good reason to sing the Psalms and, over the centuries, have attempted to do so in a variety of ways. The main approaches may be outlined under the following headings.

1. Metrical Psalms

In metrical psalm singing, the words of the Psalms are adjusted to fit various tunes, written in one of a number of popular meters. For example, in 8.6.8.6 ('Common Meter' or CM) all verses are four-lines in length. The first line contains eight syllables, the second six, the third eight syllables, and the fourth six.[2] Since the time of the Reformation, many metrical versions of the Psalms have been produced in a variety of languages – French, German, Dutch, English. In recent years, a number of contemporary metrical psalters have been produced. For example, in 1991, the Presbyterian Church of Eastern Australia produced *The Complete Book of Psalms for Singing with Study Notes* and, in 2003, the Free Church of Scotland's Psalmody and Praise Committee produced *Sing Psalms*. This adopts a similar format to the *Scottish Psalter* of 1650, but with updated vocabulary and grammar and a range of alternative meters.

---

[1] Brock, *Singing the Ethos of God*, 357.
[2] The other most frequently used (and therefore named) metres are Long Metre (LM) = 8.8.8.8., Short Metre (SM) = 6.6.8.6. and Doubled Common Metre (DCM) = 8.6.8.6.8.6.8.6. Alternative metres are simply given numerically: e.g., 8.6.8.6. or 8.7.8.7. or 11.10.11.10.

2.   Plainsong

Plainsong (or plainchant) developed during the earliest centuries of the Christian church, possibly due to the combined influence of Jewish synagogue music and the Greek modal system. In plainsong, tunes (or 'tones') are created or chosen to fit words. They are monophonic (i.e., consisting of a single melody line), chanted without accompaniment and rhythmically freer than much later Western music. Chanting is effectively a blend of speaking and singing. 'This is the key to singing text without rearranging it; most of the words are spoken in a monotone on the same note, and a small part of the text is sung to specific notes and rhythms, giving the chant its musical quality'.[3] Gregorian chant, named after Pope Gregory I (sixth century), is one type of plainsong. Byzantine chant, however, has a different heritage and involves more improvisation. In a typical plainsong psalter, the text is marked to indicate how the words are to be fitted to the music.

3.   Anglican Chant

Anglican chant (or English chant) was an elaboration of Gregorian chant. It was thus a development of the plainsong tradition that had been used in the Chapel Royal since the days of Elizabeth I. Because plainsong was sung in Latin, this contravened one of the key principles of the English Reformation: 'that all things shall be read and sung in the Church in the English Tongue, to the end that the congregation may be thereby edified'.[4] English chant, therefore, was a way of ensuring not only that the music serves the words of Scripture, but that the words were understood by those who sung or heard them. It also differed from plainsong in that it was designed to allow choirs to chant the Psalms in harmony. It has thus been described as 'harmonized plainchant'.[5] It is also likely that it

---

[3] Russell Stutler, 'Several Different Ways to Sing the Psalms', *Stutler.cc* (Last updated February, 2017): http://www.stutler.cc/russ/sing_psalms.html.

[4] These are Thomas Cranmer's words, as found in the essay, 'Concerning the Service of the Church', which follows 'The Preface' in the 1662 *BCP*. The same words appear, albeit in older English, in the 1552 *BCP*, but as part of 'The Preface'.

[5] Percy A Scholes, 'Anglican Chant', in John Owen Ward (ed.), *The Oxford Companion to Music* (Oxford: OUP, 1991), 33.

was intended to provide a way of singing the English translation of the Psalter (by Myles Coverdale), which was included in the 1662 *BCP*.

4.   Historical Adaptations

Although Isaac Watts (1674-1748) is best known for claiming that 'the Psalms were too constraining a standard for Christian worshipers',[6] and for introducing songs of personal Christian experience and extra-biblical poetry and into Protestant hymnody, he nonetheless produced a Psalter of his own in 1719. He was convinced, however, that the Psalms 'required modification for Christian worship', for the simple reason that David 'could not have fully apprehended the truth later revealed through Jesus Christ. [...] The Psalms should therefore be "renovated" as if David had been a Christian, or as Watts put it in the title of his 1719 metrical psalter, they should be "imitated in the language of the New Testament"'.[7] So, for example, Watts rendered Psalm 1:5 as follows: 'Sinners in judgement shall not stand / Amongst the sons of grace, / When Christ, the Judge, at his right hand / Appoints his saints a place'.

5.   Contemporary Adaptations

As we noted in our introductory history, the Jubilate Group, founded by Bishop Michael Baughen in the early 1960s, formed in order to meet the needs of a new generation that desired to move beyond metrical hymnody. At the same time, it also sought to revive and reform traditional worship practices. To this end, the Group published *Psalm Praise* in 1973, and *Psalms for Today* and *Songs from the Psalms* in 1990. In the last couple of decades, a string of further developments has taken place in a variety of quarters. In 2008, as we also noted, Sovereign Grace ministries released an album of 12 psalm-based-songs at the 'Rediscovering the Psalms' conference.[8] More recently, Nashville-based singer-songwriter, Sandra McCracken, has released an album of 12 songs based on a variety

---

[6] Stephen A Marini, *Sacred Song in America: Religion, Music, and Public Culture* (Urbana: University of Illinois Press, 2003), 75.

[7] Marini, *Sacred Song in America*, 76.

[8] The album, simply titled, *Psalms*, contains 12 songs written on the following psalms: 32, 23, 34, 46, 51, 68, 84, 90, 96, 130, 145 and 150.

of psalms.[9] Two other notable initiatives are *The Psalms Project* by Shane Heilman and *The Prayerbook Project* by Brian Moss. Both Heilman and Moss are aiming to write 150 new songs inspired by each of the Psalms. So far Heilman has produced four albums of 10 psalms each (i.e., Psalms 1-38),[10] and Moss two albums of 15 Psalms each (also Psalms 1-30).[11]

Conclusion

As I have argued in the body of this book, while the case for 'exclusive psalmody' is a weak one, the case for 'inclusive psalmody' is a strong one. As part of Holy Scripture, the Psalter is not only a personal gift given to every believer, but a powerful spiritual resource for the church in its worship. It is little wonder that Christians in the past have felt compelled to make use of psalms in their gatherings – albeit in a variety of different ways. We would do well to follow their lead and continue this practice today. As there are many creative possibilities, as well as innumerable resources available, this need not be done slavishly. In fact, there are even ways, as Witvliet suggests, that 'worshipers today can use the Psalms as the basis for improvising our own prayers'.[12] There may well be practical difficulties to overcome, but we neglect this gift to our detriment. For as Bonhoeffer admonishes: 'Whenever the Psalter is abandoned, an incomparable treasure is lost to the Christian Church'.[13]

---

[9] Sandra McCracken's album, also titled *Psalms*, includes songs written on Psalms 42, 43, 62, 104, 113, 119. For more information, see https://sandramccracken.bandcamp.com/album/psalms.
[10] See 'The Psalms Project': http://thepsalmsprojectband.com.
[11] For more information, see 'The Prayerbook Project': https://www.reformedworship.org/author/brian-moss.
[12] Witvliet, *The Biblical Psalms in Christian Worship*, 12.
[13] Bonhoeffer, *Psalms*, 26.

APPENDIX III: MUSIC, EMOTION AND BODILY EXPRESSION

Rob Smith with Megan Ng[1]

Singing, playing and even hearing music are bodily experiences. As Friedrich Nietzsche rightly observed: 'We listen to music with our muscles'.[2] For reasons we will see, music is also an inherently emotional medium. Song even more so. Both express and evoke emotional experiences.

But is there a link between music's physicality and its emotionality? If so, what are the precise connections? And what are the implications for corporate worship (in general) and congregational singing (in particular)?

1. Music and Bodily Movement

1.1. Involuntary gestures

It has often been observed that 'when we listen to music our bodies naturally respond with largely involuntary gestures, such as head nodding and foot tapping'.[2] The words spoken by the child of some friends of ours will resonate with many: 'This music gives me the moves!' Of course, sometimes we don't even realise what music is doing to us. Other times we are very much aware but find it difficult to resist music's power. What

---

[1] I am greatly indebted to the work of my friend and former student, Megan Ng, whose integrative project ('Body and Soul: Exploring the Relationship between Physical Expression and Emotional Response in Musical Worship') I supervised in 2012. Megan's work expanded both my understanding of the issues and my knowledge of the scholarly literature on this subject. Given my debt to her research, she is justly credited with co-authorship of this appendix. Her project is available here:
https://www.academia.edu/33621744/Body_and_Soul_Exploring_the_Relationship_between_Physical_Expression_and_Emotional_Response_in_Musical_Worship.
[2] Donald A Hodges, 'Bodily Responses to Music', in Susan Hallam, Ian Cross and Michael Thaut (eds.), *The Oxford Handbook of Music Psychology* (Oxford: OUP, 2009), 125.

lies behind this is the scientifically demonstrable fact that listening to music correlates with a marked increase in electrical activity in the body (particularly the leg muscles), even when subjects are instructed not to move.[3]

There is also growing evidence that 'our brain remembers music partly by moving our bodies, even if the movement is so slight that it can only be detected experimentally'.[4] Involuntary responses can even take place when we are remembering a song (without actually hearing it) or just imagining music in our minds (often called 'auditory imagination'). This has often been the experience of a certain driver who has a habit of 'drumming' on the steering wheel when stopped at traffic lights – much to his wife's irritation! (Names withheld to protect both the innocent and the guilty.)

1.2. Sympathetic responses

Music is also known to create a range of 'sympathetic responses' in the body's internal physiological system, such as increasing or decreasing heart rate. It can similarly generate external physical responses, such as increasing or decreasing a person's walking speed. Those who like to take their daily 'constitutional' listening to music, will know that we instinctively tend to fall into step with the tempo of whatever we are listening to. Motor reflexes are likewise stimulated by music's rhythmic qualities – a fact that is increasingly recognised as having profound therapeutic benefits for a range of conditions (e.g., helping stroke victims learn to walk again).[5]

Of course, it's also possible to be overcome (or perhaps undone) by music. As Oliver Sacks writes:

---

[3] Robert Jourdain, *Music, the Brain, and Ecstasy: How Music Captures Our Imagination* (New York: Avon Book, 1997), 148-149.

[4] Wren, *Praying Twice*, 86.

[5] Hodges, 'Bodily Responses to Music', 126. It has also proved beneficial in assisting with the clinical management of patients with neurodegenerative disorders, such as Alzheimer's disease, dementia and Parkinson's disease, and also those with a range neurological and psychiatric disorders. See further Marianna Boso, Pierluigi Politi, Francesco Barale and Enzo Emanuele, 'Neurophysiology and neurobiology of the musical experience', *Functional Neurology* 21.4 (2006), 187-191.

One of the most dramatic effects of music's power is the induction of trance states, which have been described by ethnomusicologists in nearly every culture. Trance – ecstatic singing and dancing, wild movements and cries, perhaps, rhythmic rocking, or catatonia-like rigidity or immobility – involves both motor and gross emotional, psychic and autonomic effects, culminating in profoundly altered states of consciousness.[6]

Given these powers, it is hardly surprising that, historically speaking, music has had its opponents (or, at least, those who have treated it with some caution or ambivalence) in both the Christian and the non-Christian worlds.[7]

1.3.   Group synchronisation

The physiological effects of music not only take place within persons, but between persons as well. 'On a practical level, musical melodies and rhythm make corporate speech more attractive and decisive'.[8] But there is much more to it than this. As we saw in chapter seven, singing with others increases the oxytocin levels of those involved, thereby enhancing the sense of belonging to one another. [9] Furthermore, '[p]osture, eye contact, and body language help to shape our attitudes and relationships'.[10] Rhythm, in particular, has a unique and powerful way of binding individuals together. [11] As each person's nervous system is synchronised to the music, they are also synchronised to one another. This brings about a united movement which is, in turn, productive of a united mood.[12] This phenomenon, known as 'emotional contagion' (see further 2.3. below), is greatly intensified if the bodily gestures of individuals are visible to other members of the group.[13] In short, 'no man

---

[6] Oliver Sacks, 'The Power of Music', *Brain* 129 (2006), 2528.
[7] See further Smith, 'Music, Singing, and Emotions', 475-476. Interestingly, Sacks references Leo Tolstoy as one who was 'deeply ambivalent about music' ('The Power of Music', 2529).
[8] Wren, *Praying Twice*, 84.
[9] Keeler, et al., 'The neurochemistry and social flow of singing'.
[10] Wren, *Praying Twice*, 87.
[11] Begbie, 'Faithful Feelings', 344.
[12] Sacks, *Musicophilia*, 244-247.
[13] Begbie, 'Faithful Feelings', 344.

is an island'; we are communal creatures who are affected by each other's bodily movements and are often moved to imitate each other.

1.4. The Bible and the body

With regard to the human body, the Bible does not evince any of the negativity characteristic of some strands of Greek philosophy and even some later Christian thought.[14] Although fallen, weak and limited, bodies are not inherently sinful or shameful. Human beings are psychosomatic unities by divine design.[15] While there will be a temporary separation of body and soul at death, God's purpose is to raise and transform our mortal body, just as He did for the Lord Jesus.[16] Far from being a hindrance to 'spiritual worship', our bodies are the God-given vehicles for responding rightly to the mercies of God in Christ (Romans 12:1).

We have previously noted some of the different bodily gestures associated with prayer in Scripture. Many of these are also seen to accompany blessing or praise – e.g., lifting hands or eyes to heaven.[17] The promise of David is typical:

> I will bless you as long as I live;
> in your name I will lift up my hands'
>
> *Psalm 63:4*

Furthermore, dancing is a frequent accompaniment to music and song in Scripture, as it is a natural way of expressing joy and, especially, of celebrating salvation.[18]

Without being naïve to the way in which music's powers can be misused, we have little reason to be overly suspicious of these physical gestures and bodily movements, particularly when they are a spontaneous response to

---

[14] See the brief discussion in Ian G Barbour, *Nature, Human Nature and God* (Minneapolis: Fortress, 2002), 79-83.

[15] See Gregory R Allison, 'Toward a Theology of Human Embodiment', *SBJT* 13.2 (Summer 2009), 5-17; John W Cooper, 'The Current Body-Soul Debate: A Case for Dualistic Holism', *SBJT* 13.2 (Summer 2009), 32-51.

[16] Romans 8:11, 1 Corinthians 6:14, and Philippians 3:21.

[17] Psalms 63:4, 134:2; Daniel 4:34, and Luke 24:50.

[18] Exodus 15:20-21, 1 Samuel 18:6, 29:5, and Psalms 87:7; 149:3; 150:3.

the mercies of God. Nor should we underestimate their potential beneficial impact on others, and even ourselves.

2.   Bodily Movement and Emotions

What more can be said about the link between bodily movement and emotional response? And what part might music play in their coordination?

2.1.   Probing the link

Although complex and not easily explained, the existence of a connection between somatic actions and psychological states is not in question. It is common human experience for emotions to manifest themselves bodily (e.g., in smiles or frowns, tears or laughter). Furthermore, numerous neurological studies have shown that the same part of the limbic system of the brain processes both emotions and physical movements.[19] This helps to explain why the emotion-movement 'street' runs in both directions. For just as our emotional reactions trigger various physical responses, so our bodily movements have an impact on our emotions.[20] One of the implications of this is that we have the capacity to affect our emotional states by intentionally engaging in physical activity.[21] We will return to this point shortly.

But, first, how might music and song factor into this link? According to the theory known as 'Appearance Emotionalism', one of the ways that music conveys emotion is by resembling the physical actions that normally accompany that emotion.[22] For example, human grief is often expressed by a drooping posture and a slow gait. Correspondingly, a sad tune will usually be slow, contain minor chords, and a falling melody line.[23] Otherwise put, the emotional contours of the music will seek to

---

[19] Iain Morley, *The Evolutionary Origins and Archaeology of Music* (PhD Thesis: Cambridge University, 2003), 174.
[20] Morley, *The Evolutionary Origins and Archaeology of Music*, 175.
[21] Physical exercise, for example, has a profound impact on mood, and is a well-recognised tool for helping to alleviate depression.
[22] See Davies, 'Artistic Expression and the Hard Case of Pure Music', 179-91.
[23] Begbie, 'Faithful Feelings', 341-343.

mimic expressions of emotions in human behaviour. As Begbie remarks: 'By embodying bodily motion, music embodies emotion'.[24]

But, again, there is more to be said. Recent research suggests that musical impulses are transmitted in the brain via two different routes – the 'upper' or cognitive (and relatively slower) route and 'lower' or emotional (and considerably faster) route.[25] In light of this, and by drawing on 'action-perception theory',[26] Björn Vickhoff has proposed an even richer understanding of the relationship between music, movement and emotion. He suggests that through a range of musical actions or 'vitality affects' (e.g., melodic leaps, rhythm, volume, pitch, speed, etc) emotion is embedded in music and so perceived directly by the hearer. 'This makes listening to music spontaneous and emotional – a lived experience rather than a decoding of signs'.[27] It also creates the basis of the principles and practice of music therapy.[28]

It is not our purpose to plumb the depths of the recent philosophical discussion of these matters or to synthesise the range of existing (and sometimes competing) theories. What can be said with confidence is this: *music directly affects our emotions as it also directly affects our bodies.*

---

[24] Begbie, 'Faithful Feelings', 343.
[25] Töres Theorell, 'Music for Body and Soul: Physiological Effects of Listening to Music', in *Psychological Health Effects of Musical Experiences* (SpringerBriefs in Psychology. Dordrecht: Springer, 2014), 33.
[26] This is a psychological theory which claims that perception and action are intricately related and driven by a spontaneous somatosensory process of information gathering. In other words, just as perception informs and guides action or bodily motion, so bodily motion informs and guides perception. With regard to music, what this means is that 'the human motor system and its actions can reciprocally influence the perception of music' (Pieter-Jan Maes, Marc Leman, Caroline Palmer and Marcelo M Wanderley, 'Action-based effects on music perception', *Frontier in Psychology* [January 2014]: https://doi.org/10.3389/fpsyg.2013.01008).
[27] Björn Vickhoff, 'Why Does Music Move Us?', *Philosophical Communications, Web Series* 34 (2004), 2: http://www.phil.gu.se/posters/musicmove.pdf.
[28] For further insight into both the theory and practice of music therapy, see Jane Edwards, 'Approaches and Models of Music Therapy', in Jane Edwards (ed.), *The Oxford Handbook of Music Therapy* (Oxford: OUP, 2016), 417-427. See also the website for the American Music Therapy Association: https://www.musictherapy.org/about/musictherapy.

Similarly, *our emotions directly affect our bodies, as our bodies directly affect our emotions.*

2.2. Proprioceptive feedback

This leads us to explore further the nature of 'proprioception' or 'proprioceptive feedback' – i.e., the way the brain receives information about the body's movements and the effect that this information has on our emotional states and vice versa.[29] To illustrate: while we may have reasons to question the use of Botox for purely cosmetic purposes, one of the more interesting findings of a number of studies is that people who are forced to smile (by having their cheek muscles effectively frozen) actually feel happier![30] In other words, mechanical changes to people's facial expressions lead to corresponding emotional changes.[31]

This 'feedback from the manifestation of an emotion to the emotion itself' is one of the keys to understanding how emotions are experienced and communicated.[32] Given that the limbic system of the brain processes both our emotions and the movements associated with them, this helps explain the bi-directionality of emotion and movement. Through the phenomenon of proprioceptive feedback, our movements activate the limbic system, which in turn generates an emotional response. In like manner, our emotions generate movement. The process is genuinely recursive; it is very much a 'two-way street'.[33]

This has two important implications. *First,* to the extent that we repress the physical responses that normally accompany an emotion we will curtail our experience of the emotion itself. *Second,* it is possible to

---

[29] Proprioceptors are sensors that provide information about the orientation of the body. Feedback from proprioceptors is essential for the accurate execution of movement.

[30] Richard J Davidson and Sharon Begley, *The Emotional Life of Your Brain: How Its Unique Patterns Affect the Way You Think, Feel, and Live – and How You Can Change Them* (London: Plume, 2012), 125-127.

[31] Klaus R Scherer and Marcel R Zentner, 'Emotional Effects of Music: Production Rules', in P N Juslin and J A Sloboda (eds.), *Music and Emotion: Theory and Research* (Oxford: OUP, 2001), 371.

[32] Vickhoff, 'Why Does Music Move Us?', 7.

[33] Davidson and Begley, *The Emotional Life of Your Brain*, 125.

enhance or facilitate an emotional response through intentional bodily movement normally associated with the emotion.

2.3. Emotional contagion

In corporate settings, the other element that needs to be appreciated is that of emotional contagion. This, as we noted earlier, is 'the tendency to automatically mimic and synchronize facial expressions, vocalizations, postures and movements with those of another person and, consequently, to converge emotionally'.[34] So, for example, if someone smiles or waves at us, we naturally tend to smile or wave back. This creates emotional empathy and personal connection.

What might this have to do with music? As we noted earlier, when a group of people listens to music together, or moves to it together, or sings along with it together, not only does *each person's* neurological and biological system become synchronised to the music's rhythm, but their respective systems are also synchronised to *each other*. Consequently, the emotions stimulated by these coordinated movements are felt not just by each person *individually*, but by the whole group *collectively*.

This highlights an additional implication to those mentioned above: *repressing natural bodily movements in corporate worship may in fact deprive others* (as well as ourselves) *of an important experience of empathy and short-change our relational unity.* But if, as we sing the saving truth of the gospel, we allow ourselves to move and feel together, we are reminded that 'we are not a crowd, a mob, a swarm, or a flock, not a chance agglomeration of individuals, but a united, Christ-centred community'.[35]

2.4. Facilitation or manipulation?

There is one final issue we need to consider before drawing this exploration to a close. *What is the difference between appropriate facilitation of movement and emotion and inappropriate manipulation of the same?* Otherwise put, how much should we encourage both ourselves and each other to respond bodily to the emotions embedded in a piece of

---

[34] Elaine Hatfield, John T Cacioppo and Richard L Rapson, 'Emotional Contagion', *Current Directions in Psychological Science* 2:3 (1993), 96.
[35] Wren, *Praying Twice*, 85.

music or to the emotional content of the lyrics of a song by engaging in bodily movement? For instance, is it ever appropriate for a song-leader to exhort people to clap or lift their hands or move their feet or bodies as they sing?

While there are biblical commands to do all of these things and more, the answer to this question cannot help but be situational and culturally conditioned. What is felt as undue pressure by one person or group may be welcomed by another. What seems natural on one occasion may feel forced on another. Wisdom and sensitivity are, therefore, needed and the question of *intention* is paramount – i.e., are we intending to help people for their benefit or control people for our benefit. As well as intention, perception and effect are also important measures of appropriateness. Therefore, if people are feeling manipulated by your exhortations, then you not only need to dial back their strength, but talk the issues through and, most importantly, explain your intentions and (ideally) the biblical reasons for your encouragements.[36] It is important that people respond freely, not under compulsion (cf. 2 Corinthians 9:7).

It is also important to understand that genuine emotions (and the bodily movements that flow from them and also give rise to them) are always directed toward an object. They ought, therefore, to be commensurate with the nature and significance of that object.[37] Consequently, the aim in writing, choosing or playing a song or piece of music ought to be governed by this principle. For instance, choosing sombre music for a funeral would be entirely fitting, whereas playing it at a wedding would be confusing and incongruous. In short, the emotional reality of a situation will determine the appropriate emotional response – albeit tempered by the cultural context. This in turn should inform our choices and exhortations.

Finally, when it comes to congregational song, the importance of the words cannot be overstated. Worship will only be true if it is tethered to truth. This means that *the appropriate emotional response to a particular*

---

[36] Morally speaking, the issue of intention is critical. Am I seeking to help myself and others respond authentically to genuine grief or joy, or am I seeking to manufacture an experience that has little objective basis? Clearly, the former motive is worthy, the latter unworthy.

[37] Roger Scruton, *Understanding Music: Philosophy and Interpretation* (London: Continuum International Publishing, 2009), 52.

song should be directed and determined by the lyrical content of that song. Pastoral exhortation must be sensitive to this. So, for example, in preparing a congregation to celebrate Christ's resurrection in song, it would be thoroughly appropriate to exhort them to stand on their feet, lift up their heads and 'sing lustily and with good courage' (John Wesley). If, however, the song is a raw confession of sin or an outpouring of grief, then a very different attitude and posture should be suggested. Emotion and movement will be fitting in both cases, but what movement and what emotion is most appropriate will be different in each case.

Conclusion

> Body and spirit are inseparable: when we sing with full voice our attitude changes. When body attitude combines with deepest beliefs, singers are taken out of themselves into a heightened awareness of God, beauty, faith, and one another.[38]

God desires an holistic response from His people (Deuteronomy 6:5; Mark 12:30). In personal and corporate worship, needlessly restricting our bodily movements short-circuits the emotional response that ought to be generated by the truths we are singing and the music we are making. The result is that we do not respond to God with the whole of our being. While there may be occasion for such self-imposed restriction out of sensitivity to others, usually our motives for doing so are less altruistic and more self-protective. Self-control (a vital fruit of the Spirit) is not to be equated with bodily rigidity or imperviousness to emotional reality.[39] Nor is this what the Bible means by self-denial. Rather, it is a needless short-changing of both ourselves and each other, and, most importantly, the living God. The better path is that taken by the Levites in Hezekiah's day, who 'sang praises with gladness', and also 'bowed down and worshiped' (2 Chronicles 29:30). For music, song, emotion and bodily expression naturally belong together.

---

[38] Wren, *Praying Twice*, 87.
[39] B B Warfield's essay on 'The Emotional Life of Our Lord' (in *The Person and Work of Christ* [Phillipsburg: P&R Publishing, 1989], 93-145) ably dispenses with this nonsensical equation.

APPENDIX IV: MUSIC AND LYRICS

Along more traditional lines, a hymn may be defined as 'a congregational song consisting of a sequence of units, called stanzas, with or without a repeated refrain'.[1] In contemporary compositional practice, congregational song structures are considerably more varied, often including pre-choruses, half-verses, bridges and codas. As we saw in chapter eleven, for any hymn or song (whatever its type or structure) to be useable and effective 'it must meet three criteria: text, tune, and fit'.[2] Even if not all of equal weight, each of these criteria is vital, as we shall see. It is not only song/hymn-writers who need to understand their importance, but pastors also and those who choose our songs even more so. Let us tackle these three criteria one by one.

1. Text

Because God is a God of truth and His saving work is accomplished through His Spirit-inspired Word, nothing is more important than getting the lyrics of our songs right. By 'right' I mean faithful to Scripture in terms of their meaning and comprehensible to their 'target audience' in terms of their clarity. Consequently, truth and clarity are the two non-negotiables. All of our songs, whatever their differing themes, emphases, purposes, structures and lengths must be Bible-based, Christ-centred and gospel-governed. They must also have the potential to be readily understood by those who sing them – even if some words or ideas may need to be explained and some believer may grow in their appreciation of their meaning over time.[3]

---

[1] Wren, *Praying Twice*, 253.
[2] Hughes, 'Free Church Worship: The Challenge of Freedom', 169.
[3] There is no getting around the fact that every congregation encompasses a range of individuals with varying levels of understanding – both of Christian teaching and of the local language. Inevitably, not every song will be equally comprehensible to every person present. Nevertheless, if 'every-member understanding' is the goal to strive for, then 'general intelligibility' will determine our aim.

1.1.   The problem

The problem, however, is that this is not always easily achieved in practice. Despite the myriad of resources available to most churches, the experience of many churchgoers is unsatisfying at best and confusing at worst. As author Nick Page writes:

> When I look at the words on my service sheet every Sunday morning they don't seem to connect with me. Either they're so banal as to be risible, or they're filled with more biblical imagery than any other book except, well, the Bible. They often don't scan very well; they frequently attempt rhymes that you could only call 'optimistic'; they're often little more than a collection of Bible verses, ripped out of context and shoe-horned into a lyric.[4]

David Montgomery is similarly critical, particularly of current trends in congregational songwriting. In his view,

> The standard of contemporary worship songs is embarrassingly low. In spite of much talk about the great new wave of songwriters that has emerged, when one takes time to examine the theological depth and literary quality of the songs in question, one is left with an over-riding sense of shallowness, sentimentality and sameness. The songs may be popular, even catchy, and the writers may have earned their reputations as competent guitar players (usually) and leaders of worship at mainstream evangelical events; however, it seems that in many cases their reputation far exceeds the worthiness of their compositions.[5]

For Montgomery, part of the problem is the postmodern penchant for subordinating text to music and image. As people's 'active vocabulary diminishes', he writes, 'our culture is becoming increasingly de-verbalised'.[6] This not only breeds linguistic fragmentation, but theological and relational (especially intergenerational) fragmentation as well. Then, as we become more and more 'unable to communicate with

---

[4] Nick Page, *And Now Let's Move into a Time of Nonsense: Why Worship Songs are Failing the Church* (Milton Keynes: Authentic Media, 2004), 2.
[5] David Montgomery, *Sing a New Song: Choosing and Leading Praise in Today's Church* (Edinburgh: Rutherford House, 2000), 58.
[6] Montgomery, *Sing a New Song*, 37.

God or with each other', the result is that 'Babel is revisited, and the gospel is undermined'. As a consequence, in 'many of the latest contemporary worship-songs, the lyrics are almost incidental, and probably deliberately so, with words and phrases (often clichés) chosen for their sound rather than their meaning'.[7]

Montgomery identifies additional problems as well. For example, the fact that 'many current songwriters and worship-leaders are first and foremost musicians goes some way to explaining the dual phenomena of the popular appeal of their songs, and the general weakness of many of their words'.[8] While these criticisms are strong, it is important to understand that Montgomery does not write as 'an unreconstructed traditionalist', suspicious of all things contemporary. Nor is he criticising popular songs in which the words are intended to be incidental. His main point (with which I am in full agreement) is that when it comes to congregational song, words cannot afford to be incidental. Rather, 'hymnwriters have an obligation to ensure that the people of God are edified by what they sing'.[9] For this to take place, the Word of God must be faithfully and intelligibly communicated.

1.2.   The solution

The solution, then, is to prioritise truth and clarity. Congregational songs 'are a particular genre of theological song. Like other theological work, they need to be appraised and tested for coherence, truthfulness and practicality'.[10] This does not mean that there is no place for lyrical ingenuity or poetic flare. Quite the contrary. Many of the hymns that have stood the test of time show that inventive meter, creative rhyme, evocative imagery, thoughtful repetition, and even tasteful alliteration, far from obstructing the cause of truth and clarity, can be well-used to serve it.[11] Of course, the opposite is also sometimes true. The point, then, is this: 'a hymn cannot give free rein to the poet's imagination. It is poetry in the service of its singers'.[12] Therefore, inasmuch as poetic and linguistic

---

[7] Montgomery, *Sing a New Song*, 37.
[8] Montgomery, *Sing a New Song*, 37.
[9] Montgomery, *Sing a New Song*, 38.
[10] Wren, *Praying Twice*, 365.
[11] 'My Song is Love Unknown', by Samuel Crossman (1624-1683) is an obvious case in point.
[12] Wren, *Praying Twice*, 278.

features assist communication, we should be grateful for them and make free use of them. But if and when they undermine it, they must be sacrificed. As Brian Wren writes, 'a good hymn is a poem under three monastic vows: clarity, simplicity, and obedience to strict rhythm'.[13]

As a rule, simplicity is generally better than subtlety. Faithful song writers ought then to follow the lead of the great preachers of the evangelical revival who, according to J C Ryle, 'were not ashamed to crucify their style and to sacrifice their reputation for learning ... They carried out the maxim of Augustine: "A wooden key is not so beautiful as a golden one, but if it can open the door when the golden one cannot, it is far more useful"'.[14] In a similar vein, Nick Page helpfully contrasts the 'master lyric' – 'which is deliberately confusing, opaque or subjective, expressed in a language that only the artist truly understands' – with the 'servant lyric' – words that aim 'to serve the church by leading it into greater understanding, truth and worship'.[15]

Getting practical, song lyrics ought to have a clear purpose and a coherent theme. This does not rule out narrative development, shifts in focus or even changes of address (e.g., verses addressed to God and a chorus addressed to believers). It simply means that we ought to avoid writing or choosing a song that confuses others because the song itself is confusing or, perhaps, just confused. Grammatical inconsistency is also to be avoided, as it's usually a sign of conceptual confusion. Songs that flip from 'I' to 'we' without reason are rarely helpful and songs that muddle the members of the Trinity can even fall into heresy (e.g., by thanking the Father for dying on the cross).

Obviously, it is possible to be overly scrupulous and to banish a strong hymn simply because it contains a clumsy or curious line. No extra-biblical song is perfect and, as we saw in chapter ten, no hymn can say everything or do every job. The value of individual songs needs to be assessed in light of a church's broader repertoire. Not every song will contribute as much as another. Nevertheless, there is no excuse for singing lies or singing nonsense. Problem verses need to be cut and bad songs should be dropped altogether. The words we sing matter because

---

[13] Wren, *Praying Twice*, 279.
[14] Ryle, *Christian Leaders of England in the 18th Century*, 24-25.
[15] Page, *And Now Let's Move into a Time of Nonsense*, 114-115.

truth and clarity matter. Nick Page's challenge to song-writers is, therefore, worth heeding:

> Make the words right and they will write themselves on people's hearts. Make the words right and they will form part of people's lives. Make the words right and they will open people's eyes to the reality of God. Make the words right and, as they sing them, God will come home to people's hearts.[16]

2. Tune

The words of hymns are essentially poems. Like poems, they can be read, meditated upon, and even quoted in sermons. Their intended purpose, however, is not to exist in textual form (as necessary as that might be for their use and preservation), but in oral form. They were written to be sung. In this sense Mark Evans is exactly right: 'lyrics "live" within the music'.[17] Indeed, while there are clear historic exceptions, most contemporary lyrics live or die depending on their accompanying music. The reason for this is straightforward: 'Without a memorable and evocative melody, the best hymn, song lyric, or chorus is rarely sung and soon forgotten'.[18]

2.1. Keys to success

What then makes for a good tune? This is not an easy question to answer, given that there are almost as many musical theories as there are different musical styles. Moreover, most musical genres have their own unique musical features and trademarks. When it comes to congregational song, however, there are some generally accepted 'rules of composition' (e.g., accessibility of rhythm, repeated chords and motifs, anticipated melodic sequences within a certain range) that usually have to be adhered to if a tune is going to work for congregational purposes. That said, 'the rules can occasionally be "stretched" or momentarily abandoned: in a discord, an unexpected melodic jump, or change of time or key. In fact it is these exceptions which transform a moderate tune into a great tune'.[19]

---

[16] Page, *And Now Let's Move into a Time of Nonsense*, 112.
[17] Evans, *Open Up the Doors*, 113.
[18] Wren, *Praying Twice*, 82.
[19] Montgomery, *Sing a New Song*, 43.

What can be affirmed with confidence is that the key qualities of a successful melody are *singability* and *memorability*. Like truth and clarity with regard to texts, singability and memorability are non-negotiables when it comes to tunes. This probably applies to any song of any type, but particularly to congregational compositions. Thinking along these lines, William Booth, the founder of the Salvation Army, once defined a 'good tune' in the following way:

> A melody with some distinct air in it, that one can take hold of, which people can learn, nay which makes them learn it, which takes hold of them and goes on humming in the mind. [...] That is the sort of tune to help you; it will preach to you and bring you believers and converts.[20]

A few other things can be added. In light of our discussion about music and movement in the previous appendix, we can also say that 'a good tune suggests bodily movement, moves musically in interesting ways, and mimics emotional flow'.[21] One of the ways of achieving this is by weaving tension and resolution into the melody's progression and facilitating its resolution through an appropriate melodic climax. Getting this progression 'right' (i.e., satisfying) is vital to musical success. Rhythmic variation is also essential to prevent a tune from becoming boring or overly predictable. On the other hand, too much syncopation can limit a tune's usefulness and limit its durability – despite the fact that syncopation is much more easily managed by Generation X and beyond (i.e., those born after 1963).

2.2.   Different musical genres

This last point raises the larger issue of generational, cultural and genre differences. Every type of music has its detractors and defenders – often divided along demographic lines. When it comes to providing accompaniment for congregational songs, however, different musical styles do appear to have objective strengths and weaknesses. If the aim of the tune is to serve the text, and the aim of both together is to enable God's people to sing in concert, then those musical types that best allow for corporate singing and clear communication of content are surely to be preferred. This does not tie us down to a single musical style, nor should

---

[20] Cited in Wilson-Dickson, *The Story of Christian Music*, 139.
[21] Wren, *Praying Twice*, 82.

it limit experimentation with emerging styles or new hybrids.[22] But it does steer us in the right direction, even if different decisions will be made by different people in different contexts and cultures.

What, then, is needed, is the willingness and ability to analyse the strengths and weaknesses of the musical options available to us within our cultural context. We also need to be alert to the way in which certain styles become entangled with our cultural idols in particular historical seasons. This does not necessarily render a style unusable, but it does highlight the need for care to be taken and, sometimes, for time to elapse.[23]

In his book, *Why Johnny Can't Sing Hymns*, and in a chapter titled, 'Three Musical Genres', T David Gordon helpfully distinguishes between the three genres that continue to dominate Christian music in the west: classical/high culture music, folk culture music and pop/mass culture music.[24] While he has an overly positive view of the first and an overly negative view of the last, Gordon ends the chapter with a series useful analytical questions:[25]

1. What are the characteristics of classical art and music?
2. What are the characteristics of folk art and music?
3. What are the characteristics of pop art and music?
4. Which of these genres has the steepest learning curve and is therefore less accessible than the others? Which has the least steep curve? Explain.

---

[22] I, therefore, agree with Mark Evans (*Open Up the Doors*, 159) when he writes: 'There are so many musical genres available today, an almost exponentially expanding world of musical opportunities. We must be willing to experiment with new musical forms and new timbres'.

[23] For example, for the most part, rock 'n' roll music today is no longer as volatile a genre as it was in the late 1950s. At that point in our history, it was 'the sound of a generation slipping free from the restraints of the past' (Steve Turner, *The Gospel According to the Beatles* [Westminster John Knox Press, Louisville, 2006], 58). At this point in our history, the same sounds are entirely mainstream, if not quaint.

[24] T David Gordon, *Why Johnny Can't Sing Hymns: How Pop Culture Rewrote the Hymnal* (Phillipsburg: P&R Publishing, 2010), 79-93.

[25] Gordon, *Why Johnny Can't Sing Hymns*, 92-93.

5. Which of these genres (may be more than one) is multi-generational? Explain.
6. Which of these genres (may be more than one) is communal/corporate rather than individual? Explain.
7. Which of these genres is most restrained/disciplined; which is least restrained/disciplined? Explain.
8. How, if at all, do the properties of these particular genres of music make them more appropriate or less appropriate to worship song?

However we may answer these questions, and whatever style we deem most suitable, what should not be in doubt is music's capacity to serve as a vehicle for communicating the Word of God. As was illustrated in chapter ten, few have understood this as well as Luther. In his 'Preface' to a 1542 collection of funeral hymns, he explains why it is so important to add music to the truths, indeed the very words, of Scripture:

> We have put this music on the living and holy Word of God in order to sing, praise, and honor it. We want the beautiful art of music to be properly used to serve her dear Creator and his Christians. He is thereby praised and honored and we are made better and stronger in faith when his holy Word is impressed on our hearts by sweet music.[26]

3. Fit

This, then, brings us to the issue of 'fit' – i.e., to the way in which, and the success with which, text and tune combine.

3.1.   Servant and master

If God's Word is to be 'impressed on our hearts by sweet music' then the music needs to serve the Word, allowing and assisting its voice to be 'heard'. Bonhoeffer saw this clearly:

> All devotion, all attention should be concentrated upon the Word in the hymns. The fact that we do not speak it but sing it only expresses the fact that our spoken words are inadequate to express what we want to say, that the burden of our song goes far beyond

---

[26] Luther, 'Preface to the Burial Hymns, 1542', 328.

all human words. Yet we do not hum a melody; we sing words of praise to God, words of thanksgiving, confession, and prayer. Thus the music is completely the servant of the Word. It elucidates the Word in its mystery.[27]

Understanding this relationship, as we have seen, has numerous practical implications – e.g., for music volume and song leadership, and for the use of instrumental music. But our chief concern here is to establish priorities: What needs to fit with what? The answer is that music needs to be found or written to fit with the words, not the other way around. This does not necessarily mean that the words always have to be written first; it can work the other way around and in many cases the two are written together. It simply means that music is the servant and the words are the master.

3.2.   A satisfying match

Acknowledging the importance of this order does not mean that 'any old tune will do', provided it has the right meter. Far from it. As we have seen, 'good music can make average words fly, or lift words better off grounded. It makes our best words soar, and stores them in memory'.[28] What we are looking for, then, is a 'satisfying match' or 'successful dance' between words and music.

Although some of us may feel that we have almost sung it to death, there are good reasons why, within five years of its composition, Stuart Townend and Keith Getty's 'In Christ Alone' (2001) was voted the ninth best loved hymn of all time in the UK in a 2005 BBC Songs of Praise survey and why, by 2006, it had risen to number one in the UK CCLI charts, and it remains in the top 30 to this day. In 2017, 16 years after it was first aired, it was estimated that 'over 100 million people sang this

---

[27] Bonhoeffer, *Life Together*, 49. The servant-master metaphor has obvious limitations. As we have seen, a good tune can enhance or even liberate a text and vice versa. The relationship is, therefore, more reciprocal that the servant-master metaphor might suggest. In fact, as Brian Wren (*Praying Twice*, 83) writes: 'The words of a congregational song relate to its tune like passengers to an airplane. The words cannot be sung without the tune, just as passengers cannot fly without the plane'. In this sense, the text of a hymn is thoroughly dependent on its tune. [28] Wren, *Praying Twice*, 83.

one hymn in the last 12 months'.[29] Why? What makes this hymn so popular? The reason is simple: the words are true and clear, the music is singable and memorable, and text and tune are a perfect fit.

In order to achieve this kind of fit, several things need to line up:

- The mood of the music needs to match the mood of the lyrics.
- The style of the music needs to reflect the substance of the lyrics.
- The tempo of the music needs to allow the lyrics to be digested and proclaimed.
- The emphases of the music need to align with the emphases of the lyrics.
- The emotional contours of the music need to track with the emotional contours of the lyrics.
- The musical climax of the tune needs to coincide with the lyrical climax of the words.

It is the alignment of these elements within a hymn or song that makes for a winning combination. This is precisely what 'In Christ Alone' (like many other songs and hymns beside) has going for it. It is the strength of the fit between music and lyrics that allows the former to truly serve the latter, so that the two 'languages' speak as one. As Wren notes: 'When text matches tune, the song moves, develops, and unfolds in an intensified way, because it incorporates the clearer, widely shared meanings that language provides'.[30] This ought to be the goal of every song writer.

Conclusion

At the beginning of the twentieth century, two tunes were composed for William W How's hymn, 'For all the saints'. Charles Villiers Standford (1852-1924) wrote the tune 'Engelberg' for the 1904 edition of *Hymns Ancient and Modern*, and Standford's former pupil, Ralph Vaughan Williams (1872-1958), wrote the tune 'Sine nomine' for *The English*

---

[29] Roslan & Campion, 'Queen Elizabeth Honors "In Christ Alone" Author Keith Getty for "Music and Modern Hymn Writing"', *The Gospel Herald* (June 19, 2017): http://www.gospelherald.com/articles/70972/20170619/queen-elizabeth-honors-christ-alone-author-keith-getty-music-modern.htm.
[30] Wren, *Praying Twice*, 82.

Hymnal (1906).[31] It soon became clear that Stanford's tune, although beautiful, was 'a pale if prestigious second in its ability to articulate the text'. Vaughan Williams' tune, on the other hand, was 'an ideal match, expressing dignity, gratitude and a sense of the ongoing life of the saints'.[32] In short, the combination of great text, great tune and great fit won the day.[33]

The church of Jesus Christ should be profoundly thankful for those poets and composers (and, in some cases, poet-composers) who, under God, have poured their energies into texts, tunes and the fit between them, and in so doing have created the enormous pool of musical and liturgical resources from which most of us freely draw week in, week out. Of course, the 'greatest compliment to a hymn poet is the unspoken "yes" from singers who grasp, delight in, and identify with the hymn in the act of singing it, yet rarely know or care who wrote the words or composed the tune'.[34] Therefore, Katie Barclay Wilkinson's prayer should be the prayer of every hymn-writer: 'And may they forget the channel, seeing only Him'.[35]

---

[31] LindaJo H McKim, *The Presbyterian Hymnal Companion* (Louisville: Westminster John Knox Press, 1993), 189.

[32] Bell, *The Singing Thing*, 33. Both quotes.

[33] 'Engelberg' was not wasted, however. It was later successfully paired with a number of other, more suitable, texts (e.g., John Geyer's 'We Know that Christ is Raised and Dies No More' [1967]).

[34] Wren, *Praying Twice*, 278.

[35] These are the last two lines of Katie Barclay Wilkinson's much-loved prayer-hymn, 'May the Mind of Christ My Saviour' (written 1925).

Bibliography

Adam, Peter. *Speaking God's Words: A Practical Theology of Preaching* (Leicester: IVP, 1996).

Adey, Lionel. *Hymns and Christian 'Myth'* (Vancouver: University of British Columbia, 1986).

Allison, Gregory R. 'Toward a Theology of Human Embodiment', *SBJT* 13.2 (Summer 2009), pp 5-17.

Arnold, Clinton E. *Ephesians* (Grand Rapids: Zondervan).

Ashton, Mark with C J Davis, 'Following in Cranmer's Footsteps', in D A Carson (ed.), *Worship by the Book* (Grand Rapids: Zondervan, 2002), pp 64-135.

Athanasius, 'A Letter to Marcellinus, Our Holy Father, Bishop of Alexandria, On the Interpretation of the Psalms', in Robert G Gregg (trans.), *Athanasius: The Life of Antony and the Letter to Marcellinus* (Mahway: Paulist Press, 1980), pp 101-130.

Augustine, 'The Greatness of the Soul', in Joseph M Colleran (trans. and annot.), *St. Augustine: The Greatness of the Soul, The Teacher* (New York: The Newman Press, 1978), pp 13-112.

Aune, David E. 'The Influence of Roman Imperial Court Ceremonial on the Apocalypse of John', *BR* 18 (1983), pp 5-26.

Baird, A and S Samson, 'Music evoked autobiographical memory after severe acquired brain injury: Preliminary findings from a case series', *Neuropsychological Rehabilitation: An International Journal* 24 (2014), pp 125-143.

Baker, David W and Bill T Arnold (eds.), *The Face of Old Testament Studies: A Survey of Contemporary Approaches* (Grand Rapids: Apollos/Baker, 1999).

Bale, John. 'The Examination of William Thorpe', in H Christmas (ed.), *Select Works of John Bale* (For the Parker Society; Cambridge: Cambridge University Press, 1849), pp 61-133.

Bale, John. 'The Image of Both Churches', in H Christmas (ed.), *Select Works of John Bale* (For the Parker Society; Cambridge: Cambridge University Press, 1849), pp 534-546.

Barbour, Ian G. *Nature, Human Nature and God* (Minneapolis: Fortress, 2002).

Barker, David G. 'Praise and Praxis: Doxology as the Context for Kingdom Ministry', *Baptist Review of Theology* 3:1 (Spring 1993), pp 4-17.

Barnett, Paul W. *Apocalypse Then and Now: Reading Revelation Today* (South Sydney: Aquila Press, 2004).

Barrick, William D. 'The Eschatological Significance of Leviticus 26', *MSJ* 16.1 (Spring 2005), pp 95-126.

Barth, Karl. *Church Dogmatics: Volume III, Part 4* (trans. A T Mackay et al; eds. Geoffrey W Bromiley & Thomas F Torrance; Edinburgh: T & T Clark, 1961).

Bauckham, Richard J. *The Climax of Prophecy: Studies on the Book of Revelation* (London: T & T Clark, 1993).

Baughen, Michael (ed.). *Youth Praise* (London: Falcon Press, 1966).

Bayly, David and Tim Bayly, 'John Calvin: Lifting hands helps "jolt us out of our laziness" in worship ...' (June 12, 2009): http://baylyblog.com/blog/2009/06/john-calvin-lifting-hands-helps-jolt-us-out-our-laziness-worship.

Beale, Gregory K. *The Book of Revelation: A Commentary on the Greek Text* (Grand Rapids: Eerdmans, 1999).

Beale, Gregory K. *We Become What We Worship: A Biblical Theology of Idolatry* (Downers Grove: IVP, 2008).

Beall, Todd S. 'Evangelicalism, Inerrancy, and Current Old Testament Scholarship', *DBSJ* 18 (2013), pp 67-81.

Bebbington, David W. *Evangelicalism in Modern Britain: A History from the 1730s to the 1980s* (London: Unwin Hyman, 1989).

Becon, Thomas. 'The Jewel of Joy', in John Ayre (ed.), *The Catechism of Thomas Becon with other pieces written by him on the reign of King Edward VI* (For the Parker Society; Cambridge: Cambridge University Press, 1844), pp 413-476.

Begbie, Jeremy S. 'Faithful Feelings: Music and Emotions in Worship', in Jeremy S Begbie and Steven R Guthrie (eds.), *Resonant Witness: Conversations between Music and Theology* (Grand Rapids: Eerdmans, 2011), pp 323-354.

Belcher Jr, Richard P. *The Messiah and the Psalms: Preaching Christ from all the Psalm* (Fearn: Mentor, 2006).

Bell, John L. *The Singing Thing: A Case for Congregational Singing* (Glasgow: Wild Goose Publications, 2000).

Bennett, Arthur (ed.). *The Valley of Vision: A Collection of Puritan Prayers & Devotions* (Edinburgh: Banner of Truth, 1975).

Benson, Louis F. *The English Hymn: Its Development and Use* (London: Hodder & Stoughton, 1915).

Bergland, Christopher. 'Why Do the Songs from Your Past Evoke Such Vivid Memories?', *Psychology Today* (11 December, 2013): http://tinyurl.com/hh2h5vc.

Best, Ernest. *Ephesians* (London: T & T Clark, 1998).

Best, Harold. *Music Through the Eyes of Faith* (San Francisco: Harper, 1993).

Bevan, Edwyn. 'Petition: Some Theoretical Difficulties', in H Anson, et al (eds.), *Concerning Prayer: Its Nature, its Difficulties and its Value* (London: McMillan & Co., 1916), pp 191-210.

Bickersteth, Edward. *Christian Psalmody, A Collection of Above 900 Psalms, Hymns and Spiritual Songs Selected and Arranged for Public, Social, Family and Private Worship* (London: S Staughton, 1839).

Black, C Clifton. 'The Persistence of the Wounds', in Sally Brown and Patrick D Miller (eds.), *Lament: Reclaiming Practices in Pulpit, Pew, and Public Square* (Louisville: Westminster John Knox Press, 2005), pp 47-58.

Blackaby, Henry, Richard Blackaby and Claude King, *Fresh Encounters: God's Pattern for Spiritual Awakening* (Nashville: B&H Publishing, 2009).

Block, Daniel I. *For the Glory of God: Recovering a Biblical Theology of Worship* (Grand Rapids: Baker, 2014).

Bloesch, Donald G. 'Prayer', in Walter A Elwell (ed.), *Evangelical Dictionary of Theology* (Grand Rapids: Baker Academic, 2001), pp 946-948.

Bonhoeffer, Dietrich. *Life Together* (London: SCM, 1954).

Bonhoeffer, Dietrich. *Psalms: The Prayerbook of the Bible* (Minneapolis: Augsburg, 1974).

Boring, M Eugene. 'Narrative Christology in the Apocalypse', *CBQ* 54 (1992), pp 702-723.

Boso, Marianna, Pierluigi Politi, Francesco Barale and Enzo Emanuele, 'Neurophysiology and neurobiology of the musical experience', *Functional Neurology* 21.4 (2006), pp 187-191.

Brighton, Louis A. 'Christological Trinitarian Theology in the Book of Revelation', *Concordia Journal* 34.4 (2008), pp 292-297.

Brock, Brian. *Singing the Ethos of God: On the Place of Christian Ethics in Scripture* (Grand Rapids: Eerdmans, 2007).

Brown, Callum G. *The Death of Christian Britain: Understanding Secularisation 1800-2000* (London/New York: Routledge, 2009).

Brown, Jamie. 'Is Evangelical Worship Headed for a HUGE Crash?', *Church Leaders* (November 9, 2017): https://churchleaders.com/worship/worship-articles/175020-jamie-brown-evangelical-worship-headed-for-a-huge-crash.html/2.

Broyles, Craig C. 'Psalms of Lament', in Tremper Longman III and Peter Enns (eds.), *Dictionary of the Old Testament: Wisdom, Poetry and Writings* (Downers Grove: IVP Academic, 2008), pp 384-399.

Brueggemann, Walter. *Israel's Praise: Doxology Against Idolatry and Ideology* (Philadelphia: Fortress, 1988).

Butler, Andrew. 'History of Hymns: 'Blessed Be the God of Israel', *Discipleship Ministries: The United Methodist Church* (n.d.): https://www.umcdiscipleship.org/resources/history-of-hymns-blessed-be-the-god-of-israel.

Calvin, John. 'Articles Concerning the Organisation of the Church and of Worship at Geneva (1537)', in J K S Reid (ed. & trans.), *Calvin: Theological Treatises* (London: SCM, 1954), pp 47-55.

Calvin, John. 'The Author's Preface' (1557), in *A Commentary on the Book of Psalms – Volume 1: Translated from the original Latin, and collated with the author's French version, by The Rev James Anderson* (Calvin Translation Society, 1845–1849; repr. Grand Rapids: Baker, 1979): http://www.ccel.org/ccel/calvin/calcom08.vi.html.

Calvin, John. 'The Form of Prayers and Songs of the Church, 1542: Letter to the Reader' (trans. Ford Lewis Battles), *CTJ* 15.2 (November 1980), pp 160-165.

Calvin, John. *Commentary on the Book of Psalms* (trans. Henry Beveridge; Grand Rapids: Baker, 1979).

Calvin, John. *Sermons on Ephesians* (Edinburgh: Banner of Truth, 1973).

Campbell, Alistair. 'Once More: Is Worship "Biblical"?', *Churchman* 110.2 (1996), pp 131-139.

Carothers, Merlin R. *Prison to Praise* (London: Hodder & Stoughton, 1970).

Carson, D A (ed.). *From Sabbath to Lord's Day: A Biblical, Historical and Theological Investigation* (Grand Rapids: Zondervan, 1982).

Carson, D A and Douglas J Moo, *An Introduction to the New Testament* (Leicester: Apollos, 2005).

Carson, D A. 'Matthew', in F E Gaebelein (ed.), *The Expositor's Bible Commentary: Volume 8: Mathew, Mark, Luke* (Grand Rapids: Zondervan, 1984), pp 1-599.

Carson, D A. 'Systematic Theology and Biblical Theology', in T Desmond Alexander and Brian S Rosner (eds.), *New Dictionary of Biblical Theology* (Leicester: IVP, 2000) pp 89-104.

Carson, D A. 'Worship Under the Word', in D A Carson (ed.), *Worship by the Book* (Grand Rapids: Zondervan, 2002), pp 11-63.

Carson, D A. *A Call to Spiritual Reformation: Priorities from Paul and His Prayer* (Grand Rapids: Baker, 1992).

Carson, D A. *The Gospel According to John* (Leicester: IVP, 1991).

Cartwright, Hugh. 'Does the Bible tell us what to sing?' (14 February 2000): www.fpchurch.org.uk/about-us/how-we-worship/exclusive-psalmody/does-the-bible-tell-us-what-to-sing.

Chapell, Bryan. *Ephesians* (Phillipsburg: P&R Publishing, 2009).

Chapple, Allan. 'The English Standard Version: A Review Article', *RTR* 62.2 (Aug, 2003), pp 61-96.

Childs, Brevard S. *Introduction to the Old Testament as Scripture* (Philadelphia: Fortress, 1979).

Chrysostom, John. 'Homily XIX. Ephesians V. 15, 16, 17', in Philip Schaff (ed.), *Nicene and Post-Nicene Fathers: Chrysostom: Homilies on Galatians, Ephesians, Philippians, Colossians, Thessalonians, Timothy, Titus, and Philemon* (Peabody: Hendrickson, 1999), pp 137-142.

Ciampa, Roy E and Brian S Rosner. *The First Letter to the Corinthians* (Grand Rapids: Eerdmans, 2010).

Clarke, Martin V. *John Wesley and Methodist Music in the Eighteenth Century: Principles and Practice* (Doctoral thesis, Durham University, 2008).

Clowney, Edmund P. 'A Biblical Theology of Prayer', in D A Carson (ed.), *Teach Us to Pray: Prayer in the Bible and the World* (Exeter: Paternoster, 1990), pp 136-173.

Cole, Graham. 'Lament: A Missing Practice', *The Gospel Coalition Australia* (September 22, 2016): https://australia.thegospelcoalition.org/article/lament-a-missing-practice.

Connell, Scott. '10 Things I Did Not Do that Improved My Congregation's Singing', *TGC: U.S. Edition* (March 16, 2017): https://www.thegospelcoalition.org/article/10-things-i-did-not-do-that-improved-my-congregations-singing.

Cooper, John W. 'The Current Body-Soul Debate: A Case for Dualistic Holism', *SBJT* 13.2 (Summer 2009), pp 32-51.

Coverdale, Myles. 'Goostly psalms and spirituall songes drawen out of the holy Scripture, for the comforte and consolacyon of soch as loue to reioyse in God and his worde', in George Pearson (ed.), *Remains of Myles Coverdale, Bishop of Exeter* (For the Parker

Society; Cambridge: Cambridge University Press, 1846), pp 533-590.

Cranfield, Charles E B. *A Critical and Exegetical Commentary on the Epistle to the Romans: Introduction and Commentary on Romans IX-XVI and Essays*, Vol 2 (Edinburgh: T & T Clark, 1979).

Cranmer, Thomas. 'Letter to King Henry VIII, 7 October, 1544', in J E Cox (ed.), *Miscellaneous Writings and Letters of Thomas Cranmer, Archbishop of Canterbury* (For the Parker Society; Cambridge: Cambridge University Press, 1846), p 412.

Cranmer, Thomas. 'A Preface made by the King's most excellent Majesty unto his Primer Book' (1545), in J E Cox (ed.), *Miscellaneous Writings and Letters of Thomas Cranmer, Archbishop of Canterbury* (For the Parker Society; Cambridge: Cambridge University Press, 1846), pp 496-498.

Darsey, Steven. 'John Wesley as Hymn and Tune Editor', *The Hymn* 47.1 (January 1996), pp 17-24.

Davidson, Richard J and Sharon Begley, *The Emotional Life of Your Brain: How Its Unique Patterns Affect the Way You Think, Feel, and Live – and How You Can Change Them* (London: Plume, 2012).

Davies, Horton. *Worship and Theology in England: From Cranmer to Baxter and Fox, 1534-1690* (Grand Rapids: Eerdmans, 1996).

Davies, Horton. *Worship and Theology in England: From Watts and Wesley to Maurice, 1690-1850* (Book 2, Section III, 1961; Grand Rapids: Eerdmans, 1996).

Davies, Stephen. 'Artistic Expression and the Hard Case of Pure Music', in M Kieren (ed), *Contemporary Debates in Aesthetics and the Philosophy of Art* (Oxford: Blackwell, 2006), pp 179-191.

Dawn, Marva J. *Reaching Out Without Dumbing Down: A Theology of Worship for This Urgent Time* (Grand Rapids: Eerdmans, 1995).

deClaissé-Walford, Nancy L, Rolf A Jacobson and Beth LaNeel Tanner, *The Book of Psalms* (Eerdmans: Grand Rapids, 2014).

Delitzsch, Franz. *Isaiah: Commentary on the Old Testament: Volume 7* (trans. James Martin; Peabody: Hendrickson, 2006).

Dowley, Tim. *Christian Music: A Global History* (Oxford: Lion, 2011).

du Rand, Jan A. '"... Let Him Hear What the Spirit Says ...": The Functional Role and Theological Meaning of The Spirit in The Book of Revelation', *Ex Auditu* 12 (1996), pp 43-58.

Dueck, Jonathan. *Congregational Music, Conflict and Community* (Abingdon/New York: Routledge, 2017).

Duncan III, J Ligon. 'Foundations for Biblically Directed Worship', in Philip Graham Ryken, Derek W H Thomas, and J Ligon Duncan III (eds.), *God: A Vision for Reforming Worship* (Phillipsburg: P&R, 2003), pp 51-73.

Dunn, James D G. *Romans 9-16* (Dallas: Word, 1988).

Dunn, James D G. *The Epistles to the Colossians and to Philemon* (Grand Rapids: Eerdmans, 1996).

Durham, John I. *Exodus* (Waco: Word, 1987).

Edwards, Brian. *Revival! A People Saturated with God* (Durham: Evangelical Press, 1994).

Edwards, Jane. 'Approaches and Models of Music Therapy', in Jane Edwards (ed.), *The Oxford Handbook of Music Therapy* (Oxford: OUP, 2016), pp 417-427.

Edwards, Jonathan. 'They Sang a New Song (Rev 14:3a)', in Harry S Stout (ed.), *Sermons and Discourses, 1739-1742; WJE Online Vol. 22* (New Haven: Jonathan Edwards Centre at Yale University, 2008), pp 228-244.

Eskridge, Larry. 'The "Praise and Worship" Revolution', *Christianity Today* (October, 2008): http://www.christianitytoday.com/history/2008/october/praise-and-worship-revolution.html.

Evans, Mark. *Open Up the Doors: Music in the Modern Church* (London/Oakville: Equinox, 2006).

Fee, Gordon D. *God's Empowering Presence: The Holy Spirit in the Letters of Paul* (Peabody: Hendrickson, 1994).

Fee, Gordon D. *Paul's Letter to the Philippians* (Grand Rapids: Eerdmans, 1995).

Ferguson, Everett. *The Church of Christ: A Biblical Ecclesiology for Today* (Grand Rapids: Eerdmans, 1997).

Firth, David G. 'The Teaching of the Psalms', in David G Firth and Philip S Johnston (eds.), *Interpreting the Psalms: Issues and Approaches* (Downers Grove: IVP, 2005), pp 159-174.

Wenham, Gordon J. 'The Ethics of the Psalms', in David G Firth and Philip S Johnston (eds.), *Interpreting the Psalms: Issues and Approaches* (Downers Grove: IVP, 2005), pp 175-194.

Foley, Edward. *Foundations of Christian Music: The Music of Pre-Constantinian Christianity* (Collegeville: The Liturgical Press, 1996).

Ford, Josephine M. 'The Christological Function of the Hymns in the Apocalypse of John', *Andrews University Seminary Studies*, 36 (1998), pp 207-229.

Forsyth, P T. *The Cruciality of the Cross* [London: Hodder & Stoughton, 1909).

Forsyth, P T. *The Soul of Prayer* (London: Independent Press, 1949).

Foster, Paul. *Colossians* (London: Bloomsbury, 2016).

Frame, John M. '*Review of Marva Dawn*, Reaching Out Without Dumbing Down', in Frame, *Contemporary Worship Music*, pp 155-174.

Frame, John M. *Contemporary Worship Music: A Biblical Defense* (Philipsburg: P&R Publishing, 1997).

Frame, John M. *Worship in Spirit and Truth: A Refreshing Study of the Principles and Practice of Biblical Worship* (Phillisburg: P&R Publishing, 1996).

Frere, W H and W M Kennedy (eds.). *Visitation Articles and Injunctions of the Period of the Reformation* (London, 1910).

Futato, Mark D. *Interpreting the Psalms: An Exegetical Handbook* (Grand Rapids: Kregel, 2007).

Gallusz, Laszlo. *The Throne Motif in the Book of Revelation* (London: Bloomsbury T & T Clark, 2014).

Garland, David E. *1 Corinthians* (Grand Rapids: Baker Academic, 2003).

Gerald H Wilson, *The Editing of the Hebrew Psalter* (Chico: Scholars Press, 1985)

Gillman, Frederick John. *The Evolution of the English Hymn* (London: George Allen, 1927).

Goldingay, John. *Psalms: Volume 2: Psalm 42-89* (Grand Rapids: Baker, 2007).

Goldsworthy, Graeme. *According to Plan* (Leicester: IVP, 1991).

Goldsworthy, Graeme. *Prayer and the Knowledge of God: What the Whole Bible Teaches* (Leicester: IVP, 2003).

Goldsworthy, Graeme. *Preaching the Whole Bible as Christian Scripture: The Application of Biblical Theology to Preaching* (Leicester: IVP, 2000).

Goldsworthy, Graeme. *The Goldsworthy Trilogy* (Carlisle: Paternoster, 2000).

Gombis, Timothy G. 'Being the Fullness of God in Christ by the Spirit: Ephesians 5:18 in its Epistolary Setting', *TynB* 53.2 (2002), pp 259-271.

Gordon, T David. *Why Johnny Can't Sing Hymns: How Pop Culture Rewrote the Hymnal* (Phillipsburg: P&R Publishing, 2010).

Gottfried Schimanowski, "Connecting Heaven and Earth': The Function of the Hymns in Revelation 4-5', in Ra'anan S. Boustan and Annette Yoshiko Reed, *Heavenly Realms and Earthly Realities in Late Antique Religions* (Cambridge: CUP, 2004), pp 67-84.

Grabiner, Steven. *Revelation's Hymns: Commentary on the Cosmic Conflict* (London/New York: T & T Clark, 2015).

Graham, Glenn H. *An Exegetical Summary of Ephesians* (Dallas: Summer Institute of Linguistics, 1997).

Scheer, Greg. 'Singing the Psalm in Modern Worship', *Reformed Worship* 85 (June 2007): http://www.reformedworship.org/article/june-2007/singing-psalms-modern-worship.

Grenz, Stanley J. *Prayer: The Cry of the Kingdom* (Peabody: Hendrickson, 1988).

Grindal, Gracia. 'The Rhetoric of Martin Luther's Hymns: Hymnody Then and Now', *Word & World* 26.2 (Spring 2006), pp 178-187.

Grudem, Wayne A. *1 Peter* (Leicester: IVP, 1988).

Grudem, Wayne A. *Systematic Theology: An Introduction to Biblical Doctrine* (Grand Rapids: Zondervan, 1994).

Guthrie, Donald. 'The Christology of Revelation', in Joel B Green and Max Turner (eds.), *Jesus of Nazareth: Lord and Christ: Essays on the Historical Jesus and New Testament Christology* (Grand Rapids: Eerdmans, 1994), pp 397-409.

Guthrie, Steven R. 'Singing in the Body and in the Spirit', *JETS* 46/4 (December 2003), pp 633-646.

Haenchen, Ernst. *The Acts of the Apostles: A Commentary* (trans. Bernard Noble and Gerald Shinn; Philadelphia: The Westminster Press, 1971).

Hamilton, Michael S. 'The Triumph of the Praise Songs: How Guitars Beat Out the Organs in the Worship Wars', *Christianity Today* (July 12, 1999), pp 28-35.

Harman, Allan. *Psalms: Volume 2: Psalms 73-150* (Fearn: Mentor, 2011).

Harrichand, James J S. 'Recovering the Language of Lament for the Western Evangelical Church: A Survey of the Psalms of Lament and their Appropriation within Pastoral Theology', *MJTM* 16 (2014–2015), pp 101-130.

Harris, Murray J. *Exegetical Guide to the Greek New Testament: Colossians and Philemon* (Nashville: B&H Academic, 2010).

Hassler, Mark A. 'Isaiah 14 and Habakkuk 2: Two Taunt Songs Against the Same Tyrant?', *MSJ* 26.2 (Fall 2015), pp 221-229.

Hatfield, Elaine, John T Cacioppo and Richard L Rapson. 'Emotional Contagion', *Current Directions in Psychological Science* 2:3 (1993), pp 96-99.

Hayford, Jack. *Worship His Majesty* (Waco: Word, 1987).

Hely Hutchinson, James. 'The Psalms and Praise', in David G Firth and Philip S Johnston (eds.), *Interpreting the Psalms: Issues and Approaches* (Downers Grove: IVP, 2005), pp 85-100.

Hely Hutchinson, James. 'The Psalter as a Book', in Andrew G Shead (ed.), *Stirred by a Noble Theme: The Book of Psalms in the Life of the Church* (Nottingham: Apollos, 2013), pp 23-45.

Hengel, Martin. *Between Jesus and Paul: Studies in the Earliest History of Christianity* (trans. John Bowden; London: SCM, 1983).

Hess, K. 'Serve, Deacon, Worship', in Colin Brown (ed.), *Dictionary of New Testament Theology*, Vol 3 (Exeter: Paternoster, 1978), pp 544-553.

Hicks, Zac. *The Worship Pastor: A Call to Ministry for Worship Leaders and Teams* (Grand Rapids: Zondervan, 2016).

Hill, Andrew E and John H Walton. *A Survey of the Old Testament* (Grand Rapids: Zondervan, 2000).

Hodges, Donald A. 'Bodily Responses to Music', in Susan Hallam, Ian Cross and Michael Thaut (eds.), *The Oxford Handbook of Music Psychology* (Oxford: OUP, 2009), pp 121-130.

Hoehner, Harold W. *Ephesians: An Exegetical Commentary* (Grand Rapids: Baker, 2002).

Hoenen, Alison Werner. 'How Can I Keep from Singing? An Appeal to Christians to Sing the Faith', *Journal of Lutheran Ethics* (10/01/2010): http://www.elca.org/JLE/Articles/254#_edn20.

Hughes, Philip Edgcumbe. *Theology of the English Reformers* (London: Hodder & Stoughton, 1965).

Hughes, R Kent. 'Free Church Worship: The Challenge of Freedom', in D A Carson (ed.), *Worship by the Book*. (Grand Rapids: Zondervan, 2002), pp 136-192.

Hurtado, Larry W. *One God, One Lord: Early Christian Devotion and Ancient Jewish Monotheism* (Philadelphia: Fortress, 1988).

Hustad, Donald P. 'The Psalms as Worship Expressions: Personal and Congregational', *Review & Expositor* 81 (Summer 1984), pp 407-424.

Hustad, Donald P. *Jubilate II: Church Music in Worship and Renewal* (Carol Stream: Hope Publishing, 1993).

Jacobson, Rolf. 'The Costly Loss of Praise', *Theology Today* 57:3 (October, 2000), pp 375-385.

Janata, P. 'The Neural Architecture of Music-Evoked Autobiographical Memories', *Cerebral Cortex* 19 (2009), pp 2579-2594.

Jäncke, Lutz. 'Music, Memory and Emotion', *Journal of Biology* 7.6 (2008): https://jbiol.biomedcentral.com/articles/10.1186/jbiol82.

Japhet, Sara. *I & II Chronicles: A Commentary* (Louisville: Westminster John Knox Press, 1993).

Jensen, Peter F. 'The Lord and His Church', in *Church, Worship and the Local Congregation*, ed. B. G. Webb (Homebush West: Lancer, 1987), pp 111-120.

Jenson, Robert W. *Systematic Theology II* (Oxford: OUP, 1999).

Jinkins, Michael *In the House of the Lord: Inhabiting the Psalms of Lament* (Collegeville: Liturgical Press, 1989).

Johansson, Calvin M. *Music & Ministry: A Biblical Counterpoint* [Peabody: Hendrikson, 1984).

Heitzenrater, Richard P and W Reginald Ward (eds.), *The Works of John Wesley: Volume 22: Journals and Diaries* (Nashville: Abingdon, 1983).

Johnson, Terry. 'The History of Psalm Singing in the Christian Church', in Joel R Beeke and Anthony T Selvaggio (eds.), *Sing a New Song: Recovering Psalm Singing for the Twenty-First Century* (Grand Rapids: Reformation Heritage Books, 2010), pp 41-60.

Jones, Logan C. 'The Psalms of Lament and the Transformation of Sorrow', *The Journal of Pastoral Care & Counselling* 61.1-2 (Spring-Summer, 2007), pp 47-58.

Jourdain, Robert. *Music, the Brain, and Ecstasy: How Music Captures Our Imagination* (New York: Avon Book, 1997).

Jung, Kyu Nam. 'Prayer in the Psalms', in D A Carson (ed.), *Teach Us To Pray: Prayer in the Bible and the World* (Exeter: Paternoster, 1990), pp 35-57.

Kaiser Jr., Walter C and Moisés Silva, *An Introduction to Biblical Hermeneutics: The Search for Meaning* (Grand Rapids: Zondervan, 2007).

Käsemann, Ernst. 'Worship and Everyday Life. A note on Romans 12', in *New Testament Questions of Today* (London: SCM, 1969), pp 188-195.

Kauflin, Bob. *True Worshippers: Seeking What Matters to God* (Wheaton: Crossway, 2015).

Kauflin, Bob. *Worship Matters: Leading Others to Encounter the Greatness of God* (Wheaton: Crossway, 2008).

Keach, Benjamin. *The Breach Repaired in God's Worship; or, Singing of Psalms, Hymns and Spiritual Songs, proved to be an Holy Ordinance of Jesus Christ. With an Answer to all Objections* (London: John Hancock, 1691).

Keeler, J R, E A Roth, B L Neuser, J M Spitsbergen, D J M Waters and J-M Vianney. 'The neurochemistry and social flow of singing: bonding and oxytocin', *Frontiers in Human Neuroscience* (23 September 2015): http://dx.doi.org/10.3389/fnhum.2015.00518.

Keener, Craig S. *Acts: An Exegetical Commentary: Volume 2: 3:1-14:28* (Grand Rapids: Baker, 2013).

Keller, Timothy. *Prayer: Experiencing Awe and Intimacy with God* (London: Hodder & Stoughton, 2014).

Kidner, Derek. *Psalms 1-72* (Leicester: IVP, 1973).

Kidner, Derek. *Psalms 73-150* (Leicester: IVP, 1975).

Knights, C H. 'Singing Prophets and Prophetic Songs – Isaiah's Song of the Vineyard', *ExpTim* 125.12 (Sep 2014), pp 602-604.

Koester, Craig R. 'The Distant Triumph Song: Music and the Book of Revelation', *Word & World* 12.3 (Summer, 1992), pp 243-249.

Koester, Craig R. *Revelation: A New Translation with Introduction and Commentary* (New Haven & London: Yale University Press, 2014).

Kolb, Robert and Charles P Arand. *The Genius of Luther's Theology: A Wittenberg Way of Thinking for the Contemporary Church* (Grand Rapids: Baker Academic, 2008).

Kortering, John. 'Psalm Singing: A Reformed Heritage' (16 July, 2000): http://www.prca.org/pamphlets/pamphlet_37.html.

Kreeft, Peter. 'Lewis's Philosophy of Truth, Goodness and Beauty', in David Baggett, Gary R Habermas and Jerry L Walls (eds.), *C. S. Lewis as Philosopher: Truth, Goodness and Beauty* (Downers Grove: IVP, 2008), pp 23-36.

Krentz, Edgar. 'The Early Dark Ages of the Church', *Concordia Theological Monthly* 41 (1970), pp 67-85.

Lambert, J C. 'Praise', *International Standard Bible Encyclopedia Online*: http://www.internationalstandardbible.com/P/praise.html.

Langford, Thomas A. 'Charles Wesley as Theologian', in S T Kimbrough Jr. (ed.), *Charles Wesley Poet and Theologian* (Nashville: Abingdon, 1992), pp 97-105.

Latimer, Hugh. 'Letter to Sir Edward Baynton, c. 1531', in G E Corrie (ed.), *Remains of Bishop Latimer* (For the Parker Society; Cambridge: Cambridge University Press, 1865), pp 322-333.

Le Huray, Peter. *Music and the Reformation in England, 1549-1660* (Cambridge: Cambridge University Press, 1967).

Leaver, Robin A. *Luther's Liturgical Music: Principles and Implications* (Grand Rapids: Eerdmans, 2007).

Leaver, Robin A. *The Whole Church Sings: Congregational Singing in Luther's Wittenberg* (Grand Rapids: Eerdmans, 2017).

Lee, Hee Youl. *A Dynamic Reading of the Holy Spirit in Revelation: A Theological Reflection of the Functional Role of the Holy Spirit in the Narrative* (Eugene: Wipf & Stock, 2014).

Leslie, Elmer A. *The Psalms: Translated and Interpreted in the Light of Hebrew Life and Worship* (New York: Abingdon-Cokesbury Press, 1949).

Lewis, C S. 'On Church Music', in Walter Hooper (ed.), *Christian Reflections* (London: Geoffrey Bles, 1967), pp 117-123.

Lewis, C S. *Letters to Malcolm Chiefly on Prayer: Reflections on the Intimate Dialogue Between Man and God* (London: Collins, 1966).

Lewis, C S. *Reflections on the Psalms* [London: Harper Collins, 1958).

Lightfoot, J B. *Saint Paul's Epistle to the Philippians* (London: MacMillan and Co, 1927), p 181.

Lightfoot, J B. *The Epistles of St Paul: Colossians and Philemon* (London: Macmillan, 1875).

Lincoln, Andrew T. *Ephesians* (Waco: Word, 1990).

Lindsay, Mark R. 'Thomas Cranmer and the Book of Common Prayer: Theological Education, Liturgy and the Embodiment of Prosper's Dictum', *Colloquium* 47.2 (November 2015), pp 195-207.

Lints, Richard. *Identity and Idolatry: The Image of God and its Inversion* (Downers Grove: IVP, 2015).

Lloyd-Jones, D Martyn. *Singing to the Lord* (Bridgend: Bryntirion Press, 2003).

Lohse, Eduard. *Colossians and Philemon: A Commentary on the Epistles to the Colossians and to Philemon* (Philadelphia: Fortress, 1965).

Lorenz, Edmund S. *Church Music: What a Minister Should Know About It* (New York: Fleming H Revell, 1923).

Luther, Martin. 'An Exposition of the Lord's Prayer for Simple Laymen, 1519', *Devotional Writings I* (eds. Martin O Deitrich and Helmut T Lehmann; trans. Martin H Bertram; vol. 42 of *Luther's Works*, American Edition, eds. Jaroslav Pelikan and Helmut T Lehmann; Philadelphia: Fortress, 1969), pp 15-81.

Luther, Martin. 'Concerning the Order of Public Worship, 1523', in *Liturgy and Hymns* (eds. Ulrich S Leupold and Helmut T Lehmann; trans. Paul Zeller Strodach; vol. 53 of *Luther's Works*, American Edition, eds. Jaroslav Pelikan and Helmut T Lehmann; Philadelphia: Fortress, 1965), pp 7-14.

Luther, Martin. 'Defense of the Translation of the Psalms', in *Word and Sacrament I* (eds. E Theodore Bachmann and Helmut T Lehmann; trans. Jeremiah J Schindel; vol. 35 of *Luther's Works*, American Edition, eds. Jaroslav Pelikan and Helmut T Lehmann; Philadelphia: Fortress, 1960), pp 203-223.

Luther, Martin. 'On the Councils and the Church, 1539', in *Church and Ministry III* (eds. Eric W Gritsch and Helmut T Lehmann; trans. Charles M Jacobs; vol. 41 of *Luther's Works*, American Edition, eds. Jaroslav Pelikan and Helmut T Lehmann; Philadelphia: Fortress, 1966), pp 3-178.

Luther, Martin. 'Preface to Georg Rhau's Symphonoiae iucundae, 1538', in *Liturgy and Hymns* (eds. Ulrich S Leupold and Helmut T Lehmann; trans. Ulrich S Leupold; vol. 53 of *Luther's Works*, American Edition, eds. Jaroslav Pelikan and Helmut T Lehmann; Philadelphia: Fortress, 1965), pp 321-324.

Luther, Martin. 'Preface to the *Babst Hymnal*, 1545', in *Liturgy and Hymns* (eds. Ulrich S Leupold and Helmut T Lehmann; trans. Paul Zeller Strodach; vol. 53 of *Luther's Works*, American Edition, eds. Jaroslav Pelikan and Helmut T Lehmann; Philadelphia: Fortress, 1965), p 332-334.

Luther, Martin. 'Preface to the Burial Hymns, 1542', in *Liturgy and Hymns* (eds. Ulrich S Leupold and Helmut T Lehmann; trans. Paul Zeller Strodach; vol. 53 of *Luther's Works*, American Edition, eds. Jaroslav Pelikan and Helmut T Lehmann; Philadelphia: Fortress, 1965), pp 325-331.

Luther, Martin. 'Preface', to 'Works on the First Twenty-Two Psalms, 1519 to 1521', in *Select Psalms III* (trans. Jaroslav Pelikan; vol. 14 of *Luther's Works*, American Edition, eds. Jaroslav Pelikan and Daniel E Poellot; St Louis: Concordia, 1958), p 286.

Luther, Martin. 'Sermon at the Dedication of the Castle Church, Torgau, 1544', in *Sermons I* (eds. John W Doberstein and Helmut T Lehmann; trans. John W Doberstein; vol. 51 of *Luther's Works*, American Edition, eds. Jaroslav Pelikan and Helmut T Lehmann; Philadelphia: Fortress, 1959), pp 331-354.

Luther, Martin. 'The German Mass and Order of Service, 1526', in *Liturgy and Hymns* (eds. Ulrich S Leupold and Helmut T Lehmann; trans. Augustus Steimle; vol. 53 of *Luther's Works*, American Edition, eds. Jaroslav Pelikan and Helmut T Lehmann; Philadelphia: Fortress, 1965), p 51-90.

Luther, Martin. 'The Sermon on the Mount', in *The Sermon on the Mount (Sermons) and the Magnificat* (ed. and trans. Jaroslav Pelikan; vol. 21 of *Luther's Works*, American Edition, eds. Jaroslav Pelikan and Helmut T Lehmann; Philadelphia: Fortress, 1968), pp 1-294.

Luther, Martin. 'Treatise on the New Testament', in *Word and Sacrament I* (eds. E Theodore Bachmann and Helmut T Lehmann; trans. Jeremiah J Schindel; vol. 35 of *Luther's Works*, American Edition, eds. Jaroslav Pelikan and Helmut T Lehmann; Philadelphia: Fortress, 1960), pp 75-111.

Luther, Martin. *The Table Talk of Martin Luther* (trans. and ed. William Hazlitt; London: H G Bohn, 1857).

MacCulloch, Diarmaid. *The Later Reformation in England, 1547-1603* (Basingstoke: St Martin's Press, 1990).

MacCulloch, Diarmaid. *Thomas Cranmer: A Life* (New Haven: Yale University Press, 1996).

Maes, Pieter-Jan, Marc Leman, Caroline Palmer and Marcelo M Wanderley, 'Action-based effects on music perception', *Frontier in Psychology* (January 2014): https://doi.org/10.3389/fpsyg.2013.01008.

Manetsch, Scott M. 'Is the Reformation Over? John Calvin, Roman Catholicism, and Contemporary Ecumenical Conversations', *Themelios* 36.2 (2011), pp 185-202.

Marini, Stephen A. *Sacred Song in America: Religion, Music, and Public Culture* (Urbana: University of Illinois Press, 2003).

Marshall, I Howard. 'How Far Did the Early Christians Worship God?', *Churchman* 99/3 (1985), pp 216-229.

Marshall, I Howard. 'Worship', in I H Marshall, A R Millard, J I Packer and D J Wiseman (eds.), *New Bible Dictionary* (Leicester: IVP, 1996), pp 1250.

Marshall, I Howard. *Acts* (Leicester: IVP, 1980).

Martens, Elmer A 'Impulses to Mission in Isaiah: An Intertextual Exploration', *Bulletin for Biblical Research* 17.2 (2007), pp 215-239.

Martin, Ralph P. 'Hymns, Hymn Fragments, Songs, Spiritual Songs', in Gerald F Hawthorne, Ralph P Martin, Daniel G Reid, *Dictionary of Paul and His Letter* (Leicester: IVP, 1993), pp 419-423.

Martin, Ralph P. *Carmen Christi: Philippians ii. 5-11 in Recent Interpretation and in the Setting of Early Christian Worship* (Cambridge: CUP, 1967).

Martin, Ralph P. *Worship in the Early Church* (Grand Rapids: Eerdmans, 1974).

Matyja, Jakub Ryszard. 'Music-animated body', *Avant. The Journal of the Philosophical-Interdisciplinary Vanguard* 2.1 (2011), pp 205-209.

Mays, James L. *Psalms* (Louisville: John Knox, 1994).

Mays, James L. *The Lord Reigns: A Theological Handbook to the Psalms* (Louisville: Westminster John Knox Press, 1994).

McCann, Jr., J Clinton. 'Psalms', in *New Interpreter's Bible in Twelve Volumes: Volume IV: 1 & 2 Maccabees; Introduction to Hebrew Poetry; Job; Psalms* (Nashville: Abingdon, 1996), pp 639-1280.

McCann, Jr., J Clinton. *A Theological Introduction to the Book of Psalms: The Psalms as Torah* (Nashville: Abingdon Press, 1993).

McCracken, Brett. 'The Best New Worship Songs of the 2010s,' *TGC: US Edition* (September 21, 2019): https://www.thegospelcoalition.org/article/best-new-worship-songs-2010s.

McKim, LindaJo H. *The Presbyterian Hymnal Companion* (Louisville: Westminster John Knox Press, 1993).

Meier, Samuel A. *Themes and Transformations in Old Testament Prophecy* (Downers Grove: IVP, 2009).

Merkle, Benjamin L. *Exegetical Guide to the Greek New Testament: Ephesians* (Nashville: B&H Academic, 2016).

Michaels, J Ramsay *1 Peter* (Waco: Word, 1988).

Millar, J Gary. *Calling on the Name of the Lord: A Biblical Theology of Prayer* (Downers Grove: IVP, 2016).

Miller Jr., Patrick D. "Enthroned on the Praises of Israel': The Praise of God in Old Testament Theology', *Interpretation* 39 (January, 1985), pp 5-19.

Miller, Patrick D. *Interpreting the Psalms* (Philadelphia: Fortress Press, 1986).

Montgomery, David. *Sing a New Song: Choosing and Leading Praise in Today's Church* (Edinburgh: Rutherford House, 2000).

Moo, Douglas J. *The Letters to the Colossians and to Philemon* (Grand Rapids: Eerdmans, 2008).

Moreton, Cole. 'Interview: Graham Kendrick – The Praise Maker', *Independent* (26 December, 1999): http://www.independent.co.uk/arts-entertainment/interview-graham-kendrick-the-praise-maker-1134491.html.

Morley, Iain. *The Evolutionary Origins and Archaeology of Music* (PhD Thesis: Cambridge University, 2003).

Morris, Leon L. *The Book of Revelation: An Introduction and Commentary* (Leicester: IVP, 1987).

Morris, Leon L. *The Epistle to the Romans* (Grand Rapids: Eerdmans, 1988).

Motyer, J A. *The Prophecy of Isaiah* (Leicester: IVP, 1993).

Mounce, Robert H. *The Book of Revelation* (Grand Rapids: Eerdmans, 1998).

Ng, Megan. 'Body and Soul: Exploring the Relationship between Physical Expression and Emotional Response in Musical Worship': https://www.academia.edu/33621744/Body_and_Soul_Exploring_the_Relationship_between_Physical_Expression_and_Emotional_Response_in_Musical_Worship.

Noll, Mark A. 'Praise the Lord: Song, culture, divine bounty, and issues of harmonization', *Books & Culture* (November/December 2007): http://www.booksandculture.com/articles/2007/novdec/9.14.html.

Noll, Mark A. 'We Are What We Sing: Our classic hymns reveal evangelicalism at its best', *Christianity Today* (June 12, 1999): http://www.christianitytoday.com/ct/1999/july12/9t8037.html.

Old, Hughes Oliphant. *The Reading and Preaching of the Scriptures in the Worship of the Christian Church: Volume 4: The Age of the Reformation* (Grand Rapids: Eerdmans, 2002).

Onderdonk, Julian. 'Hymn Tunes from Folk-songs: Vaughan Williams and English Hymnody', in Byron Adams and Robin Wells (eds.), *Vaughan Williams Essays* (Abingdon: Routledge, 2016), pp 103-128.

Osborne, Grant. *Revelation* (Grand Rapids: Baker, 2002).

Otte, Joshua. 'WorshipGod 08 Conference', *Eucatastrophe* (27 February, 2008): https://eucatastrophe101.wordpress.com/page/16.

Özdemir, E, A Norton & G Schlaug. 'Shared and Distinct Neural Correlates of Singing and Speaking', *Neuroimage* 33 (2006), pp 628-635.

Page, Nick. *And Now Let's Move into a Time of Nonsense: Why Worship Songs are Failing the Church* (Milton Keynes: Authentic Media, 2004).

Pao, David W. *Thanksgiving: An Investigation of a Pauline Theme* (Downers Grove: IVP, 2002).

Parrett, Gary A. '9.5 Theses on Worship: A Disputation on the Role of Music', *Christianity Today* 49.2 (February, 2005), pp 38-42.

Payne, Tony. 'Church and worship: Some questions and answers', *The Briefing* 301 (2003), pp 15-18.

Payne, Tony. 'The gathering: thinking afresh about church', *The Briefing* 302 (2003), pp 13-18.

Payne, Tony. 'Why do we worship as we do?', *The Briefing* 299 (2003), pp 15-20.

Payne, Tony, 'Confessions of a Teenage Praise Junkie', *The Briefing* (February, 1996): http://gotherefor.com/offer-search.php?pagetype=search&changestore=true&page=163&store=AU.

Pedigo, T L. *Worship Music in Three Dimensions: How to Sing Down the Presence and Power of God* (Colorado Springs: Winning Edge Publications, 2004).

Percy, Martyn. 'Sweet Rapture: Subliminal Eroticism in Contemporary Charismatic Worship', *Theology & Sexuality* 6 (1997), pp 71-106.

Pereira, C S, J Teixeira, P Figueiredo, J Xavier, S L Castro and E Brattico, 'Music and Emotions in the Brain: Familiarity Matters', *PLoS*

ONE 6.11 (November 2011):
http://www.ncbi.nlm.nih.gov/pmc/articles/PMC3217963.

Peterson, David G. 'Further Reflections on Worship in the New Testament', *RTR* 44.2 (1985), pp 34-41.

Peterson, David G. 'Prayer in Paul's Writings', in *Teach Us to Pray: Prayer in the Bible and the World* (ed. D A Carson. London: WEF, 1990), pp 84-101.

Peterson, David G. 'The Worship of the New Community', in I Howard Marshall and David G Peterson (eds.), *Witness to the Gospel: The Theology of Acts* (Grand Rapids: Eerdmans, 1998), pp 373-395.

Peterson, David G. 'Worship in the New Testament', in D A Carson (ed.), *Worship: Adoration and Action* (Grand Rapids: Baker, 1993), pp 51-91.

Peterson, David G. *Encountering God Together: Biblical Patterns for Ministry and Worship* (Leicester: IVP, 2013).

Peterson, David G. *Engaging with God: A Biblical Theology of Worship* (Leicester: IVP, 1992).

Peterson, David G. *The Acts of the Apostles* (Grand Rapids: Eerdmans, 2009).

Peterson, Jim. *Church Without Walls: Moving Beyond Traditional Boundaries* (Colorado Springs: NavPress, 1992).

Phillips, Godfrey E. *The Old Testament in the World Church* (London: Lutterworth Press, 1942).

Pierce, Ronald W. 'The Feminine Voice of God: Women as Prophets in the Bible', *Priscilla Papers* 21:1 (Winter 2007), pp 4-8.

Pierce, Timothy M. *Enthroned on Our Praise: An Old Testament Theology of Worship* (Nashville: B&H Academic, 2008).

Piper, John. *Let the Nations Be Glad! The Supremacy of God in Missions* (Grand Rapids: Baker, 2003).

Plass, Ewald M (ed.). *What Luther Says: A Practical In-Home Anthology for the Active Christian* (St. Louis: Concordia Publishing House, 1959).

Polman, Bert. 'The History of Worship in the Christian Reformed Church', in Emily R Brink and Bert F Polman (eds.), *Psalter*

Hymnal Handbook (Grand Rapids: CRC Publications, 1998), pp 109-119.

Porter, Mark. *Contemporary Worship Music and Everyday Musical Lives* (Abingdon: Routledge, 2017).

Powery, Luke A. 'Painful Praise: Exploring the Public Proclamation of the Hymns of Revelation', *Theology Today* 70.1 (2013), pp 69-78.

Rack, Henry D (ed.), *The Works of John Wesley: Volume 10: The Methodist Societies: The Minutes of Conference* (Nashville: Abingdon, 2011).

Raiter, Michael D. *Colossians & Philemon: Growing Strong in Christ* (Grand Rapids: Discovery House, 2015).

Raiter, Mike and Rob Smith, *Songs of the Saints: Enriching our singing by learning from the songs of Scripture* (Sydney: Matthias Media, 2017).

Ramshaw, Elaine J. 'Singing at Funerals and Memorial Services', *Currents in Theology and Mission* 35.3 (June 2008), pp 206-215.

Rattenbury, J Ernest. *The Evangelical Doctrines of Charles Wesley's Hymns* (London: Epworth, 1941).

Reynolds, William J and Milburn Price, *A Survey of Christian Hymnody* (Carol Stream, Illinois, 1987).

Richardson, John P. 'Is "Worship" Biblical?', *Churchman* 109/3 (1995), pp 197-218.

Richardson, John P. 'Neither "Worship" nor "Biblical": A Response to Alastair Campbell', *Churchman* 111.1 (1997), pp 6-18.

Ridderbos, Herman. *Paul: An Outline of His Theology* (Grand Rapids: Eerdmans, 1975).

Ridley, Nicholas. 'Letter VIII (Coverdale)', in Henry Christmas (ed.), *The Works of Nicholas Ridley D. D.: Sometime Lord Bishop of London: Martyr 1555* (Eugene: Wipf & Stock, 2008), p 349-356.

Riley, Matthew and Anthony D Smith. *Nation and Classical Music: From Handel to Copland* (Woodbridge: The Boydell Press, 2016).

Robinson, Donald W B. 'What Theology of Order and Ministry do the Anglican Formularies Teach?', in *Donald Robinson: Selected*

Works: Volume 2, Preaching God's Word (Sydney: Australian Church Record, 2008), pp 405-413.

Robinson, Hastings (ed.). *The Zurich Letters, Comprising the Correspondence of Several English Bishops and Others, With Some of the Helvetian Reformers, During the Early Part of the Reign of Queen Elizabeth* (For the Parker Society; Cambridge: CUP, 1842).

Roslan & Campion, 'Queen Elizabeth Honors "In Christ Alone" Author Keith Getty for "Music and Modern Hymn Writing"', *The Gospel Herald* (June 19, 2017): http://www.gospelherald.com/articles/70972/20170619/queen-elizabeth-honors-christ-alone-author-keith-getty-music-modern.htm.

Ross, Allen P. *Recalling the Hope of Glory: Biblical Worship from the Garden to the New Creation* (Grand Rapids: Kregel, 2006).

Routley, Erik. *A Short History of English Music* (Oxford: Mowbrays, 1977).

Ryle, J C. *Christian Leaders of the 18th Century* (Carlisle: Banner of Truth, 1970).

Sacks, Oliver. 'The Power of Music', *Brain* 129 (2006), p 2528–2532.

Sacks, Oliver. *Musicophilia: Tales of Music and the Brain* (London: Picador, 2007).

Sadler, Michael F. *The Acts of the Apostles* (London: Bell, 1906).

Salier, W S. 'The Temple of God in the Gospel of John', in T Desmond Alexander & Simon Gathercole (eds.), *Heaven on Earth: The Temple in Biblical Theology* (Carlisle: Paternoster, 2004), pp 121-134.

Saliers, Don E. *Worship as Theology: Foretaste of Glory Divine* (Nashville: Abingdon, 1994).

Schalk, Carl F. *Luther on Music: Paradigms of Praise* (St Louis: Concordia, 1988).

Scherer, Klaus R and Marcel R Zentner. 'Emotional Effects of Music: Production Rules', in P N Juslin and J A Sloboda (eds.), *Music and Emotion: Theory and Research* (Oxford: OUP, 2001), pp 361-392.

Schnabel, Eckhard J. *Acts* (Grand Rapids: Zondervan, 2012).

Scholes, Percy A. 'Anglican Chant', in John Owen Ward (ed.), *The Oxford Companion to Music* (Oxford: OUP, 1991), p 32-35.

Schreiner, Thomas R. *40 Questions About Christians and Biblical Law* (Grand Rapids: Kregal, 2010).

Scruton, Roger. *Understanding Music: Philosophy and Interpretation* (London: Continuum International Publishing, 2009).

Shead, Andrew G and Andrew J Cameron, 'Singing with the Messiah in a Foreign Land', in Andrew G Shead (ed.), *Stirred by a Noble Theme: The Book of Psalms in the Life of the Church* (Apollos: Nottingham, 2013), pp 158-180.

Shead, Andrew G. 'Is There a Musical Note in the Body? Cranmer on the Reformation of Music', *RTR* 69.1 (April, 2010), pp 1-16.

Smietana, Bob. 'Modern hymn writers revive lost art of Christian music', *USA Today* (April 16, 2013): https://www.usatoday.com/story/life/music/2013/04/16/christia n-hymn-writers/2089271.

Smith, Claire S. *Pauline Communities as 'Scholastic Communities': A Study of the Vocabulary of 'Teaching' in 1 Corinthians , 1 and 2 Timothy and Titus* (Tübingen: Mohr Siebeck, 2012).

Smith, J A. 'Which Psalms Were Sung in the Temple?', *Music & Letters* 71.2 (1990), pp 167-186.

Smith, James K A. *Desiring the Kingdom: Worship, Worldview, and Cultural Formation* (Grand Rapids: Baker Academic, 2009).

Smith, Robert H. '"Worthy is the Lamb' and Other Songs of Revelation', *Currents in Theology and Mission* 25.6 (Dec 1998), pp 500-506.

Smith, Robert S. 'A "Second Reformation"!? "Office" and "Charisma" in the New Testament', *RTR* 58 (1999), pp 151-162.

Smith, Robert S. 'Belting Out the Blues as Believers: The Importance of Singing Lament', *Themelios* 42.1 (2017), pp 89-111.

Smith, Robert S. 'Music, Singing and Emotions: Exploring the Connections', *Themelios* 37.3 (2012), pp 465-479.

Smith, Robert S. 'Psalms, Hymns and Spiritual Songs: What are They and Why Sing Them?', *CASE* 23 (2010), pp 26-29.

Smith, Robert S. 'Songs of the Seer: The Purpose of Revelation's Hymns', *Themelios* 43.2 (2018), 193-204.

Smith, Robert S. 'The Hymnody of John Wesley and George Whitefield', in Ian J Maddock (ed.), *Wesley and Whitefield? Wesley versus Whitefield?* (Eugene: Wipf & Stock, 2018), pp 219-242.

Smith, Robert S. 'The Role of Singing in the Life of the Church', *The Briefing* 401 (September-October, 2012), pp 15-21.

Spurgeon, Charles Haddon. *An All-Round Ministry* (Edinburgh: The Banner of Truth Trust, 1960).

Staubli, Thomas and Silvia Schroer, *Body Symbolism in the Bible* (Collegeville: The Liturgical Press, 2001).

Stetzer, Ed. 'Worship Leaders Are Not Rock Stars: Instead of performing music, we should be leading worship', *Christianity Today* (March, 2015):
http://www.christianitytoday.com/edstetzer/2015/march/worship-leaders-are-not-rock-stars.html.

Steven, James H S. *Worship in the Spirit: Charismatic Worship in the Church of England* (Carlisle: Paternoster, 2002).

Storms, Sam. 'Singing Truth (3:16)', *Sam Storms* (n.d.):
https://www.samstorms.org/all-articles/post/singing-truth--3:16-.

Stutler, Russell. 'Several Different Ways to Sing the Psalms', *Stutler.cc* (Last updated February, 2017):
http://www.stutler.cc/russ/sing_psalms.html.

Swarbrick, John. 'Jesus the Soul of Musick Is: Music and the Methodists', A lecture read at the Methodist Sacramental Fellowship Public Meeting during the Methodist Conference of 2003 at Llandudno:
http://www.sacramental.org.uk/uploads/5/0/0/9/50096105/jesus_the_soul_of_musick_is_-_john_swarbrick.pdf.

Synod of the Reformed Presbyterian Church of North America. 'The Psalms in the Worship of the Church' (June 2004):
http://www.reformedprescambridge.com/articles/Psalms_in_worship_final_version.pdf.

Taliaferro, Charles. 'Evil and Prayer: Set Prayers and Other Special Weapons', in C Meister and J K Dew Jr. (eds.), *God and Evil: The*

Case for God in a World Filled with Pain (Downers Grove: IVP, 2013), pp 152-162.

Tate, Marvin E. *Psalm 51-100* (Waco: Word, 1990).

Taylor, Dale B. *Biomedical Foundations for Music as Therapy* (Saint Louis: MMB Music, 1997).

Taylor, David. 'Resources for Exploring the Psalms', *Fuller Studio* (2017): https://fullerstudio.fuller.edu/resources-exploring-psalms.

Temperley, Nicholas. *The Music of the English Parish Church: Volume I* (Cambridge: Cambridge University Press, 1979).

Thiselton, Anthony C. *The First Epistle to the Corinthians* (Grand Rapids: Eerdmans, 2000).

Toon, Peter. 'Freedom as a Christian – ancient and modern', *Virtue Online: The Voice for Global Orthodox Anglicanism* (n.d.): http://www.virtueonline.org/freedom-christian-ancient-and-modern-peter-toon.

Töres Theorell, 'Music for Body and Soul: Physiological Effects of Listening to Music', in *Psychological Health Effects of Musical Experiences* (SpringerBriefs in Psychology. Dordrecht: Springer, 2014), pp 33-47.

Torrance, David W and Thomas F Torrance (eds.), *Calvin's Commentaries: The Second Epistle of Paul the Apostle to the Corinthians and the Epistles of Timothy, Titus and Philemon* (trans. T A Smail. Grand Rapids: Eerdmans, 1964).

Torrance, David W and Thomas F Torrance (eds.). *Calvin's Commentaries: The Acts of the Apostles: 14-28* (trans. John W Fraser. Grand Rapids: Eerdmans, 1973).

Trench, R C. *Synonyms of the New Testament* (London: Kegan, Paul, Trench, Trübner, 1880).

Trueman, Carl. *Luther on the Christian Life: Cross and Freedom* (Wheaton: Crossway, 2015).

Turner, Steve. *The Gospel According to the Beatles* (Westminster John Knox Press, Louisville, 2006).

Tyreman, Luke. *The Life of the Rev. George Whitefield*, 2 vols (London: Hodder & Stoughton, 1876).

Tyson, John R. 'The Theology of Charles Wesley's Hymns', *Wesleyan Theological Journal* 44.2 (Fall 2009), pp 58-75.

Tyson, John R. *Assist Me to Proclaim: The Life and Hymns of Charles Wesley* (Grand Rapids: Eerdmans, 2007).

Vaughan Williams, Ralph. 'Preface: The Music', to *The English Hymnal* (London: OUP, 1906), pp x-xix: https://www.ccel.org/ccel/ccel/eee/files/enghml.htm.

Vaughan Williams, Ralph. *National Music and Other Essays* (Oxford: OUP, 1987).

Verhey, Allen. *The Christian Art of Dying: Learning from Jesus* (Grand Rapids: Eerdmans, 2011).

Vickhoff, Björn. 'Why Does Music Move Us?', *Philosophical Communications, Web Series* 34 (2004), p 2: http://www.phil.gu.se/posters/musicmove.pdf.

Wainwright, Geoffrey. 'The Praise of God in the Theological Reflection of the Church', *Interpretation* 39.1 (January, 1985), pp 34-45.

Wallace, Daniel B. *Greek Grammar Beyond the Basics* (Grand Rapids: Zondervan, 1996).

Walter A Buszin, 'Luther on Music', *The Musical Quarterly* 32:1 (1946), pp 80-97.

Waltke, Bruce K, J M Houston and E Moore, *The Psalms as Christian Lament: A Historical Commentary*. (Grand Rapids: Eerdmans, 2014).

Ward, Pete. *Selling Worship: How what we sing has changed the Church* (Milton Keynes: Paternoster, 2005).

Warfield, B B. 'The Emotional Life of Our Lord', in *The Person and Work of Christ* (Phillipsburg: P&R Publishing, 1989), pp 93-145

Waters, Guy Prentiss. *Acts: EP Study Commentary* (Holywell: EP Books, 2015).

Watson, Francis. 'Theology and Music', *SJT* 51.4 (1998), pp 1-29.

Watts, Isaac. *Hymns and Spiritual Songs* (London: J. Humphreys, for John Lawrence, 1707).

Webb, Barry G. *The Message of Isaiah* (Leicester: IVP, 1996).

Wellesz, Egon. *A History of Byzantine Music and Hymnography* (Oxford: OUP, 1949).

Wenham, Gordon J. *Psalms as Torah: Reading Biblical Song Ethically* (Grand Rapids: Baker, 2012).

Wesley, John. 'On Knowing Christ After the Flesh', in Albert Outler (ed.), *The Works of John Wesley: Volume 4: Sermons IV: 115-151* (Nashville: Abingdon, 1987), pp 97-107.

Wesley, John. 'Preface' (*Oct.* 20, 1799) to *A Collection of Hymns, for the Use of the People Called Methodists* (London: John Mason, 1780).

Wesley, John. *Select Hymns with Tunes Annext: Designed Chiefly for the Use of the People Called Methodists* (London, 1761).

Westermann, Claus. *Blessing in the Bible and the Life of the Church*, trans K Crim (Philadelphia: Fortress, 1978).

Westermann, Claus. *Isaiah 40-66* (London: SCM, 1966).

Westermann, Claus. *Praise and Lament in the Psalms* (trans. K R Crim and R N Soulen. Atlanta: John Knox Press, 1981).

Westermeyer, Paul. *Te Deum: The Church and Music – A Textbook, a Reference, a History, an Essay* (Minneapolis: Augsburg Fortress, 1998).

Whitefield, George. *A Collection of Hymns for Social Worship: More particularly design'd for the Use of the Tabernacle Congregation, in London* (London, 1753).

Whitefield, Samuel. 'The Role of Prophetic Singers in God's Plan to Redeem the Nations', *Samuel Whitefield* (October 6, 2016): https://samuelwhitefield.com/1986/the-role-of-prophetic-singers-in-gods-plan-to-redeem-the-nations.

Wiersbe, Warren. *Real Worship: Playground, Battleground, or Holy Ground?* (Grand Rapids: Baker, 2000).

Wietzke, Walter R. *The Primacy of the Spoken Word: Redemptive Proclamation in a Complex World* (Minneapolis: Augsburg Fortress Press, 1988).

Williams, Donald M. *The Preacher's Commentary: Psalms 73-150* (Nashville: Thomas Nelson, 1989).

Willis, Jonathan P. *Church Music and Protestantism in Post-Reformation England: Discourses, Sites and Identities* (Farnham: Ashgate, 2010).

Wilson-Dickson, Andrew. *The Story of Christian Music: From Gregorian Chant to Black Gospel, An Authoritative Illustrated Guide to All the Major Traditions of Music for Worship* (Oxford: Lion, 1992).

Wilson, Gerald H. 'Shaping the Psalter: A Consideration of Editorial Linkage in the Book of Psalms', in J Clinton McCann (ed.), *The Shape and Shaping of the Psalter* (Sheffield: JSOT, 1993), pp 72-82.

Wilson, Gerard H. 'The Structure of the Psalter', in David G Firth and Philip S Johnston (eds.), *Interpreting the Psalms: Issues and Approaches* (Downers Grove: IVP, 2005), pp 229-246.

Witherington III, Ben. *The Acts of the Apostles: A Socio-Rhetorical Commentary* (Grand Rapids: Eerdmans, 1998).

Witvliet, John D. *The Biblical Psalms in Christian Worship: A Brief Introduction and Guide to Resources* (Grand Rapids: Eerdmans, 2007).

Wren, Brian. *Praying Twice: The Music and Words of Congregational Song* (Louisville: Westminster John Knox Press).

Wright, G Ernest. *God Who Acts: Biblical Theology as Recital* (London: SCM, 1952).

Wright, N T. *Simply Good News: Why the Gospel Is News and What Makes It Good* (New York: HarperCollins, 2015).

Wu, Dan. 'The Role of Lament in the Shape of the Psalter', in G Geoffrey Harper & Kit Barker (eds.), *Finding Lost Words: The Church's Right to Lament* (Eugene: Wipf & Stock, 2017), pp 133-147.

Recently Released by the Latimer Trust

The Anglican Ordinal. Gospel Priorities for Church of England Ministry by *Andrew Atherstone*

This book is part of our *Anglican Foundation* series, which offer practical guidance on Church of England services.

There is no better handbook for Anglican ministry than the Anglican ordinal – the authorized liturgy for ordaining new ministers. The ordinal contains a beautiful, succinct description of theological priorities and ministry models for today's Church. This booklet offers a simple exposition of the ordinal's primary themes. Anglican clergy are called to public ministry as messengers, sentinels, stewards, and shepherds. They are asked searching questions and they make solemn promises. The Holy Spirit's anointing is invoked upon their ministries, with the laying-on-of-hands, and they are gifted a Bible as the visual symbol of their new pastoral and preaching office. This booklet is a handy primer for ordinands and clergy, and all those responsible for their selection, training, and deployment.

Anglican Foundations Series

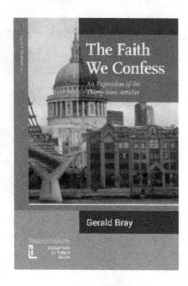

The Anglican Foundations series are a collection of booklets which offer practical guidance on Church of England services.

These include:

- *The Faith We Confess – An exposition of the Thirty-Nine Articles*
- *The 'Very Pure Word of God – The Book of Common Prayer as a model of biblical liturgy*
- *Dearly Beloved – Building God's people through morning and evening prayer*
- *Day by Day – The rhythm of the Bible in the Book of Common Prayer*
- *The Supper – Cranmer and Communion*
- *A Fruitful Exhortation – A guide to the Homilies*
- *Instruction in the Way of the Lord – A guide to the catechism*
- *Till Death Do Us Part – "The solemnization of Matrimony" in the Book of Common Prayer*
- *Sure and Certain Hope – Death and burial*
- *The Athanasian Creed*
- *The Anglican Ordinal*

Other Recommendations

Tend my sheep ed. *Keith G. Condie*

What is the connection between the doctrine and exegesis of the Scriptures on the one hand, and the theology and practice of ministry on the other? The chapters of this book each reflect the belief that authentic pastoral ministry is grounded in the ministry of the word of God. The essays collected here originated as papers given at the Annual Moore College School of Theology for 2015.

To oversee Christ's flock is 'a noble task' but also a difficult task. The responsibilities and expectations of the job are numerous and weighty. Skills in leadership and management, the ability to communicate effectively in a variety of settings, the need to be a competent listener and counsellor – these things and more are required of those who exercise pastoral oversight, even of a small congregation.

And as pastors seek resources to assist them in their vocation, it is no wonder that many have found great benefit from the insights of the social sciences. The problem, however, is the seeming lack of connection between the doctrine and exegesis of the Scriptures on the one hand, and the theology and practice of ministry on the other.
The chapters that follow do not claim to offer an extensive critique or response to this issue. Rather, as they address some of its aspects,

each reflects the belief that authentic pastoral ministry is grounded in the ministry of the word of God. Each chapter was first delivered as a lecture at the 2015 School of Theology held at Moore Theological College.

Translating the Bible by *Gerald Bray*

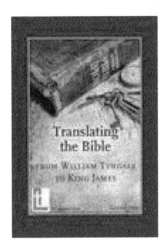

What motivated the men who gave us our Bible in English? Much of the answer lies in the turbulent religious history of the era, but there are clues which can be found in the prefaces published with each new edition.

This collection of the prefaces to the main translations of the Bible into English between 1525 and 1611 provides the historical and theological ancestry of the King James Version, and readers can hardly fail to be challenged by the spiritual concerns of the translators.

CPSIA information can be obtained
at www.ICGtesting.com
Printed in the USA
LVHW110337070721
692012LV00008B/695